AUTOMOTIVE FUEL, IGNITION, AND EMISSION CONTROL SYSTEMS

AUTOMOTIVE FUEL, IGNITION, AND EMISSION CONTROL SYSTEMS

GLEN E. IRELAND

Centennial College
of Applied Arts
and Technology

BRETON PUBLISHERS
BOSTON, MASSACHUSETTS
A Division of Wadsworth, Inc.

Breton Publishers
20 Providence Street, Boston, Massachusetts 02116
A Division of Wadsworth, Inc.

Library of Congress Cataloging in Publication Data
Ireland, Glen E   1922–
    Automotive fuel, ignition, and emission control sys-
tems.

    Includes index.
    1. Automobiles—Fuel systems—Maintenance and repair.
2. Automobiles—Ignition—Maintenance and repair
3. Automobiles—Pollution control devices—Maintenance
and repair. I. Title.
TL214.F8173   629.2′53   80-19664
ISBN 0-534-00866-6

Production and text design by Lloyd Rieber. Cover design by
Julia Gecha. Text composition in English Times Roman and
Univers by Carol Trowbridge on the Compugraphic Editwriter
7700. Page make-up, redrawn art, and camera work by Jay's
Publishers Services, Inc. Cover printed and text printed and
bound by The Alpine Press, Inc.

PREFACE

This text is the result of the author and publisher's belief that there is a pressing need for a comprehensive, up-to-date work on fuel, ignition, and emission control systems. These three vehicle systems have been most affected by government regulations, technological advances, and new information. The fuel, ignition, and emission control systems affect fuel economy and efficient engine operation. They are, therefore, increasingly important to vehicle owners and service technicians.

Most other books on the subject cover basic operation and service procedures, but fail to provide the student with a firm conceptual understanding of the principles governing these systems. Service manuals are fine for the experienced mechanic, but they are not adequate tools for learning a new subject. This text provides comprehensive coverage of the principles, components, operations, and service procedures for the three systems. After studying this text, students should be able to use manufacturers' service manuals effectively to troubleshoot and service the fuel, ignition, and emission control systems on any vehicle.

The text is organized to proceed from the general to the specific. First, each system is discussed in principle, and the concepts that underlie the system's operation are explained. Then, each component in the system is analyzed and its operation described. This is followed by troubleshooting and repair procedures for a typical system. Finally, specific differences between various models are described so that the student will know what to look for in a service manual.

Along with conventional systems, fuel injection and electronic ignition systems are covered in detail. These systems are compared to conventional systems to give the student a conceptual understanding of the differences between the two systems. Special attention is given to diagnostic and service procedures that are appropriate for both electronic ignition and fuel injection.

The author hopes that this text will result in improved work by tomorrow's service technicians and, thus, improved use of our increasingly scarce fuel resources.

Acknowledgments

This text is the product of three years' labor. Many individuals, companies, and organizations have been generous in providing support and information during this effort. I would like to thank the following companies for the illustrations, technical information, and advice that they extended as the work progressed:

American Motors Corporation
Robert Bosch (Canada) Limited
Champion Spark Plug Company of Canada, Limited
Chrysler Corporation
Echlin, Limited
Ford Motor Company, Dearborn
General Motors of Canada Limited
Holly Carburetor Division, Colt Industries
Suntester Equipment (Central) Limited

I would also like to thank Lloyd Rieber and the staff of Breton Publishers for their support and expertise.

On a personal note, many friends, colleagues, and family members have encouraged and supported me throughout my work on the text. I would especially like to thank David Coghlan for his help and advice during my writing, and for his vigilant proofreading and critiquing of the text; Mrs. Alison Edwards for her typing; my dear wife, Pauline, for her patience and support; and the administration of Centennial College, Scarborough, Ontario, for their encouragement.

INTRODUCTION

With the ever-increasing need to conserve fuel energy resources, it is important that automobile technicians understand how automobile fuel, ignition, and emission controls operate. The ability to service these systems for maximum efficiency is a critical need for today's technicians. *Automotive Fuel, Ignition, and Emission Control Systems* is an attempt to meet this need. While there are many tune-up and repair books on the market, this book goes beyond them and provides a learning tool with which you can thoroughly understand, diagnose, and repair fuel, ignition, and emission control systems.

It would be impossible for any text to cover the fuel, ignition, and emission control systems on every vehicle manufactured. Fortunately, it is not necessary to do so: every automobile manufacturer provides service manuals for its vehicles. However, the information in service manuals can only be applied by technicians who already understand how these systems operate. Service manuals are written for the professional, not for the student. This book is designed to give you the conceptual knowledge that you need in order to use service manuals to make effective repairs.

Automobile fuel, ignition, and emission control systems are closely interrelated. Every attempt is made in the text to ensure that this interrelationship is not overlooked. It does little good to attempt to repair the ignition system when the emission control system is actually responsible for the problem. A clear understanding of exactly what these systems do and how they operate will help you put your best efforts where they are needed in order to get the job done correctly.

Fuel, ignition, and emission control systems are each treated separately in the text. First, the general "how" and "why" of each system is explained. Then, diagnosis and repair are covered in a detailed (though general) manner, designed to give you the background knowledge you need in order to use the manufacturer's service manuals to repair any specific system. Each chapter has five special elements that deserve particular attention: learning objectives, assignments, self-tests, facts to remember, and illustrations.

Learning Objectives provide you with a road map for what you will learn in each chapter. Read them carefully. They explain what you should know and what you should be able to do after you have studied the chapter. The learning objectives have been selected to ensure that each chapter covers only the important and necessary material that you cannot get from a service manual.

Brief **Assignments** are presented throughout each chapter. These assignments consist of short review questions on the material that has immediately preceded the assignment. The assignments are meant to be done on a separate piece of paper. Because there are many assignments in each chapter, you will not find it difficult to go back and check your assignment answers against the text. By doing so, you will have an immediate gauge on your learning and can isolate confusion or misunderstanding early on in your study.

The **Self-Tests** are designed as an end-of-chapter check on your progress. Like the assignments, they are meant to be done on a separate piece of paper. They follow the text in wording and order of material presented and, along with the assignments, are designed to see if you have met the learning objectives for the chapter. You will probably find it helpful to review the text material before you take the self-tests. If you get any self-test answers wrong, you can increase your learning by locating the correct answer in the chapter and reviewing the material that you did not understand. Answers for the self-tests are given at the end of the book so that you can check your work.

Facts to Remember are presented throughout each text chapter. The facts to remember are short summaries of the text material. They allow you to quickly review the most important parts of the previous material and ensure that you have understood the text.

The **Illustrations** deserve a special comment. Too often students overlook illustrations and struggle to understand the material through the words alone. This is a mistake. The illustrations in this text have been carefully selected from among thousands to provide you with the best possible visual picture of the text information. Study each illustration carefully until you feel that you have a thorough understanding of the text material. In fact, you may find it helpful to look at all of the illustrations in a chapter before you actually read the chapter. This will give you an idea of what the chapter is about and what types of information you will be studying.

CONTENTS

CHAPTER 1   INTRODUCTION TO FUEL AND IGNITION SYSTEMS

Learning Objectives   1
Introduction   2
Gasoline Combustion   2
Fuel System   3
Ignition System   3
Internal-Combustion Engine Operation   4
The Multicylinder Engine   6
Driveline Components   8
Self-Test   9

CHAPTER 2   FUEL TANKS, LINES, AND PUMPS

Learning Objectives   10
Introduction   11
Fuel System Parts   11
Atmospheric Pressure and Vacuum   12
Fuel Tanks   13
Fuel Lines   16
Mechanical Fuel Pumps   17
Electric Fuel Pumps   19
Fuel Pump Testing Procedures   21
Service Tips for Fuel Pump Replacement   23
Self-Test   24

CHAPTER 3   CARBURETOR FUNDAMENTALS

Learning Objectives   25
Introduction   26
Gasoline Vaporization   26
Gasoline and Air Metering and Mixing   28
Simple Carburetor Systems   29
Float System Design and Operation   30
Idle and Low-Speed System Design and Operation   33
High-Speed System Design and Operation   37
Power System Design and Operation   39
Acceleration Pump Design and Operation   42
Choke System Design and Operation   45
Self-Test   51

CHAPTER 4   CARBURETOR DIAGNOSIS AND QUICK SERVICE PROCEDURES

Learning Objectives   52
Introduction   53
Tools and Procedures   53
Float System Problems   55
Idle and Low-Speed System Problems   56
Improper Idle Speed and Mixture Adjustment   57
High-Speed and Power System Problems   59
Acceleration Pump System Problems   61
Choke System Problems   64
Quick Service Procedures: Choke System   66
Quick Service Procedures: Minor Carburetor Repairs   69
Self-Test   71

CHAPTER 5   CARBURETOR OVERHAUL PROCEDURES

Learning Objectives   72
Introduction   73
How to Identify a Carburetor and Order the Parts   73
Carburetor Disassembly and Cleaning   74
Carburetor Reassembly and Internal Adjustments   78
External Carburetor Adjustments   80
Carburetor Installation   83
Self-Test   85

CHAPTER 6   FUEL INJECTION SYSTEMS

Learning Objectives   86
Introduction   87
Fuel Injection Systems   87
Electronic Fuel Injection   88
Bosch EFI-L and EFI-D Systems   89
Bosch Continuous Injection Systems   97
General Motors Electronic Fuel Injection System   101
Electronic Fuel Injection Service   107
Self-Test   107

CHAPTER 7   ELECTRICAL FUNDAMENTALS

Learning Objectives   **108**
Introduction   **109**
Electrical Fundamentals   **109**
Measuring Electron Flow   **110**
Magnetism   **111**
Electromagnetism   **112**
Electromagnetic Induction   **113**
Battery Theory   **114**
Self-Test   **117**

CHAPTER 8   ELECTRICAL CIRCUITS AND METERS

Learning Objectives   **118**
Introduction   **119**
Electrical Circuits   **119**
Electron Movement   **119**
Types of Electrical Circuits   **119**
Circuit Problems   **122**
Electrical Meters   **124**
Self-Test   **128**

CHAPTER 9   IGNITION SYSTEM FUNDAMENTALS

Learning Objectives   **129**
Introduction   **130**
Ignition Systems   **130**
Primary Circuit Components   **131**
Secondary Circuit Components   **134**
The Cycle of Events that Produce a Spark   **136**
Ballast Resistors and Ballast Wires   **138**
Point Gap and Dwell Angle   **139**
Self-Test   **141**

CHAPTER 10   DISTRIBUTOR ADVANCES, CABLES, AND SPARK PLUGS

Learning Objectives **142**
Introduction **143**
Ignition Timing **143**
Advance Mechanisms **143**
Ignition High-Tension Cables **148**
Spark Plugs **150**
Coil Polarity **154**
Self-Test **156**

CHAPTER 11   IGNITION SYSTEM SERVICE

Learning Objectives **157**
Introduction **158**
Compression Test **158**
Spark Plug Service **160**
Ignition System Electrical Tests **162**
Ignition Parts Inspection **164**
Distributor Service **169**
Installing an Unmarked Distributor **175**
Adjusting Ignition Timing **176**
Battery Service **178**
Battery Preventive Maintenance **180**
Battery Testing and Diagnosis **180**
Low-Maintenance Batteries **182**
Self-Test **183**

CHAPTER 12   ELECTRONIC IGNITION SYSTEMS

Learning Objectives **184**
Introduction **185**
The Chrysler Electronic Ignition System **186**
Testing Electronic Ignition Systems **189**
Chrysler Electronic Ignition Tests **190**
Ford Electronic Ignition Tests **194**
General Motors Electronic Ignition Tests **196**
Electronic Spark Advance **200**
Chrysler Electronic Spark Control **201**
Self-Test **203**

CHAPTER 13   EMISSION CONTROL SYSTEMS

Learning Objectives   **204**
Introduction   **205**
Air Pollution and Smog   **205**
Positive Crankcase Ventilation   **206**
Thermostatically Controlled Air Cleaner   **209**
Lean Carburetor Calibration   **210**
Part-Throttle and Power System   **212**
Metering Jets and Valves   **213**
Choke   **213**
Controlling Distributor Advance   **215**
Evaporative Emission Controls   **219**
Exhaust Gas Recirculating Systems   **222**
Air Injection Systems   **224**
Catalytic Converter Systems   **228**
Self-Test   **233**

CHAPTER 14   EMISSION CONTROL SYSTEMS: DIAGNOSIS AND SERVICE

Learning Objectives   **234**
Introduction   **235**
Infrared Exhaust Emision Analyzer   **235**
Propane-Assisted Idle Adjustment   **237**
Emission Control Service   **238**
PCV System Service   **239**
Thermostatic Air Cleaner Service   **240**
Electrically Heated Choke Service   **242**
Evaporative Emission Controls Service   **244**
EGR System Service   **245**
Air Injection System Service   **248**
Aspirator Air Valve Service   **250**
Catalytic Converter Service   **251**
Self-Test   **252**

SELF-TEST ANSWERS   253

INDEX   256

1

INTRODUCTION TO FUEL AND IGNITION SYSTEMS

☐ LEARNING OBJECTIVES ☐

After studying this chapter, you will be able to:

1. Describe gasoline combustion.
2. State the difference between carbon dioxide and carbon monoxide.
3. List the parts of a vehicle fuel and ignition system.
4. Describe each of the four-stroke cycles of a single-cylinder, internal-combustion engine.
5. List the major parts of a multicylinder, internal-combustion engine.
6. Describe the operation of an eight-cylinder, internal-combustion engine.
7. Explain the purpose of the parts in a vehicle driveline.
8. Define and/or discuss the following terms:

gasoline	crankshaft
octane number	camshaft
carbon monoxide	clutch
fuel system	torque converter
ignition system	transmission
four-stroke cycle	drive shaft

INTRODUCTION

The twentieth century has seen a large growth in all types of consumer goods, including automobiles. A large number of "horseless carriages" (buggies with engines) were produced before 1900. These early automobiles were powered by steam or electricity. Factory production of motor vehicles began about 1900. The modern automobile industry began with the development of the four-stroke cycle engine. It was fueled by gasoline that was ignited by a spark from an electrical source.

GASOLINE COMBUSTION

Gasoline, carefully selected and manufactured from crude petroleum, is a mixture of **hydrocarbons** (symbol HC). **Hydrocarbons** are compounds of hydrogen (a colorless gas) and carbon. Gasoline is blended during refining to give it the correct volatility (vaporization rate) and the proper octane rating, to comply with automobile industry standards. The ability of gasoline to burn properly in an engine, without knocking, is indicated by an **octane number,** such as 90 or 95.

During combustion in an engine, two parts of hydrogen from the gasoline and one part of oxygen from the atmosphere unite chemically to form water vapor (H_2O). At the same time, one part of carbon from the gasoline and two parts of oxygen from the atmosphere unite chemically to form carbon dioxide (CO_2). Water vapor and carbon dioxide, therefore, are the **byproducts** of gasoline combustion. These byproducts, along with some unburned fuel (HC) and an odorless gas, carbon monoxide (CO), are emitted from the exhaust. **Carbon dioxide** is harmless, but **carbon monoxide** is a deadly poison. If enough carbon monoxide is inhaled, death will result. This is why an exhaust ventilation system is always used when you are running a vehicle in a closed work area.

Although highly volatile, gasoline is a safe and effective fuel when burning is controlled. The automobile **carburetor** safely mixes air and fuel for controlled burning inside the engine cylinders.

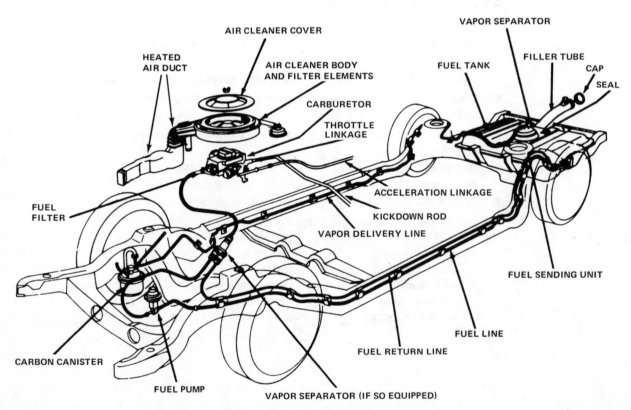

Figure 1-1.   Fuel system parts. (Courtesy of Ford Motor Company, Dearborn)

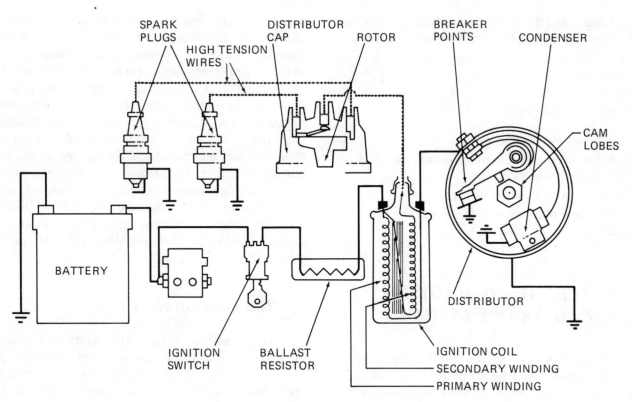

Figure 1-2. *A complete ignition system.*

FUEL SYSTEM

The **fuel system** delivers fuel from the fuel tank for use in the engine. See Figure 1-1. Gasoline is pumped by the **fuel pump** from the **fuel tank** and delivered to the carburetor through the **fuel lines**. The carburetor mixes the fuel with air and delivers it to the engine cylinders. Here the air-fuel mixture is ignited by a spark from the ignition system. These two systems— the fuel system and the ignition system—are the two major systems discussed in this text.

The fuel system consists of a fuel tank, vapor separator, fuel line, fuel pump, carbon canister, fuel filter, carburetor, throttle linkage, air-cleaner body and filter element, hot-air tube, and heated-air duct. Fuel lines, made of steel-tube or flexible fuel hose, connect the parts together.

FACTS TO REMEMBER

Gasoline is a mixture of hydrocarbons that are carefully selected and manufactured from crude petroleum. Although highly volatile, gasoline is a useful fuel under conditions of controlled burning. Gasoline must be mixed with oxygen to form a com-bustible mixture. During combustion, carbon monoxide (CO) is produced which, if inhaled, may result in death.

IGNITION SYSTEM

The **ignition system** components work together to create the ignition **spark** that ignites the air-fuel mixture. These components are shown in Figure 1-2. They increase the low battery voltage of 12 volts to the very high ignition voltage (up to 35,000 volts) needed to cause an electrical spark to jump the spark plug gap. This spark has enough heat to ignite the air-fuel mixture inside the engine cylinders.

The **battery** sends an electrical current through the ignition system at the moment that the **breaker points** in the **distributor** are closed. When the engine is in operation, this current flows through a **ballast resistor** to the **primary winding** inside the **ignition coil**. As the distributor shaft turns, the breaker points are opened by the **cam lobes** on the distributor shaft. This causes the ignition coil **secondary winding**, aided by the **condenser**, to create a high-voltage spark. This spark is delivered through the **distributor cap** and **rotor** to the **spark plugs** by the **high-tension wires**.

□   ASSIGNMENT 1-A   □

1. Describe gasoline combustion.
2. Describe the difference between carbon dioxide (CO_2) and carbon monoxide (CO).
3. List the parts of a vehicle fuel system.
4. List the parts of a vehicle ignition system.

INTERNAL-COMBUSTION ENGINE OPERATION

The most common type of automobile engine is the **four-stroke cycle, internal-combustion engine**. In order to understand the operation of a multicylinder engine, we will first discuss the design and operation of a single-cylinder engine. In Figure 1-3, notice that a **piston** is enclosed in a **cylinder**. **Piston rings** are fitted to the piston to provide a seal between the piston and the cylinder wall. The piston's reciprocating (up-and-down) motion is transferred through the **wrist pin** and **connecting rod** into rotary motion at the **crankshaft**. On top of the cylinder is a **cylinder head**. The cylinder head provides a cap and seal for the top of the combustion chamber. Located in the cylinder head are two valves: an **intake valve** and an **exhaust valve**. These valves control the incoming air-fuel mixture and the outgoing exhaust gas. Threaded into the cylinder head is the spark plug that ignites the air-fuel mixture.

The Four-Stroke Cycle

The term **four-stroke cycle** refers to a series of events that relate to the four movements (strokes) of the piston inside the cylinder. These strokes are called the intake, compression, power, and exhaust strokes. It is important to understand that the term **stroke** refers to only one movement of the piston, either up or down in the cylinder.

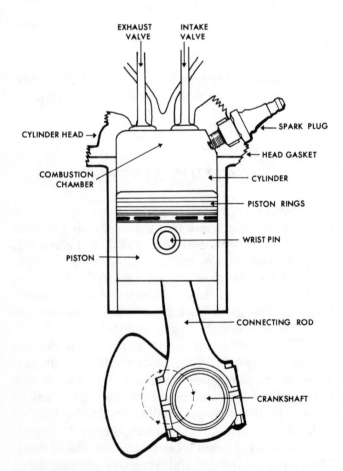

Figure 1-3.   A single-cylinder engine.

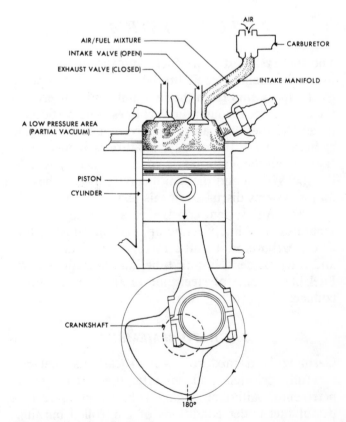

Figure 1-4.   Intake stroke.

Stroke 1–Intake: During the **intake stroke**, the piston moves down in the cylinder. During this stroke, the intake valve is open and the exhaust valve is closed, as shown in Figure 1-4. The piston movement creates a vacuum (a low-pressure area) in the cylinder. To fill this vacuum, the air-fuel mixture from the carburetor flows into the cylinder through the intake valve. When the piston has reached the bottom of the intake stroke, the crankshaft will have revolved one-half of a revolution.

Stroke 2–Compression: As the crankshaft continues to rotate, the piston moves back up into the cylinder. This is the **compression stroke**. The intake and exhaust valves are both closed, sealing the upper part of the cylinder. See Figure 1-5. The upward piston movement compresses the air-fuel mixture so that it will ignite easily and burn efficiently. When the piston has reached the top of the compression stroke, the crankshaft will have revolved one complete revolution.

Stroke 3–Power: When the piston is at the top of the compression stroke, the air-fuel mixture will be fully compressed and both valves will still be closed. See Figure 1-6. At this moment, an electrical charge, created by the ignition system, is transmitted to the spark plug. This charge creates a spark that jumps the spark plug gap, causing the compressed air-fuel mixture to burn rapidly. This forces the piston down in the cylinder for the **power stroke**. The connecting rod moves down with the piston and forces the crankshaft to rotate. At the end of the power stroke, the crankshaft will have rotated one and one-half revolutions.

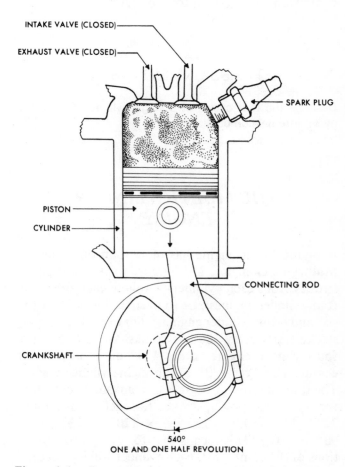

Figure 1-6.   Power stroke.

Stroke 4–Exhaust: The piston is now at the bottom of the cylinder. Due to the motion created during the power stroke, the crankshaft pushes the piston back up in the cylinder. See Figure 1-7. On this stroke, the intake valve remains closed, but the exhaust valve is opened. As the piston moves up, it forces the exhaust gas up the cylinder and out the exhaust valve. This is the **exhaust stroke**. It is immediately followed by an intake stroke. The process continues as long as fuel and spark are supplied to the cylinder. At the end of each exhaust stroke, the

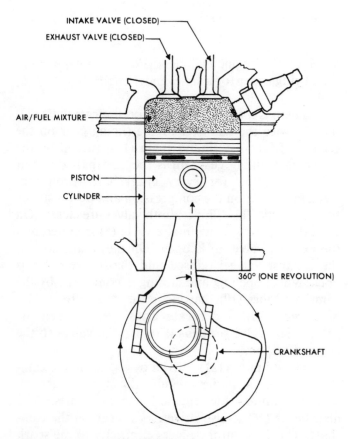

Figure 1-5.   Compression stroke.

crankshaft will have rotated two complete revolutions.

FACTS TO REMEMBER

In order to complete the four-stroke cycle, the piston must move down, up, down, and up. These four piston strokes occur in the following cycle: intake, compression, power, and exhaust. Each complete four-stroke cycle will cause the crankshaft to turn two complete revolutions, a total of 720°.

□   ASSIGNMENT 1-B   □

Describe the four cycles of a single-cylinder, four-stroke cycle, internal-combustion engine.

THE MULTICYLINDER ENGINE

A **multicylinder** engine has more than one cylinder. Multicylinder engines are designed to allow the power strokes from each cylinder to follow each other (on four-cylinder engines), or to overlap one another (on six- and eight-cylinder engines). For example, a power stroke starts every 180° of crankshaft rotation on a four-cylinder engine, every 120° on a six-cylinder engine, and every 90° on an eight-cylinder engine. The total number of degrees of crankshaft revolution for all of the power strokes for each engine totals 720° (4 × 180° = 720°, 6 × 120° = 720°, 8 × 90° = 720°). This means that for every two revolutions of the crankshaft, each cylinder will have received spark once and completed one four-stroke cycle.

To understand the operation of a multicylinder engine, look at the cutaway view of an eight-cylinder engine shown in Figure 1-8. The action of the pistons (20) is transferred to the crankshaft (18) through the wrist pins (14) and connecting rods (9). **Connecting-rod bearings** (15), positioned between the connecting-rod and **crankshaft journals**, protect the connecting rod and the crankshaft journals from wear. **Main bearings** (16) allow the crankshaft to rotate smoothly and freely.

In order to evenly distribute the power stroke from the different pistons across the length of the crankshaft, engine manufacturers stagger the **firing**

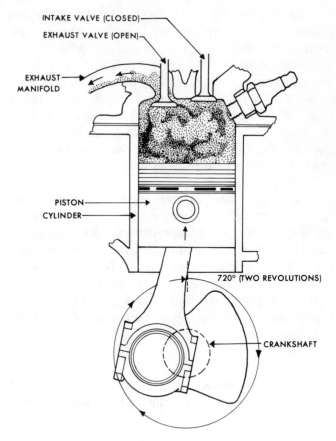

Figure 1-7.   Exhaust stroke.

order of the engine cylinders. For example, a common firing order for a six-cylinder engine is 1, 5, 3, 6, 2, 4.

There is a **timing gear** (13) on the **camshaft** (22) that is twice the diameter of the timing gear on the crankshaft (11). A **timing chain** (12), turned by the crankshaft timing gear, turns the camshaft one-half of a revolution for every crankshaft revolution. Remember that on the compression and power stroke for any particular cylinder, both valves are closed. On the exhaust stroke, the intake valve (5) is closed and the exhaust valve (6) is open. On the intake stroke, the exhaust valve is closed and the intake valve is open. Valve opening and closing is controlled by the **camshaft lobes** (19) that move the **valve lifters** (17), **push rods** (28), and **rocker arms** (29) to open the valves. The **valve springs** (4) return the valves to the closed position.

The **oil pump** (21), driven by a gear on the camshaft, forces oil under pressure through passages to lubricate all of the engine's moving parts. The **distributor** (26) is also driven by a gear on the camshaft. The distributor delivers electricity to the spark plugs (27), as each piston nears the top of its compres-

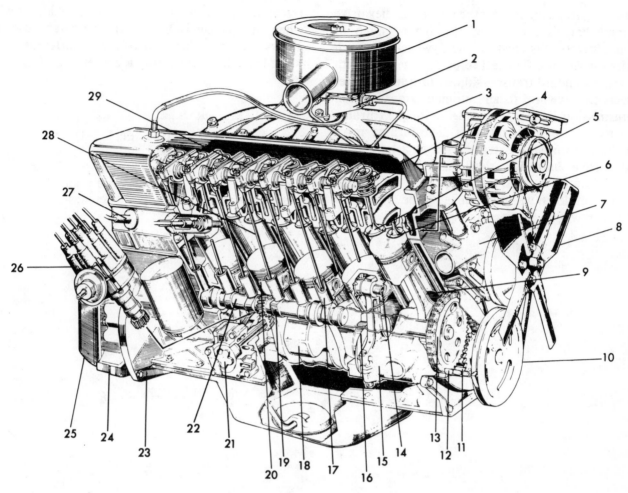

Figure 1-8. *A multicylinder engine. (Courtesy of Chrysler Corporation)*

sion stroke. Air, to be mixed with fuel, passes through the **air cleaner** (1) and mixes with fuel in the carburetor (2). The air-fuel mixture is distributed to the different cylinders through the **intake manifold** (3). The **fanbelt**, driven by the crankshaft, turns the **water pump** (7) and **cooling fan** (8) to circulate water and air that cools the engine. Water in the radiator is cooled by air from the cooling fan and from the forward motion of the vehicle. This water is circulated from the radiator through passages around the engine cylinders.

The **flywheel** (23) (a heavy metal wheel) is mounted to the rear of the engine on the crankshaft. When the engine is in operation, the turning flywheel tends to smooth out the power surges of the individual pistons. The flywheel also serves as a mounting for the clutch (24) (if the vehicle has a standard trans-

mission), or a torque converter (if the vehicle has an automatic transmission). The flywheel also contains a **ring gear** with which the **starter** (not shown in Figure 1-8) turns the crankshaft to start the engine.

□ ASSIGNMENT 1-C □

1. Review Figure 1-8 and list the numbered parts of an engine.

2. State the purpose for each of the following engine parts:

   pistons   push rods
   crankshaft   distributor
   camshaft   flywheel
   timing gears and chain

DRIVELINE COMPONENTS

The turning force created by the pistons as they drive the crankshaft is transmitted through a clutch or torque converter fastened on the flywheel. A **clutch** permits the turning flywheel to be disengaged or engaged to a standard transmission. A **torque converter** connects the flywheel to an automatic transmission. A **transmission** increases the engine torque (turning force) through a series of gears. The turning force from the transmission is transferred to a long shaft called a **drive shaft**. This shaft has a front and rear universal joint. **Universal joints** allow the rear axle to move up and down without damaging the drive shaft as the rear wheels go over bumps. The drive shaft transmits the turning action from the transmission to another set of gears inside a differential. The **differential** divides the torque evenly to each rear wheel when the vehicle is being driven straight and also allows the rear wheels to rotate at different speeds when the vehicle is turning a corner.

☐ ASSIGNMENT 1-D ☐

Explain the purpose of the following driveline parts:
clutch	drive shaft
transmission	differential

□ SELF-TEST □

Complete the following sentences by filling in the missing words.

1. The modern automobile industry began with the development of the _____-stroke cycle engine, fueled by _____ that was ignited by a _____ from an electrical source.

2. Gasoline, carefully selected and manufactured from crude _____ , is a mixture of _____ .

3. The ability of gasoline to burn properly in an engine, without knocking, is indicated by an _____ number.

4. Carbon dioxide is considered harmless, but carbon _____ is a deadly poison.

5. The automobile carburetor safely mixes _____ and _____ for controlled burning inside the engine cylinders.

6. Fuel lines, made of _____-tube or _____ fuel hose, connect the parts of the fuel system together.

7. The _____ system components work together to create the ignition spark that ignites the _____-_____ mixture.

8. The ignition system has a battery that sends an electrical current through the _____ system at the moment that the breaker points in the distributor are _____ .

9. As the distributor shaft turns, the breaker points are opened by the _____ _____ on the distributor shaft.

10. The piston's _____ (up-and-down) motion is transferred through the wrist pin and connecting rod into _____ motion at the crankshaft.

11. Located in the cylinder head are two valves: an _____ valve and an _____ valve.

12. During the intake stroke, the piston moves _____ in the cylinder. During this stroke, the intake valve is _____ and the _____ valve is closed.

13. When the piston has reached the top of the compression stroke, the crankshaft will have revolved _____ complete _____ .

14. Each complete four-stroke cycle will cause the _____ to turn _____ revolutions.

15. In order to evenly distribute the _____ stroke loads from the different pistons across the length of the crankshaft, engine manufacturers _____ the firing order of the engine cylinders.

16. There is a timing gear on the camshaft that is _____ the diameter of the _____ gear on the crankshaft.

17. The _____ pump, driven by a gear on the camshaft, forces oil under _____ through passages to lubricate all of the engine's moving parts.

18. Air, to be mixed with fuel, passes through the air _____ and mixes with fuel in the _____ .

19. The purpose of a transmission is to increase the engine _____ (turning force) through a series of gears.

20. The _____ _____ transmits the turning action from the transmission to another set of gears inside a differential.

2

FUEL TANKS, LINES, AND PUMPS

☐ LEARNING OBJECTIVES ☐

After studying this chapter, you will be able to:

1. Explain the purpose and describe the construction features of fuel tanks, fuel lines, and fuel pumps.

2. Explain the operation of a mechanical fuel pump and an electrical fuel pump.

3. Describe the inspection and testing procedures for fuel pumps, fuel lines, and fuel tanks.

4. Define and/or discuss the following terms:
   atmospheric pressure
   vacuum
   tank vent
   vapor return line
   mechanical diaphragm fuel pump
   diaphragm-type electric fuel pump
   impeller-type electric fuel pump
   fuel pump pressure test
   fuel pump flow test

INTRODUCTION

The **fuel system** brings fuel from the fuel tank to the carburetor. The carburetor mixes air with the fuel and delivers the mixture to the engine cylinders for combustion. The air-fuel mixture is regulated for varying engine conditions, such as cold and hot starting, idling, slow speeds, high speeds, acceleration, and heavy loads.

FUEL SYSTEM PARTS

The main parts of a fuel system are the fuel tank, fuel lines, fuel pump, fuel filter, and the carburetor. Figure 2-1 shows all of the fuel system parts that deal with fuel storage, delivery, venting, and vapor recovery.

The **fuel tank** stores fuel so that the vehicle can travel long distances before refueling. When the fuel system is in operation, the fuel pump produces a vacuum in the fuel line that draws fuel through the **fuel sending unit** and fuel line to the fuel pump. The **fuel pump** sends fuel through the line to the **fuel filter** where it is cleaned before entering the carburetor.

The **vapor separator** allows fuel vapors (caused by heat), along with some fuel, to return to the fuel tank through the **fuel return line**. The **carburetor** produces and delivers the proper air-fuel mixture to the engine for all driving conditions. It contains the **throttle** (controlled by the throttle linkage) that regulates the quantity of fuel and air delivered to the engine. The **heated-air duct** preheats and regulates the temperature of the air going into the air cleaner. The **air cleaner** filters and cleans the air going into the carburetor.

Fuel vapors formed in the fuel tank pass through the **vapor separator** on the fuel tank. They then travel through the **vapor delivery line** to a **carbon canister**. These fuel vapors are stored in the carbon canister until the engine is started. They are then burned during combustion.

FACTS TO REMEMBER

A vehicle fuel system stores fuel and delivers it to the carburetor. The carburetor produces and delivers the proper air-fuel mixture to the engine cylinders for various driving conditions.

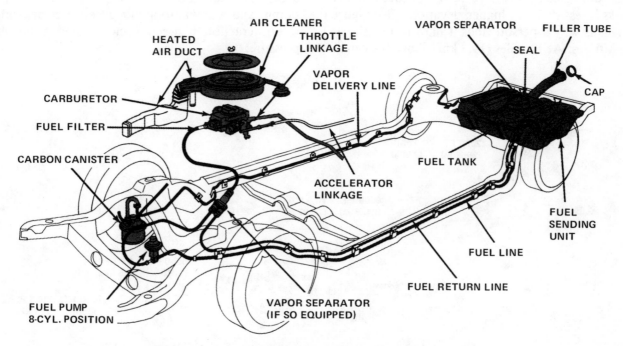

Figure 2-1. A typical fuel system. (Courtesy of Ford Motor Company, Dearborn)

State the purpose of the following fuel system parts:

fuel tank	vapor separator
fuel line	fuel return line
fuel pump	throttle
fuel filter	air cleaner
carburetor	

ATMOSPHERIC PRESSURE AND VACUUM

In order to understand the operation of a fuel system, you must understand the terms "atmospheric pressure" and "vacuum."

Atmospheric Pressure

The pressure that exists in the air mass surrounding the earth is called **atmospheric pressure**. At sea level, atmospheric pressure is about 14.7 pounds per square inch (psi). In metric measure, this figure would equal 101.34 kPa (read kilopascals).

At any given altitude, atmospheric pressure is equal in all directions. However, as elevation *increases*, atmospheric pressure *decreases*, because the air mass is less dense at higher elevations. See Figure 2-2. This is why a person finds it hard to breathe at high altitudes. At 12 miles (19.3 km) above the earth, air pressure is less than one pound per square inch (6.9 kPa). In the same way that a person finds it difficult to breathe at high altitudes, a vehicle engine finds it difficult to take in air. In fact, at 12 miles above the earth an automobile engine could not operate at all.

Vacuum

A **vacuum** can be considered a confined space from which most of the air has been removed, leaving an area where the pressure is less than atmospheric pressure. A vacuum is sometimes called a **low-pressure area**, because the pressure in a vacuum is less than atmospheric pressure.

The types of vacuums encountered in automotive situations are only partial (incomplete) vacuums. A partial, weak, or low vacuum is formed when a small difference in pressure is created between the atmosphere and the vacuum area. A strong, or high, vacuum occurs when there is a large pressure difference. In automotive work, the term **low vacuum** represents a low reading on a vacuum gauge, while a **high vacuum** represents a high reading.

There is an interaction between areas with different pressures. Air at any pressure greater than that of a vacuum will move toward a vacuum. Air at atmospheric pressure flows into low-pressure (vacuum) areas in an effort to equalize the pressure in the two areas. The operation of an engine, carburetor, fuel pump, and many automobile accessories depends on this interaction between vacuums and atmospheric pressure.

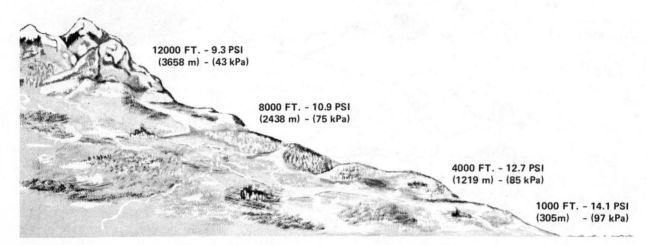

12000 FT. - 9.3 PSI
(3658 m) - (43 kPa)

8000 FT. - 10.9 PSI
(2438 m) - (75 kPa)

4000 FT. - 12.7 PSI
(1219 m) - (85 kPa)

1000 FT. - 14.1 PSI
(305m)   - (97 kPa)

Figure 2-2. *Atmospheric pressure at different elevations above sea level.*

FACTS TO REMEMBER

Air moves from high- to low-pressure areas in an attempt to equalize pressure between the two areas. This principle is important to the operation of many automotive systems. For example, if atmospheric pressure cannot enter a fuel tank because the tank is fitted with an incorrect gas cap, the automobile will stall. This is because the fuel pump will create a vacuum in the fuel line by removing most of the air from it. However, the incorrect gas cap will not allow atmospheric pressure to enter the tank, and no fuel will be able to leave the tank to fill the vacuum created in the fuel line by the fuel pump. The pressure in the system will not be able to equalize, and the car will stall. The difference between the atmospheric pressure on the outside of the tank and the vacuum created inside may even crush the tank.

□ ASSIGNMENT 2-B □

Give a brief explanation of atmospheric pressure and vacuum or a low-pressure area.

FUEL TANKS

The **fuel tank** is used to store fuel. A front-engine car usually has the fuel tank mounted at the rear under the floor. Fuel tanks are usually made from stamped sheet steel that is galvanized or plated to retard rusting. Tank capacities vary.

Most tanks have **baffles**, as shown in Figure 2-3, that reduce fuel sloshing when starting, stopping, or turning. A **filler tube** leads to a convenient spot for filling the tank. The filler tube is covered by a cap that may be vented or nonvented. Fuel is delivered to a fuel line attached to a fuel sending unit that is located either on the top or side of the tank. Most fuel tanks made after 1971 contain non-overfill-expansion chambers and vapor recovery systems. These prevent the release of gasoline vapor and fuel spillage, both of which contribute to air pollution.

Fuel Tank Venting

The fuel tank must be **vented** to allow atmospheric pressure to enter it. Atmospheric pressure

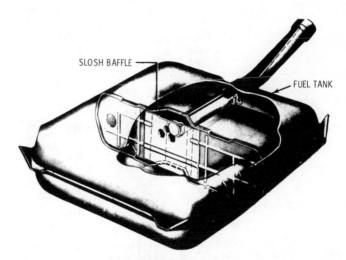

SLOSH BAFFLE

FUEL TANK

Figure 2-3. A fuel tank with baffles to reduce fuel sloshing. (Courtesy of General Motors of Canada Limited)

forces fuel into the vacuum created in the fuel line by the fuel pump. If atmospheric pressure cannot enter the tank, fuel will not be able to enter the fuel line. A tank vent, in its simplest form, could be a hole through the filler cap. However, to prevent fuel spillage, the cap is generally sealed and a vent line is located on the tank. The vent line could be a tube leading from the top of the tank to a convenient spot under the car.

On cars produced since 1971, the vent line is also a vapor delivery line that is attached to a carbon canister. See Figure 2-4. While the car is standing, vapors are directed through a **liquid-vapor separator** that removes and returns any liquid fuel to the tank through the **liquid return line**. The vapors from the separator pass through the **fuel tank vent line** to the **charcoal canister**. Activated charcoal in the canister absorbs the vapors and prevents them from escaping into the atmosphere. When the engine is running, the canister is purged of vapors by **purge air** that passes through the canister and **purge valve**, and on into the engine manifold to be burned in the cylinders. Vapors from the carburetor bowl may also be absorbed in the charcoal canister. These pass through the **carburetor fuel bowl vent tube** when the engine is not running.

The **pressure-vacuum filler gas cap** prevents excess pressure or vacuum buildup in the fuel tank. A plugged fuel tank vent line, for example, could cause an excess pressure buildup. The special valve in the filler cap allows tank pressure to escape and also allows atmospheric pressure to enter the tank when a vacuum is created inside the tank.

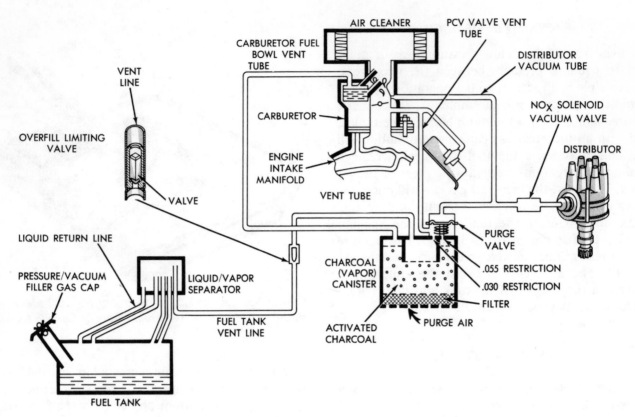

Figure 2-4. *An evaporation control system with a charcoal canister. (Courtesy of Chrysler Corporation)*

Fuel Filters

The fuel tank is designed with a **sediment area** that collects water and dirt. If dirt or water enters the fuel system, it can cause corrosion and carburetor or fuel pump failure. The **fuel pickup pipe**, part of the fuel gauge tank unit shown in Figure 2-5, is positioned slightly above the bottom of the tank. There is

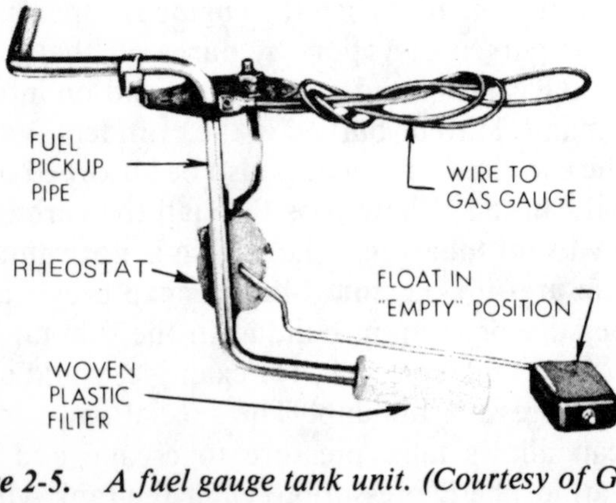

Figure 2-5. *A fuel gauge tank unit. (Courtesy of General Motors of Canada Limited)*

usually a woven plastic **filter** on the fuel pickup pipe that filters out dirt but, like any fuel filter, cannot filter water out of the fuel.

Dirt, pieces of iron oxide (rust), and particles shed from inside the fuel system parts can cause fuel system problems. Dirt lodged in fuel pump valves will cause pump failure. Dirt in the carburetor needle and seat valve can cause the carburetor to flood. It is common to have a fuel filter on the fuel pump, in the fuel line leading to the carburetor, or in the fitting where the line attaches to the carburetor. See Figures 2-6, 2-7, and 2-8.

Fuel Gauge Tank Unit

The **fuel gauge tank unit** or fuel sending unit (Figure 2-5) is installed in the top or side of the fuel tank. The tank unit sends an electrical signal to the dashboard fuel gauge that indicates the level of fuel in the tank. This unit is a type of variable-resistance rheostat that has an operating arm with a float at the end.

As the fuel supply level increases or decreases, the float rises and falls and changes the electrical resistance of the sending unit. This varies the reading on the dashboard fuel gauge. The fuel pickup pipe and filter are an integral part of this unit.

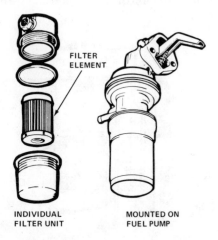

FILTER ELEMENT

INDIVIDUAL FILTER UNIT

MOUNTED ON FUEL PUMP

Figure 2-6. Some fuel pumps have a filter mounted on them, or the filter could be in the line after the pump. (Courtesy of Ford Motor Company, Dearborn)

□ ASSIGNMENT 2-C □

1. Describe the construction features of a fuel tank.
2. List the possible locations for fuel filters in a fuel system.
3. Describe the operation of a fuel gauge tank unit.

Fuel Tank Inspection and Service

A fuel tank is serviced only if it is damaged, leaking, or needs to be cleaned out. The need for fuel tank service is usually determined by visual inspection. When the tank is full, look for signs of leakage (such as clean spots where fuel has washed out) on the top or sides of the tank. Bottom leaks drip and are easily found. Look for damage such as a crush or abrasion caused by hitting ramps, curbs, or bumps. A clogged vent pipe or an unvented filler cap can cause the top or bottom of a tank to cave in. Make sure the proper filler cap is being used.

If the tank must be removed, first drain the fuel from it. Some tanks have drain plugs for draining off water and dirt or removing fuel. You must syphon the fuel out through the filler pipe or through the fuel line on a tank that does not have a drain plug.

Caution: To avoid explosion or fire, extreme caution and care must be used when handling gasoline. If you have a safety gasoline syphoning and storage unit, much of the danger is eliminated. If you have to syphon or drain fuel into open containers, keep the area well ventilated. No welding, smoking, or other types of flame should be allowed near the vehicle. Avoid using an extension lamp. A dropped lamp could start a fire. Have a fire extinguisher near-by. Put the syphoned gasoline into covered containers to prevent danger of explosion from the vapors. Wipe up spills immediately, and put the rags in a closed, metal safety container.

After removing the fuel, carefully remove the fuel line and vent lines from the tank to prevent breaking or damaging them. Next, remove the tank mounting straps. Use a jack to hold the tank in place while you are removing the straps. Lower the tank carefully to avoid spillage and to prevent sparks that might occur if the tank fell on a cement floor.

If the tank is leaking and is badly rusted, it should be replaced. Soldering the tank would be a waste of time, since it would probably soon begin

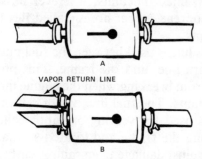

A

VAPOR RETURN LINE

B

Figure 2-7. A disposable, in-line filter (A) and a disposable, in-line filter with a vapor return line (B). (Courtesy of Ford Motor Company, Dearborn)

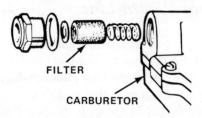

FILTER

CARBURETOR

Figure 2-8. A fuel filter in the fuel line fitting on the carburetor. (Courtesy of Ford Motor Company, Dearborn)

leaking again. A crushed, caved-in, or leaking tank that is not rusted should be sent to a radiator repair shop to be safely repaired by an expert. **Caution:** It is very dangerous to try to braze or weld a fuel tank. Such repairs should be left to a qualified expert.

□ ASSIGNMENT 2-D □

1. List three things to look for when inspecting a fuel tank.
2. Describe the procedures for removing a fuel tank.
3. List the safety precautions for removing a fuel tank.

FUEL LINES

The main fuel line carries the fuel from the fuel tank to the fuel pump. Other lines in the fuel system are: the fuel line between the fuel pump and carburetor, the vapor return line, and the vent or venting-vapor collection lines. These lines are generally made from a rust-resistant steel alloy that can withstand abrasion, crushing, or breakage. Lines may be connected to some units with metal fittings, but it is common practice to join lines and units, wherever possible, with flexible neoprene rubber hoses (called **flex lines**) held with clamps.

A flex line is used between the fuel pump, or the vapor return line, and the frame. This prevents the fuel lines from breaking when the engine moves on its rubber mounts. The fuel line, vapor return line, and other lines used for venting or vapor collection are placed along the frame and located so that they are guarded against damage from ramps, curbs, or flying stones. They are held firmly in place by spring steel clips that snap into holes in the frame. This prevents chafing or breakage of the lines due to vibrations.

Vapor Return Lines

During warm weather, engine heat can boil the gasoline in the fuel pump and lines and cause vapors to form. This can cause **vapor lock**, which will stop the fuel pump from pumping fuel. Vapor lock occurs when vapor forms faster than the pump can remove it, and the engine stalls. The vapor return line returns a metered amount of fuel, along with fuel vapors,

back into the fuel tank. This fuel circulation tends to lower the temperature of the fuel in the engine area and reduce the likelihood of vapor lock. The vapor return line may connect to a fitting containing a metering restriction in the fuel pump, or to a special vapor separator unit in the fuel line between the fuel pump and the carburetor. See Figure 2-1 and Figure 2-9.

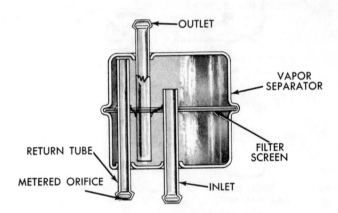

Figure 2-9. *A vapor separator that is located between the fuel pump and carburetor. (Courtesy of Chrysler Corporation)*

Fuel Line Inspection and Service

To service fuel lines, raise the vehicle by using either a jack or a hoist. If a jack is used, make sure the vehicle is properly supported on safety stands.

Procedure: Give a thorough visual inspection to all of the lines in the fuel system. Inspect steel lines for signs of breakage, abrasion, crushing, rusted-out areas, or fuel leakage. Inspect flex lines for rotting, cracking, leakage, or deteriorated clamps. If a small section of steel line needs to be repaired, the damaged area may be removed with a pipe cutter. The section can be replaced with gas line hose and clamps. If the entire line must be replaced, only steel tube should be used for safety. Be sure to use the proper flaring methods and fittings. Where flex lines are required, use only neoprene rubber fuel line hose that has been marked **For Fuel Use**, and be sure to use new clamps.

Caution: Never use rubber hose that is not marked **For Fuel Use**. This hose will swell and deteriorate when exposed to gasoline. When exposed to heat, it will become brittle and tend to crack and break. Only use neoprene fuel line hose.

☐ ASSIGNMENT 2-E ☐

1. List the fuel line conditions you should look for during fuel line inspection.
2. Explain the purpose of a vapor return line in a fuel system.
3. Explain the purpose of a flexible fuel line.
4. Describe the procedure for replacing a section of fuel line.

MECHANICAL FUEL PUMPS

Various methods have been used to bring gasoline from the fuel tank to the carburetor. Some early vehicles had a pump, similar to a bicycle tire pump, that was used to pressurize the fuel tank. This pressure pushed the fuel from the tank to the carburetor. Other early vehicles had gravity feed systems. In these systems the fuel tank was mounted at a point higher than the carburetor, usually in front of the windshield. The force of gravity caused the fuel to run through a fuel line in the bottom of the fuel tank to the carburetor.

The mechanical diaphragm-type fuel pump used today had early beginnings. It has been used for well over half a century with very little change other than improvements in the materials used to construct the diaphragm and valves. Electric fuel pumps are also used today. These are discussed later in this chapter.

Fuel Pump Construction Features

The **mechanical diaphragm fuel pump** is a practical method for bringing fuel from the fuel tank to the carburetor. Modern fuel pumps are sealed, nonrepairable units. Through a series of springs and diaphragms, activated by a mechanical rocker arm, they draw fuel from the tank and deliver it to the carburetor. Figure 2-10 is an exploded view of a typical mechanical diaphragm fuel pump. Study the illustration to become familiar with the fuel pump parts before continuing your reading.

Check Valves

Since check valves play an important part in fuel pump operation, it is important to understand how they function. **A check valve** is a one-way valve that permits fluid to flow in only one direction. The valve has a thin disc made of neoprene or fiber that is held tight against a seat by a fine spring. See Figure 2-11. With pressure in the direction shown in View A, the disc is pushed against the seat (closed) and fuel cannot pass through the valve. With pressure from the opposite direction (View B), the disc is pushed away from the seat (open), allowing fuel to pass through the valve.

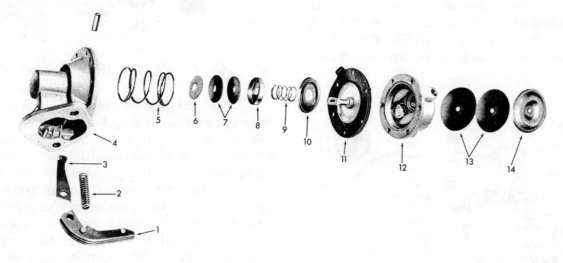

1. Rocker Arm
2. Rocker Arm Return Spring
3. Actuating Lever
4. Pump Body
5. Diaphragm Spring
6. Lower Seal Retainer
7. Oil Seal
8. Upper Seal Retainer
9. Seal Spring
10. Diaphragm Spring Upper Seat
11. Diaphragm
12. Fuel Cover and Valves
13. Pulsator Diaphragm
14. Pulsator Cover

Figure 2-10. Exploded view of a diaphragm fuel pump.
(Courtesy of General Motors of Canada Limited)

VIEW A: DISC PUSHED CLOSED
BLOCKING FLOW.

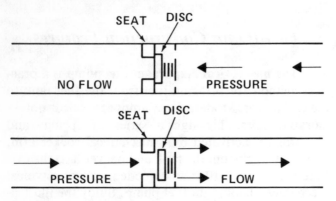

VIEW B: DISC PUSHED OPEN
ALLOWING FLOW.

Figure 2-11. Check valve operation. A check valve can be opened by pressure pushing the disc, or vacuum pulling it.

Mechanical Diaphragm Fuel Pump Operation

To understand the operation of a typical mechanical diaphragm fuel pump, study the following explanation and illustrations.

Rocker Arm Movement: The fuel pump is bolted to the engine on a mounting flange. The **rocker arm** extends inside the engine where it comes into contact with either an eccentric on the camshaft, or a push rod that rides against an eccentric on the camshaft. An **eccentric** is a circular lobe made off center to the main center of the camshaft. See Figure 2-12. While the camshaft is rotating, the eccentric rotates,

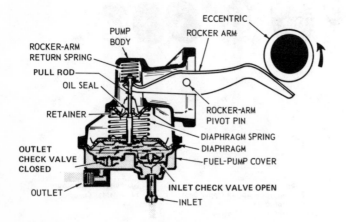

Figure 2-12. Pump intake stroke. (Courtesy of General Motors of Canada Limited)

causing the pump rocker arm to move back and forth.

Pump Intake Stroke: As the eccentric rotates, it pushes the pump rocker arm. The rocker arm moves a **pull rod** and compresses the **diaphragm spring**. As the **diaphragm spring** becomes compressed, it moves the diaphragm away from the **inlet check valve**, as shown in Figure 2-12. As the diaphragm moves away, the space between the diaphragm and the inlet check valve increases and creates a vacuum. Pressure from the outlet, trying to enter this vacuum, will close the **outlet check valve**. Atmospheric pressure in the gas tank will force gasoline into the vacuum created between the diaphragm and the inlet check valve. Gasoline will flow from the tank, through the fuel line, and into the fuel pump inlet, where it will open the inlet check valve and enter the diaphragm area.

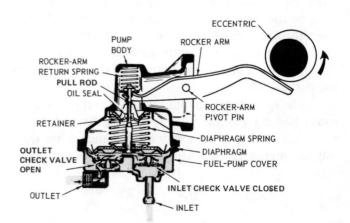

Figure 2-13. Pump pressure stroke. (Courtesy of General Motors of Canada Limited)

Pump Pressure Stroke: The eccentric continues to rotate, and the rocker arm moves back with it, as shown in Figure 2-13. This action releases the pull rod and diaphragm, and the heavy diaphragm spring pushes the diaphragm toward the check valves. This reduces the space below the diaphragm and compresses the fuel, causing an increase in pressure. The pressurized fuel, trying to escape toward a lower pressure area, will close the inlet check valve and force the outlet check valve open. Fuel will be discharged from the pump outlet and forced through the line to the carburetor float bowl. These actions, repeated each time the camshaft revolves, maintain enough fuel in the carburetor for all engine demands.

When the carburetor float bowl is full, the

needle and seat valve closes and stops the fuel flow from the fuel pump to the carburetor. The fuel pump diaphragm will remain at or near its maximum travel, because the diaphragm spring is unable to compress the gasoline further. Pressure now is maximum and is maintained by the tension of the diaphragm spring pushing against the diaphragm. The rocker arm continues to rock back and forth. As fuel demand increases, the fuel level in the fuel bowl decreases. This opens the needle and seat valve, and the fuel pump will again pump fuel to fill the carburetor.

☐ ASSIGNMENT 2-F ☐

Describe the operation of a mechanical diaphragm fuel pump during the intake stroke and the pressure stroke.

ELECTRIC FUEL PUMPS

An **electric fuel pump** can be used instead of a mechanical diaphragm fuel pump. Some manufacturers supply electric fuel pumps as original equipment on their vehicles. Electric pumps have some advantages over engine-mounted, mechanical diaphragm pumps. An electric pump works independently of the engine, using electric power supplied through the vehicle electrical system. When an electric pump is installed at the tank, the fuel is *pushed* through the fuel line by pump pressure instead of being *pulled* through the line by pump vacuum. This reduces the possibility of vapor lock.

Some electric pumps are mounted inside the fuel tank. On these pumps, gasoline flows around the pump armature and quenches the electrical arching at the brushes. Because there is no oxygen (air) in the fuel to aid combustion, there is no danger of fire with such a pump. For safety, the electrical connection is made on the outside of the tank. Other electric fuel pumps may be mounted in any convenient location on the fuel line.

When the camshaft fuel pump lobe for a mechanical diaphragm pump is badly worn, it is possible to install an electric fuel pump on the fuel line. In this way, you can avoid replacing the camshaft. A short description of the features and operation of several types of electric fuel pumps is given below.

Diaphragm-Type Electric Fuel Pump

Some manufacturers produce an electric fuel pump that has a magnetic solenoid and points. The pump uses a diaphragm unit similar to a mechanical diaphragm pump.

Refer to Figure 2-14 while reading the following description of a cycle of this pump. When the ignition switch is on, current flows through terminal (1), points (2), and through the winding (3). This magnetizes the core (4), which draws the armature (5), and pulls the diaphragm (6) over, compressing the spring (7). When the diaphragm moves, it creates a vacuum, and fuel enters the valve (8) through the inlet (9). As soon as the magnet has pulled the diaphragm to near its full travel, the points are snapped apart by the spindle (10). The open points cut off the current flow, and the magnetism collapses. The feed spring can now push the diaphragm back. As the diaphragm moves back, the pressure pushes the fuel through the valve to the outlet (11). Near the far travel of the diaphragm, the points will snap closed again by the reverse action of the spindle. This causes magnetism to pull the diaphragm again. How often the cycles occur is governed by engine needs.

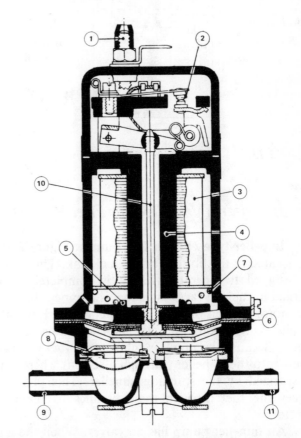

Figure 2-14.   An electric fuel pump, diaphragm type.

Bellows-Type Electric Fuel Pump

In the **bellows-type electric pump** shown in Figure 2-15, a metal bellows is used instead of a diaphragm. A bellows can cause vacuum when it is stretched (opened) and pressure when it is compressed (closed). The electrical and pumping operation of a bellows pump is similar to that of the diaphragm-type electrical pump.

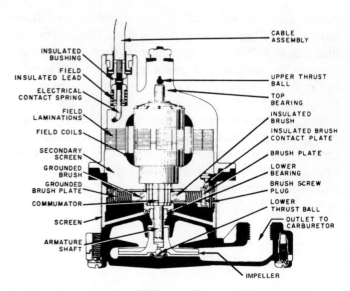

Figure 2-16.   An impeller-type electric fuel pump.

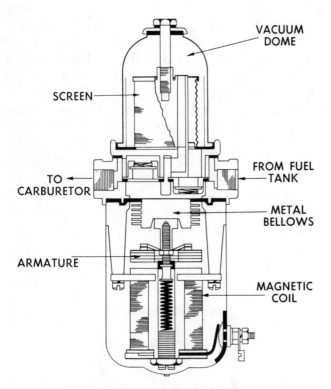

Figure 2-15.   A bellows-type electric pump.

Impeller-Type Electric Fuel Pumps

Impeller-type electric fuel pumps (Figure 2-16) are located in the bottom of the fuel tank. The pump is designed to operate while it is completely submerged in fuel. In fact, some fuel is pumped through the motor section of the pump to cool and lubricate it. The electric motor spins the **impeller blades** at high speed. Because the pump is submerged, fuel will run freely into the impeller (through a screen) where it is pressurized by the spinning impeller. This pressure forces the fuel through the fuel lines to the carburetor.

An impeller pump has no valves. When the engine is switched off, the pump stops and the pressure

in the pump drops to zero. This takes the fuel pressure off the carburetor and reduces flooding in a hot, standing engine.

Figure 2-17 shows an electric pump mounted on the fuel pickup pipe. Figure 2-18 is a cutaway view of this type of pump. This small impeller-type pump operates the same way as the larger types, but uses permanent magnetic fields to reduce its size. The motor section of this pump uses gasoline for cooling and lubrication.

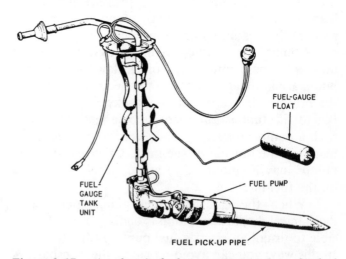

Figure 2-17.   An electric fuel pump mounted on the fuel pickup pipe. (Courtesy of General Motors of Canada Limited)

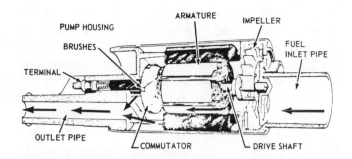

Figure 2-18. Cutaway view of an electric fuel pump mounted on the fuel pickup pipe. (Courtesy of General Motors of Canada Limited)

□ **ASSIGNMENT 2-G** □

1. Indicate whether the following electric pumps are motor or solenoid operated and whether they have valves or not:
   diaphragm electric
   bellows type
   impeller type

2. Explain the advantage of a tank-mounted, electric fuel pump.

FUEL PUMP TESTING PROCEDURES

The pressure and flow capacity of each fuel pump is engineered according to the demands of the engine-carburetor combination for which it is designed. The average pressure of most fuel pumps is in the range of 3–5 psi (21–34 kPa), and the flow capacity is at least 1 pint (.5 liter) in 30 seconds.

It is important to test fuel pump performance because too much fuel pressure can result in a high fuel level in the carburetor and a possible flooding condition. Too little pressure will result in a low fuel level in the carburetor. This may cause a loss of engine power, or cause the engine to starve (run out of fuel) at high speeds.

Test Procedure

Part I: Pump Pressure Test

The **pump pressure test** tells at what pressure fuel is delivered from the fuel pump. A vacuum-pressure gauge and a specification book or shop manual for the pump being tested are required when testing a fuel pump. Special wrenches, called **flare nut wrenches**, are designed for use on fuel lines. These should be used when connecting or disconnecting fuel pumps.

1. Use flare nut wrenches to disconnect the fuel line at the carburetor, as shown in Figure 2-19.

2. Install the vacuum-pressure gauge hose to the line, as shown in Figure 2-20.

Figure 2-19. When removing or replacing a fuel line, use flare nut wrenches to avoid twisting the line.

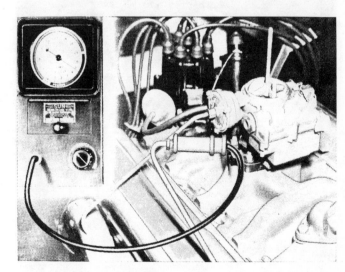

Figure 2-20. Fuel pump pressure test. (Courtesy of General Motors of Canada Limited)

3. Start the engine and observe the pressure indicated on the gauge. Record the reading, and stop the engine.

4. With the aid of the specification book or shop manual, determine if the recorded pressure gauge reading conforms to the manufacturer's specifications.

When performing tests on an electric fuel pump, you must look up the electrical specifications in the manufacturer's manual, inspect the circuit conditions, test for current draw and voltage availability, and check the fuse.

Part 2: Flow Test

The **flow test** will tell the pumping capacity (volume) of the pump. This test will tell more if the pump has first passed the pressure test. To conduct a flow test, you need a one-quart (1-liter) container and a neoprene fuel line hose about 18 inches (45 cm) long. The quart container should be graduated (have measurements marked on it).

1. Attach one end of the hose to the fuel line that you disconnected from the carburetor. See Figure 2-21.

2. Place the other end of the hose into the container.

3. Have someone run the engine at the proper speed. The specification book will state if the test

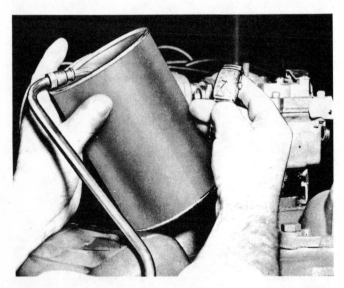

Figure 2-21. Fuel pump capacity test. (Courtesy of General Motors of Canada Limited)

should be done at cranking speed, idle speed, or at a higher engine speed. Record the time it takes the pump to pump the volume of fuel stated in the specification book. During the test, place the hose into the gasoline in the container and watch the bubbles made by the fuel stream. A stream of small bubbles is normal. Large bubbles indicate that air is leaking into the fuel system.

4. Compare the time and volume with the manufacturer's specifications. A volume higher than the amount specified by the manufacturer is acceptable and in no way harmful to engine operation. If the volume is too low, the pump will have to be repaired or replaced.

Part 3: Inlet and Outlet Vacuum and Pressure

If the fuel pump fails the flow or pressure test, it must be tested further.

1. Disconnect the lines from the fuel pump with flare nut wrenches. Install adapters in the pump fittings to allow the use of a vacuum-pressure gauge.

2. Plug or clamp the vapor return line (if so equipped).

3. Connect the vacuum-pressure gauge to the inlet side of the pump. **Caution:** For safety, install a length of hose from the outlet side of the fuel pump into a container to catch any fuel that might be discharged during this test. Run the engine, record the vacuum, and stop the engine. The vacuum should read 10 to 15 inches (34 to 51 kPa).

4. Connect the vacuum-pressure gauge to the outlet side of the pump. Run the engine, record the pressure, and stop the engine. Pressure as specified by the manufacturer is acceptable. Unacceptable pressure readings mean that the pump must be repaired or replaced.

Part 4: Fuel Tank Line

This test will determine if the fuel tank line is the cause of the fuel system problem. The test will require two people.

1. Raise the vehicle by using a hoist or a floor jack. **Caution:** If a jack is used, position the vehicle on **safety stands**.

2. Remove the fuel line connection between the fuel pump and the fuel tank line. Connect one end of a flexible hose to the fuel line. Place the other end of the hose into a container.

3. Plug or clamp the flexible part of the vent

line and vapor return line if there is one.

    4. Use shop cloths to make a large collar around an air hose nozzle.

    5. One person should blow a few short bursts of air through the tank-filler neck. Do not put too much pressure in the tank, or the tank will distort.

    6. The second person should observe the fuel discharged into the container at the fuel pump end of the line. The fuel should run out as a solid stream the full diameter of the line. If it does not, the fuel line or the in-tank fuel filter is clogged.

    7. Plug or clamp the fuel line hose at the fuel pump end of the line.

    8. Apply air again, being careful not to use too much pressure.

    9. The second person should examine the complete fuel line to see if fuel is leaking out through fittings, rusted or chafed areas, or loose or deteriorated hoses. If the fuel line is blocked or leaking, it should be repaired or replaced.

□   **ASSIGNMENT 2-H**   □

1. Explain how to test for fuel pump pressure.
2. Explain how to test for fuel pump flow capacity.
3. Explain how to test a fuel line to determine if it leaks or is plugged.

SERVICE TIPS FOR FUEL PUMP REPLACEMENT

Since rebuilt and new fuel pumps are readily available, fuel pump overhaul or installation procedures have not been included in this book. Manufacturers

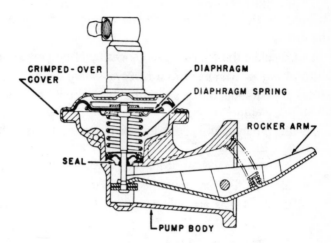

Figure 2-22. Sectional view of a fuel pump that cannot be easily disassembled for service. (Courtesy of Chrysler Corporation)

now use fuel pumps that are sealed units and cannot be disassembled for repair. In Figure 2-22, notice that instead of bolts, a crimped cover at the diaphragm holds the pump together. If it is necessary to replace a fuel pump, consult the manufacturer's shop manual. The following service tips will assist you with fuel pump replacement.

    1. Use two flare nut wrenches when removing or replacing fuel lines to avoid twisting the lines.

    2. Inspect flex lines for need of replacement.

    3. Inspect the camshaft lobe and push rod (if so equipped) for wear.

    4. Clean all traces of gasket and dirt from the fuel pump mounting flange on the engine.

    5. Always start fuel line fittings by hand before using wrenches. That way you will avoid cross-threading the lines.

    6. Test the fuel system thoroughly after a new pump has been installed.

□ SELF-TEST □

Complete the following sentences by filling in the missing words.

1. The main parts of a fuel system are the fuel _____ , fuel lines, fuel _____ , fuel filter, and the _____ .

2. The fuel pump sends the fuel through the line to the fuel _____ where it is _____ before entering the carburetor.

3. The vapor _____ allows fuel vapors, along with some fuel, to return to the fuel _____ through the fuel _____ line.

4. At sea level, atmospheric pressure is about _____ pounds per square inch.

5. The fuel tank must be _____ to allow atmospheric pressure to enter it.

6. Fuel lines are generally made from a rust-resistant _____ alloy that can withstand _____, crushing, or _____.

7. A check valve is a _____ - _____ valve that permits fluid to flow in only one _____ .

8. The fuel pump rocker arm extends inside the engine where it comes into contact with either an _____ on the camshaft, or a _____ _____ that rides against an eccentric on the camshaft.

9. Fuel is discharged from the pump _____ and forced through the line to the carburetor _____ bowl.

10. When an electric fuel pump is installed at the tank, the fuel is _____ through the fuel line by pump pressure, instead of being pulled through the line by pump _____ .

11. The average pressure of most fuel pumps is in the range of _____ - _____ psi, and the flow capacity is at least _____ pint in _____ seconds.

3

CARBURETOR FUNDAMENTALS

☐ LEARNING OBJECTIVES ☐

After studying this chapter, you will be able to:

1. Describe the atomization and vaporization of gasoline and explain how the carburetor assists in these processes.

2. Explain air-fuel ratios and demonstrate your understanding of lean and rich mixtures.

3. Name the six systems in a simple carburetor.

4. Describe the construction features of each carburetor system and explain the purpose of the parts in each system.

5. Describe the operation of a typical:

float system	power system
idle and low-speed system	acceleration pump system
high-speed system	choke system

6. Define and/or discuss the following terms:

carburetor	throttle valve
vaporization	manifold vacuum
atomization	venturi
fuel ratio	metering rod
carburetor floats	choke plate
carburetor vents	bimetallic spring

INTRODUCTION

The **carburetor** mixes a measured amount of air and fuel for combustion in the engine cylinders. The simple carburetors used on the first engines have been greatly improved. Early "Benz" engines were run on a mixture of air and gasoline. The mixture was formed by passing air through gasoline in a mixing tank called a "carburetter." Gottlieb Daimler developed the "jet carburetter," which used a small fuel jet to spray a fine stream of gasoline into the air that was being drawn into the engine. This style of carburetor was common on early automobiles. To meet the needs of different engines, carburetors were designed so that air could flow through them either downward (down-draft type), upward (up-draft type), or sidewise (side-draft type). See Figure 3-1.

Carburetors come in many different sizes for different sized engines. A **multibarrel carburetor** could have two, three, or four barrels for air to flow through. Some engines use more than one carburetor. With multibarrel carburetors, or when more than one carburetor is used, the volumetric efficiency of the engine is improved. Stated in a simple way, **volumetric efficiency** means that the engine can breathe more freely, taking in a larger charge of air-fuel mixture at a wide open throttle setting and developing greater power.

In this chapter, you will learn how air and fuel are mixed together in a carburetor. You will also learn the names, purposes, and operating ranges for the circuits or systems in a simple carburetor, and the theory behind their operation.

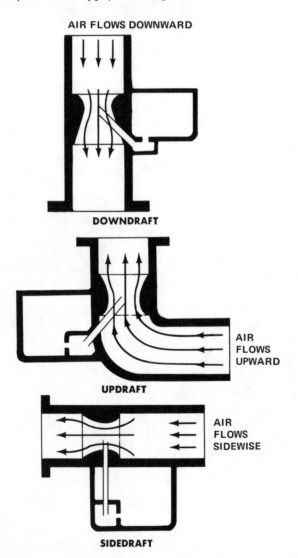

Figure 3-1.   Down-draft, up-draft, and side-draft carburetors.

GASOLINE VAPORIZATION

Air is a mixture of about 21% oxygen, 75% nitrogen, and 4% other gases. The oxygen in the air supports combustion in the air-fuel mixture. Air is a gas. Before a liquid will mix with a gas, the liquid must first be **vaporized** (turned into a gas). Gasoline (a liquid), if turned into a vapor (a gas), will combine with the air and become an **air-fuel mixture**.

As shown in Figure 3-2, when gasoline is burning in a container, the gasoline must vaporize and mix with air to form an air-fuel mixture before it will burn. In our open-container example, the area immediately above the liquid gasoline forms a vaporization area where liquid gasoline changes to a vapor.

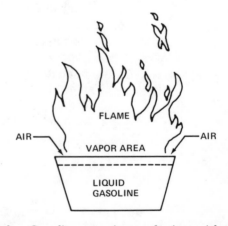

Figure 3-2.   Gasoline vaporizes and mixes with the air beneath the flame.

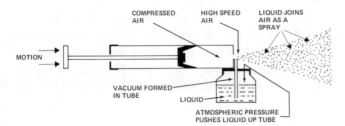

Figure 3-3. A garden sprayer atomizes a liquid.

Atomization

Atomization of gasoline aids in the vaporization process. **Atomization** is the process of breaking the fuel into tiny droplets, like the spray from a garden sprayer. See Figure 3-3. Tiny droplets of gasoline have much more surface area exposed to air for vaporization than would larger drops or a stream of gasoline.

A number of carburetor features are designed to cause or assist in gasoline atomization. As shown in Figure 3-4A, an **air bleed** allows a small amount of air to enter a fuel passage, causing bubbling that breaks up and helps atomize the fuel. The main fuel nozzle enters the carburetor at an angle to the air flow and is surrounded by a streamlined restriction called a venturi. See Figure 3-4B. The **venturi** increases air-flow velocity and vacuum at the nozzle, causing better fuel distribution and atomization. The shape of the nozzle is important as well. In Figure 3-4B, notice how the nozzle is cut off vertically in the direction of air flow to promote atomization. Other fuel outlet ports in the carburetor may be constructed to cause a spraying action.

Vacuum

A vacuum aids vaporization. Air pressure on a liquid tends to hold the liquid together. Lowering the pressure by applying a vacuum can cause a liquid to separate and vaporize more easily. Gasoline is subjected to vacuum in the carburetor venturi and also in the intake manifold before it reaches the cylinders.

Heat

A controlled amount of heat is applied to the fuel mixture to increase vaporization. **A manifold heat control system,** as shown in Figure 3-5, is used to

heat the floor of the intake manifold. These units use a thermostatic (heat-sensitive) spring to regulate a valve. When the valve is closed, exhaust gases heat the intake manifold. When the valve opens, the exhaust gases are directed away from the intake manifold.

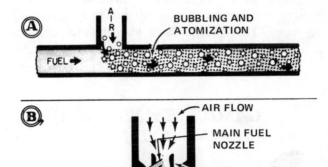

Figure 3-4. (A) An air bleed allows a small amount of air to enter a fuel passage, causing bubbling that breaks up and atomizes the fuel. (B) The main fuel nozzle is cut at an angle to air-flow direction. This promotes atomization. The nozzle is surrounded by two venturis that increase the air velocity and vacuum on the nozzle. (Courtesy of General Motors of Canada Limited)

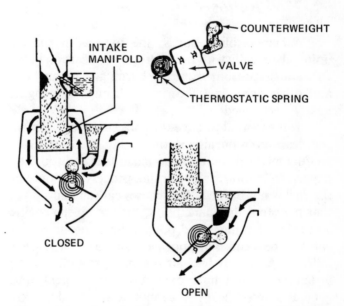

Figure 3-5. A typical manifold heat control valve. When the valve is closed, exhaust gases flow around the intake manifold, heating it. When the valve is open, exhaust gases bypass the intake manifold and flow into the exhaust pipe.

The system directs more or less exhaust gas heat to the intake manifold, depending on the engine speed and temperature.

A water-warmed flange beneath the carburetor is sometimes used as another aid to vaporization. The engine cooling system thermostat ensures that a certain temperature is maintained in the engine. Most air cleaners now have preheated air intake systems built into them. This allows warm temperature regulated air to pass through the carburetor.

GASOLINE AND AIR METERING AND MIXING

The **metering** (volume control) and mixing of gasoline and air is done in the carburetor. Fuel from the carburetor flows through **metering jets** with specific sized orifices (holes). The fuel is then discharged into the air stream entering the carburetor in a measured, controlled amount. The amount of air flow through the carburetor is determined by the throttle position. Maximum possible air flow is determined by the size of the carburetor venturi at a wide open throttle position. As air passes through the carburetor venturi, it creates a vacuum that draws gasoline into the air stream to mix with the air.

Fuel Ratios

When gasoline burns, the oxygen in the air unites chemically with the hydrogen and carbon in the fuel and is consumed during burning. The nitrogen and other gases in the air pass through the engine nearly unchanged.

It is essential to have the correct air-to-fuel ratio for clean, even burning in the engine. An overly **rich air-fuel mixture** contains too much fuel and too little oxygen to complete the burning process, so some of the fuel is not burned. This causes carbon and smoke that may foul the spark plugs, carbon up the engine and exhaust system, and pollute the environment. It can also be a cause of poor performance and low gas mileage. An overly **lean air-fuel mixture** contains too little fuel and too much oxygen. It burns quickly and generates excess heat that cannot be absorbed quickly enough by the cooling system. This could result in loss of power and heat damage to the spark plugs and engine parts.

A typical air-fuel ratio for light loads is 16 parts

of air to one part of fuel (16:1) by weight, or 9500 parts of air to one of fuel by volume. A typical air-fuel ratio for heavy loads is 12.5 parts of air to one part of fuel (12.5:1) by weight, or 7500 parts of air to one part of fuel by volume. See Figure 3-6.

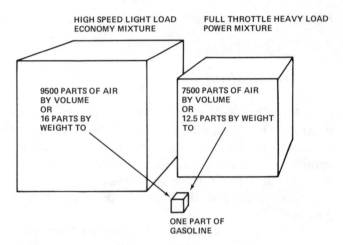

Figure 3-6.   Typical air-fuel ratios.

FACTS TO REMEMBER

An engine that has an overly rich fuel mixture will eventually become fouled with the carbon. Deposits of carbon around the valves and in the engine intake and exhaust ports will reduce the area for air to enter the cylinders, thus reducing engine power. Carbon deposits raise compression pressures, causing **detonation** (a type of knocking). They also foul spark plugs, which reduces spark plug efficiency.

Some carbon deposits in the combustion chambers remain hot enough after combustion to glow red hot on the compression stroke and can cause preignition or early ignition of the air-fuel mixture. This results in pinging (a type of knocking) and poor performance. Severe detonation and preignition can cause serious engine damage.

Rich fuel mixtures also contribute to air pollution by producing excess hydrocarbon and carbon monoxide exhaust emissions.

□   **ASSIGNMENT 3-A**   □

1. Why is it necessary to vaporize gasoline?

2. What is the reason for atomizing gasoline?

3. What carburetor features assist atomization?

4. What is meant by a lean mixture?

5. What is meant by a rich mixture?

6. What are the typical mixture ratios for light and heavy loads?

SIMPLE CARBURETOR SYSTEMS

To produce the proper air-fuel mixture for different speeds, loads, and engine temperatures, a simple carburetor generally has six systems or circuits. The names chosen for these systems suggest the part they play in the overall operation of the carburetor. Below are the names of the six systems and a brief description of their purpose and operating ranges.

Float System: This system is designed to keep a constant fuel level available in the fuel bowl for use in the carburetor under all driving conditions. Since the other carburetor systems are engineered around a specific level of fuel maintained in the float bowl, any change in that level upsets the operation of the other systems.

Fuel is supplied under pressure from the fuel pump to the carburetor. The pressure is reduced in the float system fuel bowl to atmospheric pressure.

Idle and Low-Speed System: This system supplies the proper air-fuel mixture for engine idle and low-speed driving under light-load conditions. The mixture ratio is determined by engine design and ranges between 8 to 14 parts of air to one part of fuel (8–14:1). The throttle is nearly closed at idle and only up to about 1/4 open for low speeds. This system operates alone from idle to speeds up to about 25 mph (40 km/h) if the load is light, and along with the high-speed system up to about 40 mph (65 km/h).

High-Speed System: The high-speed system (also called the **main metering system** or **part-throttle system**) supplies an economical air-fuel mixture for high-speed driving under light to medium loads. The mixture ratio supplied is in the range of 15 to 17 parts of air to one part of fuel. The throttle position can vary between 1/4 to 3/4 open, depending on engine speed and load. The speed range of the high-speed system begins at about 25 mph (40 km/h) and overlaps with the low-speed system up to about 40 mph

(65 km/h) if engine load is moderate. This system works alone at speeds between 40 to 70 mph (65–115 km/h), depending on engine size and vehicle weight. Faster speeds or heavier loads will bring in the power system.

Power System: This system increases the richness of the air-fuel mixture under conditions of heavy load or extremely high speeds. The extra fuel delivered by the power system allows the engine to develop more horsepower. The power system works along with the regular high-speed system and adds about 25% more fuel into the mixture. The mixture ratio, depending on the particular carburetor, could range from 12 to 14 parts of air to one part of fuel. The throttle position is about 3/4 to fully open. The normal speed range is above that of the high-speed system, or above 70 mph (115 km/h) to top speeds. The speed range can be much lower when the load is heavy. A heavy load (such as when climbing hills, passing, towing, or rapid acceleration) can cause a nearly wide-open throttle position.

Acceleration Pump System: This system prevents hesitation or a flat spot when the throttle is opened quickly at low speeds. It aids in the smooth transfer from the low-speed system to the high-speed and power systems. Do not confuse this system with the power system. The acceleration pump delivers a spray, or shot of fuel, for a few seconds only. The fuel supplied by the acceleration pump system is a proper amount to keep the engine operating until the high-speed system starts to deliver fuel. Whenever the throttle is opened from a position below halfway open, the acceleration pump will spray fuel into the carburetor throat to temporarily enrich the air-fuel ratio until the high-speed system cuts in.

Choke System: The choke system cuts off some of the air flow into the carburetor barrel and causes a very rich air-fuel mixture. This is necessary for starting a cold engine. The **choke** regulates the richness of the air-fuel mixture for smooth running during the engine warm-up period. It also causes a fast idle that prevents the engine from stalling during warm-up. The ratio of the air-fuel mixture when the choke is operating is extremely variable. It depends on engine temperature and loss of fuel from the air-fuel mixture as it condenses (changes from a gas back to a liquid) on the cold engine parts. The ratio at −10°F (−23°C) might be as low as one part of air to one part of fuel (1:1) in some cases.

Figure 3-7 is a graph showing the mixture ratios,

the speed of operation, and the overlapping of the systems in a typical carburetor. The information following Assignment 3–B will discuss these systems in detail.

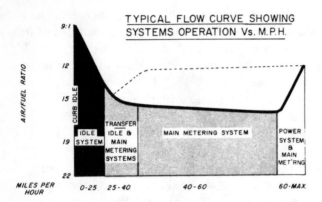

Figure 3-7. A typical flow curve showing carburetor systems operation at different speeds. (Courtesy of General Motors of Canada Limited)

FACTS TO REMEMBER

The carburetor mixes the proper ratio of air and fuel for different engine temperatures, loads, and speeds. In order to do this, the carburetor has six different systems: the float system, the idle and low-speed system, the high-speed system, the power system, the acceleration pump system, and the choke system. These six systems all work together to provide the proper air-fuel mixture for different engine conditions.

☐   ASSIGNMENT 3–B   ☐

1. What is the purpose of the float system?
2. What is the purpose, mixture ratio, and approximate mph associated with the following systems:
   idle and low-speed system
   high-speed system
   power system
   acceleration pump system
3. List three functions of the choke system.

FLOAT SYSTEM DESIGN AND OPERATION

A typical float system is shown in Figure 3-8. It consists of the **fuel bowl,** which is a reservoir for gaso-

line, a **float** on a **pivot,** and a **needle and seat valve** that is opened and closed by the action of the float. The fuel bowl has an **atmospheric vent** to let in atmospheric pressure.

When the fuel bowl is empty or has a low fuel level, the float drops and moves the **float level adjusting tang** away from the needle and seat valve. Fuel pressure forces fuel to spill into the fuel bowl through the now open needle and seat valve. As fuel fills the bowl, the float raises on its pivot until the float level adjusting tang presses the needle into its seat. This closes the valve and stops the fuel flow. As fuel is used by the engine, the fuel level lowers and relaxes the pressure of the float level adjusting tang against the needle and seat valve. This allows the needle to back out of the seat and open the valve. The system is self-regulating and insures that fuel will be supplied to the float bowl at the same rate as it is being used. In this way, the fuel level is kept as nearly constant as possible.

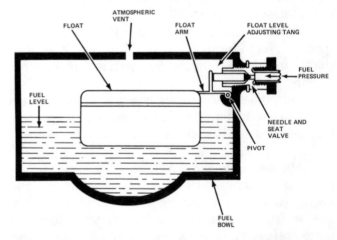

Figure 3-8.   A typical float system. (Courtesy of Chrysler Corporation)

Needle and Seat

The needle and seat can be mounted in the bowl cover, the bowl floor, or the bowl side by using a suitable lever and pivot on the float. The **needle and seat** combination serves as the valve that starts and stops fuel flow into the fuel bowl. Needle and seat assemblies are made of different materials in various sizes and shapes. Some use a steel needle and a brass seat. A spring-loaded needle, as shown in Figure 3-9, shock absorbs the float on rough roads. Some needle and seats are integral (cannot be separated). There are also needle and seats that can be adjusted from the outside of the bowl.

Rubber-tipped needles used with brass seats are common. These needles have certain advantages. The rubber tip tends to eliminate improper valve seating caused by tiny dirt particles in the fuel. The rubber can form around small dirt particles and still have a tight fit with the seat. Another advantage of a rubber-tip needle is that it cannot become magnetized as can a steel-tip needle. A magnetized steel needle will attract iron oxide (rust) from the fuel. The iron oxide will stick to the needle tip, causing the valve to leak and flood the carburetor.

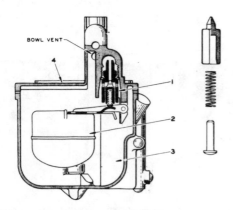

Figure 3-9. A spring-loaded needle helps to absorb road shock in a needle and seat valve. (Courtesy of General Motors of Canada Limited)

Floats

The **float** rises and falls with the fuel level in the fuel bowl, causing the needle and seat to open and close. Floats are made from various materials and come in a number of shapes and sizes. Some floats are made from very thin gauge brass, formed and soldered to make a hollow, air-filled pontoon. Other floats are hollow, air-filled plastic shells. Often buoyant molded plastic is used. Some carburetors have float systems with two floats on one arm.

Float Level

Carburetors are designed to operate with a specific fuel level in the fuel bowl. There is a means of adjusting the float to obtain that specified fuel level. Changes in the level can cause incorrect carburetor operation.

The height that the float rises before it closes the needle and seat valve determines the fuel level maintained in the fuel bowl. To adjust the float position

(or float level), the float adjusting tang must be bent toward the needle valve (to lower the level) or away from the needle valve (to raise the level). Float level must be adjusted according to manufacturer's specifications for each individual carburetor.

Float Drop

Floats designed like the one shown in Figure 3-8 rest on the bowl floor when the fuel bowl is empty or when the float drops down due to a very large fuel demand. Others have a float-drop tang. This assures that the tang opens the needle valve tip, but does not travel far enough to allow the needle to bind or fall out. This type of float is adjusted by bending a tang at the rear of the float pivot to obtain the manufacturer's specified measurement.

Fuel Bowl Venting

A **fuel bowl vent** acts as a breathing port for the carburetor. It allows air to leave the bowl as the bowl fills with fuel and to enter as the bowl empties. Fuel flow in a carburetor depends on vacuum at the discharge end and atmospheric pressure in the float bowl. The vent allows atmospheric pressure to enter the fuel bowl. The vent also provides a way for fuel vapors, formed by heat, to escape before pressure is built up. See Figure 3-9.

External Vents

Figure 3-10 shows three types of fuel bowl vents that have been used in carburetors. At one time, it

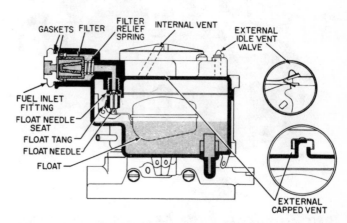

Figure 3-10. Carburetor venting methods: An external capped vent, internal or balance vent, and an external idle vent valve. (Courtesy of General Motors of Canada Limited)

was common to use only an **external capped vent** on the fuel bowl. However, this type of vent produced high-speed richening due to air cleaner restriction (particularly if the air cleaner was dirty). Because of the air cleaner restriction, the air pressure going through the carburetor barrel is reduced at higher speeds. However, fuel bowl pressure remains at atmospheric pressure. This sets up an unnecessary pressure difference between the fuel bowl and the high-speed-nozzle tip and increases fuel flow from the nozzle, and makes the mixture too rich.

Internal Vents

Replacing the external vent with an internal vent (or balanced vent) from the air horn to the fuel bowl eliminated the pressure difference caused by air cleaner restriction. See Figure 3-10. Carburetors using an internal vent have more stable air-fuel mixtures. This style vent has worked so well that it is still used today. A large four-barrel carburetor may have four, six, or eight internal vent tubes.

An **internal vent**, used alone, allows fuel vapors, formed while the engine is hot, to affect the idle. When a hot engine is not running, fuel vapors collect in the air cleaner and intake manifold. This makes the engine difficult to start. In order to prevent this prob-

lem, an external idle vent valve (or **antiperculator valve**) was used along with the internal vent for many years. This valve was opened by linkages during idle and when the engine was stopped and allowed fuel vapors to escape into the atmosphere. Thus, the amount of vapors that escaped into the intake manifold was reduced, and the engine would start and idle better. The valve was closed by linkages at driving speeds. Figure 3-11 shows a mechanically operated fuel bowl venting system that produces the same effect as the external idle vent valve.

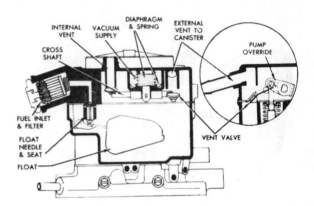

Figure 3-12. This carburetor has a vacuum-operated vent valve connected to a charcoal canister. (Courtesy of General Motors of Canada Limited)

Modern Vents

Since 1971, when emission controls were introduced, fuel vapors have to be prevented from reaching the atmosphere. One example of a system designed to meet emission controls is illustrated in Figure 3-12. The return spring inside this vacuum-operated vent valve opens the fuel bowl vapor vent passage into a tube that leads to a charcoal canister. The canister absorbs the fuel vapors. While the engine is running, manifold vacuum applied to the diaphragm closes the vapor vent, allowing the balanced vent system to function. The pump override (circled in the insert in Figure 3-12) opens the valve mechanically at idle to allow vapors to escape into the charcoal canister.

Another simple method of vapor collection, shown in Figure 3-13, uses a pressure relief valve (plastic disc) connected by a tube to a charcoal canister. Some carburetors have no external vents, but use a raised bowl cover as a vapor dome to collect vapors.

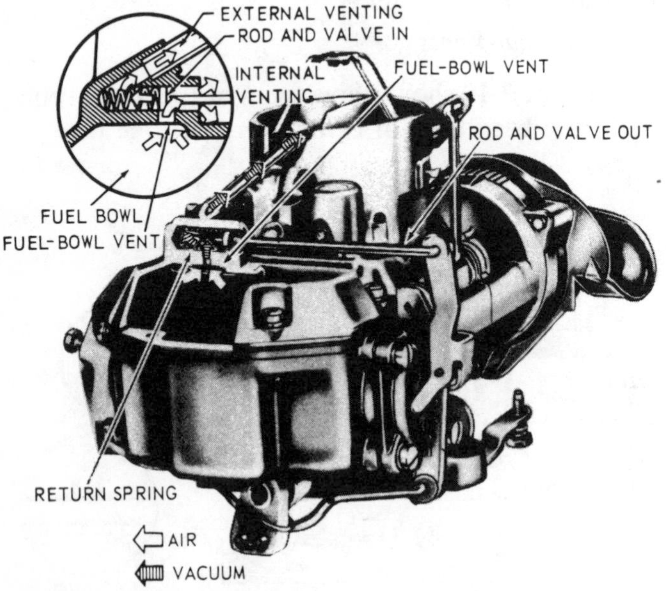

Figure 3-11. This carburetor has a mechanically operated float bowl venting system. (See insert circle.) When the rod is pushed in at idle, the internal vent is closed and the bowl is vented to the atmosphere. (Courtesy of Ford Motor Company, Dearborn)

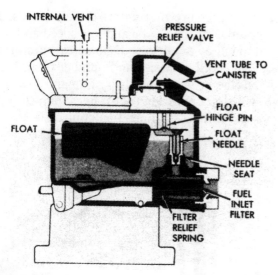

Figure 3-13. This carburetor has a pressure relief valve (a plastic disc) connected to a charcoal canister. (Courtesy of General Motors of Canada Limited)

□ ASSIGNMENT 3-C □

1. Explain the operation of a typical float system.
2. Describe three types of needle and seat combinations.
3. Describe three types of floats.
4. List the various types of fuel bowl vents described in the text.

IDLE AND LOW-SPEED SYSTEM DESIGN AND OPERATION

In order to understand the operation of the idle and low-speed system and the location of the idle fuel discharge port, we must understand the function of the **carburetor throttle valve.**

Manifold vacuum in an engine is caused by restricting the flow of air entering the engine cylinders through the intake manifold. Air enters the intake manifold through the carburetor. As the engine pistons move down on the intake stroke, they pull air out of the intake manifold. However, the carburetor throttle valve *restricts* the amount of air going through the carburetor into the manifold. A partial (incomplete) vacuum is created when the intake manifold is emptied of air, at the same time that the throttle valve is blocking the flow of additional air into the manifold.

The amount of vacuum in the intake manifold is directly related to the position of the throttle valve. When the throttle is wide open, air can pass freely through the carburetor, and manifold vacuum will be weak (or low). At part-throttle, vacuum is much stronger (or higher). When the throttle is almost closed, as in Figure 3-14, air flow is greatly restricted, and only a little air can enter the manifold. An even stronger (higher) vacuum results.

Recall that fuel flow in a carburetor depends on vacuum at the discharge end and atmospheric pressure at the fuel bowl. At idle, the nearly closed throttle prevents most of the air from reaching the intake manifold, and at the same time causes a strong vacuum below the throttle valve. The logical place for the idle fuel discharge port, therefore, is below the throttle valve where it will be exposed to vacuum at idle.

The following material explains the operation of an idle and low-speed system. It starts by describing a simple system. The necessary features and component parts are added on as needed to describe the complete system.

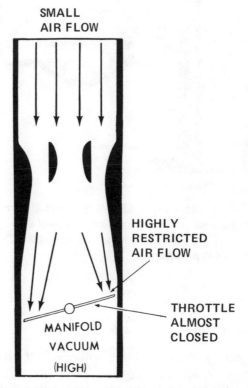

Figure 3-14. A closed throttle valve results in high vacuum.

System Design

Fuel Passage

Figure 3-15 shows a simple **idle fuel passage** from the fuel supply down to a port below the closed throttle valve. If the engine were running, a strong vacuum would form in the manifold below the closed throttle valve. Atmospheric pressure, transferred through the internal vent to the fuel in the fuel bowl, would push the fuel through the fuel passage to be discharged from the port into the vacuum area. Such a simple system would have disadvantages. It would have very poor flow control and poor atomization. It would not shut off during high-speed-system operation. It would syphon fuel and empty the fuel bowl after the engine was stopped. This would cause a flooded engine that would be hard to start again.

atmospheric pressure that enters the air bleeds. Engine vacuum is strong at idle and low speed and is not affected much by an air bleed. Some carburetors use only one air bleed. The size and number of air bleeds will determine at what speed the idle and low-speed system will stop delivering fuel. The system shown in Figure 3-16 still lacks proper fuel control.

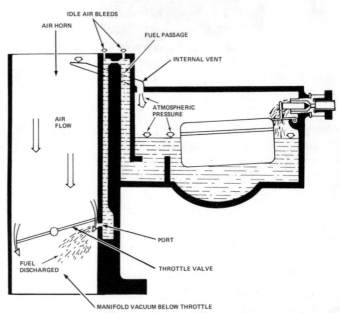

Figure 3-16.   The addition of air bleeds at the top of the idle fuel passage causes fuel atomization and stops fuel syphoning when the engine is shut off. This system still lacks proper fuel control. (Courtesy of Chrysler Corporation)

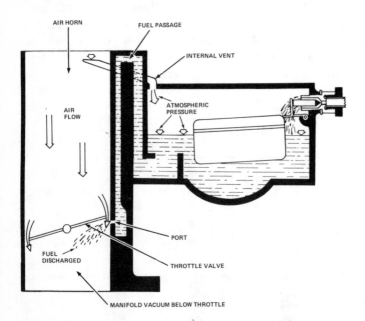

Figure 3-15.   This simple idle system would have poor flow control and poor atomization. It would also syphon the fuel bowl dry after the engine was stopped. (Courtesy of Chrysler Corporation)

Air Bleeds

Figure 3-16 shows the addition of **air bleeds** at the top of the idle fuel passage. These permit a small amount of air to enter the passage, causing bubbling and fuel atomization. Syphoning is eliminated by the

Idle Tube

Figure 3-17 shows the addition of an **idle tube** in the bowl and an **idle mixture screw** at the port end of the passageway. These parts aid in controlling the amount of fuel discharged below the throttle valve. This method would work fine for idle, but is of little use for low speeds. Manifold vacuum becomes lower when the throttle is opened. With this system, the fuel supply would *decrease* rather than *increase* when the throttle was opened during low-speed driving. However, a *larger* fuel supply is needed to support low-speed operation and small-load conditions than is needed for idle.

On modern carburetors the external vent, which is open at idle, would be attached to a vent hose leading to a carbon canister. This reduces air pollution when the engine is idling or shut down.

Low-Speed Port

Figure 3-18 shows the addition of a **low-speed port** above the edge of the throttle plate. Because it is exposed to near atmospheric pressure when the throttle is in the idle position, this port acts as an additional air bleed. If the throttle is in the slightly open, low-speed position, this port receives vacuum and will discharge fuel. Working along with the idle mixture screw port, enough fuel is supplied by the low-speed port for off-idle, low-speed operation. This port can be called a secondary idle discharge port, a low-speed port, an idle transfer port, or an off-idle port.

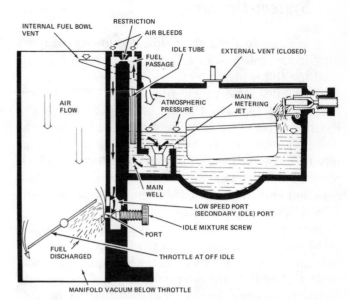

Figure 3-18. A typical idle and low-speed system. The low-speed port discharges fuel when the throttle is in the off-idle, low-speed position. (Courtesy of Chrysler Corporation)

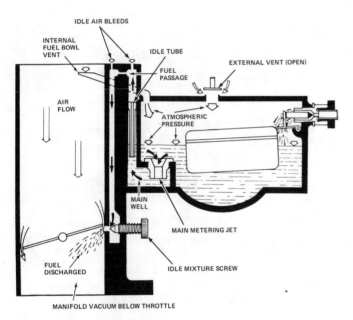

Figure 3-17. With the addition of an idle tube and an idle mixture screw, fuel flow is controlled. (Courtesy of Chrysler Corporation)

The Complete Idle and Low-Speed System

The complete idle and low-speed system contains the following parts (Figure 3-18):

Main Metering Jet: The main metering jet meters fuel flow into the high-speed system, but has no effect on fuel flow into the idle system. However, if the idle and low-speed system is overlapping the high-speed system, the two flows are metered through one jet (the main metering jet) to prevent a rich mixture.

Idle Tube: The idle tube is the metering jet that regulates the flow of fuel through the idle and low-speed system.

Air Bleeds: Air bleeds aid in atomization by allowing a small amount of air into the fuel passage. This air bubbles and breaks up the fuel. Air bleeds also prevent syphoning by the low-speed system when the engine is turned off.

Restriction: The restriction between the air bleeds assures that each air bleed is effective and aids atomization by causing a momentary speeding up of fuel flow. This tends to break the flowing fuel up into bubbles.

Low-Speed Port: This supplies fuel for low-speed operation only if the throttle is opened a fraction wider than the full idling position. When the throttle is closed to the full idling position, the low-speed port becomes an air bleed and lets air into the fuel passage.

Idle Mixture Screw: The idle mixture screw provides an adjustment for fuel mixture that will give the smoothest running at idle and give hydrocarbon and carbon monoxide exhaust readings that meet federal regulations.

System Operation

We can now put all the idle and low-speed parts into one complete picture. Refer to Figure 3-18 as you read the following.

At idle, atmospheric pressure in the fuel bowl pushes fuel through the discharge port below the throttle valve, toward the vacuum created at the manifold. The fuel passes through the main metering jet into the main well, where it enters the idle tube, which meters the flow. The fuel then passes up the fuel passage and past the air bleeds, where air is injected into it to aid atomization. It then passes down the passage to the idle mixture screw port, is discharged into the carburetor barrel, and is mixed with the air entering past the throttle. At this time, the low-speed port acts as an air bleed, aiding atomization. When the throttle is opened slightly, vacuum causes fuel to be discharged from the low-speed and the idle mixture screw port. This causes the necessary increase in fuel flow to mix with the increased air flow during low speeds.

System Variations

There are many variations to the basic idle and low-speed system. Figure 3-19 shows a carburetor with an **idle limiter needle** that is set and sealed at the

factory. If the idle adjusting screw is turned out further than necessary, the idle limiter needle will prevent excess fuel from getting through. This is an emission control. It prevents an overly rich idle mixture setting that could contribute to air pollution.

Figure 3-20 shows a carburetor with an **idle air bypass system**. In this system, the throttle valve is not adjustable and closes fully at idle. The air necessary to run the engine is supplied through the air intake and past the idle air adjusting screw. This screw controls the amount of air allowed into the engine and, therefore, the speed of the engine. With this system, fuel is supplied in the conventional manner. The carburetor shown is a two-barrel carburetor. It contains two idle fuel systems, but only one idle air bypass system.

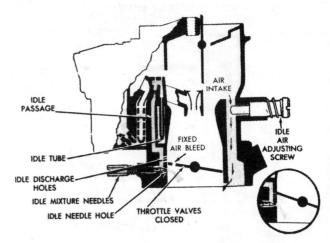

Figure 3-20. This carburetor has an idle air bypass system. (Courtesy of General Motors of Canada Limited)

Figure 3-21 is another two-barrel carburetor. Notice the **off-idle air adjusting screw** (not to be confused with the idle air bypass system). This screw is adjusted and sealed at the factory with the off-idle mixture accurately set. It is an emission control feature to prevent an overly rich off-idle mixture that could contribute to air pollution.

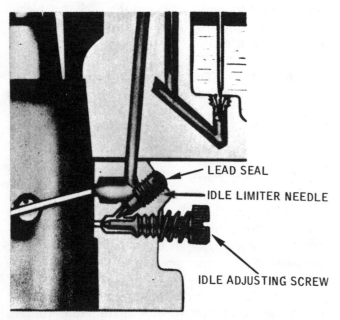

Figure 3-19. This carburetor has an idle limiter needle that is set and sealed at the factory. (Courtesy of Ford Motor Company, Dearborn)

☐   **ASSIGNMENT 3-D**   ☐

Describe the purpose of each of the following:

main metering jet	low-speed port
idle tube	idle mixture screw
air bleed	

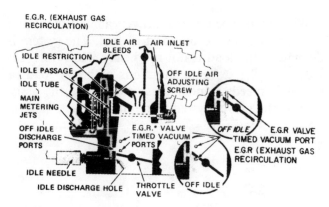

Figure 3-21. This carburetor has an off-idle air adjusting screw that is sealed and set at the factory. (Courtesy of General Motors of Canada Limited)

HIGH-SPEED SYSTEM DESIGN AND OPERATION

At a certain throttle valve position (speed or load on the engine), the idle and low-speed system will stop delivering fuel. This is because the amount of air entering the intake manifold at open-throttle positions reduces manifold vacuum so much that it can no longer draw fuel from the idle and low-speed system. Before this happens, the high-speed system will have started working. Through a certain load range, the two systems work together. Then the high-speed system takes over on its own.

Intake manifold vacuum strength is reversed as to the needs of a high-speed system. Manifold vacuum *decreases* as the throttle is opened. This would cause less fuel flow when more is needed. This problem is eliminated through the use of a venturi.

Venturi

A **venturi** is a streamlined constriction that partly closes the carburetor bore. The carburetor bore is reduced in size at the venturi. As air enters the venturi, it is forced to speed up (increase velocity) in order to pass through. This causes less pressure to be exerted by the air in the venturi area. We could say that a venturi uses air velocity to cause a vacuum. As manifold vacuum *decreases*, venturi vacuum *increases*. The venturi aids fuel atomization and vaporization by exposing the fuel to air velocity and vacuum as it leaves the high-speed nozzle. The nozzle is centered in the strongest vacuum area of the venturi.

Figure 3-22 illustrates venturi action. The arrow lines indicate the path that air must take when it is passing through the venturi constriction. Notice that the top vacuum gauge reads zero (atmospheric pressure), the center one reads about 13 inches (44 kPa) of vacuum, and the bottom one reads about 7 inches (24 kPa) of vacuum. These readings will vary over different throttle ranges, but the strongest vacuum above the throttle valve will always be in the venturi constriction where the carburetor throat is smallest.

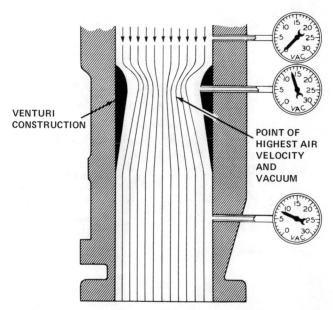

Figure 3-22. Vacuum readings taken at different points in the carburetor bore indicate that the point of greatest vacuum is in the venturi. (Courtesy of Holly Carburetor Division, Colt Industries)

Boost Venturi

Figure 3-23 shows that more than one venturi can be used. The venturi in the carburetor bore is referred to as the **primary** or **main venturi**. The smaller venturi, which further increases air speed and vacuum, is referred to as a **boost venturi**. Some carburetors have three venturis per barrel. The area of highest vacuum is inside the boost venturi, and the fuel nozzle terminates there. Boost venturis produce a highly atomized air-fuel mixture that burns efficiently and reduces exhaust emissions.

High-Speed System Parts

Refer to Figure 3-24 while you read about the following parts of the high-speed system. The **main**

metering jet meters (regulates) the flow of fuel entering the high-speed system. The **main well** is the area behind the main metering jet. It leads to the **main discharge tube** or **nozzle** and to the idle system. The **main air bleed** feeds a fine stream of air into the **main vent tube**. This air discharges from the main vent tube (because it is drawn by venturi vacuum) and causes atomization of the fuel passing through the main well. The main discharge tube or nozzle delivers the fuel into the venturi vacuum area. The nozzle shape has a lot to do with fuel control and atomization.

The high-speed system delivers a mixture ratio of 15–17 parts of air to one part of fuel. The system is adequate if the load is not too heavy. However, it is inadequate for extreme situations of heavy load or very high speeds. Under these situations, the assistance of the power system is required.

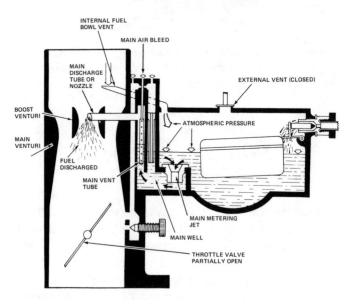

Figure 3-24. *A typical high-speed system. (Courtesy of Chrysler Corporation)*

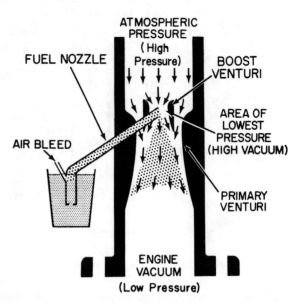

Figure 3-23. *The boost venturi further increases air velocity and vacuum. The fuel nozzle terminates in the boost venturi. (Courtesy of General Motors of Canada Limited)*

High-Speed System Operation

At a point of sufficient throttle opening, a strong vacuum is created in the boost venturi area around the main discharge tube. Atmospheric pressure coming through the internal fuel bowl vent pushes fuel through the main metering jet into the main well. The main air bleed feeds a fine stream of air through the main vent tube into the fuel passing through the main well. This atomizes the fuel. The atomized fuel passes through the passageway around the main vent tube, into the main discharge tube, and into the boost venturi. Here it meets the vacuum and high air velocity, is mixed with air, and is carried on to the engine cylinders as an air-fuel mixture.

FACTS TO REMEMBER

Changes in fuel level in the carburetor bowl can affect the operation of the carburetor systems, particularly the high-speed system. With a low fuel level in the carburetor bowl, the fuel is lower down in the high-speed nozzle (or passage to the nozzle). Therefore, it would require more vacuum and more air velocity through the carburetor (and venturi) to start and maintain the flow from the nozzle. A low fuel level in the fuel bowl causes a late-starting, lean mixture that results in poor performance.

If the fuel level is too high, the fuel is higher in the nozzle and requires less vacuum and air velocity to start and maintain the flow from the nozzle. A high fuel level causes an early-starting, rich mixture that results in poor performance and poor gas mileage. It could also result in flooding or stalling if the fuel spills from the high-speed nozzle during turning or braking.

☐ ASSIGNMENT 3-E ☐

1. Explain venturi operation.
2. Describe the fuel flow through a high-speed system.
3. What is the function of the following items:
   main metering jet
   main well
   main air bleed
   main discharge nozzle

POWER SYSTEM DESIGN AND OPERATION

During a very heavy-load or extra-high-speed situation, the lean air-fuel mixture produced by the high-speed system would cause leaning out and loss of power. To prevent this, the **power system** will come into operation to enrichen the mixture for smooth operation. The power and high-speed systems work together for as long as this rich mixture is required. The power enrichment is about 25% of the total mixture. The air-fuel ratio, as the two systems work together, is 12–14 parts of air to one part of fuel.

Power System Parts

The type of power system shown in Figure 3-25 contains a **power valve** (or jet), a **power piston** with a

stem and spring, a **power piston cylinder**, and a **passage** for manifold vacuum.

The power valve is kept closed under normal driving conditions by an internal spring. The valve leads into the main well next to the main metering jet. It may contain a metering orifice, as shown in Figure 3-25, or the metering restriction may be in the carburetor body.

The power piston, stem, and spring work together. The stem is fastened to the power piston. The spring could be on the stem, as in Figure 3-25, or inside the power piston. The **power piston cylinder** houses the power piston and allows it to slide up and down freely. The **manifold vacuum passage** brings manifold vacuum, from the base of the carburetor below the throttle valve, to the top of the power piston.

Power System Operation

Under light to medium loads, the power system does not operate. Under these conditions, manifold vacuum is strong enough to overcome the power piston spring. Atmospheric pressure pushes the piston up toward the vacuum in the vacuum passage and holds it up against the tension of the spring around the stem. The power valve is closed by its internal (bottom) spring.

Under heavy loads and extra fast speeds, the power system comes into operation. Due to the wide throttle opening under these conditions, the manifold vacuum becomes low (or weak). The strength of the power piston spring around the stem can overcome the weak vacuum in the vacuum passage and push the power piston and stem down. The power piston stem pushes the power valve open. Atmospheric pressure in the fuel bowl now forces fuel past the spindle and metering restriction in the power valve, and into the main well. This fuel mixes with the fuel flowing through the main metering jet, increasing the amount of fuel in the main well. Fuel from both the power and high-speed systems flows together out the main discharge nozzle in the boost venturi. Here it mixes with the air stream and is carried into the engine cylinders. The combined fuels cause an air-fuel mixture suitable for heavy loads with a ratio of 12–14 parts of air to one part of fuel.

It is important to realize that the amount of vacuum drop needed to make the power piston operate varies from one carburetor to another. It depends on the area of the power piston and the power piston

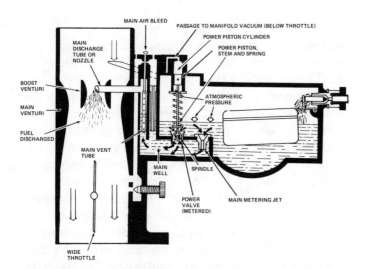

Figure 3-25. A typical power system. (Courtesy of Chrysler Corporation)

return spring tension. The critical point of vacuum for a particular carburetor may be 8 inches (27 kPa) of manifold vacuum. If the vacuum is anything above that amount, the power piston is held up. If it drops below that amount, the power piston is released.

In some cases, as shown in Figure 3-26, a diaphragm is used instead of a power piston. The diaphragm is mounted in a closed cavity. Manifold vacuum is applied to the top of the diaphragm. A stem and spring, similar to that used on a power piston, is fastened to the diaphragm. The diaphragm system operates in the same manner as the power piston system.

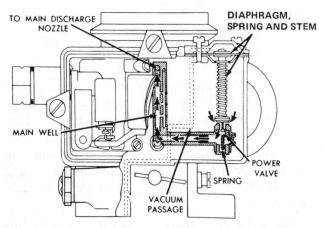

Figure 3-26. *This single-barrel carburetor has a vacuum-controlled diaphragm, stem, and spring to open the power valve. (Courtesy of Holly Carburetor Division, Colt Industries)*

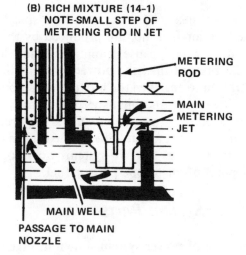

Figure 3-27. *A two-step metering rod with the large step in the jet (A) and the small step in the jet (B).*

□   **ASSIGNMENT 3-F**   □

1. Explain the function served by vacuum in a power system.

2. What is the function of the following items:
   power valve
   power piston spring
   power piston and stem
   diaphragm and spring

Metering Rod Operation

Metering rods or **step-up rods** are commonly used to regulate air-fuel mixtures for changing load conditions. A metering rod uses a stepped metal rod to control the flow of fuel through the main metering jet. This eliminates the need for a power valve.

"Metering rod" and "step-up rod" mean the same thing. Some types of metering jets must use metering rods to avoid carburetor flooding. The metering rod may have two or more steps on it that close off a portion of the jet to establish the proper mixture. Fuel flow (and mixture) depends on the size of the step that is in the jet. Figure 3-27A shows a two-step metering rod with the upper (large step) in the jet. The mixture is lean (about 16:1). Figure 3-27B shows the lower (small step) occupying the jet, making the mixture richer (about 14:1). The rod may be operated by the throttle, with linkages as shown in Figure 3-28.

Some systems use a piston and spring assembly that is inverted so that it works the opposite way to a power piston. See Figure 3-29. Other systems use a combination of both methods, as shown in Figure 3-30. Certain step-up rods remain in the jet for lean mixture, but are removed from the jet for the power mixture. This type is piston- and spring-controlled, and the metering jet is calibrated for a power mixture. See Figure 3-31.

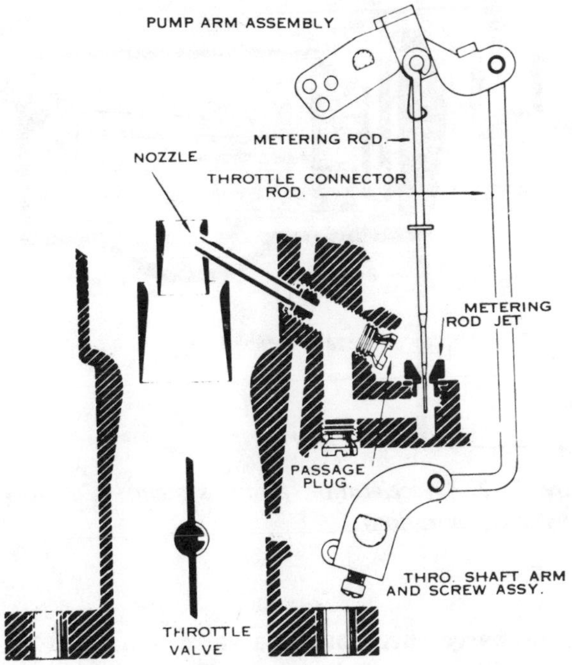

Figure 3-28. A linkage-operated metering rod. (Courtesy of General Motors of Canada Limited)

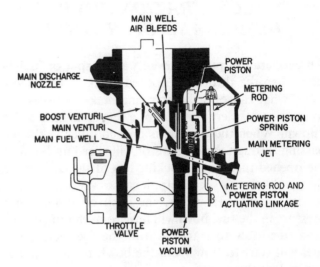

Figure 3-30. A piston- and linkage-operated metering rod. (Courtesy of General Motors of Canada Limited)

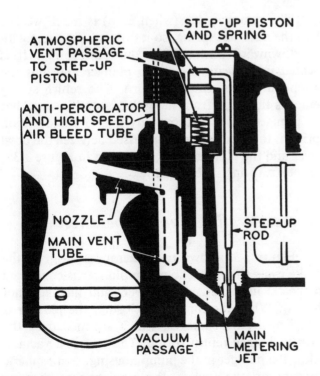

Figure 3-29. A piston-operated step-up rod. (Courtesy of General Motors of Canada Limited)

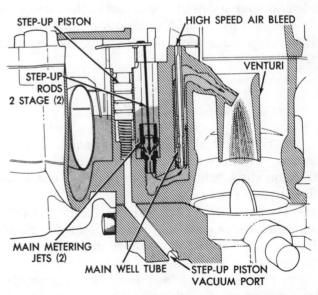

Figure 3-31. A piston-operated step-up rod that is removed from the jet orifice for the power mixture. (Courtesy of Chrysler Corporation)

☐ **ASSIGNMENT 3-G** ☐

1. Explain how a two-step metering rod regulates the mixture for changing loads.
2. List four methods used to position metering rods.

ACCELERATION PUMP DESIGN AND OPERATION

An acceleration pump prevents a **flat spot** or **hesitation** when the throttle is opened quickly. To understand what causes a flat spot and makes it necessary to have an acceleration pump, a few facts have to be known. When the throttle is opened quickly, the air passing through the carburetor will speed up because the opened throttle is blocking less of the carburetor throat. As the air speeds up, it causes venturi vacuum to rise quickly. However, the push of atmospheric pressure in the fuel bowl will have to overcome the inertia (tendency to stand still) of the fuel before the fuel will start to flow from the bowl, to the venturi, and out of the nozzle.

Put in simple terms, the fuel is heavy (compared to air) and is going to lag behind the air. When this happens, it is possible for air to reach the engine cylinders without enough fuel. If this happened, the engine would hesitate for a few seconds, until the fuel began to flow from the high-speed nozzle. The **acceleration pump** delivers extra fuel to the carburetor air stream during rapid acceleration until the fuel flow from the high-speed nozzle begins. This prevents hesitation.

Acceleration Pump Parts

A typical acceleration pump contains a pump plunger, a duration spring, an inlet check ball, a discharge check ball, and a pump discharge nozzle, as illustrated in Figure 3-32.

The pump has a **shaft** with a leather or neoprene **cup** on it. A spring coil may be used inside the cup to flare it out for a more positive seal. The **pump plunger** brings in gasoline and pushes it through the pump. The **duration spring** pushes the pump plunger down during rapid acceleration for the length of time required to prevent a flat spot. The **inlet check ball** is a valve that controls the gasoline flow into the pump.

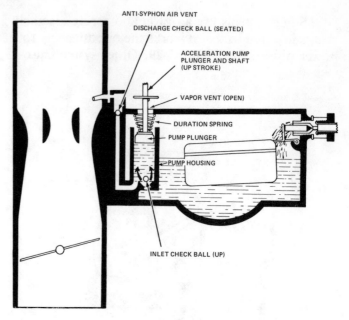

Figure 3-32. *Acceleration pump system. (Courtesy of Chrysler Corporation)*

The **discharge check ball** is a valve that controls the gasoline flow out of the pump. The **pump discharge nozzle** (sometimes called the **pump jet**) is the metering jet through which fuel is discharged. It aids in producing pressure and controlling the duration of the discharge.

The **return spring** (when used) is much weaker than the duration spring, so it does not interfere with the downward push of the duration spring. It is located underneath the pump plunger and aids the pump during its upward return. The return spring removes the slack from the linkages and insures that the plunger works without any lag. If the duration spring is the type that is compressed between the bowl cover and the plunger head, as shown in Figure 3-32, no return spring is required.

Acceleration Pump Operation

Figure 3-32 shows an acceleration pump on the intake cycle (filling). The pump plunger is connected to the throttle shaft, using levers and linkages (not shown). When the throttle is closing, the plunger is pulled up by the linkages, which are moved by the throttle linkage return spring. This causes a vacuum below the plunger in the pump housing. Atmospheric pressure on the fuel in the bowl pushes gasoline through the inlet passage, opens the inlet check ball, and fills the pump housing. At the same instant, atmospheric pressure above the discharge check ball, trying to fill the vacuum in the pump housing, presses the discharge check ball tightly closed. No air can enter from the nozzle and dilute the gasoline below the plunger.

Figure 3-33 shows an acceleration pump on the discharge cycle (emptying). As the throttle opens, the linkages stop lifting and the plunger is forced down by the duration spring. This causes pressure below the plunger that pushes the inlet check ball tightly closed. No fuel can leak back into the fuel bowl. The pressure also forces the fuel through the discharge passage, where it opens the discharge check ball, discharges from the pump discharge nozzle, and sprays into the carburetor barrel.

If the plunger was pushed directly from the throttle linkages, the gas pedal could not be pushed down quickly. There would be too much resistance involved in forcing a liquid fuel through the small discharge passage. This would cause a **hydraulic lock** and poor fuel flow duration control. To overcome this problem, instead of using a direct action on the plunger from the throttle and linkages, a telescoping plunger shaft is sometimes used.

The same effect can be achieved by having the pump operating lever slide down a slot in the shaft, or by having the operating lever slide down over the shaft. All of these methods allow the duration spring

to do the work of pushing the plunger down. They also permit a very fast throttle opening, followed by immediate plunger action of a few seconds of duration. Usually the plunger has bottomed at near half throttle, and the final half of throttle opening only compresses the duration spring as the operating link slides down the slot or over the shaft. See Figure 3-34.

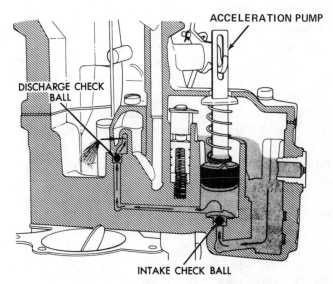

Figure 3-34. *An acceleration pump with a slotted plunger shaft. (Courtesy of Chrysler Corporation)*

Pump Pullover

The pump discharge nozzle is located in the venturi area. At high speed, the venturi vacuum is strong enough to cause fuel to flow from the nozzle continuously. This is called **pump pullover**. Pump pullover is undesirable, but is easily avoided by altering the discharge check ball. Alterations, such as using a weak spring or a needle instead of a ball, or placing a piece of metal or another ball on top of the check ball to weight the check ball against the pull of the venturi vacuum, are used to prevent this problem. Each of these alterations stops pump pullover, but still permits fuel to flow when it is needed.

One final method is to place an **antisyphon air vent** at the nozzle tip. The nozzle is placed before the air vent to permit atmospheric pressure to discharge air from the vent. This eliminates vacuum at the nozzle. Figures 3-32 and 3-33 show an antisyphon air vent.

Some variations of the plunger system are in use,

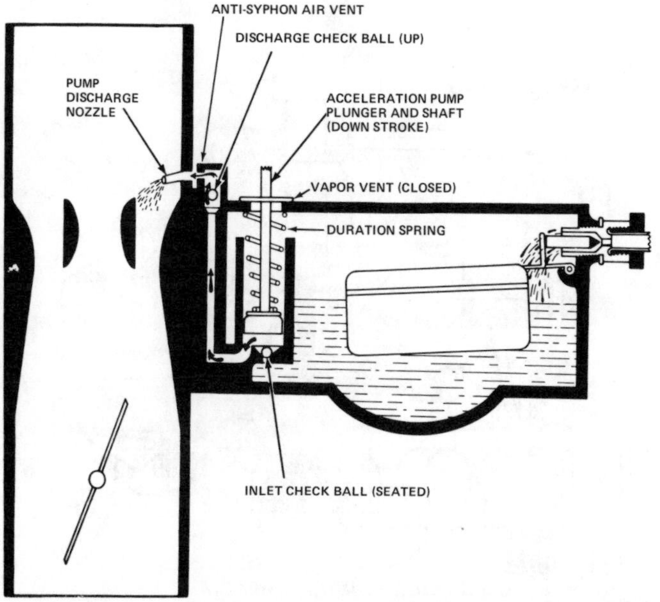

Figure 3-33. *Acceleration pump on the discharge cycle. (Courtesy of Chrysler Corporation)*

but the basic principles still apply. The plunger head may have a **vapor vent check ball** in it, as shown in Figure 3-35. This plunger system can fill with fuel through the plunger check ball, which is normally open. During periods of overheating, vapors will escape through the vapor check ball in the plunger head, instead of building up pressure that could discharge the fuel from the pump. Without a vapor check ball, vapor pressure would empty the fuel from the pump, causing hesitation on acceleration because the pump is dry. The vapor vent plunger can be used with or without the usual inlet passage and ball.

Still other plungers use a neoprene **plunger cup** that fits loosely onto the pump plunger head. The neoprene cup fits with tension to the pump cylinder. As the plunger is raised up, the cup moves down (to a stop provided on the plunger head), exposing a space at the top. See Figure 3-36, View A. Fuel enters the pump well (below the plunger) by passing over the top and down through the center of the loose cup. Fuel vapors can pass out the same way. As the plunger moves down (to operate), the loose cup moves back against the shoulder on the plunger head and seals so that fuel cannot flow back into the fuel bowl. See Figure 3-36, View B. Pressure will now build up, and fuel will discharge from the pump.

Some carburetors use a diaphragm in place of the pump plunger. It is still necessary to have check valves and the other parts used with a plunger system. Most diaphragm systems are linkage-operated from the throttle shaft, as shown in Figure 3-37.

A few models, as shown in Figure 3-38, are controlled by intake manifold vacuum. The top side of the diaphragm pumps the fuel and serves as the pump well. The bottom side of the diaphragm is exposed to

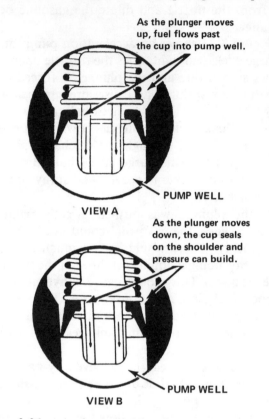

Figure 3-36.   A plunger with a loose cup. (Courtesy of General Motors of Canada Limited)

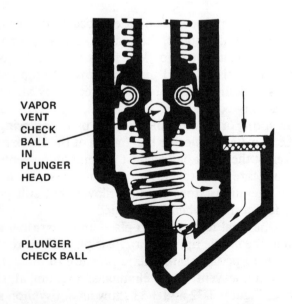

Figure 3-35.   A plunger with a vapor vent check ball. (Courtesy of General Motors of Canada Limited)

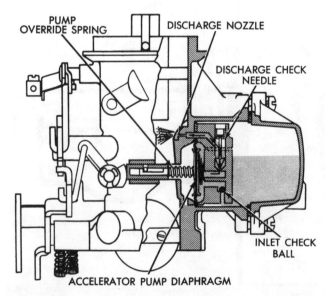

Figure 3-37.   A linkage-operated diaphragm acceleration pump. (Courtesy of Chrysler Corporation)

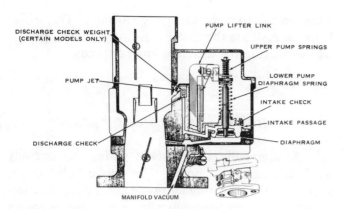

Figure 3-38. A vacuum-controlled diaphragm acceleration pump. (Courtesy of General Motors of Canada Limited)

intake manifold vacuum. Strong vacuum at part-throttle holds the diaphragm down and the pump well filled. Weak vacuum, produced during fast-throttle opening, releases the diaphragm and the spring, causing the pressure needed for the diaphragm to push fuel from the pump well to the pump jet.

□ ASSIGNMENT 3-H □

1. Explain what causes the flat spot (hesitation) that makes it necessary to have an acceleration pump on a carburetor.

2. Explain the function of the following items:
    duration spring   pump plunger
    inlet check ball   pump jet
    discharge check ball

CHOKE SYSTEM DESIGN AND OPERATION

Hand-operated chokes are the least complicated choke systems. Many methods have been used to make chokes work automatically. **Automatic chokes** eliminate the need for the operator to open the choke when the engine warms up. The design and operation of the latest automatic chokes will be presented here.

It is important to understand why a choke is needed. A **choke** causes a very rich air-fuel mixture to be delivered when starting a cold engine. Fuel coming from the carburetor is atomized into a vapor to be mixed with air before it enters the engine. When the

engine is cold, some of the atomized gasoline coming out of the carburetor condenses back into a liquid form and is deposited on the intake manifold and other engine parts before it reaches the cylinders. The colder the engine parts, the greater the condensation. The fuel mixture must be richened (more fuel added) as engine temperature becomes colder to provide for condensation and still get enough fuel in the air-fuel mixture to start the engine. The air-fuel ratio needed for starting at $-10\,°F$ ($-23\,°C$) might be as low as one part of air to one part of fuel (1:1).

The parts of an automatic choke are described below.

Choke Plate

The **choke plate** or **choke valve** is the main part of a choke system. It is a plate mounted on a shaft in the air horn at the top of the carburetor. It must be held closed when starting a cold engine. At the same time, the throttle valve must be partway open.

When the engine is being cranked over, a vacuum is caused by the moving pistons. Air cannot freely enter this vacuum, because the choke valve is restricting the flow of air into the intake manifold. This causes a strong vacuum to form in the manifold and in the carburetor throat below the choke plate. Atmospheric pressure in the carburetor bowl will force a strong fuel discharge from most of the carburetor systems to fill this vacuum. See Figure 3-39.

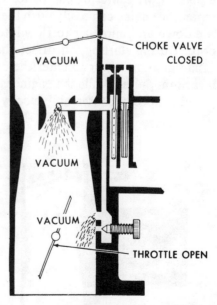

Figure 3-39. A closed choke valve and open throttle valve cause vacuum in the carburetor bore and fuel discharge from all fuel systems. (Courtesy of Chrysler Corporation)

Even though the choke valve closes off the carburetor throat, the engine must have some air to mix with the fuel when starting. On some hand-operated chokes, this air is provided by a **poppet valve** mounted on the choke plate. See Figure 3-40. The poppet valve is pushed open by atmospheric pressure and lets some air into the carburetor throat to mix with the fuel. The choke valve still must be opened slightly after the engine has started to avoid over-richening.

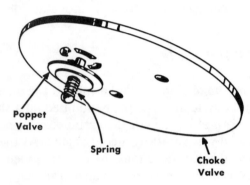

Figure 3-40. A choke plate with a poppet valve. (Courtesy of Holley Carburetor Division, Colt Industries)

Offset Choke Plate

An **offset choke plate** is often used with an automatic choke in which the choke plate is opened and closed by a spring. In Figure 3-41, the shaft of the offset choke plate is off center on the plate, so that air trying to enter the engine can easily push the long side of the plate down and allow air to flow into the carburetor bore. During starting, an offset choke plate allows a small amount of air to enter the carburetor with each vacuum pulse. While the engine is running, changing engine speeds causes air velocity past the

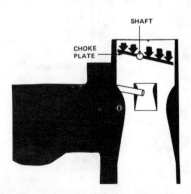

Figure 3-41. An offset choke plate. (Courtesy of Chrysler Corporation)

choke plate to vary the plate opening. The offset helps to regulate the choke position and the richness of the mixture for different engine speeds.

Bimetallic Thermostatic Spring

A **bimetallic thermostatic spring** is generally used in automatic chokes. The choke valve closes automatically by spring tension when the engine cools down and opens automatically as the engine warms up. Figure 3-42 shows a bimetallic strip and a thermostatic spring. A **bimetallic strip** is made from two different types of metal that are fused together. One metal could be spring steel (for tension), and the other could be brass or copper. These metals have different rates of expansion and contraction.

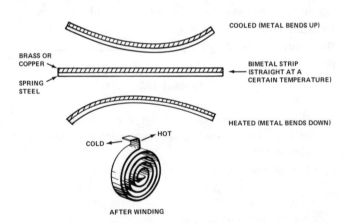

Figure 3-42. A bimetallic strip and thermostatic spring.

The way the spring works is not difficult to understand. See Figure 3-42. Assume that the bimetallic strip is perfectly straight at room temperature. If the strip is cooled, it will bend. During cooling, the copper will contract (shrink) more than the spring steel. After contracting, the longer piece (the spring steel) will be the longest surface and form the outside of the bend. If the strip is heated, it will bend the other way because the copper will expand more than the spring steel. Again, the longer piece (the copper) will be the longest surface and form the outside of the bend.

To operate the choke plate, the bimetallic strip is formed into a coil called a **bimetallic spring**, which is usually anchored to a pin and ends in a hook, as shown in Figure 3-42. The hook is used to push on an arm that closes the choke. When the choke thermostatic spring cools, it winds up (gains tension) and closes the choke plate. How far the choke closes is determined by how much the spring winds up, which is regulated by how cold the spring becomes. When heated, the spring unwinds (loses tension) and the choke opens as the temperature rises, until it reaches a fully open position. In this way, the choke thermostatic spring automatically opens and closes the choke plate.

Choke Piston or Diaphragm

If the choke plate were partially closed and the throttle suddenly opened, the increased air flow that would occur when the throttle was opened would cause extreme venturi vacuum. This vacuum would draw so much fuel out of the fuel bowl that the engine would be flooded with gasoline. The offset choke plate takes care of this problem by allowing the air velocity at high speeds to force the choke plate down and open the choke to reduce the vacuum. However, at low speeds and idle, the air velocity through the carburetor throat is too weak to move the choke plate.

To prevent overchoking during slow running when the engine is cold, a **choke piston** or **choke diaphragm** that operates off manifold vacuum is used. See Figure 3-43. These devices open the choke plate just enough to stop the flooding that could occur while the choke is closed. When the thermostatic spring has heated and relaxed the tension on the choke plate, the job of the piston or diaphragm is done. At this point, a controlled application of heat determines the choke setting. A choke diaphragm may be called by other names, such as **choke vacuum kick diaphragm** or **choke-break diaphragm**.

The pull-off distance on a choke piston may be

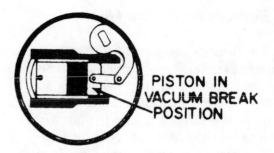

Figure 3-44. *A choke piston with vacuum brake slots. (Courtesy of General Motors of Canada Limited)*

limited by the use of a **vacuum break slot** (or slots) on the side of the piston bore, as shown in Figure 3-44. When the piston moves behind the slot, vacuum is allowed in front of the piston and piston pull is eliminated. Further opening of the choke merely pushes the piston further into its bore. The vacuum through the vacuum break slot, and atmospheric pressure at the far end of the heat tube, will cause heat to flow into the choke assembly and heat the thermostatic spring.

When a diaphragm is used, it bottoms in the vacuum chamber to limit its travel. The linkage is usually adjustable. Further choke opening is allowed by a **quadrant slot** in the choke shaft arm, as shown in Figure 3-45.

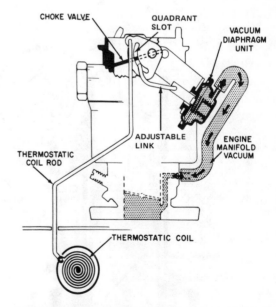

Figure 3-45. *A choke diaphragm with a quadrant slot in the operating arm that permits the choke to open after the diaphragm is bottomed. (Courtesy of General Motors of Canada Limited)*

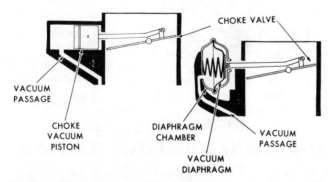

Figure 3-43. *A choke piston and a choke diaphragm. (Courtesy of Chrysler Corporation)*

Sources of Choke Heat

The thermostatic spring has to be heated to open the choke as the engine warms up and to hold it in the fully open position when the engine is hot. Chokes that have the spring enclosed in a cover on the carburetor may use a metal heat tube to draw heat from the engine to heat the spring. See Figure 3-46.

The heat may come from a **stove** (a metal cover over a cavity on the exhaust manifold or a hollow section projecting from the side of the manifold). Some automatic chokes use an inner heat tube that passes through the exhaust manifold, or the exhaust crossover in the intake manifold if the engine is a V-8. See Figure 3-47. An **electrical heating element** is often used to assist in heating the thermostatic spring. Certain chokes use only electrical heat to heat the spring. Many carburetors have a **divorced choke coil** that is mounted on a heat source such as the intake manifold exhaust crossover passage, as shown in Figure 3-48. As an aid in meeting emission standards, some of these divorced choke assemblies also have an electric assist heating element to heat the spring quickly in warm weather. See Figure 3-49.

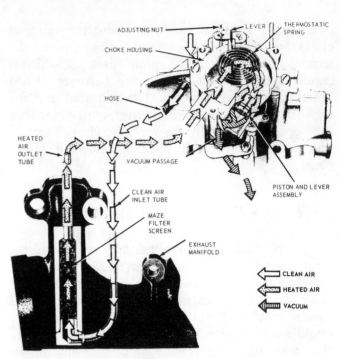

Figure 3-47. *A choke with a heat tube assembly using exhaust manifold heat. (Courtesy of Ford Motor Company, Dearborn)*

Fast Idle Cam and Unloader

More air flow is needed in a cold engine during idle. This will ensure that a well-atomized, adequate fuel supply enters the cylinders before it has a chance to condense on the cold engine surfaces. Regular hot idle throttle openings are not adequate and will cause a cold engine to stall. A fast idle is provided during warm-up by a **cam and linkage** that operate from the choke shaft. See Figure 3-50. The highest step on the cam is provided by a fully closed choke. This step can provide enough throttle opening for starting purposes and is the fastest running step. Decreasing steps provide for a tapering off of engine speed as the engine warms up and the choke opens.

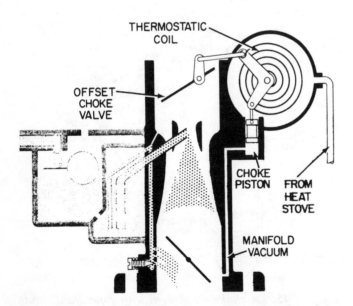

Figure 3-46. *A metal heat tube may be used to draw heat for the choke from a stove on the engine. (Courtesy of General Motors of Canada Limited)*

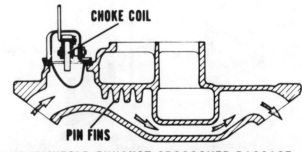

Figure 3-48. *A divorced choke coil mounted on the intake manifold exhaust crossover passage. (Courtesy of Chrysler Corporation)*

If the engine fails to start quickly, it may become flooded by a closed choke. The situation is worse if the driver is a pedal pumper. Each time the pedal is pumped, another shot of gas goes into the carburetor bore from the acceleration pump. An **unloader** is a device placed on the throttle arm or shaft that opens the choke a little at wide open throttle and lets air into the carburetor to dry out this excess fuel. See Figure 3-51. To operate the unloader, press the gas pedal to the floor and hold it there while cranking the engine until the engine starts and runs properly.

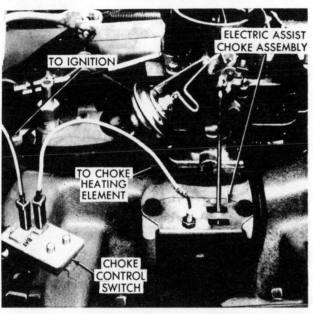

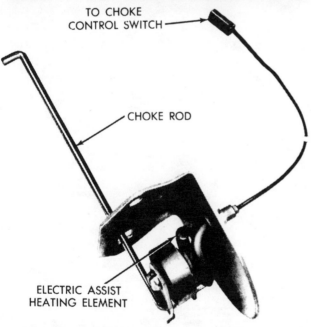

Figure 3-49.   An automatic choke with an electric-assist heating element. (Courtesy of Chrysler Corporation)

Automatic Choke Operation

It will be helpful to look at Figure 3-46 when reading this discussion of automatic choke operation.

When the engine is being started, the offset

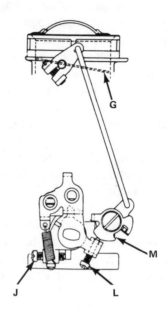

Figure 3-50.   A fast idle cam and linkage. Fast idle adjusting screw L rests on fast idle cam M and opens the throttle according to the choke-cam position. This causes a fast idle, based on engine temperature. The hot idle speed is adjusted by screw J. (Courtesy of General Motors of Canada Limited)

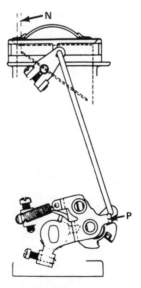

Figure 3-51.   A choke unloader. With wide open throttle, unloader lug P will push down the fast idle cam and linkage, opening the choke valve to clearance N. Air enters while cranking to dry out the flooded manifold. (Courtesy of General Motors of Canada Limited)

choke valve is closed by the cold thermostatic spring. This increases vacuum in the carburetor throat, and a strong fuel supply is discharged from most of the fuel systems. The offset choke plate will move with the intake manifold vacuum pulses and let a little air into the carburetor bore to mix with the fuel.

Once the engine has started, manifold vacuum on the choke piston (or diaphragm) will open the choke slightly against the pressure from the thermostatic spring. This will let some air into the carburetor throat to prevent flooding at idle and low speeds. At higher speeds, the air velocity in the carburetor bore will push the offset choke plate open to regulate the air-fuel mixture according to engine speed. On sudden throttle opening, the manifold vacuum drops and the choke piston will release the choke. The choke plate will partially close, momentarily giving a richer mixture for power, until increased air velocity opens it again.

By the use of vacuum in the choke housing and atmospheric pressure at the end of the choke heat pipe in the heat stove, heat is applied to the choke thermostatic spring. This heat causes the spring to relax as it warms up and eventually allows the choke plate to open all the way.

In this way, the choke plate is closed with the proper tension to assure easy starting when the engine is cold. It is positioned correctly to produce the correct air-fuel mixture for smooth running during the warm-up period. Then, when the engine is warm enough to run on normal mixtures, the choke is automatically opened.

☐ ASSIGNMENT 3-1 ☐

1. Describe the purpose of a choke.

2. Describe the operation of the following parts of an automatic choke when starting a cold engine:

    thermostatic spring   choke piston
    offset choke plate   fast idle cam
    choke diaphragm   unloader

3. Describe the effect of air velocity on an offset choke plate at idle and at high speeds.

☐ SELF-TEST ☐

Complete the following sentences by filling in the missing words.

1. Gasoline (a liquid), if turned into _____ , will combine with the _____ and become an _____-_____ mixture.

2. An overly rich air-fuel mixture contains too much _____ and too little _____ to complete the burning process.

3. The high-speed system supplies an economical air-fuel mixture for _____-_____ driving under _____ to _____ loads.

4. The power system works along with the regular _____-_____ system and adds about _____% more fuel into the mixture.

5. An air _____ permits a small amount of air to enter the fuel passage, causing bubbling and _____ of the fuel.

6. The main metering jet _____ fuel into the _____-_____ system, but has no effect on fuel flow into the _____ system.

7. At idle, _____ pressure in the fuel bowl pushes fuel through the discharge port below the throttle valve, toward the _____ created at the manifold.

8. A venturi is a streamlined _____ in the carburetor _____. As air enters the venturi, it is forced to _____ _____ in order to pass through. This causes _____ pressure to be exerted by the air in the venturi area.

9. The venturi in the carburetor bore is referred to as the _____ or _____ venturi. The smaller venturi, which further _____ air speed and vacuum, is referred to as a _____ venturi.

10. The power piston, stem, and spring work together. The _____ vacuum passage brings manifold _____ , from the base of the carburetor below the _____ valve, to the top of the power piston.

11. The duration spring in the acceleration pump pushes the pump plunger down during rapid _____ for the length of _____ required to prevent a flat spot.

12. When the choke thermostatic spring cools, it winds up (gains tension) and _____ the choke plate. When heated, the spring unwinds (loses tension) and the choke _____ as the temperature rises until it reaches a fully open position.

13. When the engine is being started, the _____ choke valve is closed by the cold _____ spring. This _____ vacuum in the carburetor throat, and a strong fuel supply is discharged from most of the fuel systems.

CARBURETOR DIAGNOSIS AND QUICK SERVICE PROCEDURES

After studying this chapter, you will be able to:

1. List the safety precautions necessary during fuel system service.

2. Discuss the importance of cleanliness during carburetor service.

3. List the common diagnostic symptoms and the quick service procedures for the following carburetor systems:
   float
   idle and low speed
   high speed, power, and metering rod
   acceleration pump
   choke

4. Define and/or discuss the following terms:
   carburetor flooding   choke heat pipe
   idle speed adjustment   fast idle cam
   infrared analysis   heat-assisted chokes
   lean-drop method   integral choke
   propane enrichment   vacuum diaphragm choke

INTRODUCTION

This chapter is about carburetor diagnosis and servicing. **Diagnosis** is the process of recognizing problems by their symptoms. Diagnosis is necessary before a problem can be isolated and service started. **Servicing** is the act of repairing, overhauling, or replacing something after diagnosis.

Unfortunately, some service technicians will try to service a carburetor without proper diagnosis. When this happens, the vehicle is generally not repaired correctly, and the customer is not satisfied. This chapter will cover general carburetor repairs that are fairly easy to perform. Chapter 5 covers major carburetor overhaul procedures.

This text only covers repairs of a general sort that apply to all carburetors. Many service needs for specific carburetors are not covered here. You will find these procedures covered in the manufacturer's shop manuals. A good tradesman takes the time to read as much as possible about his trade and seeks help from his fellow workers when necessary.

TOOLS AND PROCEDURES

Before you become involved with carburetor diagnosis and repair, you have to learn about the tools and equipment, safety precautions, and cleanliness habits necessary when you are working with carburetors.

Tools

Special tools as well as the tools used for general repair are needed when performing carburetor tuneups or repairs. Purchase good quality tools that will last and not break or bend. Many manufacturers sell sets of general mechanics tools that are suggested as starter sets for mechanics. The addition of certain special tools is necessary when working on carburetors. These tools are listed below:

1. A set of six-point flare nut wrenches.
2. Hose clamp pliers.
3. A set of special carburetor gauges, as shown in Figure 4-1 (or a set of drills to be used as carburetor gauges).
4. A set of metric tools for working on foreign cars.

A **cleaning tank** with an agitator should also be available. One that is divided for commercial cleaning

solvent and carburetor cleaner is best. A special stand made to hold two five-gallon (about 20-liter) cans, one of carburetor cleaner and one of commercial solvent, can be used in place of a cleaning tank. An **air hose** with a nozzle is needed for drying and blowing dirt out of carburetor parts. The cleaning area should have a sink with hot water for rinsing parts. Most carburetor cleaners are water soluble.

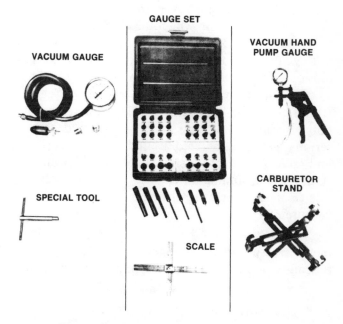

Figure 4-1. Special carburetor tools. (Courtesy of Chrysler Corporation)

Safety Precautions

The following safety precautions should be followed whenever you work on a carburetor:

1. Never run an engine in a closed shop without a vent pipe on the exhaust. Exhaust gases contain **carbon monoxide**, a colorless, odorless gas. If carbon monoxide is inhaled in small amounts, it can cause headache and nausea. Inhaling large amounts of carbon monoxide will result in death. In a closed garage, a running engine can produce enough carbon monoxide gas in a few minutes to cause death.

2. Do not leave gasoline in open pans. Store gasoline in closed metal safety containers. It is best to use a gasoline syphoning and storage unit, if one is available.

3. If gasoline spills or leaks from a car, wipe it up immediately and air out the shop by leaving the

doors open. Put gasoline-soaked rags in a closed metal safety can. Gasoline can cause a very serious explosion and fire.

4. Never disconnect a fuel line or remove a carburetor while the engine is hot. Engine heat can cause gasoline to burst into flames. Let the engine cool before working on a carburetor. Dispose of gasoline from a carburetor, filter, or pump in a safety container designed for this purpose.

5. Never crank over an engine that has an open fuel line or from which the carburetor has been removed. Seal the line first and disconnect the ignition system. Engine spark could cause a disastrous explosion and fire when exposed to an open fuel line.

6. Never prime an engine by pouring fuel in a carburetor while the engine is being cranked or running. Should the engine backfire, it could cause a serious flash fire centered around your hands, body, and face. Whenever possible, have the air cleaner installed when running an engine. The air cleaner acts as a flame arrester if the engine backfires through the carburetor.

7. Store oil- or fuel-soaked rags in a closed metal safety container. They can ignite by spontaneous combustion if left in a pile, open to the air.

8. Never bring any flame near gasoline!

9. Never smoke around gasoline!

10. Heavy concentrations of gasoline fumes can be ignited by an electric switch spark, or sparks produced while testing electrical circuits with jumper wires. Keep all electrical equipment away from gasoline.

11. Do not weld near gasoline!

12. Know the location of your fire extinguishers.

13. Do not use gasoline as a cleaning solvent. It is too volatile (bursts into flame too easily). Use a commercial cleaning solvent that is less volatile than gasoline.

14. Close the lid on the cleaning tank when the cleaning tank is not in use.

15. Carburetors are cleaned with a very strong cleaning solvent. Do not put your hands in it. Wash your hands in water if you get cleaner on them. If carburetor cleaner, solvent, or gasoline splashes in your eyes, rinse your eyes immediately with plenty of cold water. If a burning sensation lasts for more than three minutes, get medical attention. Always wear safety goggles while using or working around any fuels or cleaners.

16. An air hose is used to blow carburetor parts dry after they are cleaned and rinsed. Air pressure can make dangerous projectiles out of bits of dirt, carburetor parts, or even water or solvent. Keep the object being cleaned facing away from you and the hose blowing downward when you are using it. Wear safety goggles. Adjust the air pressure to less than 30 lbs. Never direct forced air onto your skin or use it to blow dirt or dust off your clothing. Forced air can enter your skin and form a bubble in a blood vein. This bubble will block the passage of blood to your heart and cause heart failure.

Cleanliness

Cleanliness is critically important when you are working on a carburetor. A trace of dirt left in a car-

Figure 4-2. This view of a carburetor shows the parts associated with flooding problems. The parts shown are the (1) fuel bowl, (2) fuel passage, (3) float, (4) pivot pin, (5) spray shield, (6) needle and seat, (7) gaskets, (8) filter housing, (9) spring, and (10) filter.

buretor during assembly can clog the carburetor. Pick a clean bench, wash up the area where you want to assemble the carburetor or cover the area with clean shop cloths. Make sure your tools and hands are clean. Never use dirty or linty cloths. Lint is worse in a carburetor than dirt. Don't put the clean parts in with the dirty, old gaskets and parts. Use a clean parts tray or a clean bench covered by clean shop cloths to store clean parts.

Quick Service Procedures

Proper carburetor performance depends on such things as ignition, engine compression, and correct timing. Although many things can go wrong with these systems, we will assume for the purpose of this chapter that they are all operating correctly.

After studying an engine's operation and diagnosing a carburetor problem, you will have to decide whether the carburetor should be repaired, replaced, or overhauled. **Quick service procedures** are given for problems that can be easily diagnosed and corrected.

Choke system parts are externally mounted. Therefore, choke system repairs are often easily carried out. Other minor problems, such as checking carburetor float level, venturi and fuel jets inspection, and minor acceleration pump repairs, may fall into this quick service category. Many carburetor repairs, however, require opening (dismantling) the carburetor. These should be given careful consideration before they are attempted. Such repairs should not be done unless the carburetor is fairly clean and has not been used very long.

☐ ASSIGNMENT 4-A ☐

1. Why must you put a vent pipe on the exhaust of an engine that is being run in a closed shop?
2. When should safety goggles be worn during carburetor service?
3. List five safety precautions that should be followed when working around gasoline.
4. What safety precautions should be taken when you dispose of oil- or gasoline-soaked rags?
5. Why is cleanliness important when you are repairing or overhauling a carburetor?

FLOAT SYSTEM PROBLEMS

The **float system** maintains a constant fuel level in the carburetor fuel bowl. The fuel level in the fuel bowl generally rises when any float system parts are defective. If the proper float bowl fuel level is not maintained, the carburetor floods or loads up. A **flooding carburetor** is generally indicated when gasoline spills out of the high-speed nozzle, vents, or throttle shaft. When flooding occurs, the engine will be hard to start and keep running.

An engine with a carburetor that is **loading up** will usually flood after a period of idling, or after the engine has been shut off. Carburetor loading can be the cause of poor gas mileage, stalling on turns, or sudden stalls as fuel spills from the high-speed nozzle. A catalytic-converter-equipped vehicle with a flooding or loading carburetor will give off an offensive smell from its exhaust. Some possible float system problems are listed below. Refer to Figure 4-2 when you study this list.

Needle and Seat Valve Problems

Dirt lodged between the needle and seat prevents proper sealing of the needle valve. If this happens, the fuel level becomes too high and floods the engine. A worn needle and seat valve can leak, causing high fuel level or flooding. A loose needle and seat valve body, or one with a damaged or missing gasket, will allow fuel to leak around the valve and overfill the fuel bowl. Needle and seat valves can be disassembled and cleaned or replaced if necessary.

Float or Pivot Damage

A worn or seized (stuck) float pivot can cause poor fuel-level control. A misaligned float can rub or catch inside the carburetor, causing poor fuel-level control. A damaged float does not float properly, and the fuel level becomes higher than it should be. A hollow float with a pinhole in it can fill with gasoline and sink. A solid plastic float will sink when it is saturated with gasoline. If the float sinks, the carburetor will flood. A damaged float can be easily replaced. Floats that are misaligned can be easily adjusted.

Improper Float Setting

A high float setting causes a high fuel level in the fuel bowl. A low float setting causes a low fuel level. Too much float drop will cause the needle to become misaligned and jam. This will cause flooding. When there is not enough float drop, the needle tip will restrict the opening area of the valve. This will reduce fuel flow into the fuel bowl. Float adjustments are easily made on most carburetors.

FACTS TO REMEMBER

Most float system problems result in high fuel levels in the float bowl and carburetor flooding that produces rich air-fuel mixtures. If an engine is operated for a long time with a rich mixture, engine damage will result, because the unburned fuel remains liquid and washes the oil from the cylinder walls. This will cause the walls to score and eventually destroy the cylinder. A rich mixture can also cause excess amounts of hydrocarbons to oxidize in a catalytic converter. When this happens, converter temperature rises to the point where it can destroy the converter.

□ ASSIGNMENT 4-B □

1. List four common causes of carburetor flooding.
2. What symptoms result from a high fuel level in the float bowl?

IDLE AND LOW-SPEED SYSTEM PROBLEMS

The **idle and low-speed system** provides the proper air-fuel mixture for engine idle and low speeds under light loads. Any system problems will show up in the idle and low-speed and light-load ranges. Some possible idle and low-speed system problems and the steps for correcting them are listed below.

Blocked Idle Tube

When an idle tube (or jet) is blocked on a single-barrel carburetor, the engine will stall at engine speeds below approximately 1500 rpms. You can easily identify a blocked idle tube by adjusting the idle mixture screw. If adjusting the screw produces no difference in response from the engine, an idle tube is blocked. Keep in mind, however, that a blocked idle tube will not affect engine speeds above 1500 rpms, since the high-speed system supplies the fuel to run the engine at these high engine speeds. A two- or four-barrel carburetor has two idle systems. If one

side is blocked, the engine will idle more slowly than normal, vibrate more, and tend to stall frequently. The engine will not respond when the idle mixture adjusting screw on the blocked circuit is turned.

It is not an acceptable practice to try to clear an idle tube by forcing air into the idle adjusting screw hole. The dirt blown out of the idle system will remain inside the main well of the carburetor and is sure to be picked up again. A blocked idle tube can be cleared during a carburetor overhaul.

Improper Idle Jet

An improper idle jet (or pickup tube) will affect low-speed operation. A **lean jet** (too small) causes the engine to run rough and gives rough low-speed operation. A **rich jet** (too large) allows too much fuel through. This causes poor low-speed operation, fouling of the spark plugs, and excess exhaust emissions. Adjusting the idle mixture screw cannot compensate for the wrong idle jet. The jet must be replaced with the correct jet.

Blocked Idle Air Bleed

Blocked idle air bleeds usually result in extremely rich idle mixtures even though the idle mixture screw is properly adjusted. If an air bleed is blocked, some idle systems may syphon (drain) the fuel from the fuel bowl after the engine is stopped. A dirty or missing air cleaner element can cause blocked idle air bleeds. Blocked idle air bleeds can be opened during a carburetor overhaul.

Damaged Idle Adjusting Needles

Damaged idle adjusting needles (screws) may have grooves worn into them from being over-tightened. If this happens, the air-fuel mixture cannot be adjusted correctly and the engine will not meet emission standards. Replacing the needles will correct this problem.

Intake Manifold Air Leaks

If the engine idles poorly or will not run at idle and low speeds, but will keep running at high engine speeds, check for and repair any air leaks into the intake manifold. An air leak into the intake manifold can be caused by a cracked line or hose, or a defective power brake booster. Intake manifold air leaks have the same symptoms as a blocked idle system.

To find out if air leakage is the cause of the problem, disconnect the lines or hoses from their manifold fittings. Cover each manifold fitting with masking tape, and run the engine. If the engine idles correctly, the cause of the problem is in the manifold lines and vacuum devices.

If the engine still does not idle correctly, inspect the intake manifold for cracks, loose bolts, or bad gaskets. Look up proper tightening procedures in the manufacturer's shop manual before you tighten a manifold. Running the engine while pouring small amounts of an equal mixture of cleaning solvent and oil onto the flanges at the engine and carburetor will determine if a leak is present. As the solvent is drawn through a leaking gasket flange or crack, temporarily plugging the leak, engine speed will momentarily change.

Presetting the Carburetor Idle

If you are satisfied that there are no air leaks in the intake manifold, perform the following adjustment procedure for presetting the carburetor idle. This will serve as a rough test to determine whether the idle mixture is improperly adjusted, or the idle circuit is blocked. Refer to Figure 4-3 when you make this adjustment.

1. Stop the engine. Turn the **idle speed adjusting screw** out (counterclockwise) until the throttle is completely closed. Then turn the idle speed adjusting screw in (clockwise) until it just contacts the

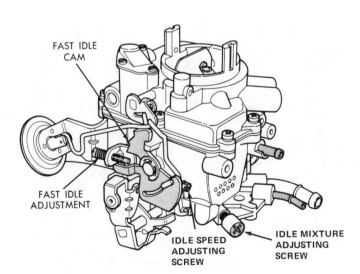

Figure 4-3. The idle speed adjusting screw and idle mixture adjusting screw on a carburetor. (Courtesy of Chrysler Corporation)

throttle stop. Now turn in the idle speed adjusting screw two more revolutions (clockwise) to open the throttle.

2. Turn the **idle mixture adjusting screw** clockwise until it is seated. Be careful not to damage the mixture screw or the fuel port by overtightening the screw into the seat. Now turn the idle mixture screw counterclockwise three complete revolutions to open the fuel port. For a two- or four-barrel carburetor, adjust both idle mixture screws in this manner.

3. The engine should idle with these settings, but it may still require a fine adjustment of idle speed and idle mixture. If the engine does not idle, the idle system is blocked. If the carburetor is multibarrel (two or four), both idle systems are blocked.

FACTS TO REMEMBER

Engine idle and low-speed operation are affected by the idle and low-speed system. There are several common faults that can occur in this system. You can find where the fault lies by presetting the carburetor idle. Remember when you are doing this not to tighten the idle mixture screw against its seat. This will score and distort the seat or the tip of the idle mixture screw.

☐ ASSIGNMENT 4-C ☐

1. List four common idle and low-speed system problems.
2. Describe the procedure for determining if there is a manifold air leak.
3. Outline the adjustment procedure used to determine if the idle circuits are plugged.

IMPROPER IDLE SPEED AND MIXTURE ADJUSTMENT

Improper idle mixture adjustment and/or idle speed setting can cause many problems. For example, an engine that has a lean mixture and idles faster than it should will probably **diesel** (keep running) after the ignition is turned off. Too rich an idle setting can foul the spark plugs, and the engine will not meet emission

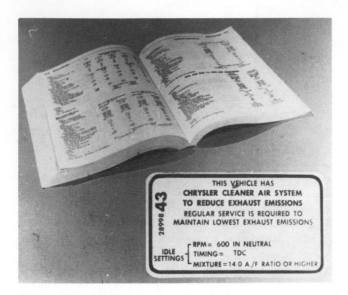

Figure 4-4.   The hood decal or shop manual will give carburetor specifications. (Courtesy of Chrysler Corporation)

standards. These problems can be corrected by adjusting the idle mixture and idle speed. Below are the procedures for adjusting the idle speed and idle mixture. It is important to realize that the idle *speed* adjustment controls the *minimum throttle opening* at idle with a throttle stop screw. The idle *mixture* adjustment, on the other hand, controls the *air-fuel mixture* at idle. These two systems work together and must be adjusted together.

Quick Service Procedure: Idle Speed and Mixture Adjustment

1.   Warm the engine up to operating temperature. Look up the specifications for the vehicle you are working on. This information can be found on a decal under the hood, or in the manufacturer's shop manual. See Figure 4-4.

2.   Attach a **tachometer** to the ignition distributor lead on the ignition coil and to a ground (or where specified for electronic units).

3.   Adjust the engine idle speed as specified, using the idle speed adjusting screw or idle stop solenoid. Have an automatic transmission in or out of drive and have the proper hoses removed and plugged as stated in the manufacturer's specifications.

4.   Turn the idle mixture screw *out* first (counterclockwise). If the engine speeds up, it was set for too lean a mixture. Readjust the idle speed screw

before continuing the procedure. If the engine starts to slow down and run rough, you have turned the screw out too far and the mixture has become too rich. From this overrich point, slowly turn the idle mixture screw *in* (clockwise). Keep an eye on the tachometer. If the engine speed rises more than 75 rpm from the present idle speed, readjust the idle speed screw to slow the engine down before you continue to turn in the idle mixture screw.

When the engine starts to slow down, you will have reached the **lean-drop** position. As soon as this happens, *stop* turning the idle mixture screw in. Now *back out* the idle mixture screw (counterclockwise) 1/4 to 1/2 turn to regain the highest engine speed without overrichening. If overrichening occurs, the engine will start to slow down again. It is usually necessary to reset the idle speed screw for the recommended idle speed after the idle mixture screw is set.

5.   A multibarrel carburetor has two idle mixture adjusting screws. See Figure 4-5. Treat them as you would two separate carburetors. Adjust one side as outlined above and then adjust the other one. However, the idle mixture screw settings can affect each other because the manifold and/or carburetor flange have **balance passages** between the two carburetor bores. Because of this, you will have to repeat the adjustment on both mixture screws to maintain a balance between the two idle systems.

Coordinated idle speed and idle mixture adjustments will result in the correct air-fuel mixture at idle and acceptable carbon monoxide and hydrocarbon exhaust emissions.

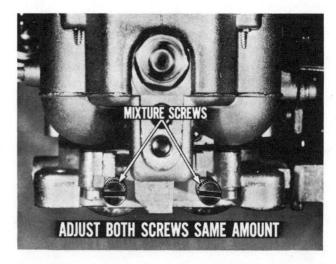

Figure 4-5.   Maintain the balance between the two idle systems on multibarrel carburetors. (Courtesy of Chrysler Corporation)

Infrared Analysis

Most emission specifications suggest **infrared analysis** of the tail pipe exhaust for carbon monoxide and hydrocarbon content. To learn how to operate the equipment for these tests, study the manufacturer's handbook and practice with the infrared analyzer. There is an outline on the use of an infrared analyzer in the emission controls chapter of this book. If the specifications require you to check the carburetor adjustment with infrared analysis, you should use an already warmed-up and zero-adjusted infrared exhaust emissions tester. The exhaust hydrocarbon and carbon monoxide content should match specifications for the vehicle. Further adjustment of the mixture screw may be needed to meet these specifications. Correct idle speed and mixture adjustments result in passable exhaust emissions.

Lean-Drop Method

Sometimes the **lean-drop method** is suggested as an alternative to using the infrared analyzer. The lean-drop method is simple to use. When you have arrived at the point where the mixture screw is set at the standard setting (1/4 to 1/2 turn from the lean-drop position), turn the mixture screw slowly in again until the idle speed drops down as specified in the shop manual. *Then leave it there.*

For example, suppose the speed is adjusted to 620 rpm at a regular idle mixture setting, but the specifications call for a lean-drop setting of 600 rpm. On a single-barrel carburetor, the mixture screw should be turned in until the engine speed drops 20 rpm. On a dual-idle system (two- or four-barrel carburetor), one mixture screw is turned in to drop the idle speed 10 rpm. Then the other screw is turned in to drop the idle speed another 10 rpm. In both cases, the idle speed will be reduced to 600 rpm by leaning out the idle mixture. Lean mixtures produce less exhaust emissions.

Propane Enrichment

Many late model carburetors require **propane enrichment** to assist in idle adjustment. The air-fuel mixture supplied by the idle system on these carburetors is so lean that it is difficult to detect a lean-drop position when you adjust the idle mixture. This lean mixture is required to meet emission standards. A lean mixture is also needed if a catalytic converter is used in the exhaust system. Catalytic converters produce such low hydrocarbon and carbon monoxide readings that an infrared emissions tester cannot detect carburetor misadjustment. If the carburetor produces a rich mixture, the catalytic converter will produce an offensive, rotten-egg smell at the exhaust. This is reduced when the mixture is corrected.

By using a special metering valve attached to a propane torch, you can direct propane into the carburetor through the air cleaner or a vacuum port. This propane will enrich the air-fuel mixture during idle adjustment. The idle speed is checked and adjusted by adjusting the throttle position while supplying enough propane enrichment to gain maximum idle speed. When the propane is turned off, the idle speed should drop to the manufacturer's specified speed. If the engine speed is incorrect, turn the idle mixture adjuster(s) to obtain the proper speed. Further discussion of catalytic converters and propane-assisted idle adjustment is found in Chapter 14.

□ ASSIGNMENT 4-D □

1. Explain how you would adjust the idle mixture and idle speed on a single-barrel carburetor.
2. Explain how you would do a lean-drop setting on an adjusted carburetor.

HIGH-SPEED AND POWER SYSTEMS PROBLEMS

The **high-speed system** provides the proper air-fuel mixture for high speeds under moderate loads. Extreme speeds, or heavy loads at lower speeds, require extra fuel. This is supplied either by the power system or by metering rods working along with the high-speed system. Because of the close relationship of their functions, high speed, power, and metering rod system problems are discussed together in this section. Figures 4-6 and 4-7 show the layout of the parts of the high-speed and power systems.

Incorrect Main Metering Jet

A main metering jet that is too large can cause poor gas mileage, smoke, carbon deposits, spark plug fouling, and excess exhaust emissions. A jet that is

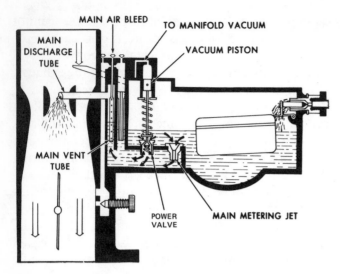

Figure 4-6. A high-speed system that has a main jet and a power valve or power bypass jet. (Courtesy of Chrysler Corporation)

too small can cause power loss, hesitation, and pinging. The spark plugs and engine can also be damaged due to extreme heat caused by burning an overly lean mixture. Installing the right main metering jet will correct this problem.

Blocked High-Speed Air Bleed

A blocked high-speed air bleed usually causes a rich mixture and uneven running because of improper fuel atomization. This suggests an air cleaner problem, where dirt from the air coming into the carburetor has clogged the carburetor air bleed hole. The air cleaner should be checked and serviced. The air bleed will have to be cleared during a carburetor overhaul.

Incorrect or Leaking Power Valve

The wrong power valve can cause the same symptoms as a wrong main jet, but at wider open-throttle positions. A leaking power valve causes poor gas mileage, because it fails to completely close off the flow of fuel during light-load, part-throttle operation. Incorrect or leaking power valves should be replaced.

Sticking Power Piston

If seized in a down position, the power piston will hold the power valve open. This will cause the constant production of a power mixture at high speeds and a reduction of about 25% in gas mileage. If the power piston is seized in the up position, the power valve will always be closed and no power mixture can be obtained. This results in poor heavy-load or fast-speed performance. Seized power pistons can be freed and replaced, if necessary, during carburetor overhaul.

Loss of Manifold Vacuum

When no manifold vacuum reaches the power piston, the piston fails to move, holds the power valve open, and constantly produces a power mixture. Manifold vacuum could be lost through carbon build-up in the passage between the manifold and the piston. See Figure 4-7. Vacuum can also be lost if the gasket is installed backward, the manifold vacuum hole in the gasket is not punched out, or the wrong gasket is installed. Any of these problems can be corrected during a carburetor overhaul.

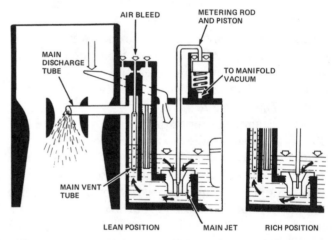

Figure 4-7. A high-speed system controlled by a metering rod that is vacuum-piston operated. (Courtesy of Chrysler Corporation)

Metering Rod and Piston Position Problems

Some carburetors have metering rods, as shown in Figure 4-7. If the operating piston is seized in the up position, the metering rod is always in the power (rich) position, and fuel is wasted. If seized in the down position, the metering rod is always in the lean position, and no power mixture can be produced. With loss of manifold vacuum, the piston and metering rod stay in the rich position. If the wrong metering rod is used, the air-fuel mixture ratio is upset. If the return spring is missing from a power or metering rod piston, the piston will not respond as the vacuum drops, and no power mixture will be available. If the power or metering rod piston return spring is broken, deformed, stretched, or incorrect, the power system will begin to function at the wrong time. All of these problems can be corrected during carburetor overhaul.

Metering Rod Adjustment

Certain metering rods are moved by throttle movement and can be adjusted. If they are adjusted incorrectly, the engine will not run properly. Proper metering rod adjustment can solve this problem.

Dirt in a Carburetor Passage

Dirt is one of the worst enemies of a carburetor. Dirt lodged in a jet, passageway, or in a pickup tube can lead to performance problems, such as cutting out at high speeds. Passageways and tubes should be thoroughly cleaned during overhaul.

Power Valve Problems

Some Ford and Holley carburetors have a diaphragm and power valve as an integral part. See Figure 4-8. This means that the two are connected together and cannot be repaired. The diaphragm has vacuum on one side and fuel on the other. If there is a hole in the diaphragm or a poor seal where it is crimped together, or if it is not tight enough to compress the gasket, fuel will pass through the diaphragm or bypass the power valve. The engine will run poorly

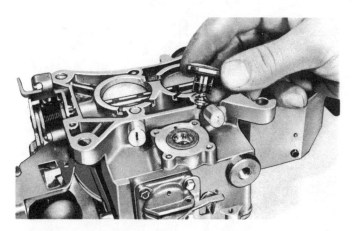

Figure 4-8. A typical Ford carburetor power valve. The power valve diaphragm has vacuum on one side and fuel on the other. (Courtesy of Ford Motor Company, Dearborn)

and produce black smoke. The manifold will become flooded while the engine is shut off, causing hard starting. This condition can be mistaken for a float system flooding problem. Defective power valves should be replaced during carburetor overhaul.

FACTS TO REMEMBER

A faulty power system prevents the power mixture from being delivered and causes the engine to cut out under load. A very low fuel level in the carburetor bowl or a weak fuel pump could cause the engine to act in much the same way. A power system problem that keeps the power system in operation continuously wastes gas.

☐ ASSIGNMENT 4-E ☐

Describe the symptoms caused by a:
1. main metering jet that is too small
2. main metering jet that is too large
3. blocked high-speed air bleed
4. power piston stuck in the down position
5. power piston stuck in the up position
6. missing power piston spring
7. stuck metering rod piston
8. leaking power valve diaphragm.

ACCELERATION PUMP SYSTEM PROBLEMS

The **acceleration pump** prevents hesitation when the throttle is opened quickly. Defects in the operation of the acceleration pump will show up on acceleration, or pull away. The following is a list of some common acceleration pump problems. See Figure 4-9 for the layout of the acceleration pump parts.

Improper Pump Stroke

Too short a pump stroke (or travel) can cause **hesitation** (a lag in acceleration). Too long a pump stroke wastes fuel. It could also cause a momentary lag in power, because the engine is supplied with more fuel than it can efficiently consume. On some carburetors, the plunger stroke is adjusted by selecting

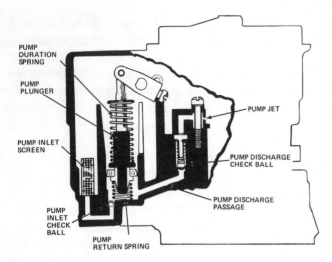

Figure 4-9. An acceleration pump. (Courtesy of General Motors of Canada Limited)

the proper hole for the pump linkage rod, (Figure 4-10). On other carburetors, it is adjusted by bending the linkage rod (Figure 4-11). Some accelerator pumps have a fixed pump travel that is not adjustable.

Worn or Shrunken Pump Plunger

A worn or shrunken pump plunger cup causes hesitation on acceleration. Some fuel will pass around a loose-fitting pump cup on the downward stroke. A rubber cup can wear out. A leather cup can both wear and shrink. Always flare out the leather cup on a plunger (even a new one) when installing it. Worn or shrunken pump plungers must be replaced.

Leaking or Missing Check Ball, Spring, Weight, or Needle

A leaking inlet check ball causes hesitation because some of the fuel backs up into the fuel bowl on the discharge stroke. Dirt in the check valve, or an etched (scored) or corroded seat or ball, causes a check valve to leak. A leaking or missing discharge check ball (or needle) causes a flat spot, because some air enters the pump from the fuel nozzle. This reduces the amount of fuel drawn into the pump on the intake stroke.

Venturi vacuum can draw fuel past a leaking discharge check ball, causing **pump pullover** at high speeds. A missing spring or weight, needle, or check ball from the discharge check valve causes pump pullover. The spring or weight prevents the ball from being lifted by the venturi vacuum. If the spring or

weight is missing, unwanted fuel will be drawn through the pump nozzle.

The pump fuel discharge nozzle is located in the venturi area. At high speed, the venturi vacuum may be strong enough to cause fuel to flow from the nozzle if any of the parts in the discharge side of the pump are missing, worn, or defective. Missing or bucking under extreme load conditions and poor gas mileage are symptoms that indicate trouble in the discharge side of the pump. Leaking or missing check balls or parts can be repaired or replaced during pump overhaul.

Duration and Return Spring Problems

A weak duration spring allows the fuel discharge to be lean and sustained too long. This will cause a slight hesitation at times. A spring that is too strong causes the fuel discharge to be too rich and the duration too short. This causes a lag after initial accelera-

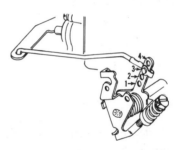

Figure 4-10. Some acceleration pumps are adjusted by selecting the correct holes on the linkage rod. (Courtesy of Ford Motor Company, Dearborn)

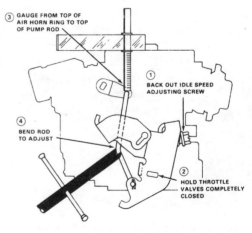

Figure 4-11. Some acceleration pumps are adjusted by bending the operating rod. (Courtesy of General Motors of Canada Limited)

tion. If the duration spring is missing, there will be no fuel discharge from the acceleration pump until the throttle is almost completely open. Then the discharge is too late to be effective. This causes very bad hesitation.

The pump return spring under the plunger removes the slack from the linkages. When it is weak or missing, plunger operation will lag, causing hesitation on slight acceleration. On diaphragm-type acceleration pumps, as shown in Figure 4-12, the return spring pushes back the diaphragm to fill the pump. The pump will be inoperative if the spring is missing. Defective or missing springs can be replaced during pump overhaul.

Plugged Pump Jet

A plugged pump jet (nozzle) causes a flat spot during acceleration. On a dual pump nozzle (two- and four-barrel carburetors), if one side is plugged, the engine will miss on initial acceleration. Half of the cylinders will respond normally while the others will lack fuel. Plugged pump jets can be cleaned during pump overhaul.

Diaphragm Problems

On diaphragm operated acceleration pumps, a hole in the diaphragm causes a flat spot on accelera-

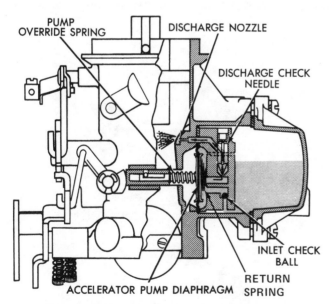

Figure 4-12. A diaphragm-type acceleration pump. Fuel will drip from the pump if the diaphragm has a hole in it. If the return spring is missing, this type of pump will not operate. (Courtesy of Chrysler Corporation)

tion because of the fuel lost out of the hole as the pump is operating. When there is a hole in the diaphragm, fuel continuously drips from the pump onto the engine. This is a very dangerous situation and could cause a fire. Pump diaphragms are easily replaced, often without disassembling the carburetor.

Checking Acceleration Pump Discharge

A momentary hesitation or engine stumble is often caused by an improperly operating acceleration pump. Pump operation can be checked by watching the fuel discharge from the pump nozzle.

Caution: Extreme caution is required when you are operating around an acceleration pump. The pump shoots a stream of fuel into the carburetor bore. If exposed to heat from cigarettes, hot drop lights, hot engine parts, or any other source, this fuel stream could burst into flames. **Never** look down a carburetor throat while the engine is running and try to open the throttle to watch the acceleration pump discharge. Engines usually hesitate and backfire through the carburetor if the acceleration pump is faulty. If the engine backfires, the flames could burn your face, eyes, and hair.

If you want to do an acceleration pump test by snapping open the throttle while the engine is running, make sure that the air cleaner is installed on the carburetor. The air cleaner will arrest a backfire through the carburetor. The air-fuel mixture is leaner when the air cleaner is removed, and the tendency to backfire is increased. Always wear safety glasses when working around gasoline. The stream of fuel from an acceleration pump could burn your eyes and cause blindness.

Procedure

To observe the fuel discharge from the acceleration pump nozzle, you should proceed as follows:

1. Shut off the engine.

2. Remove the air cleaner.

3. Look down the carburetor throat (use a flashlight if needed).

4. Open the throttle quickly with the throttle control linkage. Then close it and reopen it slowly.

5. Assess the acceleration pump stream(s). A single-barrel carburetor could have one or two nozzles spraying into the venturi. A two- or four-barrel carburetor will have a dual nozzle to spray into each venturi. On the first (quick) opening, there should be a solid stream of fuel that lasts a few seconds. There should be an equal discharge into each venturi on two- and four-barrel carburetors. See Figure 4-13. On the second (slow) opening, the stream should be weaker but steady to about half throttle, then it should stop.

If the stream of fuel from the acceleration pump is not adequate, the cause of the problem should be found, and the pump should be repaired or replaced.

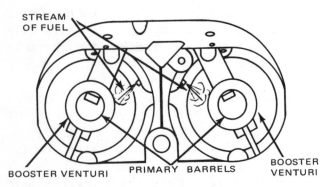

Figure 4-13. When an acceleration pump discharges, there should be a solid stream of fuel and an equal discharge pattern on two- or four-barrel carburetors. (Courtesy of Ford Motor Company, Dearborn)

FACTS TO REMEMBER

Faults in the acceleration pump will show up during pull-away or rapid acceleration. The acceleration pump discharge can be checked with the carburetor installed on the engine, but care is necessary during this process.

☐ ASSIGNMENT 4-F ☐

What symptoms are caused by:

1. The spring or weight missing from the discharge check ball.
2. A shrunken pump plunger cup.
3. Improper pump linkage rod adjustment.
4. Dirt in the pump jet (nozzle).

CHOKE SYSTEM PROBLEMS

The **choke system** provides a very rich air-fuel mixture to start a cold engine. It also regulates the richness of the air-fuel mixture according to engine temperature during the warm-up period. While the choke is in operation the fast idle speed is regulated by a step cam system to prevent stalling. Defects in the choke system are most apparent during starting and warm-up. Many common choke system problems are listed below. While studying this material, refer to Figures 4-14 and 4-15.

Broken, Distorted, or Misadjusted Thermostatic Spring

If the thermostatic spring is broken, the choke plate will not operate. This will cause hard starting when the engine is cold, poor cold-engine performance, and stalling until the engine warms up. When the engine is warm, it will run normally. When the thermostatic spring is distorted, it is impossible to set the choke tension correctly by using the index marks on the spring housing. The spring must be replaced.

A distorted spring can cause a rich or lean air-fuel mixture, depending upon which way it is distorted. If the spring tension is set too strong, the engine will smoke, flood easily while starting, and the choke plate may never fully open. If the spring tension is set too weak, the engine may be hard to start when cold and hesitate during warm up because the choke plate will open too quickly.

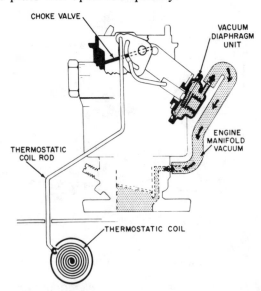

Figure 4-14. A typical choke system with a diaphragm and a separated choke thermostatic spring or coil. (Courtesy of General Motors of Canada Limited)

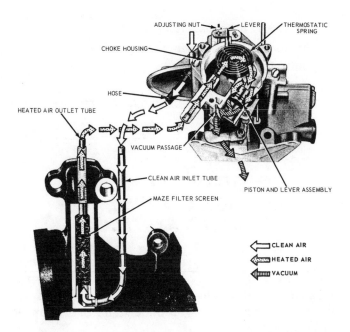

Figure 4-15.   A choke system with a piston and an integral thermostatic spring. (Courtesy of Ford Motor Company, Dearborn)

Choke Plate Seized

When the choke plate is seized and remains wide open, the symptoms are the same as a broken thermostatic spring. If the choke plate is seized partway open, the position of the choke plate will only be right for one specific engine temperature. The mixture will be too lean before this temperature is reached and too rich after the engine warms up. This could cause flooding and smoking. It is sure to cause poor gas mileage. A seized choke piston is often the cause of a stuck choke plate.

Defective Heat Pipe

If the choke heat pipe is defective, the engine will flood and smoke very badly moments after starting, and the choke will fail to fully open. The heat pipe may not deliver enough heat to the choke if the pipe is broken, rusted out, plugged, or has become disconnected from the manifold stove. If the engine is equipped with an internal heat pipe inside the exhaust crossover, the pipe may be burned through. If this is the case, the choke housing will be contaminated with carbon, water, and corrosion from the exhaust fumes drawn into the housing. The manifold heat control valve may also be seized. A seized manifold heat control valve can reduce choke heat from the exhaust crossover passage.

On carburetors with internal choke assemblies, a bad gasket or warped choke housing cover will let cold air reach the heat pipe or spring. This eliminates the vacuum to the heat pipe and also cools the spring so that the choke will never fully open.

Defective Choke Piston or Diaphragm

A defective choke diaphragm is usually obvious, because it fails to move the choke plate and the plate will not be kicked open after a cold start. The engine will flood and smoke for a few minutes, but may run properly from then on. If not corrected, this situation could load the engine with carbon and cause severe damage. Loss of vacuum to the piston or diaphragm causes the same symptoms as a defective diaphragm. The vacuum could be cut off by a plugged vacuum passage. Chokes with a loose housing, a missing gasket, or a poor seal behind the housing will allow air to leak into the vacuum passage. This will eliminate the vacuum. On heat pipe heated chokes, loss of vacuum results in loss of the heat necessary to heat the choke.

Some choke pistons and linkages are adjustable. They can be set to control the amount of choke pull-off when the engine is cold. Choke diaphragms are adjustable and can be set to open the choke a predetermined amount when the engine is cold. If the diaphragm is set too wide, the engine may start and stall several times and hesitate on pull-away once started. If the diaphragm is not set wide enough, the engine will smoke badly for the first few minutes. This could also cause the engine to flood and stop.

Fast Idle Cam Seized or Out of Adjustment

If there is an improper fast idle after a cold start, the fast idle cam may be seized or out of adjustment. A seized fast idle cam prevents a fast idle. If it is seized at the slow idle speed end of the cam, it also locks out the choke. If the cam is seized at a faster idle speed, the choke plate will close to that spot (halfway if seized at half open, or fully closed if the cam is seized at the fastest step). The fast idle speed will hold this fast idle, making the engine race at idle even when it warms up. The engine will probably diesel when it is shut off after the engine is warm. A choke linkage and fast idle cam is shown in Figure 4-16.

Faulty Electric Heater Element

The heating of many automatic chokes is electrically assisted. The electric heater element on such chokes can become faulty. If this happens on an electrically assisted choke that has the choke spring mounted on the engine, the choke spring will not warm up quickly. This will keep the choke plate closed longer than necessary. Because the choke spring is mounted directly on the engine, it will eventually warm up enough to open the choke plate, but the choke plate will have been closed longer than necessary.

Electrically heat-assisted chokes which have the thermostatic spring mounted on the carburetor receive heat from a heat pipe as well as the heater element. If the electric heater element on this type of choke is defective, the choke will eventually open from the heat of the heater pipe. However, the choke opening will be delayed. Fully electrically heated chokes with carburetor-mounted choke springs have no heat pipe assist. If the electric heater element on these types of chokes is faulty, the choke plate will never fully open and the engine will run rich when warm.

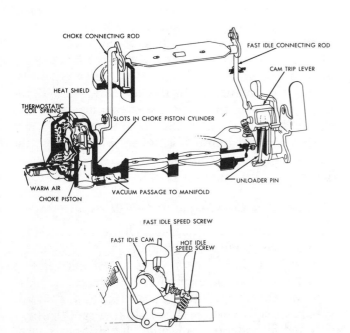

Figure 4-16. *A choke with a fast idle cam and linkage. If the fast idle cam is seized, it can prevent the choke from closing properly. (Courtesy of Ford Motor Company, Dearborn)*

☐ ASSIGNMENT 4-G ☐

Describe the symptoms caused by the following choke system faults:

1. Broken thermostatic spring.

2. Defective choke diaphragm.

3. A bad gasket or warped choke cover.

4. Defective heater element on a heat-pipe-assisted choke.

5. Defective heater element on a fully electrically heated choke.

QUICK SERVICE PROCEDURE: CHOKE SYSTEMS

Because most choke system parts are external, there are many quick service procedures that can be performed on automatic chokes. Refer to the illustrations provided to help you understand the following procedures.

Integral Choke

On these chokes, the choke spring is mounted on the carburetor.

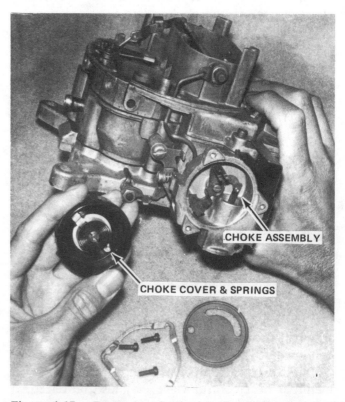

Figure 4-17. *Remove and examine the choke cover and thermostatic spring for signs of distortion or cracking.*

1. Remove the thermostatic spring cover and spring, and inspect them for signs of distortion or cracking, as shown in Figure 4-17. If the choke assembly shows signs of corrosion, carbon, rust, or piston seizure, you should suspect that the heat pipe is burned or rusted out. Inspection of the heat pipe is advisable on all choke servicing.

If the choke cover contains an electric heater, determine if the element is functional. When you are testing electrically assisted chokes, it may be necessary to warm the choke cover before an ohmmeter will indicate a closed circuit. On fully electric heated chokes, the heating element should indicate a closed circuit on the ohmmeter whether the choke is hot or cold.

Follow the specifications and procedures in the manufacturer's manual. Use a voltmeter to check the supply voltage to the heating element. The voltage may be supplied directly from the ignition switch. Some vehicles receive the voltage from the ignition switch and through the oil pressure switch. On these vehicles the engine must be running to make the test. On other vehicles, voltage is supplied from the alternator only while the alternator is being driven by the engine.

2. Repair the heat pipe if necessary. If the pipe appears to be in usable condition, blow the dust out of it with an air hose. **Caution:** cover the pipe opening with a shop cloth to avoid getting dirt in your face and eyes.

3. Inspect and, if necessary, free the manifold heat control valve. This valve affects the heat supply for the choke.

4. Inspect all linkages, cams, levers, and the choke valve shaft for free movement, as shown in Figure 4-18. When cleaning these parts, use a nonoily cleaner. Use a solvent specified for this purpose, or lacquer thinner. **Caution:** solvents and thinners tend to be toxic (poisonous), so avoid breathing fumes from them. Thinners are also very flammable. Never use solvents or thinners on or near a hot engine. Never smoke while using thinners.

5. Flush out the piston. Move the shaft rapidly (causing the piston to move in and out of its bore) while squirting solvent into the bore. See Figure 4-19.

6. Any fast idle cam that is corroded and does not drop down freely should be removed. Clean the cam pivot hole and attachment screw with crocus cloth (a very fine abrasive paper) to free up the cam movement.

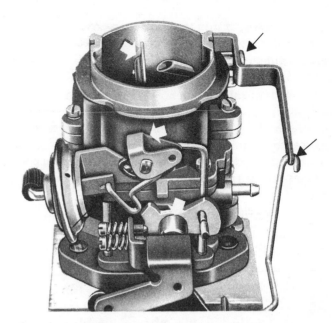

Figure 4-18. The cam, linkages, levers, and choke valve shaft (arrows) should be clean and free-moving. (Courtesy of Chrysler Corporation)

Figure 4-19. To flush out the piston, squirt a nonoily solvent into the piston bore and work the piston in and out.

7. Any piston that is carbon-covered or badly corroded must be removed and cleaned. Often replacement of the choke housing and piston is necessary. See Figure 4-20.

8. Install the choke thermostatic spring. Align the mark on the cover with the specified mark on the housing, as shown in Figure 4-21. Use a new gasket to assure a good seal. A rule of thumb for adjusting spring tension is that the choke plate should be gently, but fully, closed when the choke spring is at room temperature.

9. Adjust the choke rod, choke plate pulldown, and unloader according to manufacturer specifications. Each manufacturer has his own adjustment names and procedures.

10. Run the engine and observe the choke in operation.

11. Adjust the idle mixture, the idle speed, and the fast idle speed after the engine warms up. Fast idle speeds are somewhat slower when the engine is cold because they are affected by engine temperature. You must adjust fast idle and slow idle speeds when the engine is warm.

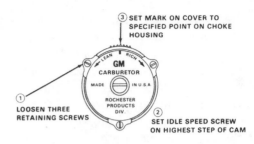

Figure 4-21.   Automatic choke spring adjustment: Set the mark on the cover to the proper mark on the housing. (Courtesy of General Motors of Canada Limited)

Vacuum Diaphragm Choke

On vacuum diaphragm chokes, the choke spring is mounted on the engine.

1. To test the choke diaphragm, connect a hand-operated vacuum pump to the diaphragm, as shown in Figure 4-22. Pump the vacuum pump to create a vacuum in the diaphragm unit. The diaphragm should pull in until it is seated. See if the pump holds the reading. If the reading drops, the diaphragm unit has a leak in it and should be replaced. If no vacuum pump is available, put a length of hose on the unit. Draw air through the hose until the diaphragm is seated. Then put your finger over the open end of the hose. The diaphragm will stay seated if no air is leaking into the unit. If the diaphragm moves out again you will feel the loss of vacuum on your finger. This means that it is leaking and should be re-

Figure 4-20.   It is often necessary to remove the choke piston for cleaning or replacement.

Figure 4-22.   Connect a hand-vacuum pump to test the choke diaphragm. (Courtesy of Chrysler Corporation)

placed. If the diaphragm unit is old, it is advisable to replace it.

2. The choke coil or thermostatic spring is separate from the carburetor on vacuum diaphragm chokes. Remove the spring from the engine, inspect it, and check its adjustment (if it is adjustable). Typical choke coil rod adjustments are shown in Figure 4-23. If the spring has an electric heating element, test the element continuity with an ohmmeter. Check the electrical supply, using recommended procedures from the manufacturer's shop manual.

3. The remaining procedures are the same as those used when servicing an integral-type choke. Follow steps 4, 6, 8, 9, 10, and 11 of the integral choke service procedure.

□   ASSIGNMENT 4-H   □

Describe the following choke service procedures:

1. Vacuum testing a choke diaphragm.
2. Freeing up a sticking choke piston.
3. Freeing up a sticking fast idle cam.

QUICK SERVICE PROCEDURE: MINOR CARBURETOR REPAIRS

Common carburetor repairs that require partial carburetor disassembly are often undertaken. Below is a list of quick service procedures that can be done without a major carburetor disassembly and overhaul.

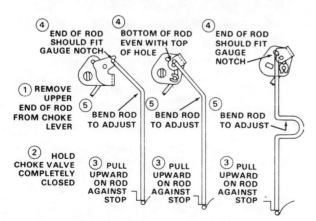

Figure 4-23. Typical choke coil rod adjustments. (Courtesy of General Motors of Canada Limited)

Disassembly

1. Clean around the carburetor cover to avoid getting dirt inside the carburetor during service.

2. Remove the necessary linkages and screws, and take off the carburetor cover.

3. Examine the fuel bowl contents for signs of dirt or other particles.

Float System

1. Measure the float level and float-drop setting before disassembling the float system. This will serve as a reference for diagnostic purposes.

2. Determine the condition of the float. Make sure it is not loaded with gasoline, misaligned, or damaged.

3. Inspect the needle, seat, and fuel passage for dirt, lint, or other particles. Examine the needle and seat. Replace them if they are in poor condition.

Idle System

1. Disconnect the necessary parts, and remove the idle pickup tube(s). See Figure 4-24.

2. Examine the idle pickup tube(s) and idle restriction(s) for dirt or lint. This is done by looking through them at a light.

Figure 4-24. This view of a carburetor shows the location of the idle pickup tubes and related idle passages.

Main and Power System

1. Remove the main jet(s) for inspection. Examine them for wear or dirt, and check to make sure they are the right ones for the carburetor.

2. On power-valve-type carburetors, examine the power valve by pressing on it with your finger to make sure it is not sticking. Then remove it and look for dirt or lint. Press the valve open to examine the wear on the spindle and determine if the valve needs to be replaced.

3. Examine the power or metering rod piston to see if it is stuck. Do this by gently pressing and pulling the piston with your fingers.

4. Remove the power piston and spring for inspection, even if it is not seized. A special tool is often needed to remove the piston retainer. However, sometimes you can depress the piston and snap it against the retainer to knock the retainer out.

5. On metering-rod-type carburetors, remove the metering rod(s) for inspection. Examine them for wear, and check to make sure that they are the correct size.

Pump System

1. Inspect the pump nozzle for dirt or clogging.

2. Inspect the check balls (or needle).

3. Inspect the pump plunger.

4. Inspect the pump system springs.

5. Use the procedure outlined in Chapter 5 to test the check valves for leakage. This procedure also covers how to repair check valves if they are leaking.

Cleaning

1. Clean all the removed parts in carburetor cleaner and dry them.

2. Soak up the fuel from the carburetor float bowl with a clean, lintless cloth. **Caution:** Dispose of gasoline-soaked cloths only in a sealed metal safety container.

3. Blow out the fuel bowl and fuel passages with compressed air. **Caution:** Cover the carburetor with a rag when cleaning it with air, and wear goggles or a face shield.

Reassembly

1. Reassemble all the internal parts.

2. Check the float adjustment.

3. Reinstall the carburetor, using a new gasket on the flange.

4. Install a new gas filter if one is needed.

Adjusting and Testing

Run the engine and make the necessary adjustments to obtain the correct idle speed and idle mixture. Use either the standard adjustment, lean-drop method, infrared analyzer, or propane-assisted method, as recommended by the manufacturer.

☐ SELF-TEST ☐

Complete the following sentences by filling in the missing words.

1. Never run an engine in a closed shop without a _____ pipe on the exhaust.

2. Store oily rags in a closed _____ safety container. They can ignite by _____ _____ if left in a pile, open to the air.

3. Proper carburetor performance depends on such things as _____, engine _____, and correct _____ .

4. A flooding carburetor is generally indicated when gasoline spills out of the _____ -_____ nozzle, vents, or throttle _____ .

5. The fuel level in the fuel bowl generally _____ when any float system parts are defective.

6. An air leak into the _____ manifold can be caused by a _____ line or hose, or a defective power brake booster. Intake manifold air leaks have the same symptoms as a _____ idle system.

7. Presetting the carburetor idle will serve as a rough test to determine whether the _____ mixture is improperly adjusted, or the idle circuit is _____ .

8. An engine that has a _____ mixture and idles faster than it should will probably _____ after the ignition is turned off. Too _____ an idle setting can foul the _____ _____ .

9. When no manifold vacuum reaches the power piston, the _____ fails to move, holds the _____ valve open, and constantly produces a _____ mixture.

10. A faulty power system prevents the _____ mixture from being delivered and causes the engine to _____ _____ under load.

11. Too short a pump stroke (or travel) on an acceleration pump can cause _____. Too long a pump stroke _____ fuel and could cause a momentary _____ in power.

12. The choke system provides a very _____ air-fuel mixture for starting a _____ engine. It also regulates the _____ of the air-fuel mixture according to engine temperature during the warm-up period.

13. If the choke heat pipe is defective, the engine will _____ and _____ very badly after starting, and the choke will fail to fully _____ .

5

CARBURETOR OVERHAUL PROCEDURES

☐   LEARNING OBJECTIVES   ☐

After studying this chapter, you will be able to:

1. Explain how to identify a carburetor and order the parts needed for a carburetor overhaul.

2. Describe the steps for:
    removing a carburetor from the engine
    disassembling a carburetor and inspecting the parts
    cleaning a carburetor
    reassembling a carburetor
    making the necessary carburetor adjustments
    installing a carburetor

3. Explain how to adjust the:
    float level   choke rod
    float drop   choke-break
    acceleration pump   unloader
    idle vent valve   choke spring
    fast idle cam

4. Define and/or discuss the following terms:
    overhaul kit   vacuum hose diagram
    carburetor overhaul   carburetor cleaner

INTRODUCTION

This chapter covers the proper method of overhauling a carburetor. If a carburetor fails to adjust to specifications when you test it with an infrared analyzer, consumes more fuel than necessary, floods constantly, gives poor performance (stalling, excess fuel consumption, poor idle, hesitation, etc.), or is dirty from years of use without service, a carburetor overhaul may be called for. Do not, however, rule out the possibility of installing a rebuilt carburetor rather than performing an overhaul. Rebuilt carburetors are useful in situations where the vehicle cannot be off the road for a long period, the old carburetor has high mileage on it, or it needs expensive major parts beyond those supplied in the overhaul kit.

HOW TO IDENTIFY A CARBURETOR AND ORDER THE PARTS

You must properly identify the carburetor you are

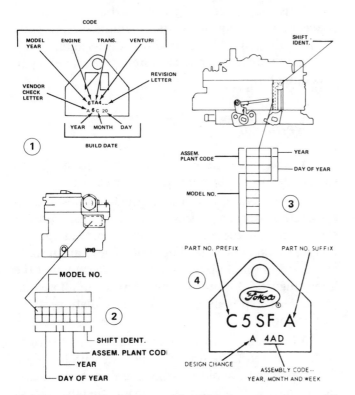

Figure 5-1. Carburetor identification numbers: (1) American Motors, tag; (2) General Motors, stamped number; (3) Holly, stamped number; (4) Ford Motor Co., tag.

working on in order to buy the correct repair parts and overhaul kit. The manufacturer's name is stamped on the carburetor. The part number or model number is stamped on a metal tag fastened to the carburetor, or into the metal on one of the carburetor castings, as shown in Figure 5-1. If the tag is missing, or the number is not legible, refer to the carburetor reference manual for the carburetor number.

When buying carburetor parts, supply the carburetor name and number and the number of barrels the carburetor has. Also supply the vehicle make, model, and year, the number of cylinders, and the engine size or displacement. This information can be found in the owner's manual, on a decal under the hood, on the engine rocker cover, or on the air-cleaner housing. It is always contained in the manufacturer's shop manual. If the vehicle is equipped with power steering, power brakes, or air conditioning, this information should also be supplied when ordering carburetor parts.

To summarize, when you are ordering parts, the parts department must be supplied with the:

1. vehicle make, model, and year;
2. number of cylinders and displacement of the engine and engine equipment (such as air conditioning, power brakes, etc.);
3. carburetor make and the number of barrels;
4. carburetor number; and
5. the proper names and description of any parts needed that are not contained in the overhaul kit.

Careful consideration is required if, when checking the carburetor number, you find it is not the correct carburetor for the vehicle it is mounted on. Cross-reference the carburetor number using a carburetor catalog to find the type of vehicle and engine for which it is designed. If the engine for which the carburetor is designed is the same make and size but a different year than the one on which it is installed, the carburetor should perform reasonably well. However, if the carburetor is designed for a much larger or much smaller engine, it will not perform correctly. Carburetors are designed and calibrated for the engine on which they are to be used. If the carburetor is not designed for the engine you are working on, replace it.

Standard Overhaul Kits

Standard overhaul kits can be ordered for most carburetors. The usual parts found in such a kit are:

1. all necessary gaskets;

2. a pump plunger or cup (for carburetors that contain a plunger pump system);

3. a diaphragm for the pump (for carburetors that have a diaphragm pump system);

4. needle and seat valve(s) (some four-barrel types will have two sets);

5. pump check valves;

6. power valve(s) on Ford and Holley carburetors (some four-barrel types will have two sets);

7. linkage clips and fasteners; and

8. information sheets.

Some kits are universal and may contain parts that are not needed for the carburetor you are overhauling. A typical tune-up and carburetor overhaul kit is shown in Figure 5-2. Any parts needed that are not contained in the overhaul kit must be ordered with a good description and/or the proper name. Look in the manufacturer's shop manual for this information.

Figure 5-2.   The parts included in a typical tune-up and carburetor overhaul kit. (Holly Carburetor Division, Colt Industries)

FACTS TO REMEMBER

Before attempting a carburetor overhaul, you must decide whether you should buy a rebuilt carburetor or overhaul the one you have. There are several different types of information you must have in order to buy a carburetor overhaul kit. The kit must match the carburetor you are working on.

□   **ASSIGNMENT 5-A**   □

1. Explain how to identify a carburetor.

2. List the information that must be supplied when ordering carburetor parts.

3. List the possible locations of carburetor numbers and information.

CARBURETOR DISASSEMBLY AND CLEANING

The information sheets in a carburetor overhaul kit generally contain only limited instructions. They may show an exploded view of the carburetor parts. They seldom include the step-by-step information needed to disassemble, overhaul, or reassemble a carburetor. The manufacturer's shop manual usually is more detailed. Most kits and manuals have information about required carburetor adjustments. A few kits have no information sheets, and you must rely completely on the shop manual.

This chapter covers general carburetor overhaul procedures. Along with the manufacturer's shop manual, they should enable you to disassemble, overhaul, and reassemble any carburetor you are likely to encounter.

Removal

1. Remove the hoses and pipes connected to the air cleaner. Then remove the air cleaner.

2. Study the layout of all the lines, hoses, linkages, clips, springs, wires, and solenoids. Draw a sketch showing these details. You can also use manufacturer's **vacuum hose diagrams**. These are usually contained in the shop manual or on a decal under the hood. Figure 5-3 is an example of a vacuum hose diagram. This step is necessary for reinstallation of the carburetor.

3. Clean any dirt from around the fuel fittings at the carburetor. Remove the fuel line with two flare nut wrenches to avoid twisting the line or damaging the fittings. With a cloth, wipe up any fuel that sprays out of the hoses. Dispose of the shop cloth in a metal safety container.

4. Check the tightness of the hoses, lines, and

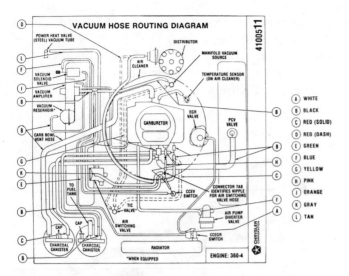

Figure 5-3. When removing and replacing a carburetor, make a sketch of the details or use the vacuum hose diagram for that model carburetor. This vacuum diagram is for a Chrysler engine. (Courtesy of Chrysler Corporation)

fittings. Look for air leaks that would affect carburetor performance.

5. Check the condition of all hoses, lines, springs, heat tubes, automatic choke units, air filter elements, the Positive Crankcase Ventilation (P.C.V.) hoses, valve, and filter. If any of these parts are defective, they should be ordered when you order the overhaul kit.

6. Remove the carburetor from the engine.

Disassembly and Inspection

After removal, keep the carburetor upright to avoid spilling out the gasoline. A stand to hold the carburetor upright is helpful at this point. Study the layout of the carburetor parts to aid you during reassembly. Drawing a sketch of the parts layout is helpful. Include part numbers on the sketch if they are available. Inspect each part as you remove it.

Bowl: After removing the carburetor cover, inspect the bowl for dirt, water, or corrosion. Water in a zinc carburetor bowl causes zinc oxide corrosion. This can etch the pump cylinder and check ball seats, and block fuel passages, air bleeds, vent tubes, and jets. Carburetor cleaner does not remove corrosion very well. If the carburetor has a great deal of corrosion damage, replace it with a new or rebuilt carburetor.

Gaskets: Inspect the gaskets for proper impressions. Lack of impression in an area on a gasket indicates warpage, poor seating, and a possible leak point for gasoline, air, or vacuum.

Any bits of gasket should be scraped off parts or fittings to prevent misalignment during reassembly. Be very careful not to gouge or score the parts when you are scraping off old gaskets.

Inspect all mating surfaces for nicks, burrs, corrosion, and warpage. Use a straightedge (metal ruler) to see if they are within a few thousandths of an inch of being perfectly flat. See Figure 5-4. Any flat flange or casting that is only slightly warped can be resurfaced and leveled. Work the part back and forth across a sheet of fine emery cloth that has been fixed to a flat surface. Use a straightedge frequently to check for flatness. A casting with a badly warped surface must be replaced.

Throttle Shaft: Inspect the throttle shaft arm for looseness. Check the throttle shaft for wear or binding on the throttle plate. See Figure 5-5. If there

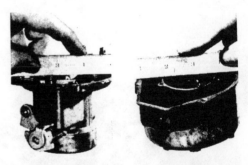

Figure 5-4. Check all mating surfaces with a straightedge to see if they are flat. (Courtesy of General Motors of Canada Limited)

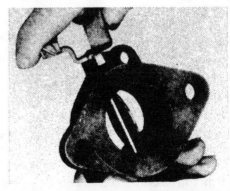

Figure 5-5. Inspect the throttle shaft arm for looseness and wear. (Courtesy of General Motors of Canada Limited)

is a fault in the throttle body, the complete throttle unit should be replaced. When adjustment procedures call for backing out the idle speed adjusting screw to completely close the throttle, count the turns needed to unthread the screw so it can be reinstalled in the same exact position.

Do not remove the throttle shaft and valve. Correct alignment between the throttle valve and the fuel and vacuum ports is difficult to achieve if the throttle valve is removed. There is no reason to remove the throttle valve unless it is damaged. Do not remove the choke shaft and plate unless the choke piston is seized or very dirty. If it is necessary to remove a choke shaft, file the ends of the screws where they are staked over, to prevent breaking them off in the holes.

Do not remove cams and links unless it is necessary, especially on four-barrel carburetors. This will save time and confusion when you are reassembling the carburetor.

Power Piston: Check the power piston for seizure, wear, and fit. It must be free, but should not have excess play. Also inspect the tapered seat on the upper end of the piston. See Figure 5-6.

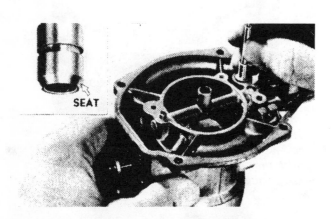

Figure 5-6.   The power piston must be free in the cover, but without excess play. Check the condition of the seat. (Courtesy of General Motors of Canada Limited)

Needles: Inspect the idle mixture adjusting needle(s). They should not be bent or ridged. A ridged needle will provide irregular air-fuel mixtures and cause rough idling. See Figure 5-7. When you remove idle mixture screws for cleaning or inspection, turn them in and count the turns until they are seated. Then remove them. On reassembly, you can return them to the same position.

Inspect the float needle and seat for indications of wear or improper seating. This could be a cause of flooding and indicate the need for overhaul. A carburetor kit has a replacement needle and seat assembly. See Figure 5-8.

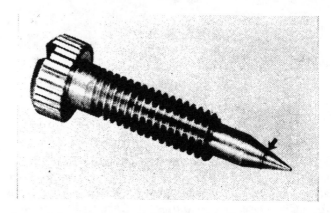

Figure 5-7.   Check the idle mixture adjusting needle for ridges. Replace a ridged needle. (Courtesy of General Motors of Canada Limited)

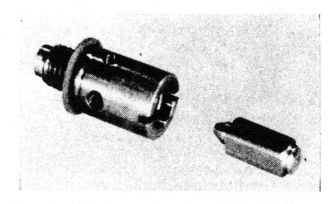

Figure 5-8.   Inspect the float needle and seat for wear. If they are worn or damaged, they should be replaced. (Courtesy of General Motors of Canada Limited)

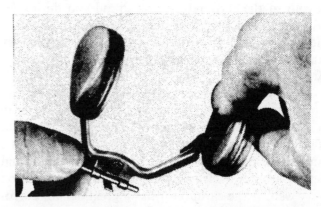

Figure 5-9.   Inspect the float assembly for signs of leaks. (Courtesy of General Motors of Canada Limited)

Float: Inspect the float assembly for signs of leaks in the float or gasoline saturation. See Figure 5-9. Also, check for wear on the float pivot and pivot pinhole in the carburetor casting.

Pump Plunger: Inspect the pump plunger for wear or a damaged spring. See Figure 5-10. A badly fitting plunger could be the cause of a flat spot during acceleration and justify a carburetor overhaul. A new plunger or cup is included in the repair kit.

Choke: Check the choke piston (if so equipped) for excess wear or seizure. The fast idle cam and other links and levers should also be checked.

If the carburetor is equipped with choke diaphragm(s), inspect their condition and leak test them with a vacuum. See Figure 5-11. A hand-operated vacuum pump connected to the choke diaphragm can be used to produce sufficient vacuum. The diaphragm should respond, and the vacuum should not drop after it has been formed. If the vacuum does drop, replace the unit. A vacuum drop indicates that there is a hole in the choke diaphragm.

Other Parts: Inspect the condition of all jets, metering rods, check valves, power valves, and springs.

Carburetor Cleaning

The manufacturer's carburetor servicing procedures usually make little or no reference to the cleaning process. The following steps may be used as a guide when cleaning parts. **Caution:** Always wear goggles and work in a well-ventilated area when using cleaners and solvents.

1. If carburetor parts are very dirty, wash them in a commercial solvent before washing them in carburetor cleaner. This will save costly carburetor cleaner and cleaning time.

2. Soak the parts for at least 30 minutes in carburetor cleaner. Place small parts in a fine mesh tray so they do not get lost in the cleaning tank, and use an agitator to speed up the process.

3. Do not put rubber, plastic, or Bakelite parts in the carburetor cleaner. Do not put electric choke heaters in *any* liquid. Do not immerse solenoids, dashpots, or choke diaphragms. Clean them with a shop cloth moistened with solvent. Floats should not be put in the cleaning tank because they will be

damaged if they bump against other parts, the tank walls, or the agitator. Wash floats by hand.

4. When the parts are clean, remove them from the carburetor cleaner and rinse them in hot water.

5. Blow out all passages, air bleeds, and jets with compressed air. Then dry all the parts. If they are not clean and free from carbon deposits, return them to the cleaner bath for further cleaning.

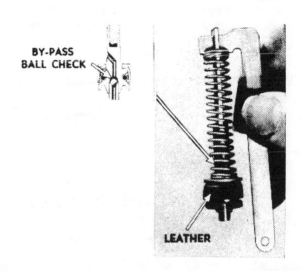

Figure 5-10. Inspect the pump plunger and spring for damage or wear. (Courtesy of General Motors of Canada Limited)

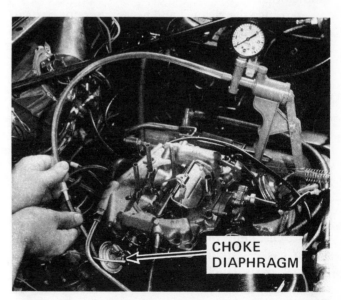

Figure 5-11. Test a choke diaphragm with a hand-operated vacuum pump. This test can be done with the choke diaphragm on the car or on the bench. (Courtesy of Chrysler Corporation)

When you are disassembling a carburetor, the parts must be carefully examined for wear. All parts must be carefully and completely cleaned before they are reinstalled. Worn parts should be replaced.

☐ ASSIGNMENT 5-B ☐

1. List at least ten parts that must be removed and inspected when you are disassembling a carburetor.

2. List the steps and precautions to be taken when removing a carburetor.

3. What carburetor settings should be recorded during disassembly?

4. Describe the method for cleaning carburetor parts in carburetor cleaner.

CARBURETOR REASSEMBLY AND INTERNAL ADJUSTMENTS

Cleanliness is essential during carburetor reassembly. Choose a work area that is spotlessly clean. If you are working on a shop bench, cover the bench with clean shop cloths.

Arrange the cleaned and new carburetor parts in order of their relationship to each other. Place screws in order of type, size, and length, and place the gaskets beside the parts they are used on. Follow the exploded views and instructions supplied with the overhaul kit and in the shop manual. If you made a sketch of the parts layout when disassembling the carburetor, use it to aid you in reassembly.

Be sure to install the proper gaskets on jets where needed. Remove any old gaskets which are stuck to jet seats. Some jets do not use gaskets. Compare each gasket you install with the original gasket that you removed during disassembly. Be certain that you are installing the correct gaskets. Often, several similar gaskets are included in an overhaul kit.

All parts (such as jets, needle valves, power valves, etc.) and screws must be tightened firmly to compress the gaskets and prevent the parts from working loose when exposed to engine vibration.

When installing a pump plunger, be certain that it fits tightly in the pump cylinder. If the plunger ap-

pears to be loose, turn the leather cup inside out for a moment to expand the cup. Then turn it back the way it should be, and try fitting it into the pump cylinder again.

Acceleration Pump Test

Assemble the acceleration pump. Pour approximately 1/2 inch (12 mm) of fuel into the open fuel bowl. Press the discharge ball or needle with a suitable rod, and work the plunger by hand. No fuel should leak past the check balls and none should back up into the fuel bowl. See Figure 5-12. If leakage occurs, gently tap a rod down on the leaking check ball or needle to compress the seat and form a better seal. Install a new ball if the ball is dented, and test the system again for leaks.

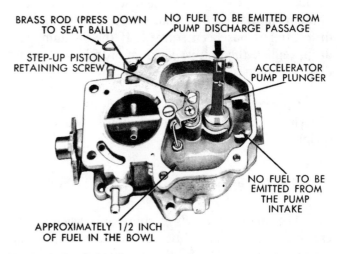

Figure 5-12. *Testing the acceleration pump check balls for leakage. (Courtesy of Chrysler Corporation)*

Float System Adjustments

Check the float-level and float-drop adjustment, and adjust them, if necessary, before installing the float bowl cover.

Float-Level Adjustment: The carburetor **float-level adjustment** controls the fuel level in the carburetor bowl. Each carburetor is engineered around a specific fuel level in the carburetor bowl. Changes in the fuel level in the bowl can affect carburetor operation.

To adjust float level, turn the bowl upside down, allowing the float arm to rest on the needle valve. By bending a tab on the float arm, or by bending the float arm itself, the level of fuel maintained in the carburetor bowl can be adjusted. Manufacturer specifications will give proper float level and indicate where to measure it. Figure 5-13 shows this method of float-level adjustment.

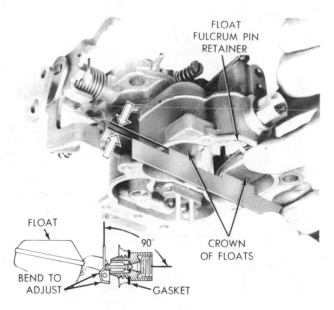

Figure 5-13. Float-level adjustment. (Courtesy of Chrysler Corporation)

Float-Drop Adjustment: **Float drop** determines how far the needle valve will open. The opening is set to give proper clearance between the needle point and the seat for a steady gas flow. If float drop is set correctly, there is no danger of the needle binding or falling out of the seat. Some carburetors do not have a float-drop adjustment.

Float drop is set by bending a tang at the float pivot to position the amount the float hangs down from the carburetor bowl cover. Manufacturer specifications will give the required float-drop measurement and indicate where to measure it. Figure 5-14 shows this method of float-drop adjustment.

External Parts Assembly

Be sure to tighten the screws in the bowl cover and other flanges a little at a time in a staggered pattern until they are tight. This prevents distortion of the parts. A typical tightening sequence is shown in Figure 5-15.

Install all external parts and linkages, and operate them by hand to insure that they are correctly installed, free moving, and operating correctly. Make

all the necessary carburetor adjustments as outlined in the following section under external carburetor adjustments.

□ ASSIGNMENT 5-C □

1. List the steps to follow during carburetor reassembly.
2. Describe the procedures for adjusting the float level.
3. Describe the procedures for adjusting the float drop.
4. Explain why a specific tightening sequence is used when installing a carburetor bowl cover.

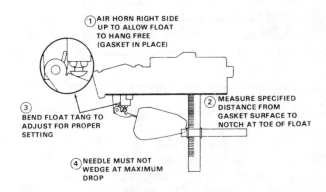

Figure 5-14. Float-drop adjustment. (Courtesy of General Motors of Canada Limited)

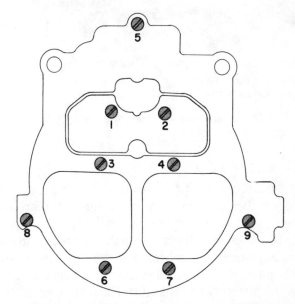

Figure 5-15. The proper bowl cover tightening sequence should be followed during carburetor assembly. (Courtesy of General Motors of Canada Limited)

EXTERNAL CARBURETOR ADJUSTMENTS

The idle air-fuel mixture and idle speed must always be adjusted on an overhauled carburetor. Certain mechanical adjustments must also be performed both during and after carburetor reassembly. Some of these adjustments are done even if the carburetor has not been overhauled, but they *all* must be done after an overhaul. Each adjustment plays a specific role in proper carburetor operation. Some adjustments can affect others. Therefore, they must be done in a specific order.

The following adjustments are of a general nature and can be applied to any carburetor. Always use the manufacturer's specified settings for the model and year carburetor you are working on. The following is an explanation of what each adjustment does and how it should be performed.

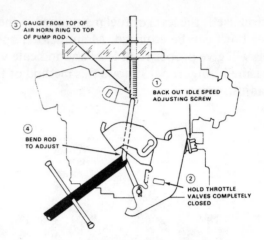

Figure 5-17. *A plunger-type pump is adjusted by bending the rod. (Courtesy of General Motors of Canada Limited)*

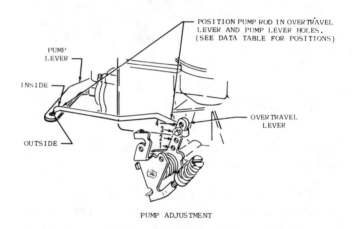

Figure 5-18. *A diaphragm-type pump is adjusted by selecting holes. (Courtesy of Ford Motor Company, Dearborn)*

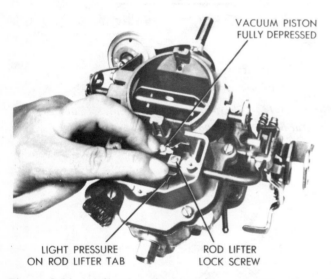

Figure 5-16. *Adjusting the metering rods. (Courtesy of Chrysler Corporation)*

Metering Rod Adjustment: Metering rods that are controlled only by vacuum on the piston are not adjustable. If they are mechanically operated, they have to be set in relationship to the throttle position. This adjustment synchronizes the light-load and power air-fuel mixtures. Typically, the arm that controls the metering rod is adjustable. The throttle stop screw should be backed out to close the throttle. The metering rod clearance is then adjusted to specifications, as shown in Figure 5-16.

Acceleration Pump Adjustment: The distance the acceleration pump plunger (or diaphragm) travels up or back controls how much fuel is taken into the acceleration pump to supply the discharge when the throttle opens. To get the correct amount of discharge, the pump plunger must have the correct setting. Generally the adjustment is made by bending the linkage or arm that works the plunger. Some plungers are adjusted by selecting the proper combination from a series of holes in the pump arm and/or lever. The correct holes must be used.

Manufacturer specifications give the correct measurement for pump plunger travel, tell where to measure it, and describe the adjustment. On pumps that are adjusted with hole combinations, the correct holes to use will be indicated by the manufacturer. Pump-travel adjustment methods are shown in Figures 5-17 and 5-18.

Idle Vent Valve Adjustment: Newer carburetors do not have external vents of any kind. However, the vent valve, where used on older model carburetors, should open a predetermined amount when the throttle is in the idle position or shut off. This vent lets vapors escape when the engine is hot. Manufacturer specifications give the amount of opening needed and describe how to set it. Some vents are adjusted by turning the valve with a screwdriver, as shown in Figure 5-19. Others are adjusted by bending a tang, as shown in Figure 5-20.

Fast Idle Cam or Choke Rod Adjustment:

This adjustment sets the fast idle cam for the correct relationship with the choke valve. If this adjustment is not made, the fast idle speed will not taper off cor-rectly. This will cause periods of racing or stalling, depending on the direction the idle cam is out of adjustment. When you are checking this setting, the fast idle screw should usually rest on the second step of the fast idle cam, against the shoulder of the high step. Manufacturer specifications will indicate the proper step for the cam. The choke valve should be lightly pressed closed, and the clearance left at the edge of the choke plate should be as stated in the specifications.

Manufacturer specifications will show whether you should take this measurement at the top or bottom edge of the choke plate. Use a carburetor gauge or a drill to take this measurement. Bend the cam operating rod or the lever on the choke shaft as stated in the manufacturer specifications. This adjustment is shown in Figure 5-21.

Choke-Break or Vacuum-Kick Adjustment:

To prevent overchoking at slow engine speeds and idle when a cold engine is started, a vacuum diaphragm opens the choke slightly. This is called **choke break**. If the choke is not allowed to open enough, it over-chokes, causing smoking and flooding for a few minutes.

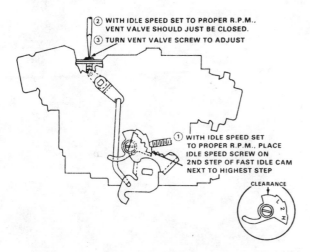

Figure 5-19. Vent adjustment by turning the valve with a screwdriver. (Courtesy of General Motors of Canada Limited)

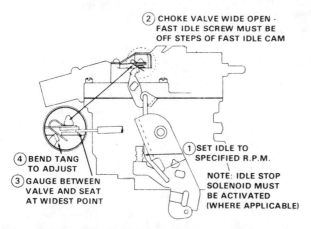

Figure 5-20. Vent adjustment by bending the tang. (Courtesy of General Motors of Canada Limited)

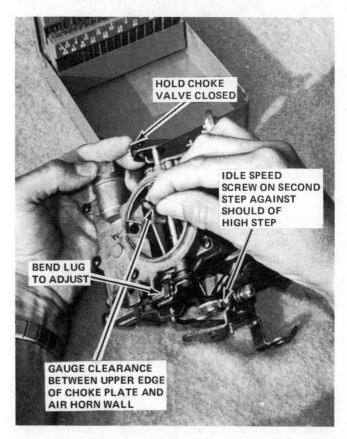

Figure 5-21. Checking the fast idle cam adjustment.

To adjust for proper choke break, apply vacuum from a vacuum pump to the diaphragm to pull the diaphragm in. Then open the throttle slightly, and gently press the choke closed. Measure the distance the choke plate is open with a carburetor gauge or a drill of the specified size. Adjustment is usually made by bending the rod between the diaphragm and the choke-shaft quadrant, as shown in Figure 5-22.

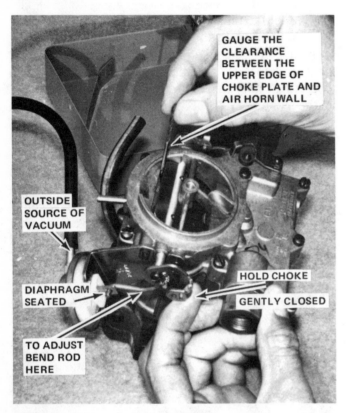

Figure 5-22.   Adjusting the choke-break diaphragm.

Unloader Adjustment: This adjustment sets the distance the choke plate is mechanically pulled open when the throttle is wide open and the engine is cold. If the choke plate does not open far enough, it is difficult to dry out a cold, flooded engine. If it opens too wide, the mixture will be too lean under heavy-load, wide-throttle openings. This will result in poor, cold engine performance. Figure 5-23 shows how this adjustment is done. To make this adjustment, the choke valve must be closed and the throttle valve must be in the wide-open position. Check the choke valve opening with a carburetor gauge or a drill of the specified diameter. Bending the unloader lug on the throttle arm is the usual method of changing the amount of choke-plate opening.

Choke Spring Adjustment: This adjustment sets the choke thermostatic spring tension. If the tension is too strong, the engine will flood, stall, and be difficult to start when cold. If the tension is too weak, the engine may be hard to start, because the air-fuel mixture is too lean and could hesitate, backfire, and stall during warm-up.

On integral-type chokes, as shown in Figure 5-24, the tension adjustment is made by setting a mark on the choke thermostatic spring cover to a specified mark on the choke housing. On chokes that

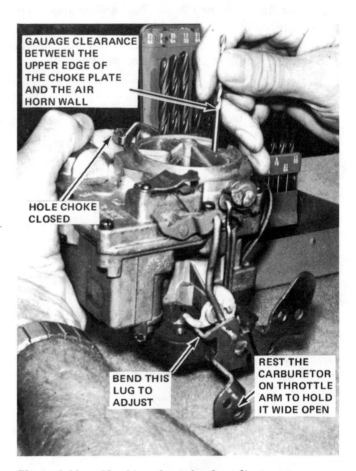

Figure 5-23.   Checking the unloader adjustment.

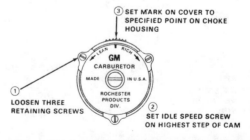

Figure 5-24.   Choke coil adjustment for an integral-type choke. (Courtesy of General Motors of Canada Limited)

have the spring mounted on the manifold, the adjustment is made with the choke installed on the car. This is done by bending the rod between the choke spring and the choke valve shaft, as shown in Figure 5-25, or by bending the lever on the choke shaft, as shown in Figure 5-26. Some springs have an adjustment nut and index inside the choke assembly. If the choke assembly has an electric-assist heating element, the element must be checked, using the tests outlined in the manufacturer's service manual. Further information about testing electric chokes is given in Chapter 14 of this text.

FACTS TO REMEMBER

There are several internal and external adjustments that must be made on a carburetor as it is being re-assembled. These adjustments must be made carefully and in the correct order if the carburetor is going to work properly. Always consult the manufacturer's specification manual for the exact adjustments that need to be made and the procedures to use when making them. No two carburetors are exactly alike. There is no room for guesswork when making carburetor adjustments.

☐ ASSIGNMENT 5-D ☐

What is controlled by the:
    acceleration pump adjustment
    fast idle cam adjustment
    choke-break adjustment
    unloader adjustment
    choke spring adjustment

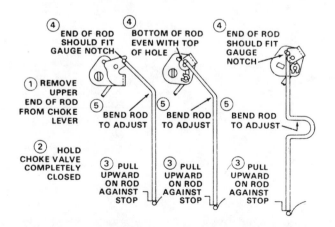

Figure 5-25. *Choke coil rod adjustment by bending the rod. (Courtesy of General Motors of Canada Limited)*

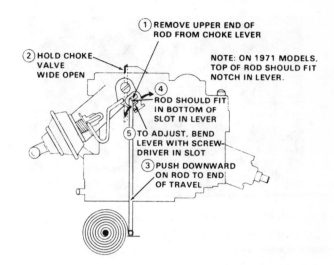

Figure 5-26. *Choke rod adjustment by bending the lever. (Courtesy of General Motors of Canada Limited)*

CARBURETOR INSTALLATION

After the carburetor is overhauled, it must be installed. Certain checks and adjustments should be made during installation, as indicated below.

1. Scrape the old gasket off the manifold flange if necessary. Any gasket left on the flange could cause an air leak that would affect carburetor operation.

2. Attach metal fuel lines before you bolt the carburetor in place. This will help you avoid cross-threading and binding the line fittings. Start the fittings with your fingers. Use flare nut wrenches to turn them only when you are certain the threads are not crossed. Use two flare nut wrenches to avoid twisting a line.

3. Tighten the carburetor flange a little at a time in a staggered pattern to avoid warping or breaking the flange.

4. Install all hoses, linkages, springs, clips, the automatic choke unit, wires, and other parts to complete the installation. Use your sketch and vacuum diagram to aid you during this step.

5. Check the throttle linkage for sticking, binding, and proper adjustment. With the engine shut off, check to see if the throttle opens fully. Have another person push the accelerator pedal to the floor while you look down into the carburetor bore to make this check. See Figure 5-27.

Figure 5-27.   Check throttle linkage for sticking, binding, and proper adjustment. (Courtesy of Ford Motor Company, Dearborn)

Figure 5-28.   Observe the choke in operation during the warm-up period. (Courtesy of Ford Motor Company, Dearborn)

6. The choke should be closed and working freely. Check this before starting the engine.

7. Run the engine, and observe the choke operation during the warm-up period. See Figure 5-28.

8. Shut off the engine, and install the air cleaner and related parts, hoses, and ducts.

9. Correct the dwell and initial timing if necessary. If they are out of adjustment, the carburetor will not perform well.

10. Set the slow idle speed and adjust the idle mixture screw(s) to obtain the smoothest idle. At this point it will be necessary to follow the manufacturer's recommended adjustment procedures, as there are several possible adjustment methods. Some require propane enrichment. Others require the use of an infrared exhaust analyzer.

11. Set the fast idle speed to specifications if it is adjustable.

12. Road test the vehicle. Check engine response under idle, low speed, high speed, and load conditions. Start and stop the engine several times to check carburetor operation during starting and to check for dieseling.

□   ASSIGNMENT 5-E   □

List the checks and adjustments that should be done after an overhauled carburetor has been installed on the engine.

□ SELF-TEST □

Complete the following sentences by filling in the missing words.

1. When buying carburetor parts, supply the name and _____ and the number of barrels the carburetor has. Also supply the vehicle _____ , _____ , and _____ , the number of cylinders, and the _____ or displacement of the engine.

2. After removing the carburetor _____ , inspect the bowl for _____ , water, or _____ .

3. Inspect the gaskets for proper _____ .

4. Any bits of gasket should be _____ off parts or fittings to prevent misalignment during reassembly.

5. Inspect the idle mixture adjusting needle(s). They should not be _____ or _____ .

6. Always wear _____ and work in a well-_____ area when using cleaners and _____ .

7. Be sure to install the proper _____ on jets where needed.

8. Be sure to tighten the screws in the bowl _____ and other flanges a little at a time in a _____ pattern until they are tight.

9. The distance the acceleration pump _____ (or diaphragm) travels up or back controls how much _____ is taken into the acceleration pump to supply the discharge when the _____ opens.

10. The fast idle cam or choke rod adjustments set the fast idle cam for the correct relationship with the _____ valve.

11. The choke spring adjustment sets the choke _____ _____ tension.

12. Attach metal fuel lines before you bolt the _____ in place. This will help you avoid _____-_____ and _____ the line fittings.

FUEL INJECTION SYSTEMS

☐   LEARNING OBJECTIVES   ☐

After studying this chapter, you will be able to:

1. Explain the function of the separate sections, and describe the operation of the parts in each section on the following fuel injection systems:

    Bosch Electronic Fuel Injection Systems, types EFI-D and EFI-L

    Bosch Continuous Injection Systems (CIS)

    General Motors Electronic Fuel Injection System (EFI)

2. Define and/or discuss the following terms:

electronic fuel injection	continuous fuel injection
direct fuel injection	detecting sensor elements
manifold injection	electronic control unit
port injection	injection valve
timed fuel injection	injection distributor

INTRODUCTION

Carburetor systems all operate on the same principles and have the same types of problems. One of the main problems with carburetor systems is the difficulty of delivering the same exact air-fuel mixture to each cylinder. Air easily flows through the passages, bends, ports, and various lengths of the intake manifold. However, gasoline vapor, which is much heavier than air, has more difficulty going through manifold bends and sharp corners. Some of the fuel does not get to certain cylinders, causing leanness in those cylinders. Other cylinders are enriched. Engines with **in-line cylinders** (in which all the cylinders line up one behind the other) are most affected by this problem.

Fuel injection systems spray fuel under pressure directly into the manifold close to the intake valve, or into the cylinder itself. This prevents uneven air-fuel mixtures in the cylinders, fuel condensation, and poor performance (particularly during the warm-up period). The amount of fuel sprayed into the engine is based on information received from engine sensors. These sensors report engine conditions. Therefore, fuel injection systems have several advantages over typical carburetor systems.

FUEL INJECTION SYSTEMS

There are several different fuel injection systems on the market. One of the differences between them is based on the location of the injection fuel spray. A fuel injection system can be categorized as follows:

1. **Direct fuel injection**, where fuel is sprayed directly into the cylinder.
2. **Manifold injection**, where fuel is sprayed into the intake manifold.
3. **Port injection**, where fuel is sprayed at the intake port of each cylinder.

The most commonly used system is the port injection system. Two different methods of fuel discharge are used:

1. **Timed fuel injection**, where the fuel is injected for a controlled time interval each time it is needed.
2. **Continuous fuel injection**, where the fuel is injected continuously in a controlled flow rate.

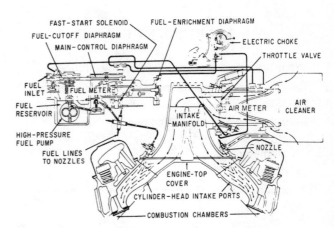

Figure 6-1. *Sectional view of an early model General Motors fuel injection system. (Courtesy of General Motors of Canada Limited).*

General Motors offered a fuel injection system as an option on certain model cars during the late fifties and early sixties. The system was a continuous-flow system designed by the Rochester Products Division of General Motors. Figure 6-1 shows a sectional view of the Rochester system.

This system is no longer used, and we will not discuss it in great detail. From Figure 6-1 you can pick out the various system components. The **air meter** contains the throttle to control the air flow, power, and speed. It also contains the idle speed and mixture adjustments, and a venturi for a vacuum signal to the fuel meter. Venturi vacuum and manifold vacuum work on separate diaphragms attached to the fuel meter to aid in fuel-flow control. The **fuel meter** regulates the fuel flow from the nozzles according to engine needs. The **fuel nozzles** have no valves and are open at all times to give a continuous flow. Sensing devices are used to regulate the flow for starting, warm-up, acceleration, deceleration, and other operating conditions.

FACTS TO REMEMBER

Fuel injection systems may deliver fuel directly into the cylinders, or at the intake port of each cylinder, or into the intake manifold. This provides an even air-fuel mixture to each cylinder at all engine speeds and loads. Fuel can be sprayed continuously, or there can be a fuel spray for a timed interval.

---

1. What are two advantages of fuel injection?
2. Describe three possible methods of fuel injection.
3. List the function of the following parts of the Rochester system described above.
   air meter
   fuel meter
   fuel nozzles

ELECTRONIC FUEL INJECTION

The early fuel injection systems were mechanically operated. Some newer types still are. Electronic circuitry has been used for controlling fuel injection on many systems. Systems with electronic control are called **electronic fuel injection systems**. Studying two Bosch electronic systems will illustrate the basic principles of electronic fuel injection.

The following information and illustrations are taken in part from information supplied by Robert Bosch Gmb.

In electronic fuel injection systems, **detecting elements** sense engine operating conditions and pass this information, in the form of electric signals, to an electronic control unit. The **control unit** processes these signals, determines the amount of fuel required by the engine, and controls the injection valves. The **injection valves** inject the required amount of fuel into the engine.

Electronically controlled fuel injection systems were developed in order to reduce exhaust emissions and improve engine performance. This had to be done with no loss of engine power. Fuel injection systems made it possible to meet these goals. A well-designed, properly functioning fuel injection system increases engine torque (turning power), saves fuel, and reduces harmful exhaust emissions.

Engine torque is increased by the design of the fuel intake system. The rise in torque at low and high

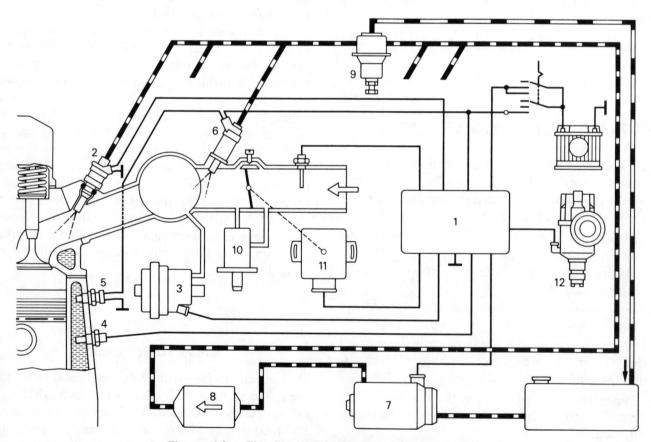

Figure 6-2. The Bosch EFI-D fuel injection system.
(Courtesy of Robert Bosch [Canada] Ltd.)

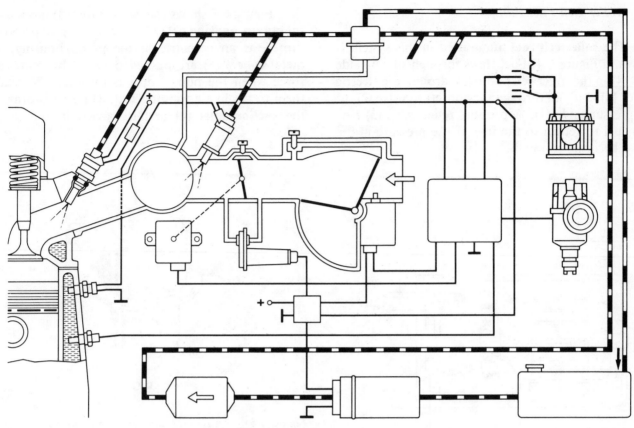

Figure 6-3. The Bosch EFI-L fuel injection system. (Courtesy of Robert Bosch [Canada] Ltd.)

engine speeds improves engine performance. In comparison with a carburetor fuel system, fuel consumption in injection systems is somewhat reduced during general driving. Fuel savings during city driving, depending on traffic conditions and driving characteristics, can be even greater.

BOSCH EFI-L AND EFI-D SYSTEMS

Two fuel injection systems with a number of similar features are designed by Robert Bosch. These are the **manifold-pressure-sensitive** type (EFI-D), and the **air-flow-sensitive** type (EFI-L). The fact that the air sensor flap is L-shaped in the EFI-L system will serve as a clue to help you remember that the EFI-L is the air-flow type.

Figures 6-2 and 6-3 are diagrams of the EFI-D and EFI-L systems. Both the EFI-D and EFI-L are timed port injection systems. They can each be divided into three basic sections:

1. The **fuel delivery system** is responsible for fuel delivery, pressure generation, regulation, and filtering. The injection valves are part of the fuel delivery system.
2. The **detecting sensor elements** collect all engine operating information needed to calculate fuel needs.
3. The **electronic control unit** processes the information from the detecting elements, determines injection duration (the amount of time fuel is to be sprayed), and controls the injection valves.

Fuel Delivery System

An electric **fuel pump** in the fuel delivery system draws fuel from the tank and delivers it to the **injection valves**. The fuel pressure at the valves is kept constant by a **fuel pressure regulator**. Excess fuel flows back to the tank. A **fuel filter**, between the pump and the injection valves, filters the fuel.

Roller Cell Fuel Pump

The **roller cell fuel pump** used in this system is shown in Figure 6-4. Fuel flows through suction side inlet (4) to the roller cell pump (5), around the electric motor (6), and out through the nonreturn valve (2), to the pressure side (1). A pressure relief valve (3) permits fuel to return to the inlet if the pressure in the pump becomes too high.

Figure 6-5 shows the **pump rotor** (3) mounted in the **pump housing** (2). Note that the pump rotor is turned as an eccentric in the pump housing. The **metal rollers** (5) are pushed outward by centrifugal force when the pump rotor is turning. This causes them to act like a rotating seal. The fuel is drawn in the **suction inlet** (4) and is carried in the cavities

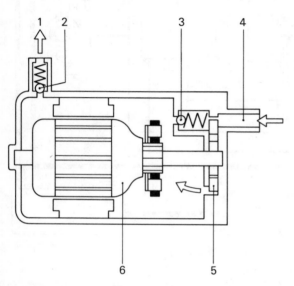

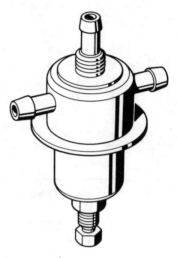

Figure 6-6. *An EFI–D fuel pressure regulator. (Courtesy of Robert Bosch [Canada] Ltd.)*

Figure 6-4. *A roller cell fuel pump. (Courtesy of Robert Bosch [Canada] Ltd.)*

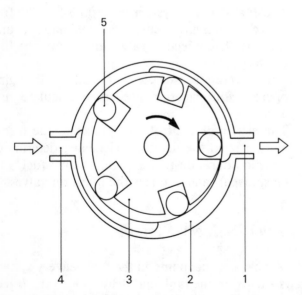

Figure 6-5. *Schematic of a roller cell fuel pump: (1) pressure side, (2) pump housing, (3) pump rotor, (4) suction side, (5) roller, (6) electric motor armature. (Courtesy of Robert Bosch [Canada] Ltd.)*

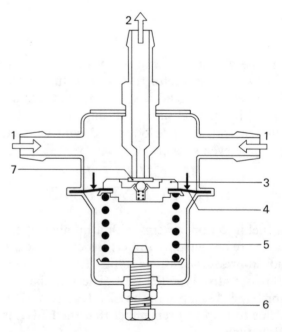

Figure 6-7. *Cross-sectional drawing of the EFI–D fuel pressure regulator: (1) fuel connection, (2) return flow to fuel tank, (3) valve support, (4) diaphragm, (5) pressure spring, (6) adjustment screw, (7) valve. (Courtesy of Robert Bosch [Canada] Ltd.)*

formed between the rollers and the rotor. It is then forced through **pressure side** (1) into the fuel line. There is no danger of explosion in the motor, because there is never enough air mixed with the fuel to produce combustion.

Fuel Pressure Regulator

Figures 6-6 and 6-7 show the type of **fuel pressure regulator** used in the EFI–D system. Fuel pressure is adjustable by **adjustment screw** (6), as shown

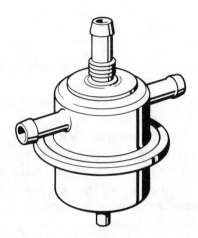

Figure 6-8. *An EFI–L fuel pressure regulator. (Courtesy of Robert Bosch [Canada] Ltd.)*

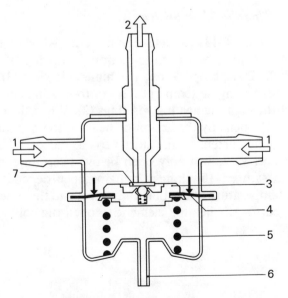

Figure 6-9. *Cross-sectional drawing of the fuel pressure regulator: (1) fuel connection, (2) return line to fuel tank, (3) valve support, (4) diaphragm, (5) pressure spring, (6) connection to intake manifold, (7) valve. (Courtesy of Robert Bosch [Canada] Ltd.)*

in Figure 6-7. Fuel under pressure enters the regulator through the **fuel connections** (1) and pushes the **diaphragm** (4) against the **pressure spring** (5) to open the **valve** (7) at the correct pressure. Excess fuel returns through the **return flow** (2), into a line back to the tank.

Figures 6-8 and 6-9 show the type of fuel pressure regulator used in EFI-L systems. This type of pressure regulator is not adjustable, but it has a more advanced pressure regulation system than the EFI-D pressure regulator. Pressure in the system works the diaphragm (4) in a manner similar to the EFI-D system. Excess fuel is delivered to the fuel tank return line. Manifold vacuum is brought into the spring chamber (5) from the connection to the intake manifold (6), below the diaphragm. The diaphragm reacts to changing manifold vacuum strength, and varies the pressure in the fuel supply lines according to engine loads and throttle positions. The difference between the fuel line pressure and the vacuum pressure in the intake manifold is held constant. This provides an equal pressure drop across the injection valves for all load conditions and helps to reduce exhaust emissions.

Injection Valve

Figure 6-10 is a picture of an injection valve. Figure 6-11 shows a cross-sectional view of the valve.

Figure 6-10. *A fuel injection valve. (Courtesy of Robert Bosch [Canada] Ltd.)*

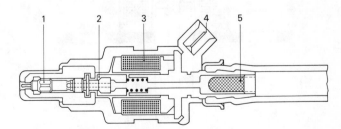

Figure 6-11. *Cross-sectional drawing of the injection valve: (1) nozzle valve, (2) solenoid armature, (3) solenoid winding, (4) electrical connection, (5) filter. (Courtesy of Robert Bosch [Canada] Ltd.)*

The electrical pulses received from the control unit flow into the **solenoid winding** (3) and cause a magnetic field, which draws back the **solenoid armature** (2) and pulls the **nozzle valve** (1) from its seat. This opens the channel for fuel. The fuel flows through the **filter** (5) and through the center of the unit to the manifold. The amount of time that the valve remains open is controlled by the electronic control unit and depends on engine operating conditions.

When the EFI-D fuel injection system is used in four-cylinder engines, two groups of injection valves are used. Each group contains two injection valves. The valves in each group are electrically connected and open at the same time. The same principle applies for six- and eight-cylinder engines. Six-cylinder engines have two groups of three valves, and eight-cylinder engines have two groups of four valves.

When the EFI-L fuel injection system is used, all of the injection valves are combined into a single group. This makes the system somewhat simpler. In this system, half the fuel required for each operating cycle is injected two times during each camshaft revolution.

Start Valve

Figure 6-12 shows a cross-sectional drawing of a start valve. The **start valve**, located near the air throttle valve, sprays finely atomized fuel into the air in the intake manifold. This valve acts like a choke on a carburetor system. It only sprays fuel when the starting motor is turned on and when a thermoswitch or thermo–time switch, located in the engine coolant, is closed. When the engine is cold, the **thermoswitch** allows an electrical flow to reach the **start valve windings** during starting. This produces a magnetic field that pulls the **solenoid armature** (4) in and pulls open the **valve seal** (3). Fuel passes through the start valve and sprays from the **swirl nozzle** (6).

□   ASSIGNMENT 6-B   □

1. Explain the operation of the fuel pump on Bosch electronic fuel injection systems.
2. Compare the fuel pressure regulator on the EFI-D and the EFI-L fuel injection systems.
3. Explain how an electronic fuel injector operates.
4. Compare the grouping of the fuel injectors on the EFI-D and the EFI-L fuel injection systems.
5. Explain the function of the start valve and how it works with the thermo-time switch.

Detecting Sensor Elements

Thermo–Time Switch

Figure 6-13 is a picture of a thermo–time switch. Figure 6-14 shows a cross-sectional drawing of the switch. During operation, the **bimetallic strip** (3) responds to engine temperature and to heating current sent through the **heating windings** (2). When the **contact** (1) opens by the action of heat on the bimetallic strip, the current to the start valve is cut off. Thus, the start valve will only open below a certain engine temperature. How long it remains open depends on the temperature of the bimetallic strip and the time required for the heating element to open the contact.

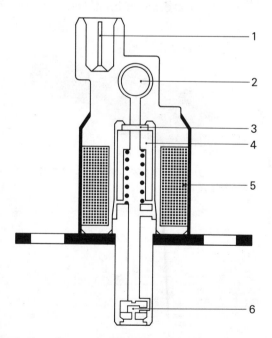

Figure 6-12.   Cross-sectional drawing of a start valve: (1) electrical connection, (2) fuel inlet, (3) seal, (4) solenoid armature, (5) solenoid winding, (6) swirl nozzle. (Courtesy of Robert Bosch [Canada] Ltd.)

Figure 6-13.   A thermo–time switch. (Courtesy of Robert Bosch [Canada] Ltd.)

Temperature Sensor

Figure 6-15 is a picture of a typical temperature sensor. Figure 6-16 shows typical installations of temperature sensors on air- or water-cooled engines. The **temperature sensor** reports engine temperature to the

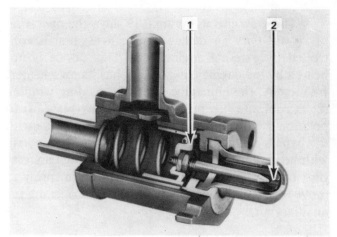

Figure 6-17. An auxiliary air device with an expansion element (1) and piston (2). (Courtesy of Robert Bosch [Canada] Ltd.)

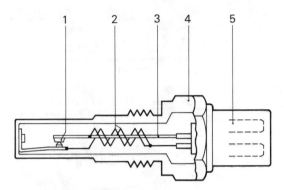

Figure 6-14. Cross-sectional drawing of the thermo–time switch: (1) contact, (2) heating windings, (3) bimetallic strip, (4) housing, (5) electrical connection. (Courtesy of Robert Bosch [Canada] Ltd.)

control unit so that the proper amount of fuel is injected for different engine temperatures.

Auxiliary Air Devices

Figures 6-17 and 6-18 show two types of auxiliary air devices. Based on engine temperature, **auxiliary air devices** provide a controlled amount of air that bypasses the throttle to cause a fast idle. The correct amount of fuel to mix with this extra air is automatically added by the control unit.

The auxiliary air device in Figure 6-17 has a wax-like **expansion element** (2) that expands with engine heat and pushes out the pin fastened to the **spring-loaded piston** (1). As the piston moves back, it reduces the size of the auxiliary air channel until the channel is closed. The expansion element is immersed in the engine coolant and "reads" engine temperature from the coolant.

Figure 6-15. A temperature sensor. (Courtesy of Robert Bosch [Canada] Ltd.)

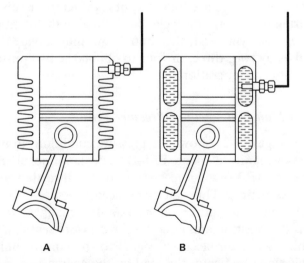

Figure 6-16. A temperature sensor installed in an (A) air-cooled and (B) water-cooled engine. (Courtesy of Robert Bosch [Canada] Ltd.)

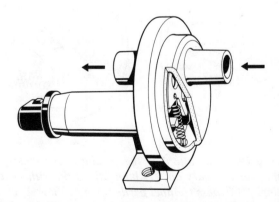

Figure 6-18. An auxiliary air device with external heating. (Courtesy of Robert Bosch [Canada] Ltd.)

The diagrams in Figure 6-19 show the operation of an auxiliary air device (Figure 6-18) that is controlled by external engine heat. This device is not heated by the engine coolant, but has its own heater. In View A, the bimetallic strip with **heating winding** (2) is cool and has pushed the **blocking plate** (4) to position the opening for **auxiliary air** (1), in line with the **bypass channel** (3). In View B, the bimetallic strip with heating winding is at normal operating temperature and has moved. This allows the return spring to move the blocking plate and close off the opening for auxiliary air.

Injection Distributor

Figure 6-20 shows a distributor with trigger contacts. This type of distributor is used with the EFI–D injection system. There are two separate **trigger contacts** (2) mounted on a plate that fits below the distributor mechanism. The **points** (4) are opened 180° from each other by a **cam** (6). Point openings determine the start of injection for each injector group and also give the control unit information about engine speed. Trigger contacts may influence the basic quantity of fuel delivered to the engine, but other devices monitor and provide fuel requirements for various engine-load, air-flow, and temperature conditions.

The distributor used on the EFI–L system does not have trigger contacts. Instead, pulses from the ignition points are used to determine the start of each injection. All injection valves in the EFI–L system are connected electrically and inject half of the required

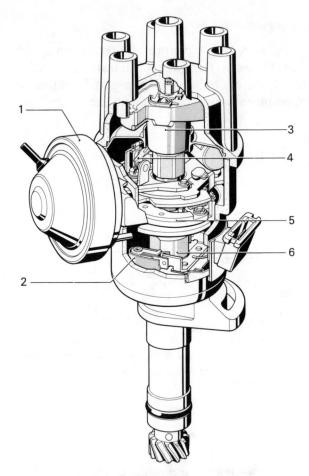

Figure 6-20. *EFI–D ignition distributor with trigger contacts: (1) vacuum unit, (2) trigger contacts, (3) distributor rotor, (4) distributor contact points, (5) centrifugal advance mechanism, (6) cam (opens trigger points). (Courtesy of Robert Bosch [Canada] Ltd.)*

amount of fuel two times during each camshaft rotation. Since there are four, six, or eight ignition pulses during one operating cycle (depending on the number of engine cylinders), the control unit must divide the pulses by two, three, or four to obtain the two pulses for injector operation.

Manifold Vacuum Pressure Sensor

Figure 6-21 shows the pressure conditions in the intake manifold of an EFI–D system. Atmospheric pressure (P_0) is reduced because of the **throttle valve** (1) restriction. This causes reduced pressure (P_1) in the common intake manifold. P_1 changes with throttle position and operates the **pressure sensor** (3), which sends an electrical signal to the control unit. This signal indicates the load on the engine.

Figure 6-22 is a cutaway view of the type of pressure sensor used on an EFI–D system. The pressure

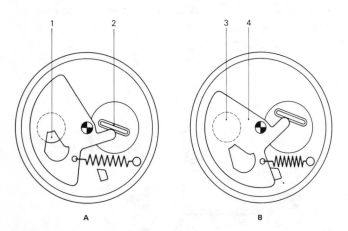

Figure 6-19. *Operation of the auxiliary air device: (1) opening for auxiliary air, (2) bimetallic strip with heating winding, (3) bypass channel partly open in View A, closed in View B, (4) blocking plate. (Courtesy of Robert Bosch [Canada] Ltd.)*

sensor is contained in a sealed metal housing that is supplied with manifold vacuum from the **common intake manifold**. This is a part of the intake manifold before the cylinder branches.

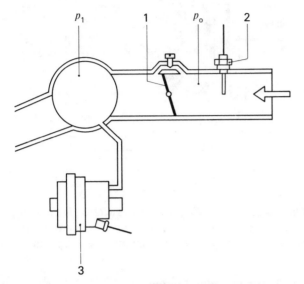

Figure 6-21. Pressure conditions in the EFI–D intake manifold: (P_0) atmospheric pressure, (P_1) pressure in the common intake manifold, (1) throttle valve, (2) temperature sensor, (3) pressure sensor. (Courtesy of Robert Bosch [Canada] Ltd.)

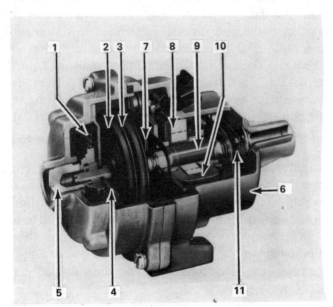

Figure 6-22. EFI–D pressure sensor with additional diaphragm for full-load enrichment: (1) full-load enrichment diaphragm, (2) diaphragm cell, (3) diaphragm cell, (4) part-load stop, (5) full-load stop, (6) housing, (7) flat spring, (8) coil, (9) armature, (10) core, (11) valve. (Courtesy of Robert Bosch [Canada] Ltd.)

The **diaphragm cells** (2) and (3) are **vacuum aneroids**. This means that when a strong vacuum is applied to them, they expand, and when a weak vacuum is applied to them, they contract. The amount of pressure they receive from the common intake manifold determines the amount of expansion or contraction movement produced in these diaphragm cells. If the load is light, the absolute pressure in the common manifold is decreased and the vacuum on the diaphragm cell is increased. The **armature** (9) is moved out of the **coil** (8) by the expanded diaphragm cells. As a result, the inductance of the coil decreases. As engine load increases, the pressure in the common intake manifold increases and the vacuum on the diaphragm cell decreases. The armature is moved into the coil by the compressed diaphragm cells. As a result, the inductance of the coil increases. The decreasing or increasing inductance signals an electronic timer in the control unit to reduce or increase the length of the injection signal to the injectors.

The **full-load enrichment diaphragm** (1) has atmospheric pressure applied to its outside surface through a vent passage. The diaphragm seals the pressure sensor and has the operating (manifold) vacuum on its inside surface. At part throttle, manifold vacuum pulls the full-load enrichment diaphragm toward the diaphragm cells, preventing full travel of the armature into the coil. At full throttle, the vacuum inside the pressure sensor is near atmospheric pressure. The full-load enrichment diaphragm relaxes and moves away from the diaphragm cells. This permits the armature to move further into the coil, pushing the full-load enrichment diaphragm against the **full-load stop** (5). Since more of the armature enters the coil, more inductance occurs, and a longer pulse for a power mixture is supplied by the control unit. Some pressure sensors do not have a full-load enrichment diaphragm. Instead, these sensors use a full-load contact in the throttle valve switch.

Air-Flow Sensor

The EFI-L system uses an air-flow sensor instead of a manifold vacuum-operated pressure sensor. Figure 6-23 shows an air-flow sensor. Figure 6-24 is a cross-sectional diagram of the sensor. The air-flow sensor generates a voltage signal based on the amount of air being drawn into the engine. This signal and information on engine speeds are the main inputs to the control unit. The control unit uses this information to regulate the duration of the fuel injection. The spring-loaded, **air-flow sensor flap** (2) is held in different positions, depending on the air flow across the flap. The position of the air flow sensor flap is sensed by a built-in measuring device (5). A **compensation flap** (7) is attached to the air-flow sensor flap. The compensation flap works together with the **dampening chamber** (6) to eliminate oscillations caused by air pressure pushing against the back of the air-flow sensor flap. The idle range is regulated by a mixture adjustment screw (1).

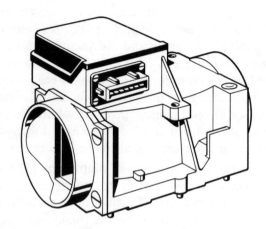

Figure 6-23. An EFI-L air-flow sensor. (Courtesy of Robert Bosch [Canada] Ltd.)

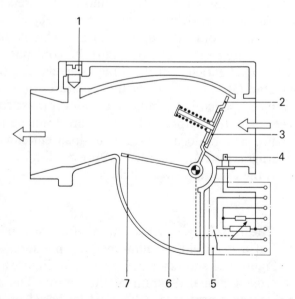

Figure 6-24. Cross-sectional drawing of the EFI-L air-flow sensor: (1) idle mixture adjustment screw, (2) air-flow sensor flap, (3) nonreturn valve, (4) air temperature sensor, (5) electrical connections, (6) dampening chamber, (7) compensation flap. (Courtesy of Robert Bosch [Canada] Ltd.)

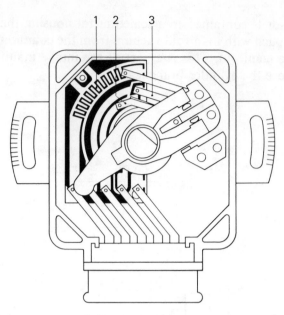

Figure 6-25. An EFI-D throttle switch: (1) contact path for acceleration enrichment, (2) full-load contact, (3) idle contact. (Courtesy of Robert Bosch [Canada] Ltd.)

Throttle Valve Switch

Figure 6-25 shows the type of throttle valve switch used on the EFI-D system. The switch is fitted with sliding contacts and a **contact path** (1) for acceleration. It is activated directly by the throttle shaft, based on throttle valve movement. During acceleration, the sliding contact moves across the face of the contact paths and produces extended injection time and additional injection pulses for acceleration enrichment. The **full-load contact** (2) signals the control unit when the throttle is fully open and triggers enrichment for heavy loads. The **idle contact** (3) signals the control unit when the throttle is closed and calls for an idle mixture.

Figure 6-26 shows the type of throttle valve switch used on EFI-L systems. It is simpler in construction than the one used for EFI-D systems. The switch signals the control unit when the throttle is closed for idle and when it is fully open for full load. Contact paths for temporary enrichment have been eliminated on this switch. The switch has two main features—the **idle contact** (1) and the **full-load contact** (2).

Control Units

Figures 6-27 and 6-28 are open views of the control units. Control units have a large number of elec-

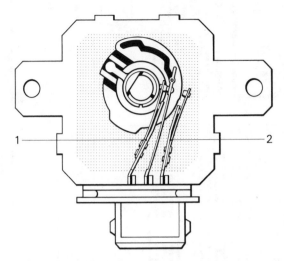

Figure 6-26. *An EFI–L throttle valve switch: (1) idle contact, (2) full-load contact. (Courtesy of Robert Bosch [Canada] Ltd.)*

Figure 6-27. *Control unit in the EFI–D. (Courtesy of Robert Bosch [Canada] Ltd.)*

Figure 6-28. *Control unit in the EFI–L. (Courtesy of Robert Bosch [Canada] Ltd.)*

tronic components working together to process the signals from the various engine sensors and devices. They process the information and produce electrical pulses that operate the injector valves for the correct injection duration at all engine conditions. The EFI-D control unit contains about 300 electrical components. The EFI-L control unit contains about 80 electrical components. Both units use printed circuitry. Control units are not intended to be repaired by a mechanic and should be replaced or sent to an authorized repair shop if they are defective.

FACTS TO REMEMBER

The Bosch EFI-D and EFI-L fuel injection systems are "electronic" in that fuel delivery is electronically controlled. This is accomplished through the use of various engine sensors that "read" engine needs and send signals to a control unit. The control unit monitors these signals and controls the length of time that the injectors open to provide the proper air-fuel mixture for the engine.

☐ ASSIGNMENT 6-C ☐

1. Explain the purpose of a temperature sensor.
2. Explain the purpose of an auxiliary air device.
3. Explain the purpose and operation of the EFI-D trigger contacts.
4. Describe the origin of the pulses used to start injection in the EFI-L system.
5. Explain the function of the pressure sensor in the EFI-D system and its relation to manifold pressure.
6. Explain the purpose of the air-flow sensor in the EFI-L system.
7. Compare the throttle valve switch in the EFI-D injection system with the one in the EFI-L system.

BOSCH CONTINUOUS INJECTION SYSTEM

Robert Bosch also manufactures a mechanically operated fuel injection system that does away with the electronic control unit and the timing signal from the distributor. The system is a **continuous port injection**

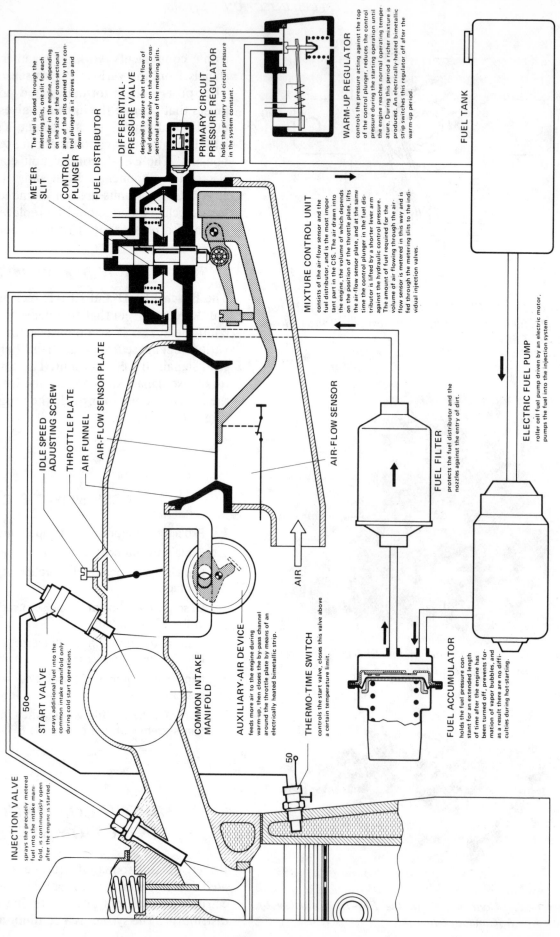

Figure 6-29. A continuous injection system. (Courtesy of Robert Bosch [Canada] Ltd.)

METER SLIT
The fuel is dosed through the metering slits, one slit for each cylinder in the engine, depending on the size of the cross-sectional area of the slits opened by the control plunger as it moves up and down.

CONTROL PLUNGER

FUEL DISTRIBUTOR

DIFFERENTIAL-PRESSURE VALVE
designed to assure that the flow of fuel depends only on the open cross-sectional areas of the metering slits.

PRIMARY CIRCUIT PRESSURE REGULATOR
holds the primary fuel circuit pressure in the system constant.

WARM-UP REGULATOR
controls the pressure acting against the top of the control plunger, reduces the control pressure during the starting operation until the engine reaches normal operating temperature. During this period a richer mixture is produced. An electrically-heated bimetallic strip switches this regulator off after the warm-up period.

FUEL TANK

MIXTURE CONTROL UNIT
consists of the air-flow sensor and the fuel distributor, and is the most important part in the CIS. The air drawn into the engine, the volume of which depends on the position of the throttle plate, lifts the air-flow sensor plate, and at the same time the control plunger in the fuel distributor is lifted by a shorter lever arm against the hydraulic control pressure. The amount of fuel required for the volume of air flowing through the air-flow sensor is metered in this way and is fed through the metering slits to the individual injection valves.

ELECTRIC FUEL PUMP
roller cell fuel pump driven by an electric motor, pumps the fuel into the injection system

IDLE SPEED ADJUSTING SCREW

THROTTLE PLATE

AIR FUNNEL

AIR-FLOW SENSOR PLATE

AIR-FLOW SENSOR

AIR

FUEL FILTER
protects the fuel distributor and the nozzles against the entry of dirt.

START VALVE
sprays additional fuel into the common intake manifold only during cold start operations.

COMMON INTAKE MANIFOLD

AUXILIARY-AIR DEVICE
feeds more air to the engine during warm-up, then closes the by-pass channel around the throttle plate by means of an electrically heated bimetallic strip.

THERMO-TIME SWITCH
controls the start valve, closes this valve above a certain temperature limit.

FUEL ACCUMULATOR
holds the fuel pressure constant for an extended length of time after the engine has been turned off, prevents formation of vapor bubbles, and as a result there are no difficulties during hot-starting.

INJECTION VALVE
sprays the precisely metered fuel into the intake manifold, is continuously open after the engine is started

50

50

98

type, which means that it injects fuel into the intake valve ports continuously during engine operation. The fuel flow rate is regulated by the flow rate of the air coming into the engine.

The Bosch continuous injection system (CIS) is mechanically operated, but does not have to be driven from the vehicle engine. The volume of intake air is measured by an air-flow sensor installed in front of the throttle plate. Based on the volume of air measured, a fuel distributor meters fuel to the individual engine cylinders to produce the correct air-fuel mixture for engine power needs, proper fuel consumption, and correct exhaust emissions. This precisely metered amount of fuel is then fed to the injection valves, which continuously spray the finely atomized fuel in front of the intake valves. The heart of the system is the mixture control unit.

Figure 6-29 is a schematic of the continuous injection system. Study this illustration and the paragraphs of explanation about each part in the system for a short description of its operation.

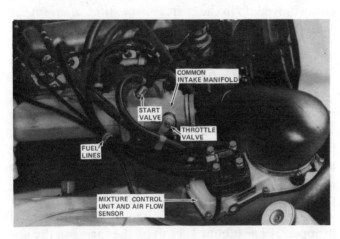

Figure 6-30. *Installation of a continuous injection system. (Courtesy of Robert Bosch [Canada] Ltd.)*

A picture of a continuous injection system installed in an automobile is shown in Figure 6-30. The mixture control unit with the air-flow sensor is in the foreground. It is joined by a flexible rubber pipe to the common intake manifold on the engine block. Four fuel lines lead from the mixture control unit to the four injectors mounted on the engine. The throttle valve is in the right-hand end of the common manifold, and the start valve is above it to the left.

Air-Flow Sensor

As shown in Figure 6-31, the **air-flow sensor** section of the mixture control unit consists of the **air funnel** and the **air-flow sensor plate** mounted on a **lever** that is supported at its **fulcrum** (pivot point). The weights of the lever and air-flow sensor plate together are balanced by a **counterweight**. The **control plunger** transmits the fuel pressure force (opposing the force of the air in the air funnel) through the lever to the air-flow sensor plate. Thus, the control plunger is trying to push the sensor plate down. The intake air, flowing through the intake funnel, lifts the air-flow sensor plate up until the force of this air and the opposing force of the plunger are equal.

A particular position of equilibrium is shown in Figure 6-32. In this diagram, the control plunger is positioned at a specific point in the **fuel barrel**. Its horizontal control edge has opened the rectangular **metering slits** by a specific amount. Fuel will now flow through these openings and be fed to the injection valves.

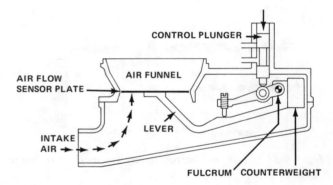

Figure 6-31. *Schematic diagram of the air-flow sensor. (Courtesy of Robert Bosch [Canada] Ltd.)*

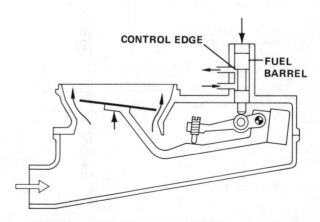

Figure 6-32. *Fuel control in the mixture control unit. (Courtesy of Robert Bosch [Canada] Ltd.)*

Fuel Barrel

Figure 6-33 is a picture of the fuel barrel in the mixture control unit. The barrel has as many metering slits (slot-shaped openings) as there are engine cylinders. The control plunger moves up and down inside the barrel, opening more or less slit area for gasoline flow. Figure 6-34 is a diagram of the barrel and control plunger. This diagram shows the control plunger, in the down position, blocking the metering slits.

Figure 6-35 illustrates the source of fuel pressure on the control plunger. This force is indicated in the drawing by five arrows pointing down on the control plunger. The amount of pressure applied to the plunger is a result of the pressure allowed by the warm-up regulator, which is regulated by engine temperature. This pressure is transmitted through the **dampening restriction** above the plunger and provides the force needed to oppose the force of the air on the air-flow sensor plate (represented by a single arrow

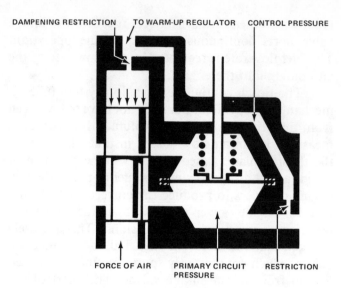

Figure 6-35. Pressure balance on the control plunger. (Courtesy of Robert Bosch [Canada] Ltd.)

below the plunger in the illustration). The **warm-up regulator** lowers the pressure against the plunger when the engine is cold, permitting the plunger to be easily moved up in the barrel by the force of air on the sensor plate, and providing a richer mixture.

Differential Pressure Valves

Figure 6-36 shows two differential pressure valves. There are always the same number of valves in the fuel distributor as there are injectors on the engine. **Differential pressure valves** regulate the pressure across the metering slits and keep it as constant as possible, regardless of the amount the slit is open.

As indicated in the illustration, the pressure is dropped .1 bar (about 1.5 psi) by the spring in the upper chamber. This .1 bar drop results from the dif-

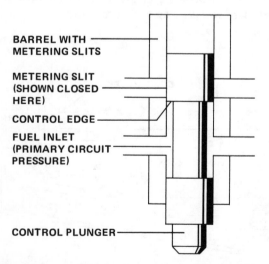

Figure 6-33. The fuel barrel. (Courtesy of Robert Bosch [Canada] Ltd.)

Figure 6-34. Barrel with metering slits and control plunger. (Courtesy of Robert Bosch [Canada] Ltd.)

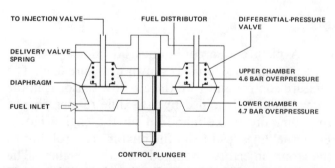

Figure 6-36. A fuel distributor with differential pressure valves. (Courtesy of Robert Bosch [Canada] Ltd.)

ference between the 4.7 bar overpressure (about 66 psi) on the bottom of the diaphragm (and also inside the control barrel) and the 4.6 bar overpressure (about 64.5 psi) on the top of the diaphragm (and outside of the barrel slit). These diaphragms are made of steel, are very small in diameter, and move only a few hundredths of a millimeter.

A **bar** is the international measurement for pressure. For practical purposes, 1 bar is about 14 psi, or 1 atmosphere of pressure. Figure 6-37 shows how the diaphragms flex down to let a greater flow through as the metering slits open, maintaining the same pressure (View A). As the flow decreases, the metering slit closes, and the diaphragm flexes back again, maintaining the same pressure (View B).

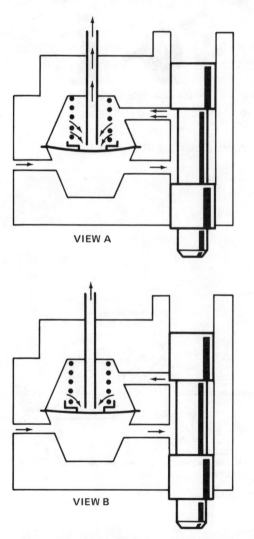

VIEW A

VIEW B

Figure 6-37. Operation of the metering slit and diaphragm. (Courtesy of Robert Bosch [Canada] Ltd.)

□ **ASSIGNMENT 6-D** □

1. Explain the operation of the air-flow sensor plate against the pressure on the control plunger on the continuous injection system.

2. Describe the operation of the metering slits and the action of the control plunger in the continuous injection system.

3. State the purpose of the differential pressure valves.

4. Describe the source of the variable pressure on the control plunger and its relation to the action of the warm-up regulator.

GENERAL MOTORS ELECTRONIC FUEL INJECTION SYSTEM

Another fuel injection system on the market is the General Motors Electronic Fuel Injection System (EFI). This system operates similarly to the Bosch EFI-D fuel injection system. The following information and illustrations are taken in part from information supplied by General Motors of Canada Limited.

Figure 6-38 shows a typical General Motors timed port injection EFI system. The injectors open in time with the engine pistons and inject a predetermined amount of fuel according to engine needs, as determined by engine temperature, load, and speed.

The General Motors system is a two-group system where the eight port injectors are divided into two groups of four each. Injectors for cylinders 1, 2, 7, and 8 form one group. The other group consists of injectors for cylinders 3, 4, 5, and 6. All four injectors in each group are opened and closed at the same time, and the two groups operate alternately. Each of the groups are opened once during every camshaft revolution. Their operation is timed by a special timing switch called a **speed sensor** that is mounted on the distributor body and works in conjunction with the electronic control unit.

The **electronic control unit (ECU)** calculates engine fuel requirements, based on inputs from the sensors. Using these inputs, the control unit determines injection duration and provides accurate control of the air-fuel mixture.

The EFI system consists of four major subsystems: (1) fuel delivery, (2) air induction, (3) sensors, and (4) electronic control unit.

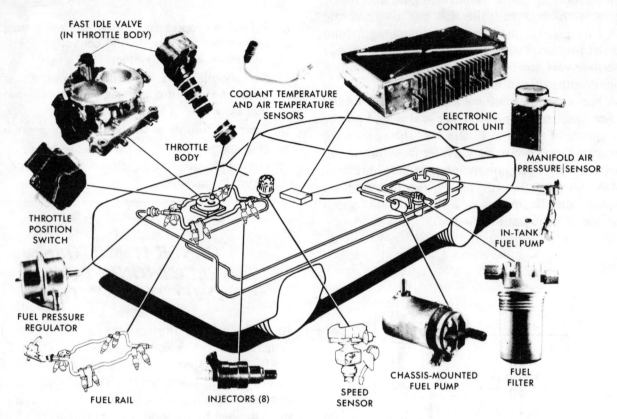

Figure 6-38. *Installation of the EFI system. (Courtesy of General Motors of Canada Limited)*

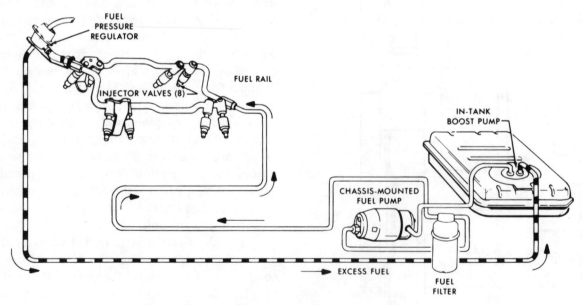

Figure 6-39. *The EFI fuel delivery system. (Courtesy of General Motors of Canada Limited)*

Fuel Delivery Subsystem

The **fuel delivery subsystem** is illustrated in Figure 6-39. Fuel is picked up by the **in-tank boost pump** (illustrated in Figure 6-40) and sent to the **chassis-mounted fuel pump**. This prevents vapor lock on the vacuum side of the main pump. The fuel pump pushes fuel through a **fuel filter** and fills the **fuel rail** with fuel at a pressure above the manifold vacuum pressure. The **fuel pressure regulator** maintains the correct fuel rail pressure, based on manifold vacuum pressure. The regulator also returns excess fuel to the tank (see dotted fuel line, Figure 6-39). The injection valves are solenoid operated. They open and spray a fine mist of fuel. Their **pulse** (opening and closing) is triggered by electrical signals received from the electronic control unit. **Pulse width** is the length of time electrical current flow lasts during each pulse. It is regulated according to engine needs by various signals fed into the electronic control unit.

Air Induction Subsystem

The **air induction subsystem** is illustrated in Figure 6-41. The **throttle valves** (similar to those in a

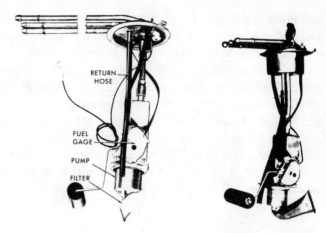

Figure 6-40. In-tank fuel pumps. (Courtesy of General Motors of Canada Limited)

carburetor) control the air-flow rate. They are assisted by an adjustable idle bypass air passage in the throttle body. This allows a regulated amount of air to bypass the throttle valves and provide idle speed adjustment. The air allowed through the throttle body enters into the cylinders through the intake manifold.

The **fast idle valve** (shown mounted in the throttle body in Figure 6-41, and in an exploded view

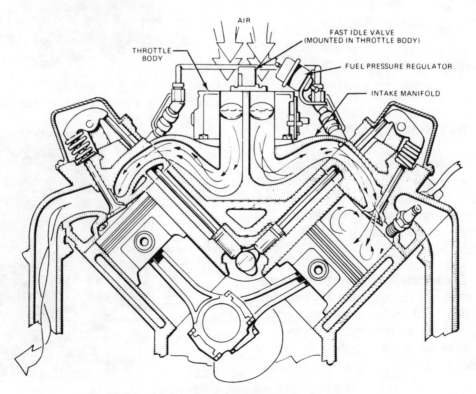

Figure 6-41. An air induction system. (Courtesy of General Motors of Canada Limited)

in Figure 6-42) allows additional air for cold starts and warm-up periods. The additional air is provided with fuel enrichment from the injectors through signals from temperature sensors into the electronic control unit. The fast idle valve contains a temperature sensitive element, a spring and plunger, and an electric heater. When the engine is cold, the valve opens and allows some air to bypass the throttle valves. This will produce a fast idle. Because the valve is electrically connected to the fuel pump circuit, it will heat up and close off after the engine warms up.

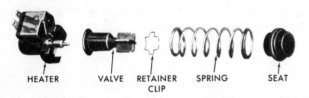

HEATER   VALVE   RETAINER   SPRING   SEAT
                            CLIP

Figure 6-42.   The fast idle valve. (Courtesy of General Motors of Canada Limited)

□   ASSIGNMENT 6-E   □

1. List the parts in the fuel delivery subsystem and explain their purpose.
2. What is the purpose of the air induction subsystem?
3. Describe the operation of the throttle valve, idle bypass air passage, and the fast idle valve.

Engine Sensors Subsystem

The **engine sensors** are electrically connected to the electronic control unit, and all operate independently. Each sensor sends a signal to the control unit, relating a specific engine operating condition. The control unit analyzes all the signals and sends out the appropriate commands.

Manifold: The **manifold absolute pressure sensor** (Figure 6-43) monitors changes in intake manifold vacuum pressure that result from variations in engine speed and load, barometric pressure, or changes in altitude. Information on these pressure changes is supplied to the electronic control unit in the form of electrical signals.

As the throttle is opened and manifold pressure increases, additional fuel is needed, and the manifold

absolute pressure sensor electrically signals the control unit. The control unit sends a signal to increase the pulse width (time) at the injectors. As the throttle closes and manifold pressure decreases, less fuel is needed, and the pulse width is shortened.

Throttle: The **throttle position switch** (Figure 6-44) is mounted on the throttle body and connected to the throttle valve shaft. Accelerator movement causes the throttle shaft to rotate and turn the throttle position switch. The switch senses shaft movement and position and sends electrical signals to the electronic control unit. The control unit processes these signals to determine the fuel requirement for any particular throttle position.

Figure 6-43.   The manifold absolute pressure sensor. (Courtesy of General Motors of Canada Limited)

Figure 6-44.   The throttle position switch. (Courtesy of General Motors of Canada Limited)

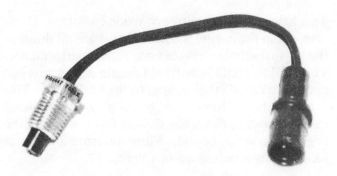

Figure 6-45. A temperature sensor. (Courtesy of General Motors of Canada Limited)

Temperature: The **temperature sensors** for liquid coolant or air are identical. See Figure 6-45. These sensors consist of a coil of nickel wire sealed into an epoxy case. The case is molded into a brass housing with two wires and a connector extending from it. The electrical resistance of the nickel wire changes with temperature changes. Low temperature provides low resistance. As temperatures increase, so does the resistance. The voltage drop across each sensor is monitored by the electrical control unit.

The **coolant temperature sensor** increases the air-fuel mixture enrichment according to engine temperature when the engine is cold and decreases enrichment as the engine temperature rises. The **air temperature sensor** accomplishes the same thing, but reads air temperature rather than coolant temperature. The air temperature sensor is located in the intake manifold, and the coolant temperature sensor is located in a coolant passage.

Speed: The **speed sensor** is in the distributor assembly. See Figure 6-46. It consists of two com-

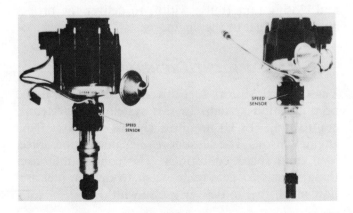

Figure 6-46. Fuel injection distributors. (Courtesy of General Motors of Canada Limited)

ponents. The first component has two reed switches mounted in a plastic housing. The second component is a rotor with two magnets that rotate with the distributor shaft. The rotor magnets rotate past the reed switches, causing the switches to open and close. The operation of these two switches allows the electronic control unit and the injector groups to work together with the intake valve timing (phasing). The switches also signal engine rpm to the control unit for determining fuel needs.

Electronic Control Unit Subsystem

A picture of an electronic control unit is shown in Figure 6-47. The control unit is a computer consisting of electronic circuits housed in a steel case. Different control units are used for each body style and vehicle equipment package and cannot be interchanged.

Figure 6-47. The electrical control unit. (Courtesy of General Motors of Canada Limited)

The diagram in Figure 6-48 shows that the input signals coming into the control unit from the various sensors are the: (1) absolute manifold pressure (vacuum), (2) engine rpm, (3) coolant temperature, (4) intake manifold air temperature, and (5) throttle position.

The output signals from the control unit regulate the operation of the (1) EGR solenoid, (2) fuel pumps, (3) fast idle valve, (4) injectors, and (5) the vacuum retard solenoid (not shown on the diagram—found on some California models only).

The electronic control unit is designed to provide the desired air-fuel mixtures for various driving and atmospheric conditions. As sensor signals are received, the control unit processes them and computes engine fuel requirements for various conditions. The control unit issues commands to the injection valves,

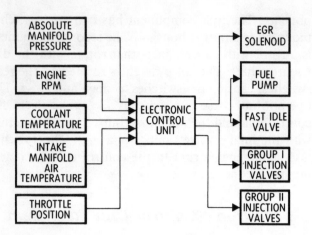

Figure 6-48. Functional block diagram showing the operation of the EFI system. (Courtesy of General Motors of Canada Limited)

opening them for a specific time duration. The width (duration) of the pulses varies with engine needs. All injection valves in each group open at the same instant on command from the control unit.

Electronic Fuel Injection System Operation

The electronic fuel injection system is activated when the ignition switch is turned on. The following events occur at that moment:

1. The electronic control unit receives battery voltage.

2. The fuel pumps are activated by the control unit. The pumps will operate for only about one second, unless the engine is cranking or running.

3. All engine sensors are activated and begin sending signals to the control unit.

4. The electrically heated fast idle valve is activated. The fast idle valve is connected to the fuel pump electrical circuit and will only operate for about one second, unless the engine is cranking or running.

5. The EGR solenoid is activated to block the vacuum signal to the EGR valve at coolant temperatures below 110° to 130°F (depending on the model).

An **EGR solenoid** is an electrically operated switch in the vacuum line that operates the **Exhaust Gas Recirculation valve** (EGR valve). The EGR valve allows some exhaust gas to recirculate through the intake manifold and into the combustion chambers.

This helps to reduce nitrogen oxide emissions. However, when the engine is cold, exhaust gas dilution of the air-fuel mixture causes poor engine performance. The EGR solenoid is activated during cold engine operation to cut off the vacuum to the EGR valve. This prevents the EGR valve from opening and allowing exhaust gases to dilute the air-fuel mixture during the engine warm-up period. More information about EGR valves is contained in Chapter 13.

6. On some California models, the vacuum retard solenoid is activated to route vacuum to the retard side of the vacuum advance unit. This is accomplished at the same temperature as the EGR activation and uses the same signal.

The following events occur when the engine is started:

1. The fuel pumps are activated for continuous operation.

2. The heater element of the fast idle valve is activated for continuous operation.

3. The throttle body air bypass controls the air flow to the intake manifold with the throttle valves closed. When the accelerator pedal is depressed, the throttle valves open, creating an air flow.

4. The fuel pressure regulator maintains the fuel pressure in the fuel rail and returns excess fuel to the fuel tank.

The following sensor signals are continuously being received and processed by the electronic control unit:

1. engine coolant temperature;
2. intake manifold air temperature;
3. intake manifold absolute pressure;
4. engine speed and firing position; and
5. throttle position changes.

The control unit sends signals alternately to each injector group, precisely controlling injector opening and closing time (pulse width) to deliver the proper amount of fuel to the engine.

FACTS TO REMEMBER

The General Motors fuel injection system is a timed port injection system. In this system, an electronic control unit (ECU) monitors signals sent to it from engine sensors. The sensors read engine temperature, load, and speed conditions. The control unit uses these signals to determine when to deliver fuel and how much fuel to deliver (pulse width).

ELECTRONIC FUEL INJECTION SERVICE

Special electronic equipment and exact instructions are needed to inspect and diagnose problems in any fuel injection system. Because of the complexity of these systems, it is not possible to cover the service procedures for them in this book. Manufacturers publish this type of information for service technicians. No attempt to service a fuel injection system should be made without the proper equipment, manufacturer instructions, and specifications.

☐ ASSIGNMENT 6-F ☐

1. Explain the operation of the manifold absolute pressure sensor.
2. Explain the purpose of the air and coolant temperature sensors.
3. What two types of information are supplied to the electronic control unit by the speed sensor?
4. What input signals come into the electronic control unit, and what output signals does it send out?

☐ SELF-TEST ☐

Complete the following sentences by filling in the missing words.

1. One of the main problems with a carburetor system is the difficulty of delivering the same exact _____-_____ mixture to each _____ .

2. Fuel injection systems _____ fuel under pressure directly into the _____ close to the _____ valve, or into the _____ itself.

3. Two fuel injection systems with a number of similar features are designed by Robert Bosch. These are (1) the _____ _____ sensitive type (EFI-D) and (2) the _____ _____ sensitive type (EFI-L).

4. Both the EFI-D and the EFI-L are timed _____ _____ systems.

5. The start valve on Bosch fuel injection systems only sprays fuel when the _____ _____ is turned on and when a _____ switch, located in the coolant, is closed.

6. Auxiliary air devices on Bosch systems provide a controlled amount of air that _____ the _____ to cause a _____ idle.

7. On a distributor used on the EFI-D injection system, there are two separate _____ contacts.

8. The distributor used on the EFI-L system does not have _____ contacts. Instead, pulses from the _____ _____ are used to determine the start of injection.

9. The throttle valve switch on the EFI-D system is activated directly by the _____ shaft, based on throttle _____ movement.

10. The Bosch continuous injection system (CIS) is a continuous _____ injection type, which means that it injects fuel into the _____ _____ ports continuously during engine operation.

11. Differential pressure valves regulate the _____ across the metering slits and keep it as _____ as possible.

12. The General Motors EFI system consists of four major subsystems. These are the: (1) _____ delivery system, (2) _____ induction system, (3) _____ , and (4) _____ control _____ .

13. In the General Motors EFI system, the fuel pump pushes fuel through a fuel _____ and fills the fuel _____ with fuel.

14. The manifold absolute pressure sensor monitors changes in intake manifold _____ pressure that result from variations in engine _____ and _____ , barometric pressure, or changes in _____ .

7

ELECTRICAL FUNDAMENTALS

☐ LEARNING OBJECTIVES ☐

After studying this chapter, you will be able to:

1. Describe the important facts about electrons and electron theory.

2. Define voltage, current, resistance, and the way each is measured.

3. List the important facts about magnetism and electromagnetism.

4. Describe the construction features of a lead-acid battery.

5. Define and/or discuss the following terms:

electron theory	voltage
matter	current
molecule	resistance
atom	permanent magnet
electron	electromagnet
conductor	electromagnetic induction
insulator	lead-acid battery

INTRODUCTION

Early automobiles had only a few electrical components. They used the simplest of ignition systems. They were started by a hand crank and used coal-oil or carbide lights. As people demanded larger engines and easier starting methods, electric starters were installed to crank the engine. Since a battery was needed to operate the starter motor, a generator had to be installed to charge the battery. Once electricity from the battery was available, an ignition coil and a distributor with breaker points and spark-advance features were installed. The lighting was also improved, and electric lamps replaced coal-oil or carbide lights.

These basic items are still used today, although they have been greatly improved. Many new electrical devices have also been added. Some of these items are stop and turn signals, horns, fuel and temperature gauges, warning lights, radios, heating and air conditioning systems, transmission controls, emission control devices, and electronic circuits for voltage regulation and electronic ignition. These items have been added for convenience, comfort, and safety.

It would be difficult to service a vehicle electrical system without some basic knowledge about electricity. This chapter will deal with basic electrical principles and terms. Magnets and battery operation will also be covered here.

ELECTRICAL FUNDAMENTALS

Electron Theory

Electron theory states that the observed results of electricity are produced by a **flow of electrons** through an **electrical circuit**. These electrons flow from the negative side to the positive side of the electrical supply. Electron theory assumes that everything on earth consists of some form of matter that has electrical properties (such as positive and negative charges). In order to understand this theory, we need some general knowledge of the terms used when discussing electricity.

Definitions

Matter: **Matter** is anything that has weight and takes up space. It may be solid, liquid, or gas. Wood, iron, oxygen, and water are all examples of matter.

Molecules: A **molecule** is matter broken down into its smallest form without changing its properties. Molecules are made from two or more atoms of one or more types. If you tore a piece of paper in half, then one of the remaining parts in half again, and continued this process until you made the smallest possible piece of paper that has all of the properties of the original piece of paper, you would have a molecule of paper.

Elements: **Elements** are substances that contain only one type of atom. Some examples of elements are pure hydrogen, oxygen, copper, carbon, or iron.

Atoms: An **atom** is the smallest portion of any element. Atoms contain **positive** and **negative charges.** Different types of atoms can be combined to form different kinds of molecules. An atom contains one or more electrons, one or more protons, and one or more neutrons. The **nucleus** of the atom contains the protons and neutrons. **Neutrons** contain both negative and positive charges, but the charges in the neutron are equal and cancel each other. This means that neutrons have no electrical charge. Therefore, they are considered electrically neutral. **Protons** are positively charged particles. Therefore, the nucleus of an atom has a positive charge equal to the number of protons it contains. **Electrons** are negatively charged particles that orbit (spin) around the nucleus of the atom.

Electron Movement

Under certain conditions, one of the electrons spinning around the nucleus in one atom can transfer to another atom and spin around its nucleus. Electrons that move from atom to atom are referred to as **free electrons**. It is the movement of these free electrons that provides electrical current.

Some materials conduct electricity (allow for electron movement) better than others. Based on its ability, or inability, to conduct electricity, a material may be considered a conductor, an insulator, or a semiconductor.

Conductor: A material is considered an electrical **conductor** when it contains free electrons that move easily from one atom to another atom. Metals, such as copper and aluminum, have free electrons and are good conductors.

Insulator: An **insulator** is a material that contains electrons that do not easily move from atom to atom. Insulators will not easily conduct electricity. Some examples of insulators are glass, plastic, rubber, wood, oil, paper, and air.

Semiconductors: A **semiconductor** conducts electricity less easily than a conductor, but more easily than an insulator. Germanium and silicon, commonly used in constructing diodes and transistors, are considered semiconductors.

☐   ASSIGNMENT 7-A   ☐

1. Define molecule, atom, and element.
2. Discuss the terms neutron, proton, and electron.
3. Define conductor, insulator, and semiconductor.

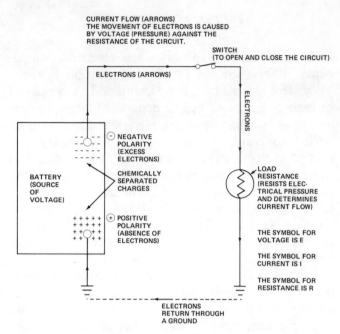

Figure 7-1.   *The flow of electricity in an electrical circuit.*

MEASURING ELECTRON FLOW

There are a number of different measurements of electron flow through a material or a **circuit** (path for electron flow). When diagnosing an electrical problem, it is often necessary to know more than just whether electricity is flowing. The serviceman may also need to know how much electricity is being delivered to the circuit and how much electricity is being used up by the electrical devices in the circuit. Tests for circuit voltage, current flow, and resistance provide these answers.

Voltage

Voltage is considered electrical pressure. In electron theory, voltage is the force that causes movement of electrons from atom to atom in an electrical circuit. The unit of measurement for voltage is the **volt**, measured with a **voltmeter**. The symbol for voltage is E (electromotive force) or V (voltage).

Current

Current is the flow of electrons that results from the electrical force or pressure (voltage). As illustrated in Figure 7-1, current flows from the negative side of the voltage source (which has an excess of electrons), through the electrical circuit, and back to the positive side of the voltage source (which has a shortage of electrons). Current is measured by the number of electrons per second that pass a single point in a circuit. The unit of measurement for electrical current is the **ampere**. Current is measured with an **ammeter**. The symbol for current is I. The term **amperage** means the amount of current flow measured in amperes.

Resistance

Resistance is anything that resists the flow of electrons (current) in an electrical circuit. An electric motor or a light offers some resistance to electron flow. See Figure 7-1. Some devices resist electron flow very little. Such devices are said to have a low resistance and allow a large amount of current flow. Some devices greatly resist electron flow. Such devices have a high resistance and allow only a small amount of current flow. The unit of measurement for electrical resistance is the **ohm**. Resistance is measured with an **ohmmeter**. When writing about electricity, the word "ohm" may be substituted by the Greek letter **omega** (Ω). In a schematic drawing, resistance is shown by a zigzag line ($-\Lambda\Lambda\Lambda-$). The symbol for resistance is R.

1. Define the terms voltage, current, and resistance.
2. How are voltage, current, and resistance measured?

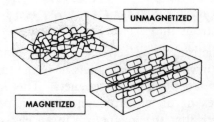

Figure 7-3. When iron or steel is unmagnetized, their molecules are disarranged, but when magnetized their molecules are parallel and their magnetic fields line up. (Courtesy of Ford Motor Company, Dearborn)

MAGNETISM

There is a direct relationship between electricity and magnetism. Magnetism can be produced with electricity, and electricity can be produced with magnetism. The alternator or generator in a car uses magnetism to produce electricity.

The earth is a huge magnet that has a magnetic field surrounding it, as shown in Figure 7-2. The magnetic field has **polarity** (direction). It ends at the poles and causes any suspended magnet to hang in a north-south direction. A compass needle is nothing more than a suspended magnet. The north-seeking end of the compass needle will always point north.

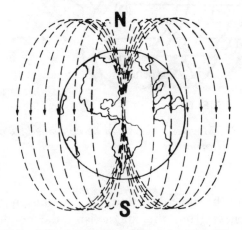

Figure 7-2. The earth is a huge magnet. (Courtesy of Ford Motor Company, Dearborn)

Most of us, at one time or another, have handled a magnet and found that it will pick up bits of metal, such as nails and tacks. The molecules in unmagnetized soft iron are small magnets, but they are completely disarranged, as shown in Figure 7-3. When a magnet is brought in contact with a magnetizable material like iron or steel, the iron or steel molecules can become arranged parallel to the magnetic field produced by the magnet. When the magnet is removed from the soft iron, the iron molecules will return to their disarranged state and the iron will lose

its magnetism. Steel, unlike soft iron, will keep its molecules lined up longer and can become permanently magnetized. Magnetizable metal can be magnetized using a permanent magnet or an electromagnet.

Important Facts About Magnets

1. A magnet has polarity. There is a **north pole** (symbol N) at one end of a magnet and a **south pole** (symbol S) at the other end.

2. A **magnetic field** surrounds a magnet with lines of force traveling from north to south outside the magnet, and from south back to north inside the magnet.

3. Like-magnetic poles or fields repel each other.

4. Unlike-magnetic poles or fields attract each other.

5. Magnetic force is strongest at the poles of a magnet. See Figure 7-4.

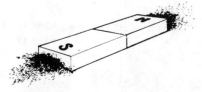

Figure 7-4. Magnetic force is strongest at the poles of a magnet. (Courtesy of Ford Motor Company, Dearborn)

1. Explain the difference between unmagnetized iron and magnetized iron.
2. List the important characteristics of magnets.

ELECTROMAGNETISM

The magnetism in an electromagnet is produced by an electric current. Electromagnets have the same characteristics as permanent magnets. The important advantages of an electromagnet over a permanent magnet are that the magnetism in an electromagnet can be turned on and off, its magnetic strength can be controlled, and if required, its magnetic polarity can be reversed.

An **electromagnet** is a conductor with electric current flowing through it that produces a magnetic field. This field is referred to as an **electromagnetic field**. The field has lines of force and direction. Figure 7-5 shows a current-carrying conductor that passes through a card. Iron filings sprinkled on the card arrange themselves as shown, because a magnetic field exists around the wire conductor. This field consists of millions of circular lines of force along the whole length of the conductor. The compass is pointing in the direction of the magnetic swirls.

Figure 7-6 shows the effect when the wires are reversed at the battery. The current flows in the opposite direction, and the magnetic field reverses. Notice that the compass needle also reverses direction, because the magnetic lines of force are reversed. The iron filings appear the same as before, but the compass needle shows that the magnetic field has reversed direction.

Figure 7-7 shows the combining effect of the magnetic fields around several conductors carrying

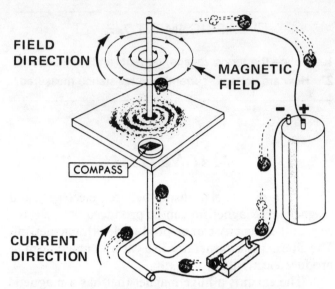

Figure 7-6. *The magnetic field reverses when the current is reversed. (Courtesy of Ford Motor Company, Dearborn)*

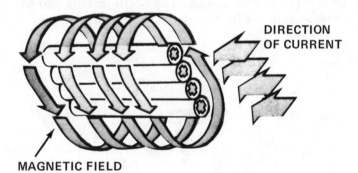

Figure 7-7. *Magnetic fields can be combined. (Courtesy of Chrysler Corporation)*

current in the same direction. To get an even greater effectiveness from the magnetism, the conductors could be wrapped into loops. Figure 7-8 shows the magnetic field around a single-loop conductor. The field can be made much stronger with the addition of a larger number of loops to form a **winding**. The magnetic field in Figure 7-9 has many lines of force forming a magnetic north and south pole. The lines of force travel from north to south on the outside of the winding, and from south back to north on the inside of the winding.

To make this winding into a more effective magnet, an iron core could be added inside the winding, as shown in Figure 7-10. Iron has much less resistance to the flow of magnetic force than does air. Therefore, iron will concentrate the strength of the magne-

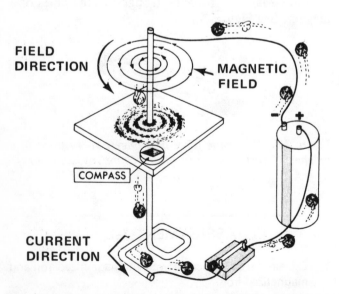

Figure 7-5. *A magnetic field circles a current-carrying conductor. (Courtesy of Ford Motor Company, Dearborn)*

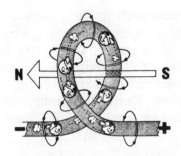

Figure 7-8. *The magnetic field around a loop has direction. (Courtesy of Ford Motor Company, Dearborn)*

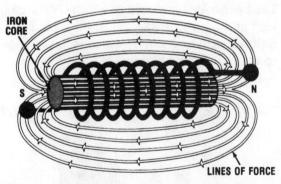

LINES OF FORCE

CURRENT FLOW
THROUGH WINDING
CAUSES A MAGNETIC
FIELD

Figure 7-9. *The magnetic fields around a winding. (Courtesy of Chrysler Corporation)*

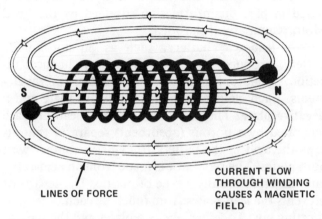

IRON CORE

LINES OF FORCE

Figure 7-10. *The iron core intensifies the magnetic field and becomes magnetized. (Courtesy of Chrysler Corporation)*

tic field. The iron core, itself, becomes magnetized when current is flowing through the winding. If the flow of electricity through the winding is reversed, the magnetic polarity reverses, too. Automobile alternators, electrical motors, generators, and ignition coils all contain windings.

□ ASSIGNMENT 7-D □

1. Describe the magnetic field around a current-carrying conductor and the effect of reversing the current in the conductor.
2. Describe the magnetic field around a current-carrying winding.

ELECTROMAGNETIC INDUCTION

As has been mentioned, magnetism can be used to produce electricity. This process is called **electromagnetic induction**.

Rules of Electromagnetic Induction

To produce electricity by electromagnetic induction, you need: (1) a magnetic field, (2) a conductor, and (3) movement of either the field or the conductor. The movement must cause the lines of force in the magnetic field to be cut by the conductor. The most effective voltage induction occurs when the motion causes the angle that the field is cut to be at a 90° angle across the magnetic field lines. Induction decreases as this angle decreases and becomes zero when the conductor movement is parallel to the magnetic lines of force.

As shown in Figure 7-11, the magnet (magnetic

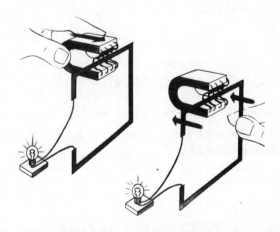

Figure 7-11. *Electromagnetic induction can be caused by moving either the magnetic field across the conductor or the conductor across the magnetic field. (Courtesy of Chrysler Corporation)*

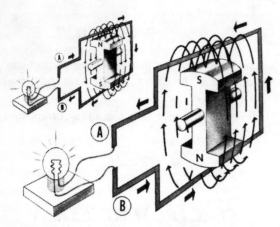

Figure 7-12. Electromagnetic induction can be caused by rotating a magnet inside a loop of wire. (Courtesy of Chrysler Corporation)

field) can be moved across the stationary conductor, or the conductor can be moved across the stationary magnet (magnetic field) to produce electromagnetic induction. Electromagnetic induction produces voltage. Current flow results when a circuit is connected to the conductor as shown in Figure 7-12. **Alternators** and **generators** use electromagnetic induction to produce electricity while the car is running.

Electromagnetic induction is affected by:

1. The speed of the field or conductor motion. (Slow speeds give poor induction. Faster speeds give better induction.)

2. The strength of the magnetic field (the stronger the field, the better the induction).

3. The number of conductors (turns) in a winding (the more turns, the more voltage the winding will produce).

□ ASSIGNMENT 7-E □

1. Describe electomagnetic induction.
2. What are the three main factors affecting electromagnetic induction?

BATTERY THEORY

Electricity can be produced by methods other than electromagnetic induction. In an automobile battery,

electricity is produced chemically. The battery is used to start the engine. With a charging system attached to the automobile's engine, the battery can be recharged and kept fully charged at all times. The battery helps meet current demands when the engine is idling or shut off. During these times, the charging system is not able to supply the full demand for electrical current.

Battery Principles

The following information and illustrations are based in part on information supplied by the Ford Motor Company, Dearborn.

A **lead-acid battery**, such as an automobile battery, produces electricity through a chemical reaction. An automobile battery consists of several **elements**. Each element contains a **positive plate** and a **negative plate**. The plates are made of lead and are separated by a porous (absorbent) **separator** that allows the acid in the battery to come in contact with both plates. The separator is made from an acid-resistant material, usually a type of plastic. The separator prevents the lead plates from touching each other and shorting out. Together, the two plates and the separator are called a **cell**. See Figure 7-13. The cell is immersed in an **electrolyte** (acid diluted in water).

The chemicals and materials that make up the active ingredients in a lead-acid battery are:

1. **Lead peroxide** (or dioxide), which is derived from lead and used to make the positive plate.
2. **Sulfuric acid** and water, which is mixed together to make the electrolyte.

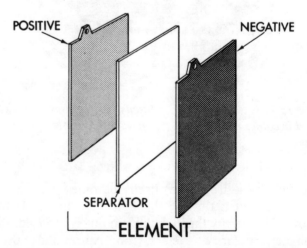

Figure 7-13. A simple battery cell. (Courtesy of Ford Motor Company, Dearborn)

3. **Sponge lead,** which is lead that has been made porous. This is used for the negative plate.

Battery Elements

Figure 7-14 shows a positive plate of lead peroxide and a negative plate of spong lead, which have been put into an acid-proof container. The container is filled with an **electrolyte** made up of 36% sulfuric acid and 64% water. The plates in the electrolyte make an electric cell that will produce approximately two volts of electricity. Electricity will flow when the plates are connected to an electrical device. Figure 7-14 shows a lamp connected to the plates of this simple battery cell.

much electrical energy as a single two-volt cell, or a total of twelve volts. See Figure 7-16.

Notice that each heavy lead element is supported by **plate bridges**. The plate bridges also form **sediment chambers** to collect any particles that are shed from the plates. These particles would short the positive and negative plates if they formed a contact between them. **Cell partitions** keep each element in its own acid supply and make up the separate battery cells. **Cell connectors** join the individual cells together. **Terminals** connect the battery to the automobile electrical system. Figure 7-17 is a cutaway view of a battery showing the battery case, cover, and filler caps.

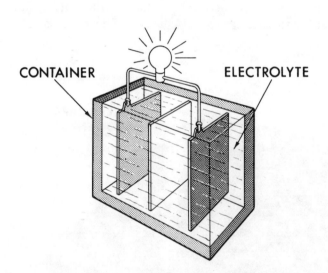

Figure 7-14. *A two-volt battery cell. (Courtesy of Ford Motor Company, Dearborn)*

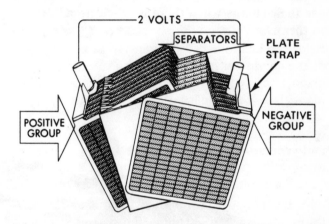

Figure 7-15. *A compound battery element. (Courtesy of Ford Motor Company, Dearborn)*

You can make a **compound battery element** by increasing the number of positive and negative plates in a cell. See Figure 7-15. This cell will still produce only two volts, but it will produce more energy (a longer current flow) than the simple cell with less plates. Figure 7-15 shows the **plate straps** that join all the positive plates into one group and all the negative plates into another group. Note the **separators** between all of the plates to keep them from touching. Should any pair of negative and positive plates touch, the whole cell would be shorted out.

When six cells are connected together in a series (so that the voltage produced in each cell is added to the voltage produced in every other cell), a **battery** of cells is formed. This battery produces six times as

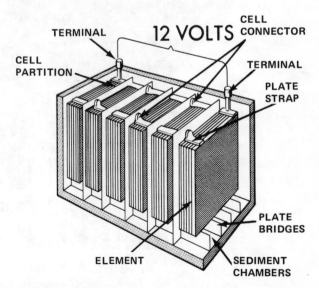

Figure 7-16. *A typical 12-volt battery cell. (Courtesy of Ford Motor Company, Dearborn)*

Battery Grids

The very soft battery plate active material has to be pasted into **lead grids** that stiffen the plates and conduct electrical energy. In regular automobile batteries, the lead in the grids is stiffened with a small amount of **antimony**. The amount of antimony used is reduced in some low-maintenance batteries. In other maintenance-free batteries, **calcium** is used as a stiffener instead of antimony. The use of calcium or reduced antimony as stiffening agents reduces the amount of **gassing** (bubbling of the battery electrolyte) during battery charging and discharging. This reduces battery water loss. Calcium and low-antimony stiffened plates also have reduced **self-discharge**. This means that once charged, these batteries do not easily lose their charge when there is no electrical demand on them.

Low-maintenance and maintenance-free batteries also have each positive plate surrounded by a porous plastic envelope that is sealed on three sides and serves as a separator. This not only keeps the soft lead in place, but allows the plates to be completely lowered into the battery case, nearly doubling the amount of electrolyte above them. Because of these features, it is not necessary to add water to a low-maintenance battery. Filler caps are not even installed on many models.

Battery Operation

Chemical reactions take place in a battery whenever current flows from it. These reactions cause changes in the active materials in the battery, and cause the battery to "discharge." This process can be

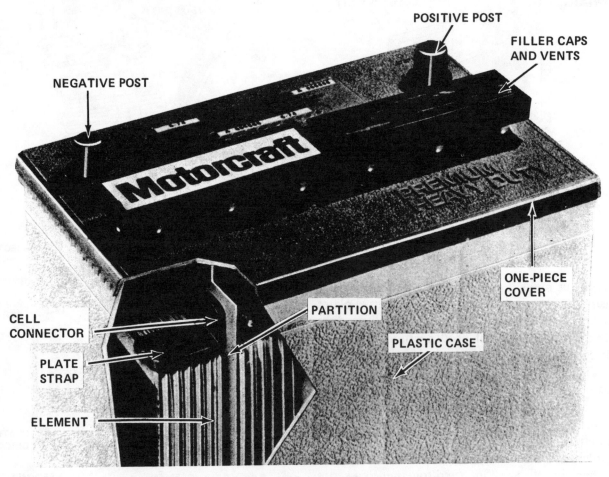

Figure 7-17. *Cutaway view of a battery. (Courtesy of Ford Motor Company, Dearborn)*

reversed by **charging** the battery with electricity to cause a "reversed current" through the battery. This reversed current reverses the chemical reactions and restores the battery chemistry. An automobile battery is often called a **storage battery** because of the way it can be charged and have its chemical action restored. Battery service procedures are covered in Chapter 11.

FACTS TO REMEMBER

A storage battery produces electricity through a chemical reaction. This chemical reaction can be reversed by charging the battery. A twelve-volt battery is made up of six, two-volt cells.

□ ASSIGNMENT 7-F □

1. What is the purpose of an automobile battery?
2. What materials are the following battery parts made of:

   positive plate   electrolyte
   negative plate   separator

3. Describe a battery cell.
4. What is the purpose of plate bridges?
5. What is the purpose of sediment chambers?
6. What are cell connectors?
7. What are battery terminals?

□ SELF-TEST □

Complete the following sentences by filling in the missing words.

1. Electron theory states that the observed results of electricity are produced by a _____ of electricity through an electrical _____ . These electrons flow from the _____ to the _____ side of the electrical supply.
2. An insulator is a material that contains _____ that do not easily _____ from atom to atom.
3. Voltage is considered electrical _____ .
4. The unit of measurement for voltage is the _____ , measured with a _____.
5. Current is the flow of _____ that results from the electrical _____ or pressure (voltage).
6. The unit of measurement for electrical current is the _____.
7. Resistance is anything that _____ the _____ of electrons in an electrical _____ .
8. Magnetizable metal can be magnetized using a _____ magnet or an _____ .
9. An electromagnet is a conductor with an electric _____ flowing through it that produces a magnetic _____.
10. If the flow of electricity through a winding is reversed, the magnetic polarity _____ .
11. Alternators and generators use electromagnetic _____ to produce electricity while the car is running.
12. A lead-acid battery, such as an automobile battery, produces electricity through a _____ reaction.
13. Should any pair of negative and positive plates in a battery cell touch, the whole cell would be _____ _____.
14. Chemical _____ take place in a battery whenever _____ flows from it.

ELECTRICAL CIRCUITS AND METERS

☐   LEARNING OBJECTIVES   ☐

After studying this chapter, you will be able to:

1. Describe electron flow through an electrical circuit.
2. List the characteristics of a simple circuit, a series circuit, and a parallel circuit.
3. Describe leakage, open circuits, short circuits, and excess resistance in a circuit.
4. Describe the care and use of a voltmeter, an ammeter, and an ohmmeter.
5. Define and/or discuss the following terms:

simple circuit	excess resistance
series circuit	leakage
parallel circuit	voltmeter
open circuit	ammeter
short circuit	ohmmeter
grounded circuit	

INTRODUCTION

You should now be familiar with the basics of electricity, voltage, current, and resistance. In order to deal with automotive electrical system problems, it is necessary to have a thorough understanding of electric circuits. Below is a list of facts about electric circuits. Study them carefully in order to understand how electrons move through an electrical circuit.

ELECTRICAL CIRCUITS

You will recall from Chapter 7 that an electrical circuit is a path through which electrons flow. All automobile electrical devices (such as motors, lights, horns, coils, spark plugs, etc.) are part of some type of electrical circuit. There are several things that you should know about electrical circuits and the behavior of electrons in a circuit.

1. An electrical circuit must provide a completed electrical path with a voltage applied to it before current will flow. In an automobile, this voltage is supplied by a battery or a magnetic device. A battery produces voltage by separating electrical charges through chemical reaction. Magnetic devices, such as alternators, generators, and transformers, produce voltage through electromagnetic induction.

2. The negative side of the source voltage has an excess of electrons in its atoms and, therefore, a negative charge.

3. The positive side of the source voltage has an absence of electrons in its atoms and, therefore, a positive charge.

4. Like-electrical charges repel each other, and unlike-electrical charges attract each other.

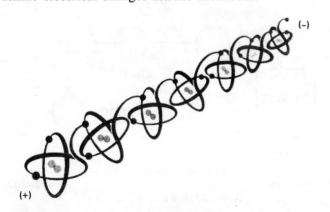

Figure 8-1.   Current flow is a stream of electrons from atom to atom. (Courtesy of Chrysler Corporation)

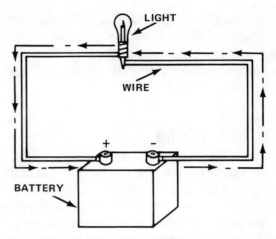

Figure 8-2.   Electrons move through the circuit from the negative to the positive pole.

5. When an atom loses an electron, its positively charged proton attracts negatively charged electrons from other nearby atoms. (Remember that unlike charges attract each other.)

ELECTRON MOVEMENT

At the negative side of a circuit, the accumulated electrons from the voltage source repel one another and crowd into the atoms in the circuit. As they do so, they collide with and repel free electrons from these atoms. Each atom that loses an electron is left with an extra proton, which attracts another electron to itself. These repulsions, collisions, and attractions of electrons proceed all of the way through the circuit in a kind of chain reaction.

The first electron that enters the circuit is not the first one to leave the other end of the circuit, but is part of a stream of electrons moving from atom to atom throughout the whole circuit, as shown in Figure 8-1. Note that the electron flow is from negative to positive. At the positive end of the circuit, the protons in the source voltage are attracting electrons. See Figure 8-2.

TYPES OF ELECTRICAL CIRCUITS

An **electrical circuit** is the complete path through which electrons move (current flows) from the source, through the circuit, and back again to the source.

Electrical devices can be designed to be connected into electrical circuits in many different ways. The most common automobile circuits are discussed below.

Simple Circuit

A **simple circuit** is a circuit that has only one electrical device in it. The wiring and switch, if one is used, are also part of the circuit. Many simple circuits are used in automobiles. The dome light, map light, or glove box light are all connected in simple circuits.

Simple Circuit Characteristics

A simple circuit has:

1. One source of electrical voltage.
2. One complete electrical path.
3. One electrical load or device (resistance).

The diagrams in Figure 8-3 are simple circuits. The circuit in View A shows a wire from the **source** (battery) to the **load** (an electrical device such as a lamp) and a wire from the load back to the source. In View B, a **ground return** from the load back to the source has been added. In an automobile, the battery is **grounded** (connected) to the automobile frame. The load (electrical device) is also grounded to the frame. The automobile frame and body replace the

return wire, as shown in View B. A switch is often used to turn off the electrical device in a circuit. View C shows that the switch can be put on either side of the load, depending on the circuit design.

The resistance of the load in the circuit determines the amount of current that can flow through the circuit from the source. If a load of higher resistance is installed in the circuit, the current flow in the circuit decreases. If, on the other hand, a load of lower resistance is put in the circuit, load resistance decreases and current flow increases. If the load resistance is left the same and the circuit voltage is increased, the current through the load increases. Decreased voltage will decrease the current through the load. Notice that current flow changes with a change in either circuit voltage or circuit resistance.

Series Circuit

A **series circuit** has two or more electrical devices (series of resistances) connected in one electrical path, as shown in Figure 8-4.

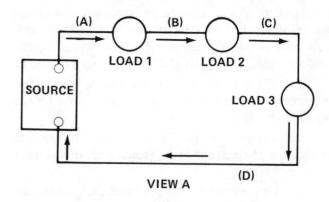

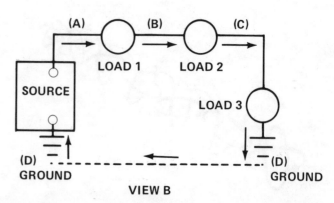

Figure 8-4. *A series circuit with a wire return (View A), and a frame ground (View B).*

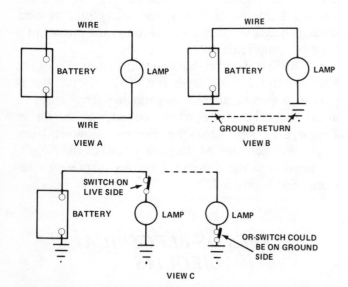

Figure 8-3. *A simple circuit with a wire return (View A), a frame-grounded return (View B), and switch (View C).*

Series Circuit Characteristics

A series circuit has several characteristics:

1. One source of voltage.

2. One path for current flow.

3. Two or more loads.

4. Total circuit resistance equals the sum of all the load resistances in the circuit.

5. Voltage drop in the separate loads is different if the resistance values of the loads are different, but the same if the resistance values of the loads are equal. **Voltage drop** is the amount of voltage used by a device in an electrical circuit.

6. Total voltage (supply voltage) in the circuit is the sum of the voltage drops at the loads.

7. Current flow is the same in all parts of the circuit.

To make the series circuit shown in Figure 8-4 easier to understand, we will ignore electrical polarity and assume that the current flows through the top wire and returns through the bottom one. In View A, the voltage from the source (battery) causes current to flow through connecting wire (a) and through Load 1. Load 1 resists the current flow a certain amount, causing a certain amount of voltage drop. The current then flows through wire (b) and through Load 2. Load 2 further resists the current flow, causing a further voltage drop. Current flow then goes through wire (c) and through Load 3, which again resists the flow a certain amount, causing a final voltage drop. After Load 3, the current flows through the connecting return wire (d) back to the source. This completes the electrical path. The total resistance of three loads determines the amount of current flow in the circuit. In View B, the wire (d) has been removed and the battery return side has been connected to the automobile's frame. Load 3 is also grounded to the metal frame. This completes the circuit, and the current flow returns through the frame.

Each load in a series circuit uses a certain amount of the source voltage. If the resistance values of the loads are unequal, the voltage drops on each load are unequal, because each load uses up a different amount of the source voltage. If the resistance values of the loads are all the same (like a series of the same size and voltage lights), then the load voltage drops are equal at each load, since each load uses up an equal amount of the source voltage. *If one electrical device in a series circuit burns out, the circuit becomes open and all the devices stop working.*

☐ ASSIGNMENT 8-A ☐

1. Draw a simple circuit.
2. Describe the characteristics of a series circuit.

Parallel Circuit

Parallel circuits have more than one path for current flow. The parallel circuit has two or more connected loads. Each load has a separate electrical path, but each uses a common supply voltage. Parallel circuits have several identifying characteristics.

Parallel Circuit Characteristics

1. One source of voltage.

2. Two or more paths for current flow.

3. Two or more loads.

4. The current can be the same or different in each path. Equal loads will produce current that is equal in each path. Unequal loads will produce current that is different in each path.

5. Total current is the amount of current sent from the supply (battery, generator, etc.) and is equal to the sum of the current flow through each path.

6. The voltage across any load is the same as the source or supply voltage.

7. Total circuit resistance is less than the lowest single load resistance.

Figure 8-5 shows how a parallel circuit functions. As shown in View A, the source voltage causes current to flow through the top wire (a) where it divides at the wire to the lamp. Some current flows through the wire and the lamp. The amount of current that flows through the lamp is determined by the resistance of the lamp. This current passes from the lamp into the bottom wire (b) to return to the source.

The remaining current (total current minus the current that went to the lamp) flows further along wire (a) where it divides at the wire to the resistor. Some current flows through the wire and the resistor. The amount of current that flows through the resistor depends on the resistance value of the resistor. This current passes through the resistor into the bottom wire (b) to return to the source.

The remainder of the current (total current

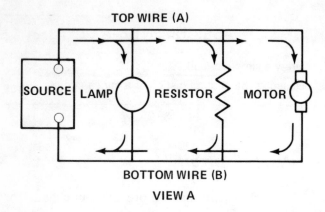

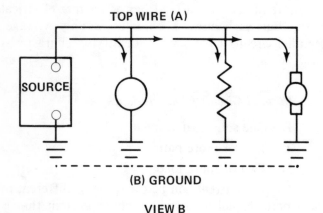

Figure 8-5.   A parallel circuit with a wire return (View A) and a frame ground (View B).

minus what the lamp and the resistor used) flows further along wire (a) where it goes into the motor. The amount of current used in the motor depends on the resistance of the motor. This current passes through the motor and into the bottom wire (b) to return to the source.

If one electrical device in a parallel circuit burns out, the other devices in the circuit are not affected and will continue to operate. In View B, the loads have been connected to the metal frame (grounded). The source is also grounded to the metal frame. The current from each unit returns to the source through this ground.

☐ ASSIGNMENT 8-B ☐

1. Draw a parallel circuit.
2. Why would it be a good idea to use a parallel circuit rather than a series circuit in a circuit that contained the parking lights, turn lights, and brake lights?

FACTS TO REMEMBER

An electrical circuit is the complete path through which current flows from the source, through the circuit, and back to the source. The amount of current that flows through a circuit depends on the amount of voltage supplied to the circuit and the amount of resistance in the circuit. Circuits can be simple, series, or parallel.

CIRCUIT PROBLEMS

Occasionally, a mechanic has to trace a circuit to find an electrical problem. Every electrical problem is different, but there are some common electrical problems that we can discuss here.

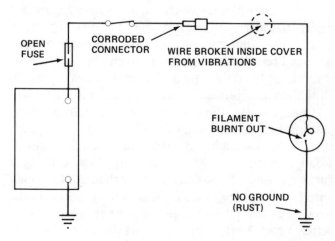

Figure 8-6.   Open circuits. Not all of these examples would occur at the same time.

Open Circuit

An **open circuit** is a break or an open area in the electrical path. Open circuits prevent current from flowing through the circuit. When the switch in a circuit is off, the circuit is open. As shown in Figure 8-6, a number of things can cause an open circuit. Some of these are: a broken wire inside an insulation cover, a badly corroded connector, a burned-out bulb, a rusty or corroded light socket that prevents a good ground connection, a loose connection, or a blown (overheated and open) fuse. When a circuit is open, no current will flow through it.

Short Circuits and Grounds

A short circuit means that there is a short path for current to flow between the two ends of the electrical circuit. It is often difficult to tell the difference between a short circuit and a ground. An example of a short circuit and a ground is shown in Figure 8-7.

In a burnt motor winding, the current flows across the burnt wire coils instead of through them. The circuit is said to be **short circuited** or **shorted**. If the wire leading to a lamp or other electrical device is worn through and touching the metal anywhere on the vehicle, the circuit would be **grounded**. A shorted or grounded circuit will blow the fuse in the circuit. Therefore, if a fuse is blown, look for a short circuit or a ground. If no fuse was included in the circuit, the wires in the circuit could burn. Fuses protect a circuit by opening (blowing) and stopping current flow through the circuit before the circuit wires get hot enough to overheat and burn.

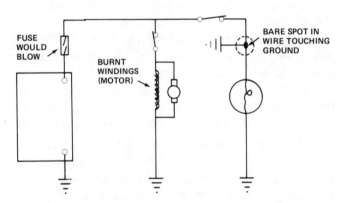

Figure 8-7. *Short circuits and grounded circuits.*

Resistance in a Circuit

All circuits have resistance. In fact, it is the resistance to electron flow through the electrical device in the circuit that causes the device to operate. The resistance of the filament in a light bulb causes the filament to glow and provide light. However, a circuit is faulty if it has excess (too much) resistance. Excess resistance reduces current flow through an electrical device. Excess resistance can be caused by corrosion on wires, connectors, or battery cables, as shown in Figure 8-8. Corrosion (or oxidation) causes electrical resistance between two contacting metals. This reduces the total current flow through the circuit. The effect of corrosion cannot be stressed too strongly.

A loose connection can also cause excess resistance. In a loose connection, electricity arcs across and burns the connection, creating excess resistance. This can cause lights to dim or go out and other types of electrical problems. If a loose connection is not repaired, electrical arcing will eventually burn the connector enough so that the circuit will become open.

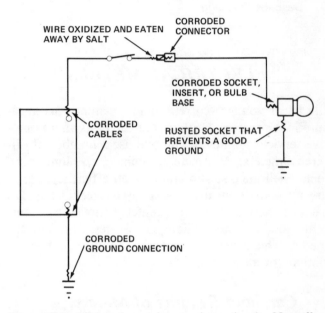

Figure 8-8. *Excessive resistance in a circuit. Not all of these examples would occur at the same time.*

Leakage

Leakage means that some electrical current is flowing even though all the electrical circuits are turned off (open). Leakage could cause a run-down battery. Examples of problems that cause leakage are:

1. A dirty or wet battery cover and case that allow current to pass between the two battery terminals.

2. An accumulation of dirt and road-salt corrosion around the terminals of electrical devices or on a connection assembly such as the fire-wall plugs.

3. Wires that have been in oil and dirt or water (road salt) and dirt for so long that their insulation is destroyed may have leakage.

4. High-voltage wires in the ignition system can have leakage when they are old, cracked, and dirty.

□ ASSIGNMENT 8-C □

1. What is meant by an open circuit?
2. What effect is produced by a short circuit?
3. What is the difference between a shorted and a grounded circuit?
4. What is meant by excess resistance in a circuit?
5. What will happen if there is excess resistance in a circuit?
6. Describe "leakage."

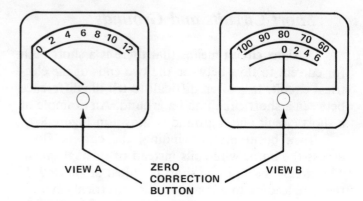

Figure 8-9. *Before you connect a meter for use, check the pointer for a zero reading. Turn the zero correction button to "zero" the meter.*

ELECTRICAL METERS

Electrical voltage, current, and resistance are measured with **meters**. During your career as an automotive service technician, you will use a number of different meters. Voltmeters, ammeters, ohmmeters, tach-dwell meters, and combustion-efficiency meters are all commonly used by a service technician. On each of these meters, the pointer is moved by a current flow of one milliampere or less through the meter. The general care and reading of meters is similar for all meters.

Care and Reading of Meters

1. If a meter is dirty, clean and dust it before you use it by wiping it with a soft cloth dampened with window cleaner. **A static charge** will collect on the glass as you rub it with a dry cloth. If you touch the glass with your fingers, static electricity from your body will transfer to the glass. Inaccurate meter readings can be caused by the static charge attracting the meter pointer. To remove the static charge, wipe the meter face with a damp cloth or use an antistatic spray designed for use on meters.

2. Meters must be **zeroed**. Meter needles should always point to zero when the meter is at rest (not being used to take a measurement). If a meter is used with the needle off zero at rest, it will be in error throughout the range of readings. To zero a meter, you have to observe the position of the pointer when the meter is at rest (while the meter is switched off or disconnected from the electrical source).

Figure 8-9 shows the position of the **zero correction button** on two meters. To adjust a left zeroing pointer (View A), turn the zero correction button right or left until the pointer is pointing to zero on the left side of the scale when the meter is at rest. To adjust a meter that zeros in the middle of the scale, turn the correction button left or right until the pointer is pointing to the zero in the middle of the scale.

3. On meters that operate from a battery, you should check the battery before you use the meter. The instruction book will tell you which position on the selector switch to use and if you should join the leads together when checking the battery. The test will cause the pointer to move all the way to the right hand side of the scale. Adjust the pointer to the last line on the right side of the scale by turning the control on the front of the meter. Ohmmeters and portable tach-dwell meters usually contain batteries.

4. Before connecting a meter to a circuit, be certain that you know how it should be connected and which scale to select on the selector switch. This knowledge will prevent meter damage. Read the instruction book and ask for assistance if you are uncertain about how to use the meter.

5. Take the time to study the scales on the meter. As shown in Figure 8-10, you should count the lines between the numbers and calculate the value per division. When there are ten divisions between single numbers, each division represents .1 or one-tenth of a unit that the meter is designed to measure (volts, ohms, amps, etc.). When there are five divisions between single numbers, each division represents .2 or two-tenths of a unit. When there are four divisions, each division represents .25 or one-quarter of a unit. When there are ten divisions between numbers by tens (10, 20, 30, etc.), each division is worth one. When there are five divisions between numbers by tens, each division is worth two. It will help you understand this system if you look at and count the divisions on several different meters.

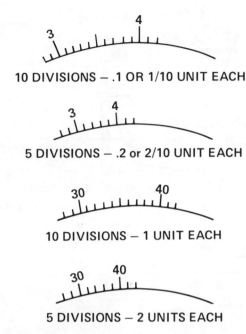

10 DIVISIONS – .1 OR 1/10 UNIT EACH

5 DIVISIONS – .2 or 2/10 UNIT EACH

10 DIVISIONS – 1 UNIT EACH

5 DIVISIONS – 2 UNITS EACH

Figure 8-10. *Study the meter face to learn the value of the divisions between the numbers.*

Voltmeter

A **voltmeter** is used to measure the electrical voltage (pressure) in a circuit. Voltmeters indicate the voltage applied to a point in the circuit. Voltmeters are designed to be connected in parallel with the device being checked.

A voltmeter can be a self-contained unit, be a section of an Amps-Volts Tester, as shown in Figure 8-11, or be a selected scale on a **multimeter** (a meter that has several functions). Be sure to select a high enough scale on the scale selector knob before connecting a voltmeter to a voltage source. This will prevent damage to the meter. To use the meter, you must connect the meter test clips to the circuit from which you want to take a voltage test. The red test clip, which is positive (+), must be connected to the positive side of the voltage. The black test clip, which is negative (−), must be connected to the negative side of the voltage.

If you do not know the polarity of the circuit, the voltmeter can determine it for you. The meter will register **downscale** (backward) if the clips are connected backward. If you reverse the test clips, the meter will register correctly. Figure 8-12 shows a voltmeter test for available voltage. Since the battery is negatively grounded, the black (−) test clip is connected to the ground, and the red (+) test clip is connected to the battery's positive post.

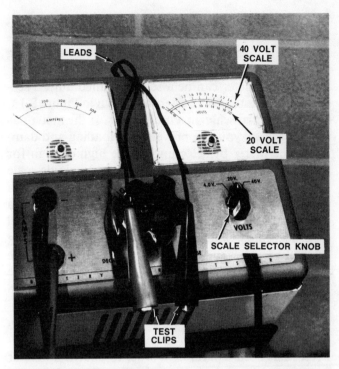

Figure 8-11. *This voltmeter is part of an Amps-Volts Tester. (Courtesy of Ford Motor Company, Dearborn)*

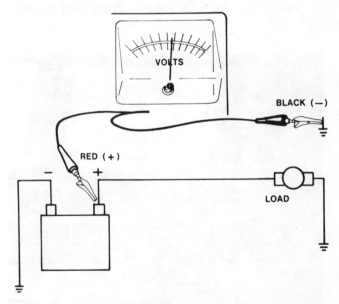

Figure 8-12. *Testing for available voltage. (Courtesy of Ford Motor Company, Dearborn)*

Ammeter

An ammeter is used to measure the amount of current flowing in an electrical circuit and indicates this flow in amperes. Ammeters are designed to be connected in series with the device being checked. When in use, the ammeter becomes part of the electrical circuit. It carries and measures the current flowing to the device.

An ammeter can be a self-contained unit, a section of an Amps-Volt Tester, as shown in Figure 8-13, or be a selected scale on a multimeter. If the meter has several scales, you can prevent overloading and damaging the meter by selecting a scale high enough for the estimated current. If you are using a single-scale meter, be certain the meter has a scale that is high enough for the estimated current. Use a meter with a low scale to measure a small current flow. This will give accurate readings. Use a high enough reading meter for heavy current flow to avoid damaging the meter. On a multiscale meter, you would use the 100-amp scale for alternator tests, but the 500-amp scale for battery and starter tests.

Figure 8-14 shows how to check current flow through a circuit with an ammeter. Notice that a connector has been separated in order to put the ammeter in series in the circuit. Since the negative (−) post of the battery is grounded, the red (+) test clip is connected to the battery side of the connector and the black (−) test clip is connected to the wire going to the lamp. The meter is actually connected in series

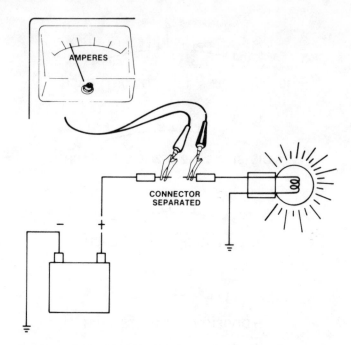

Figure 8-14. *An ammeter connected to measure current flow. (Courtesy of Ford Motor Company, Dearborn)*

with the lamp and will carry and measure the current flowing to the lamp.

When using an ammeter that has an **inductive amps pickup**, it is not necessary to separate the connector to connect the meter in series into the circuit. You can simply place the clamp-on amps pickup over the wire that you are measuring for current flow. Figure 8-15 shows an ammeter with inductive amps pickup connected to the battery ground wire for testing starting and charging systems. When it is clamped in place, the amps pickup will circle the wire

Figure 8-13. *The ammeter shown is part of an Amps-Volts Tester. (Courtesy of Ford Motor Company, Dearborn)*

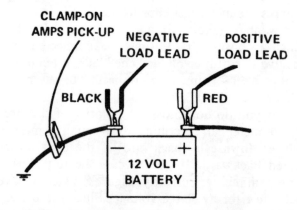

Figure 8-15. *An ammeter with an inductive amps pickup. The clamp-on amps pickup is clamped over the wire to measure the current in the wire.*

with a magnetized iron frame. A winding is wound on this frame. As current flows through the wire, the magnetic field that surrounds the wire induces a small voltage signal into the winding. A circuit in the meter translates this induced voltage into an ampere reading on the meter face.

Ohmmeter

An **ohmmeter** is used to measure the amount of ohms of resistance in a circuit or electrical device. Ohmmeters are designed with their own internal batteries and can be seriously damaged if they are connected to a live circuit. Therefore, the circuit or device being tested must always be disconnected from the voltage supply. When you are using an ohmmeter, always disconnect the ground battery cable before beginning the test, or remove the electrical supply wires from the device you are checking.

To use an ohmmeter, or a multimeter that contains an ohmmeter, you must first zero the pointer and then calibrate the meter. To do this, select a suitable ohms scale on the scale selector knob, as shown in Figure 8-16. Then, join the test clips together and adjust the calibrator knob until the pointer points to the set line, or to the full-scale reading. This must be repeated each time you select a different scale.

Figure 8-17 shows how you would check the resistance of an ignition coil primary winding. This

winding will have a low amount of resistance (1 to 3 ohms). Place the scale selector at x1, join the test clips, calibrate the meter, and connect the test clips to the coil primary terminals. Take a reading directly from the scale.

Figure 8-18 shows how you would check the resistance of an ignition coil secondary winding. The

Figure 8-17. Checking the resistance of an ignition coil primary winding. (Courtesy of Suntester Equipment [Central] Limited)

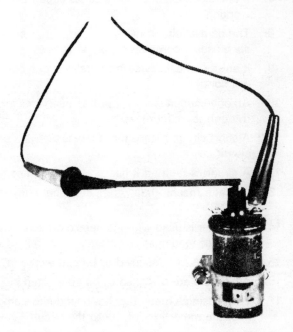

Figure 8-18. Checking the resistance of an ignition coil secondary winding. (Courtesy of Suntester Equipment [Central] Limited)

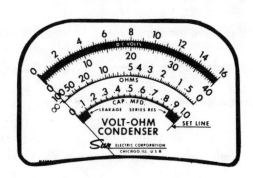

Figure 8-16. A multitester that contains an ohmmeter. (Courtesy of Suntester Equipment [Central] Limited)

secondary winding will have a high amount of resistance (7,000 to 15,000 ohms). Place the scale selector at x1000, join the test clips, and calibrate the meter again. Then connect one test clip to a primary terminal and the other to the coil tower terminal, using a suitable probe. Take a reading and multiply it by 1000 (a reading of 7 on the x1000 scale would be a reading of 7000 ohms).

FACTS TO REMEMBER

Meters are delicate, sensitive instruments. They must be kept clean and used properly. The three electrical meters that an automobile repairman uses most often are the voltmeter, ammeter, and ohmmeter. Each of these meters must be zeroed before it can be used in order to get accurate readings.

☐ ASSIGNMENT 8-D ☐

1. Describe how you would clean a meter.
2. What is meant by "zeroing" a meter?
3. Explain how you would use a voltmeter, ammeter, and ohmmeter.
4. What special precautions should you take when using an ohmmeter?

☐ SELF-TEST ☐

Complete the following sentences by filling in the missing words.

1. The negative side of the source voltage has an _____ of electrons in its atoms.
2. The positive side of the source voltage has an _____ of electrons in its atoms.
3. An electrical circuit is the complete _____ through which electrons move from the _____ , through the _____ , and back again to the source.
4. A simple circuit is a circuit that has only _____ electrical _____in it.
5. Current flow (in a simple circuit) changes with a change in either circuit _____ or circuit _____.
6. A series circuit has _____ or more electrical devices connected in _____ electrical path.
7. If one electrical device in a series circuit burns out, the circuit becomes _____ , and all the devices _____ working.
8. The parallel circuit has _____ or _____ connected loads. Each load has a separate electrical _____, but each uses a common supply voltage.
9. If one electrical device in a parallel circuit burns out, the other devices in the circuit are _____ affected and will continue to _____.
10. An open circuit is a _____ or an open area in the electrical path. Open circuits prevent _____ from flowing through the circuit.
11. A short circuit means that there is a _____ path for _____ to flow between the two ends of the electrical circuit.
12. A circuit is faulty if it has _____ resistance.
13. Leakage means that _____ electrical current is _____ even though all the electrical circuits are turned _____ .
14. If a meter is used with the needle off zero when the meter is at _____, it will be in _____ throughout the _____ of readings.
15. Voltmeters are designed to be connected in _____ with the device being checked.
16. Ammeters are designed to be connected in _____ with the device being checked.
17. When using a meter that has an inductive amps pickup, it is not necessary to _____ the connector to connect the meter in _____ into the circuit.
18. When you are using an ohmmeter, always disconnect the _____ battery cable before beginning the test, or _____ the electrical supply wires from the device you are checking.

9

IGNITION SYSTEM FUNDAMENTALS

□   LEARNING OBJECTIVES   □

After studying this chapter, you will be able to:

1. List the ignition parts in the primary and secondary circuits.
2. Explain the purpose of the ignition condenser.
3. Describe the operation of the complete ignition system in the production of the ignition sparks.
4. Explain the purpose of a ballast resistor.
5. Explain the relationship between point gap, dwell angle, and initial timing.
6. Define and/or discuss the following terms:

ignition system	ballast resistor
primary circuit	distributor cap
secondary circuit	spark plugs
ignition coil	point gap
condenser	dwell angle
breaker points	

INTRODUCTION

Internal-combustion engine operation depends on a cycle of events that deliver a combustible air-fuel mixture and a precisely timed high-voltage spark to the engine cylinders. The spark has enough heat to ignite the air-fuel mixture. It causes the mixture to burn very rapidly and release the energy necessary to drive the piston down and turn the crankshaft. The **ignition system** components work together to raise the low battery voltage to the very high voltage (up to 35,000 volts if required) needed to produce this spark.

We are now familiar with fuel system operation and service. With our knowledge of electricity and electrical circuits, we can now consider ignition system design and operation and the cycle of events that produce the ignition spark.

IGNITION SYSTEMS

The ignition system is actually two circuits that are common only in the ignition coil. These are the primary circuit and the secondary circuit. Figure 9-1 shows a complete ignition system.

Primary Circuit: The **primary circuit** is the **low-voltage** or battery side of the system. See Figure 9-2. The primary circuit contains the:

1. battery (the source of electricity);
2. ignition switch (a device to turn the system on or off);
3. primary wiring (16 or 18 gauge, lightly insulated wire that connects the parts together);
4. ballast resistor (to help regulate current flow in the primary circuit);
5. ignition coil primary winding;
6. distributor points and condenser; and
7. ground return circuit, back to the battery.

Secondary Circuit: The **secondary circuit** is the **high-voltage** or high-tension side of the system. See Figure 9-3. The secondary circuit contains the:

1. ignition coil secondary winding (the source of electricity for the secondary system);
2. distributor cap and rotor;
3. special high-tension, heavily insulated wires that

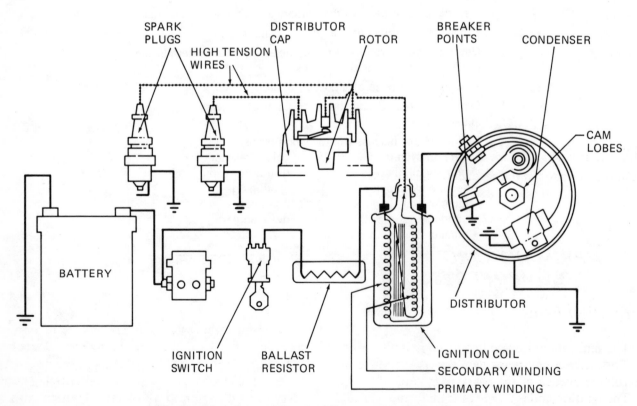

Figure 9-1. A complete ignition system. (Courtesy of Echlin, Limited)

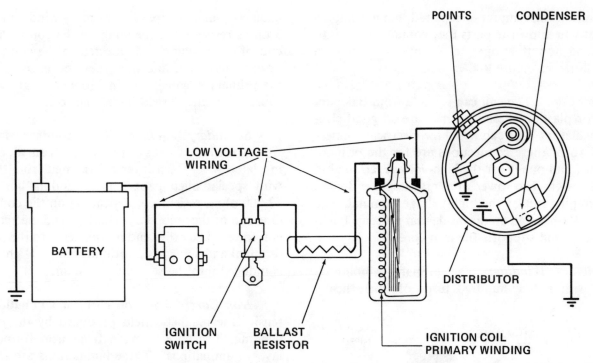

Figure 9-2. *The primary circuit. (Courtesy of Echlin, Limited)*

connect the ignition coil, distributor cap, and spark plugs;

4. spark plugs; and

5. ground return, back to the ignition coil secondary winding.

☐ ASSIGNMENT 9-A ☐

1. List the seven parts in the primary ignition circuit.

2. List the five parts in the secondary ignition circuit.

PRIMARY CIRCUIT COMPONENTS

Ignition Coils

The ignition coil is the heart of the ignition system. The other components help the coil produce the high voltage needed at the spark plug gap.

The ignition coil is a type of transformer called a **pulse transformer** or an **induction coil**. It works on pulses of direct current. **Pulses** are current flow that is

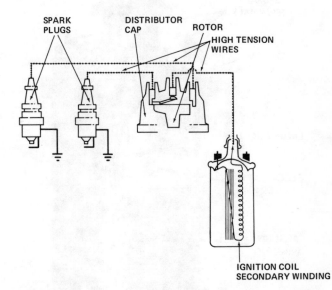

Figure 9-3. *The secondary circuit. (Courtesy of Echlin, Limited)*

interrupted. **Direct current** (DC) flows in only one direction and is supplied by the battery. Some types of transformers work on alternating current (AC), such as the electricity in a house. **Alternating current** reverses its direction at a fast rate. Ignition coils and transformers produce voltage by electromagnetic induction.

Ignition coils cannot be repaired, but it is important that you know the parts they contain in order to understand how they operate. A cutaway view of a coil is shown in Figure 9-4.

Coil Cap: The **coil cap** is made from Bakelite, epoxy, or plastic. These materials are all good electrical insulators. The cap has three electrical connections. Two of these connections are for the primary terminals, and one is for the high-voltage terminal in the coil tower. The tower prevents flashover sparks from jumping out of the high-voltage terminal. The cap has a flash shield on the inside that prevents flashover sparks and supports the iron core.

Primary Winding: The **primary winding** is wound with a few hundred turns of fairly heavy

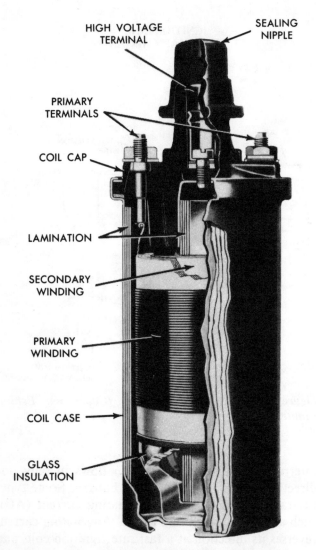

Figure 9-4. *A cutaway view of an ignition coil. (Courtesy of General Motors of Canada Limited)*

enamel-insulated wire. The primary winding has 1 to 3 ohms resistance, depending on the coil make. One end of the winding is connected to the coil primary positive terminal, and the other end is connected to the primary negative terminal. The primary winding causes a magnetic field inside the coil.

Secondary Winding: The **secondary winding** is wound with thousands of turns of very small, enamel-insulated wire. Each layer is insulated from the next with special oiled paper. This winding has 7,000–12,000 ohms resistance, depending on the coil make. One end of the secondary winding is connected to the coil tower. The other end is connected to the primary terminal and serves as a ground return. High voltage is induced into the secondary winding.

Iron Core: The **iron core**, or **laminations**, intensify the magnetic field produced by the primary winding. The core is made from iron formed into layers (laminations). These laminations are sensitive to magnetic change and reduce eddy currents that are induced in the iron core. **Eddy currents** cause heat that increases the resistance of the coil.

Iron Shield: The **iron shield** also intensifies the magnetic field in the coil. It is laminated like the iron core.

Glass Insulation: The **glass insulation** is cup shaped to support the laminations and the windings and to insulate the high voltage away from the case.

Coil Case: The **coil case** encloses all the parts in an air-tight container. The case is filled with hot oil and sealed. Oil is a good insulator and reduces high-voltage arcing inside the coil. Some coils are filled with tar instead of oil.

☐ ASSIGNMENT 9-B ☐

Describe the construction and purpose of the following ignition coil parts:

cap and tower	secondary winding
primary winding	iron core

Condensers

The **condenser** plays an important role in the operation of the ignition system. Without a condenser, the spark produced by the coil would be so weak that the engine would not operate. Moreover, in a short time the breaker points would burn because of the arcing that would occur between them. Proper condenser operation is vital.

Condenser Construction

A condenser may also be called a **capacitor**. As shown in Figure 9-5, in its most basic form, a condenser could be constructed from two thin, flat metal plates. The plates would be located next to each other, but separated by an insulator called a **dielectric**. In the simple condenser shown in Figure 9-5, air serves as the dielectric.

The type of condensers used in an automobile, as shown in Figure 9-6, are constructed from two sheets of metal foil, separated by a very thin, oiled paper. The paper serves as the dielectric. The foil and paper are rolled together. This allows both surfaces of the foils to be used in making the condenser work. Because the foils and paper are rolled, the condenser has a large capacity, but a small physical size. The two foils are rolled slightly off center to each other so that one edge of one foil is exposed at one end of the roll, and one edge of the other foil is exposed at the opposite end of the roll. The foils cannot touch each other because of the paper insulation that separates them.

On automotive condensers, one end of the roll contacts on a wavy washer spring in the bottom of the

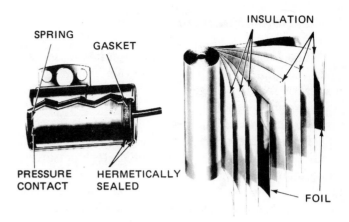

Figure 9-6. Condenser construction. (Courtesy of General Motors of Canada Limited)

condenser can. A contact disc from the condenser wire touches the other end of the roll. The top of the can, which is crimped over, seals on the insulating washer and completes the construction. The spring washer keeps tension on the roll to ensure a good electrical contact. The can contacts one foil, and the wire contacts the other foil. The condenser must be firmly fastened in place to ensure a good electrical connection to ground.

Condenser Operation

There is no electrical path through a condenser. The condenser blocks the flow of electricity between the foils, but allows electrons to enter and leave them. To put that in electrical terms, the condenser can become charged and discharged. The word **charged** means that the condenser has been filled with electrical energy. **Discharged** means that the electrical energy has been allowed to leave the condenser. Remember that electricity never actually passes through from one foil to the other because the foils are separated by the oiled paper dielectric.

Condenser Capacity

As a reference regarding condenser capacity, a **one farad** condenser will take in one **coulomb** of electrical energy if one volt is applied to it. One coulomb equals 6.24×10^{18} (over six trillion electrons). All condensers are given a value related to the farad. It is extremely important that the correct-capacity condenser be installed on a vehicle.

The breaker points and the condenser work together to produce the ignition sparks. Their close association will be discussed in this chapter.

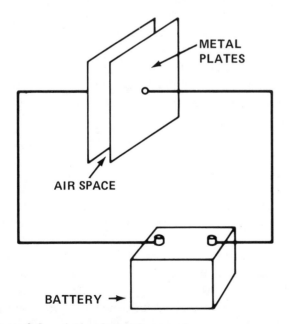

Figure 9-5. A simple condenser.

Breaker Point Set

The **breaker points** or **contact points** close and open the ignition circuit, forming the current pulses necessary for high-voltage induction in the ignition coil secondary winding.

As shown in Figure 9-7, the breaker point contact surfaces are made from **tungsten** (a very hard metal able to withstand extremely high temperatures). Tungsten resists wear, heat, and metal transfer. It is a good conductor and lasts longer than softer metals. The **rubbing block** may be made from fiber or nylon. It must withstand the friction from the point opening cam that rubs against it to open the points. The **contact lever** or arm is made from a light, strong, thin steel and has a bushing as a pivot point. It also has a flat **spring arm** that forces the points to close quickly and keeps the tension on them. The **stationary arm** is made from soft steel and can be bent for alignment purposes.

□   ASSIGNMENT 9–C   □

1. Describe the internal construction of a condenser.
2. Explain the purpose of the breaker points.
3. Describe the type of material used in breaker points and the reason for using it.

Ballast Resistor

The **ballast resistor** is connected in series with the ignition coil primary windings and helps regulate current flow in the ignition primary circuit. The ballast resistor on some vehicles is a **resistance wire** mounted in a ceramic block that is bolted to the fire wall or to the coil. Other vehicles use a ballast resistor that is a length of resistance wire covered with asbestos. This wire is located with the other wires in the wiring harness.

The ignition coil only has enough windings to use approximately nine volts of electricity from the battery. Most batteries produce twelve volts of electricity. The ballast resistor, wired in series with the ignition coil, uses the remaining voltage. Certain cars do not have a separate ballast resistor. In these cars, either the ignition coil has enough windings to operate on the full-battery voltage, or the ballast resistor is

built into the coil. Ballast resistors come in a number of values. Some examples are 1.35 ohms resistance for Ford, 1.82 for G.M., and .56 for Chrysler products.

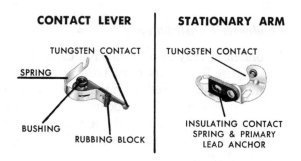

Figure 9-7. Contact point construction. (Courtesy of General Motors of Canada Limited)

SECONDARY CIRCUIT COMPONENTS

Up to this point, we have dealt with the ignition coil and the parts in the primary circuit. We can now study the secondary circuit components before discussing the overall operation of the ignition system.

Secondary Wiring

Secondary wiring carries very high voltages. Secondary wires have a thick covering of good-quality insulation to prevent high-voltage sparks from arcing through to ground, or across from one wire to another. The secondary wiring carries the secondary voltage and current from the ignition coil to the distributor cap and rotor, and from the distributor cap to each spark plug.

Spark Plugs

Spark plug types, construction, heat range, and service will be covered in Chapter 10. **Spark plugs** insulate the high voltage from grounding, and direct it to a **gap** between two **electrodes** on the spark plug. The **insulator** is a piece of ceramic material that extends from the top of the plug to the inside tip, or **core nose**. The insulator can withstand high combustion temperatures. The center electrode is inside the core nose. There is a space, or gap, between the center electrode and the ground electrode fastened to the plug's metal body. The high voltage in the secondary circuit causes a spark to jump across this gap.

Distributor Cap and Rotor

The **distributor cap and rotor** are made from insulating materials such as Bakelite, plastic, or epoxy that are easily molded to the required shapes. Figure 9-8 shows an eight-cylinder engine distributor cap and rotor. The top picture shows the **towers** into which the secondary wires (high-tension cables) are inserted. The towers prevent the high voltage from jumping between the wires. The bottom picture shows the **contacts** that receive voltage from the rotor's metal strip and **finger**.

Figure 9-9 shows how the rotor and cap distribute the secondary high voltage. Read the steps on the illustration and the information below to understand this process.

1. The coil tower (center tower on the distributor cap) receives high voltage from the coil through the coil high-tension cable.

INSULATED TOWERS
PREVENT FLASHOVER

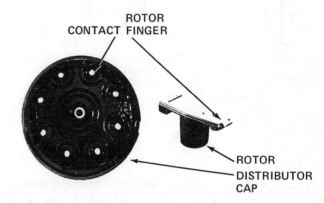

ROTOR
CONTACT FINGER

ROTOR

DISTRIBUTOR
CAP

Figure 9-8. *A distributor cap and rotor. (Courtesy of Ford Motor Company, Dearborn)*

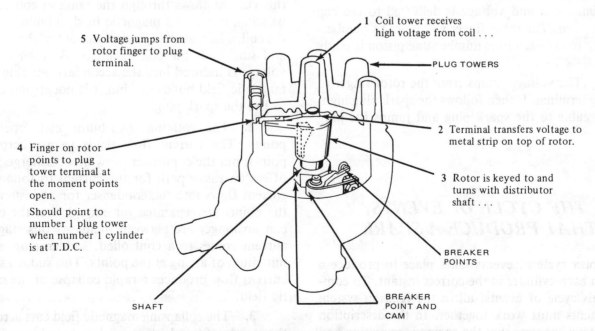

5 Voltage jumps from rotor finger to plug terminal.

1 Coil tower receives high voltage from coil . . .

PLUG TOWERS

4 Finger on rotor points to plug tower terminal at the moment points open.

Should point to number 1 plug tower when number 1 cylinder is at T.D.C.

2 Terminal transfers voltage to metal strip on top of rotor.

3 Rotor is keyed to and turns with distributor shaft . . .

BREAKER POINTS

SHAFT

BREAKER POINT AND CAM

Figure 9-9. *The distributor cap and rotor work together to distribute the high voltage to each cylinder. (Courtesy of Ford Motor Company, Dearborn)*

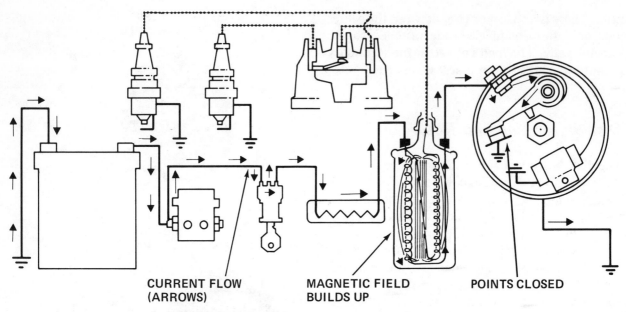

CURRENT FLOW   **MAGNETIC FIELD**   **POINTS CLOSED**
(ARROWS)   **BUILDS UP**

Figure 9-10. Current flow in the primary circuit.
(Courtesy of Echlin, Limited)

2. A terminal below the center tower, generally made of carbon, transfers the voltage to the metal strip on the top of the rotor.

3. The rotor is keyed to and turns with the distributor shaft.

4. The rotating finger or tip on the rotor points to a plug tower terminal at the precise moment that the points open and voltage is delivered to the cap from the coil. The rotor finger will point to number-one plug tower each time number-one piston is ready to fire.

5. The voltage jumps from the rotor finger to the plug terminal. It then follows the spark plug high-tension cable to the spark plug and jumps the plug gap.

THE CYCLE OF EVENTS THAT PRODUCE A SPARK

A complex cycle of events takes place to produce a spark in each cylinder at the correct instant. To complete this cycle of events, all of the ignition system components must work together. In the description that follows, assume that the engine is operating and we are viewing the cycle during the instant required to produce one spark for one cylinder.

1. The distributor cam rotates, the breaker points close, and a current flows through the primary circuit. As shown by the arrows in Figure 9-10, the current flows from the battery, through the ignition switch, the ballast resistor, the coil primary winding, and through the breaker points to ground. The current returns through the ground to the battery. As this current flows through the ignition coil primary winding, it causes a magnetic field to build up inside the coil. The magnetic field passes out of the iron core and surrounds the coil windings. A small surge of voltage is induced into the secondary winding as the magnetic field builds up, but it is not strong enough to fire the spark plug.

2. The rotating distributor cam opens the points. The current flow tends to arc across the points, but the condenser (now in a discharged state) offers an easier path for the current to follow. The current flows into the condenser for an instant until the points are separated far enough that the current can no longer arc between them. At this stage, the current comes to a controlled, sudden stop, with a minimum of arcing at the points. This sudden stop of current flow produces a rapid collapse of the magnetic field.

3. The collapsing magnetic field cuts across the thousands of conductors in the secondary winding. This induces voltage in each turn of wire in the winding. The total effect is that a very high voltage is produced in the coil. This is called **mutual induction**. As shown by the arrows in Figure 9-11, the high voltage causes current to flow from the secondary winding, through the coil tower, into the coil wire. From the coil wire it flows into the distributor cap center tower and to the rotor. At this instant, the rotor is in line with one cap cylinder tower and plug wire, permitting the current to flow to one spark plug where it jumps the gap between the spark plug electrodes. As the current jumps this gap, it causes a spark that ignites the air-fuel mixture in the cylinder.

4. The collapsing magnetic field cuts across the conductors in the primary winding (at the same instant as it cuts across the secondary winding) and induces a voltage in the primary winding. This is called **self-induction**. The voltage can be 250 volts or more. This voltage tries to keep current flowing in the winding. The condenser absorbs this voltage (becomes more charged) and prevents arcing across the point gap.

5. The self-induced voltage is present only as the magnetic field collapses. When the field has completely collapsed, the charge in the condenser discharges out of the condenser through the primary winding. This produces a magnetic field for an instant (in reverse) in the coil and causes another surge of voltage in the secondary and the primary circuits. This

surge produces another condenser charge and discharge (in the opposite direction). These voltage surges continue back and forth for from five to seven times. The voltage decreases with each new surge. These repeated surges are called **coil-condenser oscillations** and can be observed on an ignition oscilloscope.

6. The points close again, and the next cycle of events begins.

FACTS TO REMEMBER

From the sequence of events described above, you can see that the condenser is an important part of the ignition system. The condenser (1) reduces arcing at the breaker points, giving them longer life; (2) causes a rapid stopping of the current, producing a fast collapse of the magnetic field; and (3) absorbs the self-induced voltage in the primary circuit.

Breaker Point Wear

The condenser also keeps the breaker point contact surfaces smooth and level. This helps them maintain a clean, gray color and a long, trouble-free life. A condenser that is the wrong capacity can cause

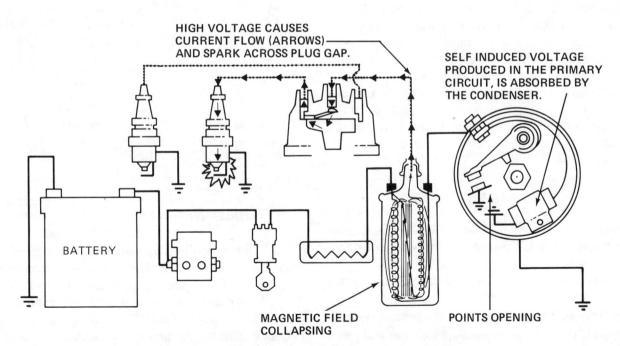

HIGH VOLTAGE CAUSES
CURRENT FLOW (ARROWS)
AND SPARK ACROSS PLUG GAP.

SELF INDUCED VOLTAGE
PRODUCED IN THE PRIMARY
CIRCUIT, IS ABSORBED BY
THE CONDENSER.

BATTERY

MAGNETIC FIELD
COLLAPSING

POINTS OPENING

Figure 9-11. Voltage and current flow in the secondary circuit. Self-induced voltage in the primary circuit. (Courtesy of Echlin, Limited)

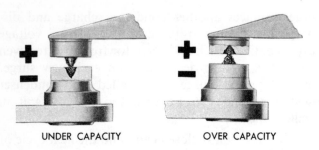

UNDER CAPACITY   OVER CAPACITY

Figure 9-12. The condenser must be the correct type and capacity, or the points will become pitted. (Courtesy of General Motors of Canada Limited)

uneven metal transfer. This will result in a buildup of metal on one point and a matching hole in the other. Figure 9-12 shows that, on a negative ground system, the buildup is on the stationary point if the condenser is over capacity. The buildup would be on the moving point if the condenser were under capacity. Different capacity condensers are used by different car manufacturers. Make sure that the condenser used in a vehicle is the proper one for that vehicle. Each type of condenser has a certain range of acceptable capacity.

There are other causes of uneven breaker point wear. If you connect a radio interference condenser to the distributor side of the coil, instead of the battery side, condenser capacity across the points is at least three times the usual amount. Uneven point wear will also occur if the wrong ignition coil is installed. In this case, the condenser will not match the coil. A primary wire that is wrapped around the high-tension leads, or is too long and laying on the engine metal, can also cause uneven point wear.

A condenser that has a slight leakage through the dielectric paper, or excess resistance between a foil and its connection, may cause the points to turn black from arcing. Blackened points make poor contact.

☐ ASSIGNMENT 9-D ☐

1. In the cycle of events that produce a spark, what happens in the coil primary winding while the points are closed?

2. What happens in the coil secondary winding as the points open?

3. What does the condenser do in the ignition system?

4. What is the function of the distributor cap and rotor?

5. What does an under- and over-capacity condenser do to the breaker points?

BALLAST RESISTORS AND BALLAST WIRES

You are probably familiar with the term "ballast." Ballast is used to stabilize a loaded ship when it is in the water. A **ballast resistor** in an electrical circuit stabilizes current flow in the circuit. The ballast resistor protects the points at low engine speeds by reducing the coil primary winding current and voltage. This reduces arcing at the points. The ballast resistor increases coil output at higher speeds by increasing coil current and voltage.

When the vehicle is being started, the ballast resistor or wire may be bypassed. This will allow maximum ignition voltage to be supplied while the engine is being cranked. As shown in Figure 9-13, voltage can be applied to the coil primary terminal directly from the starter solenoid, or from a special terminal on the ignition switch. This terminal is a part of the circuit only when the ignition key is turned to the cranking position. Bypassing the ballast resistor puts the full voltage directly into the coil and results in higher coil voltage for easier starting.

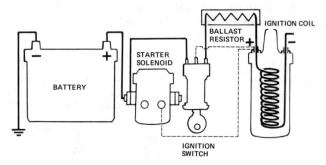

Figure 9-13. Two methods (dashed lines) can be used to bypass the ballast resistor or wire during cranking. (Courtesy of Echlin, Limited)

Ballast Resistor

A **heat-sensitive ballast resistor** is enclosed in a ceramic or metal case that is mounted either on the coil or on the engine compartment fire wall.

Electrical conductor resistance changes with changes in temperature. The higher the temperature of a conductor, the higher the electrical resistance in the conductor. Lower temperature results in lower resistance. The **resistance wire** inside a ballast resistor heats up as current flows through it.

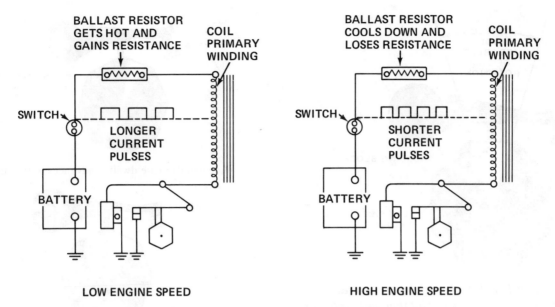

Figure 9-14. Heat-sensitive ballast resistor operation.

Figure 9-14 shows how a heat-sensitive ballast resistor operates. The length of the current pulses through the ignition system varies with engine speed. At slow engine speeds, the current pulses are long. These long heat pulses heat up the ballast resistor. As it heats up, the ballast resistor gains resistance. This increased resistance reduces current flow in the coil primary winding during slow engine speeds. At high speeds, the current pulses are short. The ballast resistor cools down and loses resistance. This reduced resistance tends to increase current flow in the coil primary winding. This results in more voltage output from the coil at higher engine speeds.

Ballast Wires

Instead of a coil or fire-wall mounted ballast resistor, a **ballast wire** is sometimes mounted in the wiring harness between the ignition switch and the ignition coil primary terminal, or between the fire-wall plug and the ignition coil primary terminal. A ballast wire does the same thing as a heat-sensitive ballast resistor. A ballast wire is not sensitive to heat, but it is sensitive to changes in current flow.

A change in current flow results in a winding if the frequency of the electricity passing through the winding is changed. In the ignition system, this frequency changes with the speed of the pulses produced by the opening and closing breaker points at different engine speeds. During slow engine speeds, the current flow increases. At higher engine speeds, the current

flow decreases. At slow engine speeds this increased primary current flow produces a greater voltage drop across the ballast wire. This reduces the voltage applied to the coil primary winding. At faster engine speeds, the decreasing primary current flow produces less voltage drop across the ballast wire. This increases the voltage applied to the coil primary winding.

POINT GAP
AND DWELL ANGLE

We have learned that the ignition points open and close to cause the ignition spark to occur. In order to understand the operation of the points, you must understand point gap and dwell angle and the effect they can have on the ignition system.

Points must have their opening distance adjusted to manufacturer's specifications. This is done by adjusting the **point gap** (opening distance) between the points.

Dwell angle, also called dwell, cam angle, or cam dwell, is given in degrees. Dwell angle is the number of degrees the distributor cam rotates between the instant the points close and the instant they reopen. See Figure 9-15. Put another way, dwell angle represents the number of degrees of distributor cam rotation while the points are closed and "dwell" together. Remember that current flows through the primary

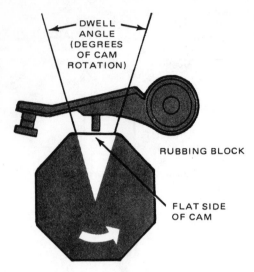

Figure 9-15. *Dwell angle is the number of degrees of distributor cam rotation from the instant that the points close to the instant they reopen. (Courtesy of Ford Motor Company, Dearborn)*

Wide gap decrease dwell — advances initial timing

Small gap increases dwell — retards initial timing

Figure 9-16. *Point gap is directly related to dwell angle and initial timing. (Courtesy of Ford Motor Company, Dearborn)*

winding during the dwell period when the points are closed.

Figure 9-16 shows that point gap is directly related to the dwell angle and initial timing. If the point gap is too small, dwell angle is larger than necessary. With a large dwell angle, the points have a tendency to burn. They do not open far enough to stop the current from arcing between them and do not have enough time to cool between current pulses. If the point gap is too wide, dwell angle is reduced. In this case, the points remain closed for too short a period of time. This reduces coil output, because the current does not flow long enough to create the strongest possible magnetic field in the coil.

A change in dwell angle (point opening) will also change the initial timing. A point gap that is too large (less dwell) will cause advanced timing. A point gap that is too small (larger dwell) will cause retarded timing. Anytime the points are adjusted, initial timing should be checked. This is why you always set dwell

angle before you set initial timing. **Initial timing** is set with a timing light focused on the crankshaft pulley timing marks.

☐ ASSIGNMENT 9-E ☐

1. What is the purpose of a ballast resistor?
2. What effect does a ballast resistor have on current flow through the coil at high speeds?
3. Define dwell angle.
4. What effect does point gap have on dwell?
5. What effect does point gap have on initial timing?

☐ SELF-TEST ☐

Complete the following sentences by filling in the missing words.

1. Internal-combustion engine operation depends on a cycle of events that deliver a combustible _____ _____ mixture and a precisely timed high-voltage _____ to the engine cylinders.

2. The ignition system is actually _____ circuits that are common only in the ignition _____ .

3. The primary winding in the ignition coil causes a _____ _____ inside the coil.

4. The high voltage is induced into the _____ _____ of the ignition coil.

5. Without a condenser, the spark produced by the _____ would be so _____ that the engine would not operate.

6. The breaker points or contact points _____ or _____ the ignition circuit, forming the current necessary for high-voltage induction in the ignition coil secondary windings.

7. The secondary wiring carries the secondary voltage and current from the ignition _____ to the _____ _____ and rotor, and from the distributor cap to each _____ _____ .

8. The high voltage in the _____ circuit causes a spark to jump across the _____ _____ gap.

9. As current flows through the ignition coil _____ winding, it causes a _____ _____ to build up inside the ignition coil.

10. A condenser that is the wrong _____ can cause uneven metal transfer. This will result in a buildup of metal on one _____ , and a matching _____ in the other.

11. A ballast resistor in an electrical circuit _____ current _____ in the circuit.

12. The ballast resistor protects the _____ at low engine speeds by _____ the coil primary winding current and _____ .

13. When the vehicle is being started, the ballast resistor or wire may be _____ . This will allow _____ ignition voltage to be supplied while the engine is being cranked.

14. Dwell angle is the number of _____ the distributor _____ rotates between the instant the points _____ and the instant they reopen.

15. Current flows through the primary winding during the dwell period when the points are _____ .

10

DISTRIBUTOR ADVANCES, CABLES, AND SPARK PLUGS

☐ LEARNING OBJECTIVES ☐

After studying this chapter, you will be able to:

1. Explain the relationship between initial timing, centrifugal advance, and vacuum advance.
2. Describe the construction and operation of centrifugal and vacuum advance mechanisms.
3. Describe ignition high-tension cable construction.
4. Describe the construction features of a typical spark plug.
5. Explain the term "heat range," and describe how it relates to spark plugs.
6. Describe and demonstrate how to check secondary polarity.
7. Define and/or discuss the following terms:

initial timing	spark plug heat range
centrifugal advance	charge cooling
vacuum advance	resistor plugs
ignition cables	coil polarity
suppression resistance	

INTRODUCTION

Chapter 9 described how the ignition system parts work together to produce the ignition spark. In this chapter, we will learn about ignition-spark timing. Remember that the ignition spark is delivered to the cylinders when the breaker points open. Breaker-point opening is timed so that it occurs at the proper instant during the compression stroke to give the best engine performance. The exact time the ignition spark should occur, however, varies during engine operation. When the spark should occur depends on such factors as engine speed and load.

IGNITION TIMING

The ignition spark ignites the fuel charge in the cylinders. As the fuel burns, it superheats the gases in the cylinder. These superheated gases expand and produce the pressure needed to push the piston down in the cylinder. It takes some time (about 1/300th of a second) for the gases to superheat. The exact amount of time it takes is determined by the type of fuel being burned and the quantity of air and fuel in the cylinder.

The power push on the piston must begin early in the power stroke in order to push the piston down with the greatest amount of force. If the ignition spark occurs at the proper moment, the fuel charge burns evenly until all of the fuel is used and releases power smoothly and efficiently. If the ignition spark

occurs later than it should, the power is released after the piston is partway down in the cylinder, and some power is lost. This is called **retarded** (late) timing. If the ignition spark takes place earlier than it should, the pressure on the piston is released too soon. This is called **advanced** (early) timing. Advanced timing causes extreme cylinder pressures, because the expanding gases are trying to push the piston down while it is still moving up in the cylinder. With advanced timing, the fuel tends to burn unevenly and usually explodes into spontaneous combustion from the extreme heat in the cylinder. Correct ignition timing results in fuel economy and reduced exhaust emissions.

ADVANCE MECHANISMS

Engine speed affects the time that the spark should occur. The **initial timing** is set with a timing light. Initial timing fixes the starting position for the ignition spark. It usually is set so the spark occurs when number-one piston is near top dead center (TDC), as the engine is idling. Since the distributor shaft cam lobes that open the points are an equal distance apart, the sparks will occur at exactly the right moment in each cylinder at idle once the spark has been timed at idle for number-one cylinder. However, as engine speed increases, the pistons move faster, and the sparks have to occur sooner (be advanced) to allow enough time for complete combustion.

On the engine shown in Figure 10-1, the spark should occur at 18° before top dead center (BTDC) at 1200 revolutions per minute (rpm) so that combustion ends by 23° after top dead center (ATDC) and releases a smooth, even power push. The "degrees" referred to in the illustration are the degrees of crankshaft revolution in relation to the top dead center position of the piston.

When the engine speed reaches 3600 rpm, the piston is moving so rapidly that the spark must occur at 40° BTDC to allow enough time for complete combustion by the 23° ATDC position. Notice that the crankshaft in the engine shown turns 41° during combustion at 1200 rpm and 63° at 3600 rpm, but in both cases combustion ends at 23° ATDC. These numbers will vary from one engine to another. An advance mechanism causes the ignition spark to occur sooner at higher engine speeds. This allows for the full-time interval necessary for complete combustion at high engine speeds and loads.

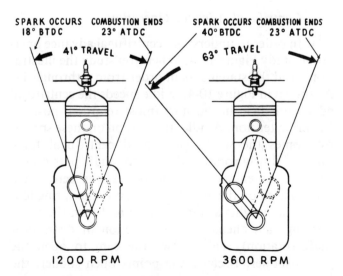

Figure 10-1. Ignition advance requirements.

Centrifugal Advance

The amount that the ignition is advanced to allow for engine speed is controlled by a **centrifugal advance** on the distributor shaft. This part of the distributor (sometimes called the **mechanical advance** or **governor advance**) is controlled by the changing centrifugal forces that are developed as the distributor shaft turns at different engine speeds. The centrifugal advance insures the correct spark timing at any engine speed, but is engineered around a full-throttle load on the engine. In other words, the centrifugal advance causes the correct spark advance for heavy loads at different engine speeds. Most centrifugal advances work in a similar manner, but they may differ in construction.

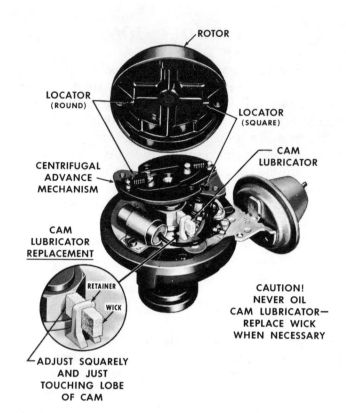

Figure 10-3. A General Motors centrifugal advance with the advance mounted above the breaker plate. (Courtesy of General Motors of Canada Limited)

The distributor shown in Figure 10-2 has the centrifugal advance mounted below the breaker plate. The distributor shown in Figure 10-3 has the centrifugal advance located above the breaker plate. On this model, the rotor is fastened to the advance and acts as a protective cover for it.

Centrifugal Advance Operation

In order to understand centrifugal advance operation, study Figure 10-4. When you study the illustration, read the statements in order from 1 through 11. As shown in Figure 10-4, at idle speeds the centrifugal advance is held in the start (most retarded) position by spring tension. At idle, the tension on these springs overcomes the weak, slow-speed centrifugal force that the slowly rotating distributor shaft puts on the weights. As engine speed increases, the centrifugal force placed on the weights overcomes the spring tension. The weights swing outward and turn the point opening cam ahead (in the direction of distributor shaft rotation). This causes the cam to open the points sooner. Because the points open sooner, the

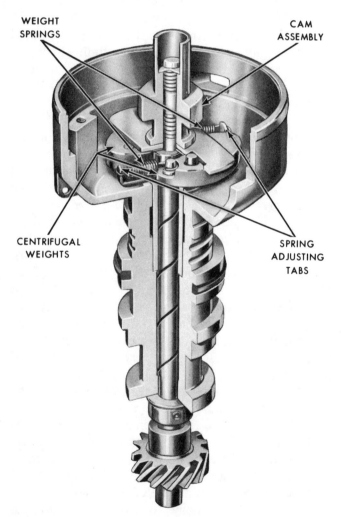

Figure 10-2. A Ford centrifugal advance with the advance mounted below the breaker plate. (Courtesy of Ford Motor Company, Dearborn)

spark is advanced. As the engine slows down, the decreasing centrifugal force causes the weights to move back in on their mounting, thus reducing the amount of spark advance (retarding it) the correct amount for slower engine speeds.

☐ ASSIGNMENT 10-A ☐

1. Why is spark advance needed as engine speed increases?
2. Explain the operation of a centrifugal advance.

Vacuum Advance

Spark timing is affected by engine load as well as engine speed. At part-throttle operation, only a small amount of a fairly lean air-fuel mixture is allowed into the engine. This causes less compression pressure and, since the fuel particles are less dense (spaced more widely apart), they take longer to burn and require more advanced timing to burn completely. The centrifugal advance does not supply enough spark advance for part-throttle openings. A **vacuum advance** provides the extra advance needed at part-throttle openings.

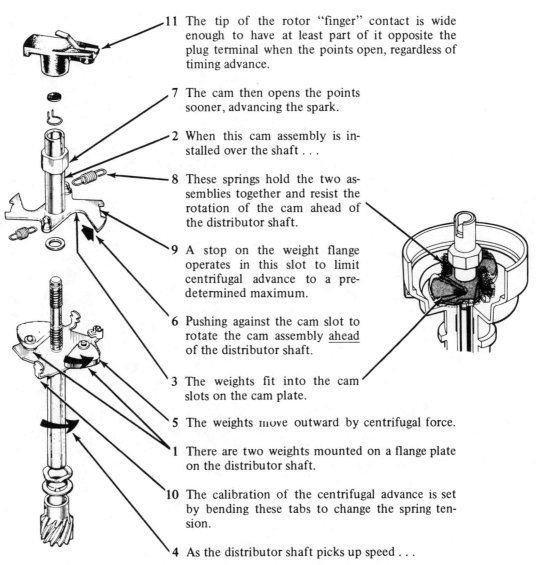

11 The tip of the rotor "finger" contact is wide enough to have at least part of it opposite the plug terminal when the points open, regardless of timing advance.

7 The cam then opens the points sooner, advancing the spark.

2 When this cam assembly is installed over the shaft . . .

8 These springs hold the two assemblies together and resist the rotation of the cam ahead of the distributor shaft.

9 A stop on the weight flange operates in this slot to limit centrifugal advance to a predetermined maximum.

6 Pushing against the cam slot to rotate the cam assembly <u>ahead</u> of the distributor shaft.

3 The weights fit into the cam slots on the cam plate.

5 The weights move outward by centrifugal force.

1 There are two weights mounted on a flange plate on the distributor shaft.

10 The calibration of the centrifugal advance is set by bending these tabs to change the spring tension.

4 As the distributor shaft picks up speed . . .

Figure 10-4. Centrifugal advance operation. (Courtesy of Ford Motor Company, Dearborn)

Manifold vacuum varies with engine load. Therefore, manifold vacuum is generally used to control part-throttle spark advance. On a vacuum advance, manifold vacuum is supplied to a spring-loaded diaphragm that regulates the spark timing according to the strength of the vacuum. Figure 10-5 is a cutaway view of a distributor with a vacuum advance. The diaphragm spring is calibrated against the pull of manifold vacuum applied to the diaphragm. The balance of the spring pushing on the diaphragm and the vacuum pulling on it determines the amount of spark advance given to the points.

Vacuum Advance Operation

Figure 10-6 will help you understand vacuum advance operation. Study the illustration by reading the

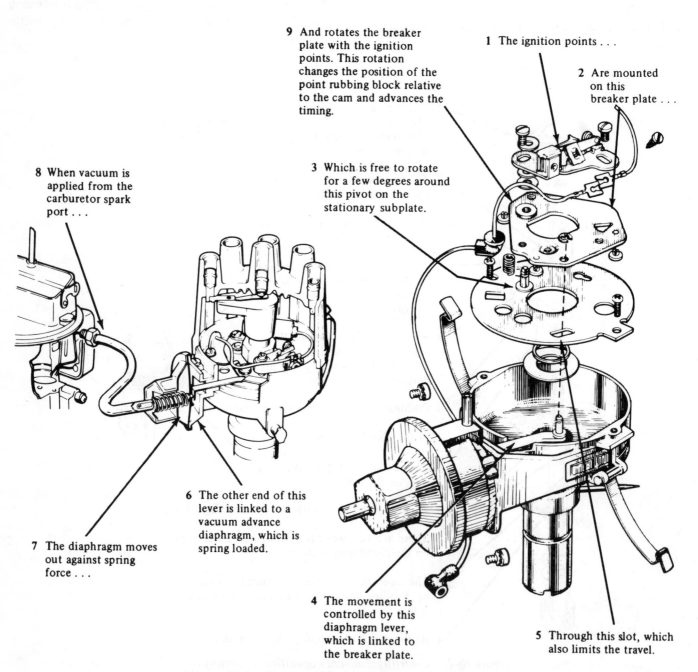

9 And rotates the breaker plate with the ignition points. This rotation changes the position of the point rubbing block relative to the cam and advances the timing.

1 The ignition points . . .

2 Are mounted on this breaker plate . . .

8 When vacuum is applied from the carburetor spark port . . .

3 Which is free to rotate for a few degrees around this pivot on the stationary subplate.

6 The other end of this lever is linked to a vacuum advance diaphragm, which is spring loaded.

7 The diaphragm moves out against spring force . . .

4 The movement is controlled by this diaphragm lever, which is linked to the breaker plate.

5 Through this slot, which also limits the travel.

Figure 10-6. Vacuum advance operation. (Courtesy of Ford Motor Company, Dearborn)

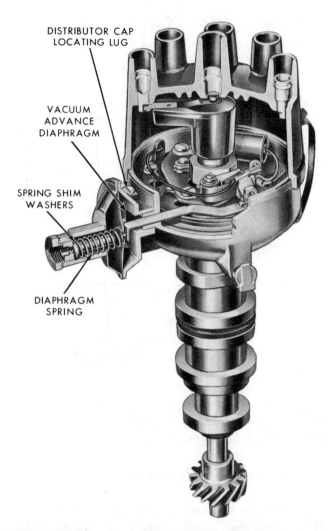

DISTRIBUTOR CAP
LOCATING LUG

VACUUM
ADVANCE
DIAPHRAGM

SPRING SHIM
WASHERS

DIAPHRAGM
SPRING

Figure 10-5.   A cutaway view of a Ford distributor, show-ing the vacuum advance diaphragm and spring. (Courtesy of Ford Motor Company, Dearborn)

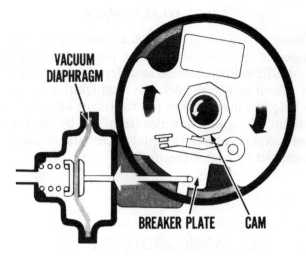

VACUUM
DIAPHRAGM

BREAKER PLATE   CAM

Figure 10-8.   High manifold vacuum moves the breaker plate in an advanced direction as indicated by the arrows. Reduced vacuum causes less advance. Weak vacuum causes no advance. (Courtesy of Chrysler Corporation)

statements in order from 1 through 9. Figure 10-7 shows that the vacuum advance port is located in the carburetor throat just above the edge of the throttle plate, when the throttle plate is in the idle position. This location prevents manifold vacuum from af-fecting the vacuum advance when the engine is idling. Most engines idle better and give off less exhaust emissions when the spark is retarded at idle. At open-throttle positions, the throttle valve is above the vacuum port so that manifold vacuum can be sup-plied to the vacuum advance. In this way, the vacuum advance only affects breaker point opening when the throttle plate is at least partway open.

Both the engine load and speed affect the strength of manifold vacuum. Slow engine speeds with light loads result in high vacuum. High vacuum causes maximum spark advance. Faster speeds and medium loads (highway driving, for example) de-crease manifold vacuum strength and spark advance. Extra fast speeds or heavy loads cause wide throttle openings. These reduce manifold vacuum so much that the vacuum advance may not respond at all. During extra fast speeds or heavy-load conditions, the centrifugal advance will provide all the advance needed.

Figure 10-8 shows the breaker plate movement according to the strength of the manifold vacuum ap-plied to the vacuum advance. The arrows indicate the direction of advance (opposite the direction of shaft rotation). The overall advantage of the vacuum ad-vance is that it provides good part-throttle operation and maximum gas mileage.

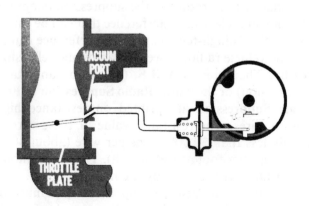

VACUUM
PORT

THROTTLE
PLATE

Figure 10-7.   The vacuum advance port is located just above the throttle plate when the throttle is at idle. (Courtesy of Chrysler Corporation)

FACTS TO REMEMBER

Timing devices time the breaker point opening and cause the spark to occur at the proper time for the most efficient combustion at different engine speeds. As shown in Figure 10-9, the total ignition advance includes the initial timing (set for engine idle) plus the amount of vacuum advance (regulated by the manifold vacuum), plus the amount of centrifugal advance (regulated by engine speed).

☐ ASSIGNMENT 10-B ☐

1. Explain vacuum advance operation.
2. Explain how spark advance requirements are satisfied during idle, at part-throttle position, and at full-throttle position.

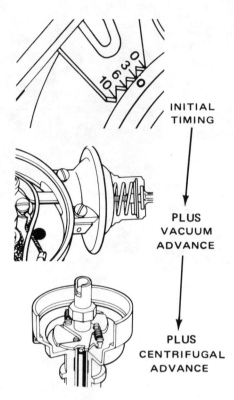

Figure 10-9.   Total spark advance equals initial timing, plus centrifugal advance, plus vacuum advance. (Courtesy of Ford Motor Company, Dearborn)

IGNITION HIGH-TENSION CABLES

The high voltage produced by the ignition coil is often referred to as **high-tension voltage**. This voltage has to be delivered from the secondary terminal in the coil cap tower to the distributor cap and rotor, and from the distributor cap towers to the spark plugs.

The type of wire used to connect the coil, distributor, and spark plugs must be able to withstand the high voltage produced by the ignition system. These wires need a thick covering of insulation to prevent the high voltage from arcing through them to ground, or across from one wire to another.

At one time, ignition high-tension cables had a copper-center wire covered with thick, natural rubber. These cables presented some problems, however, because rubber breaks down from exposure to heat, oil, road salt, and water. A cotton covering, well saturated with lacquer, was added to the wire. This helped, but the lacquer tended to dry out and crack. Wiring improved with the production of a copper- and steel-center wire, covered first by rubber, then with a layer of synthetic (man-made) rubber called neoprene. **Neoprene** is resistant to heat, oil, salt, and water.

Suppression Resistance

For many years now, it has been mandatory for all automobile manufacturers to install **static-suppression resistance** in the secondary wiring on their vehicles. Some manufacturers use carbon resistors fastened on the plug end of copper wires, along with a resistor in the distributor cap or rotor. Other manufacturers use resistance high-tension wires.

Adding a controlled amount of resistance in the secondary circuit results in the suppression (stopping) of radio and television interference that can be caused by a vehicle's high-tension wires. Interference can affect the vehicle radio, as well as radios and televisions nearby. The letters **T.V.R.S.** (Television and Radio Suppression) or the words **Radio Suppression** or **Electronic Suppression** are printed on resistance high-tension wires. The resistance value of these wires is usually less than 30,000 ohms per wire (about 4000–8000 ohms per foot of wire length). The exact amount of resistance is specified by the manufacturers.

To better understand suppression, you must understand the stages of voltage in the secondary circuit. The spark is produced in two stages—capacitive and inductive. The **capacitive** stage is very brief and consists of a sudden, initial rise in voltage. The **inductive** stage is longer and of a lower, but oscillating (varying) voltage. It is during the inductive stage that current jumps across the spark plug gap. Some portions of these oscillations are in the radio frequency range and will broadcast a signal that will cause static on nearby radios and televisions. This inductive stage of the spark is suppressed by the secondary resistance wires or suppressors.

Beyond providing radio interference suppression, resistance wires also increase spark plug life, because the current intensity across the plug gap is reduced by the resistance wire. This means that, with resistance wires, the spark plugs will maintain their correct gap for a longer period of time. If you are replacing secondary wires, do not use copper wires in place of resistance wires. Copper wires will not suppress radio and television interference.

Resistance High-Tension-Wire Construction

Internal-resistance wires used before electronic ignition have a conductor in the center of the wire. The conductor is made from carbon-impregnated cotton, nylon, or figerglass string and covered with a thick rubber inner insulator. The rubber inner insulator is covered with a synthetic outer insulator for toughness and durability. See Figure 10-10. The plug covering and distributor boots are usually made from silicone rubber to withstand heat and resist moisture.

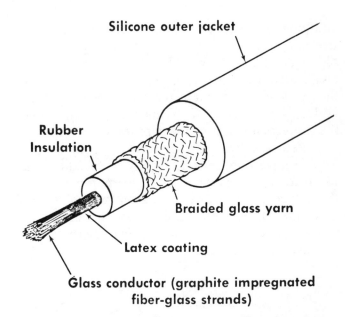

Figure 10-11. *An electronic ignition system high-tension wire. (Courtesy of General Motors of Canada Limited)*

Figure 10-11 shows the construction of the type of wires used on electronic ignition systems. These wires have special resistance cores made from flexible materials (such as graphite-impregnated fiberglass strands) that are covered with a core of natural rubber and then covered with braided glass yarn (for added strength). They are then covered with a heavy outer jacket of hypalon or silicone rubber for better insulation quality and heat resistance.

Unlike rubber that deteriorates very quickly, some synthetic materials are highly resistant to heat, oil, salt, moisture, and the corrosive action produced by ozone. **Ozone** is created by high-tension voltage leaking along the surface of the wire or passing through the air. If you looked at the ignition cables with the engine operating in total darkness, you might see a bluish halo around the wires. This is an electrical **corona** caused by electrical leakage. Ozone is a powerful oxidizing agent. If moisture and ozone combine, the result is ozonic acid, which can be responsible for eating away at a high-tension wire terminal end that was not pushed in far enough and was arcing. The arcing itself is destructive, but ozonic acid speeds up the destruction process.

Care must be exercised when you are handling resistance high-tension wires. They are not as strong as wires with an inner metal conductor. Always remove resistance high-tension wires by grasping and rotating the rubber plug boot until the seal is released and then using the boot to pull the wire off the plug.

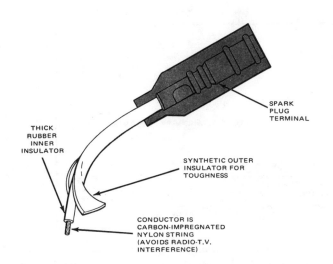

Figure 10-10. *A standard resistance high-tension wire. (Courtesy of Ford Motor Company, Dearborn)*

Grasping the wire and pulling directly on it will stretch the rubber, and the inner core may break and separate. The spark would have to arc across this break. Because of the heat produced by this arcing, the gap would burn and increase until the spark could no longer jump across it. While this was happening, the suppressor effect of the wire would be lost.

Resistance wires can burn out. The metal insert in the rubber boot may be slightly corroded and fail to make proper contact with the carbon particles in the wire core. This causes arcing that gradually burns away the carbon core until the spark cannot pass through to the plug. If there is arcing, the rubber can become brittle and crack.

□   ASSIGNMENT 10-C   □

1. Why are resistance wires used to add a controlled amount of resistance in the secondary circuit?
2. Describe the construction features of a resistance high-tension wire.
3. What possible results can be caused by rough treatment of resistance wires?

SPARK PLUGS

Properly operating spark plugs provide a good spark for the best power, acceleration, gas mileage, and easy starting. They can only do this when they are backed up by an ignition system that is operating correctly.

A spark plug conducts the high-tension current from the ignition secondary into the engine cylinder, where it sparks between the electrodes in the spark plug to ignite the air-fuel mixture in the cylinder. If spark plugs begin missing (not sparking when they should), they seriously affect engine performance, gas mileage, and exhaust emissions. Figure 10-12 gives the percentage of gasoline lost due to spark plug misfiring.

Spark Plug Construction and Operation

Terminal: The **terminal** is the electrical connection that connects the high-tension wire to the spark plug. See Figure 10-13.

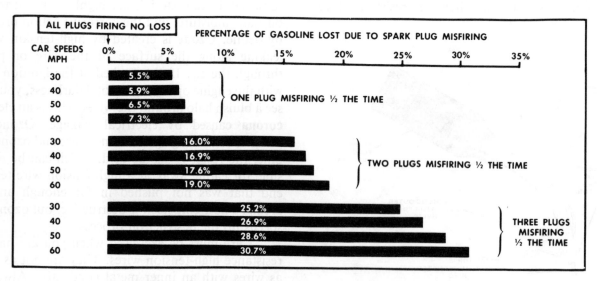

Figure 10-12.   The percentage of gasoline lost due to spark plug misfiring. (Courtesy of General Motors of Canada Limited)

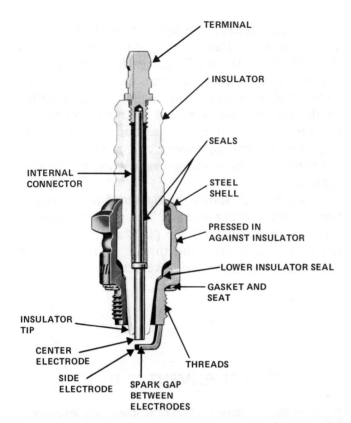

TERMINAL

INSULATOR

SEALS

STEEL SHELL

INTERNAL CONNECTOR

PRESSED IN AGAINST INSULATOR

LOWER INSULATOR SEAL

GASKET AND SEAT

INSULATOR TIP

CENTER ELECTRODE

SIDE ELECTRODE

SPARK GAP BETWEEN ELECTRODES

THREADS

Figure 10-13. Spark plug construction. (Courtesy of Champion Spark Plug Company of Canada, Limited)

Internal Connector: The **internal connector** brings the electrical current to the center electrode. Some plugs use a spring for the internal connector. Some plugs have a special seal between the connector and center electrode. This seal is made from particles of metal mixed with a glass binder.

Insulator: The **insulator** protects against voltage loss from the spark plug. It usually has a number of circular ribs to reduce **flashover** (flashing of the spark from the plug to ground) in damp weather. The insulator is made from one piece of very hard ceramic material. The insulator has excellent heat-resistance and heat-dissipating (spreading) qualities.

Seals: The plug shown in Figure 10-13 has a compound called **sillment** that is fused in place as a seal. Other plugs use a metal ring crimped under the edge of the shell for a seal. The lower insulator seal cushions and seals the ceramic insulator against combustion-pressure loss, expansion, and contraction.

Steel Shell: The **steel shell** is threaded to hold the plug into the engine. It permits the heat from the insulator tip to pass through the cylinder head and into the engine cooling system. The shell is pressed in against the insulator to form a good heat path. It holds the side electrode and electrically connects it to ground.

Gasket and Seat: The **gasket and seat** seal the plug against the cylinder head, preventing combustion-pressure loss and assuring a good heat path between the shell and the engine block. Some gaskets are permanently installed on the plug. Others are removable and must be replaced each time the plug is removed. Many spark plugs use a tapered seat that has no gasket. These plugs are designed to fit into a matching taper in the engine.

Insulator Tip: **Insulator tips** are made in a large variety of shapes and lengths to suit different engine heat ranges and head designs. The spark plug shown in Figure 10-13 has an extended tip. A conventional insulator tip would not extend past the shell. The insulator tip is exposed to combustion heat and corrosive action. It must be able to withstand a wide range of heat and fuel-mixture changes without becoming electrically conductive or destroyed by the intense heat.

Center Electrode: The best type of steel available is used in the **center electrode**. The center electrode is subject to the same conditions as the insulator tip, but it must also conduct the electrical spark.

Ground Electrode: The **ground electrode** is made from the same material as the center electrode. It is also exposed to combustion heat and must receive the electrical spark.

Spark Gap: The **spark gap** is the single-most-important feature of the spark plug. The electrical current must jump this gap to cause the flame that ignites the air-fuel mixture. The instant before the spark jumps, the voltage soars to a value high enough to cause molecules of air and gas to release electrons around the plug gap. This is called **ionization**. The electricity ionizes a path for itself to jump across the gap.

Threads: Figure 10-14 illustrates thread size. Plugs come in different thread sizes from 10 mm to

7/8″ (about 22 mm), according to manufacturer's preference and design limitations. The 14 mm and 18 mm sizes are the most common.

Plug threads are also supplied in different lengths or **reach**, as shown in Figure 10-15. Selection of the correct plug thread length is important. If a plug with too short a reach is installed in an engine, the unused threads in the cylinder head will fill with carbon, and installation of the correct plugs will be difficult. Plugs with too long a reach can cause engine damage if the pistons hit them. Even if the pistons clear the plugs, if plugs with too long a reach are left in the cylinder for a period of time, the unused threads on them fill up with carbon. This will make the plugs difficult to remove and probably damage the threads in the cylinder heads when they are removed.

Spark plugs should be tightened to the proper degree with a torque wrench. This prevents plug distortion and cracking. If the plugs are tightened too much, you may strip the thread. If they are not tightened enough, they will overheat.

Figure 10-14. Thread size is the outside diameter of the threaded part of the plug. Popular sizes are 14 mm and 18 mm. (Courtesy of General Motors of Canada Limited)

□   ASSIGNMENT 10-D   □

1. Describe the construction of a spark plug insulator.
2. Explain the function of the spark plug steel shell.
3. Explain how the spark jumps across the spark gap in a plug.

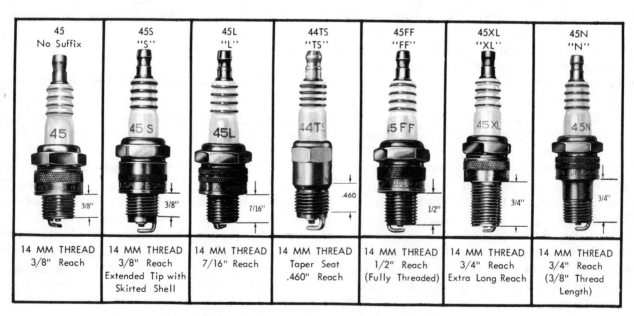

Figure 10-15. This row of spark plugs shows different thread lengths (reach) and a number of different spark plug styles. (Courtesy of General Motors of Canada Limited)

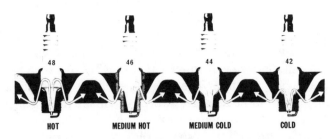

Figure 10-16.   This row of plugs illustrates heat range. Follow the arrows to the cooling system. Notice that the hot plugs have longer insulator tips than the cold plugs. (Courtesy of General Motors of Canada Limited)

Spark Plug Heat Range

One of the things you must learn in order to determine a spark plug's condition is how to identify whether the plug is operating at the correct heat range.

The difference between a **hot** and **cold** plug is the difference in temperature at which each is designed to operate. It is not, as many people seem to believe, a difference in the intensity of the spark produced by the plug. The proper temperature at which a given plug will operate depends on the amount of the insulator tip that is exposed to cylinder heat.

To prevent the insulator tip from reaching a temperature that will cause preignition (igniting the air-fuel mixture before the spark jumps the plug gap), the heat in the insulator tip must be dissipated (spread) along a heat path to the cooling system. Note the arrows shown in Figure 10-16. However, the tip of the insulator must remain hot enough to burn off the combustion deposits that collect on it.

Plug heat ranges are indicated by numbers. The higher the number for a particular type of plug, the hotter the plug, as shown in Figure 10-16. A plug with a heat range that is too hot for a certain engine has too long an insulator tip, cannot dissipate enough heat, and runs too hot. The insulator tip will become badly blistered, gray to white in color, and have a spotty appearance. The electrodes will be burned blue (overheated) and, in extreme cases, the electrodes and tip will be destroyed by the excess heat. See Figure 10-17.

The proper heat range plug has an insulator tip with the proper length to conduct away just the right amount of heat. When inspected, the insulator tip is usually a light tan to gray color and has only a few gray deposits on it. A plug that has too cool a heat range has too short an insulator tip, dissipates too

OVERHEATING

Identified by a white or light gray insulator with small black or gray-brown spots and with bluish-burnt appearance of electrodes. Caused by engine overheating, wrong type of fuel, loose spark plugs, too hot a plug, low fuel pump pressure or incorrect ignition timing. Replace the plug.

CARBON FOULED

Identified by black, dry fluffy carbon deposits on insulator tips, exposed shell surfaces and electrodes. Caused by too cold a plug, weak ignition, dirty air cleaner, defective fuel pump, too rich a fuel mixture, improperly operating heat riser or excessive idling. Can be cleaned.

NORMAL

Identified by light tan or gray deposits on the firing tip.

Figure 10-17.   These three pictures illustrate the effect of heat range on the spark plug appearance. Only three possible plug conditions are illustrated. (Courtesy of Ford Motor Company, Dearborn)

much heat, and runs cold. When inspected, the tip will be covered with carbon deposits and be black in color. This condition usually causes the spark to short out. The carbon deposits will conduct electricity, and the spark will arc through them to the steel shell, rather than jumping across the plug gap. Carbon-coated, misfiring plugs waste fuel and cause excess exhaust emissions.

Charge Cooling

A conventional firing end on a spark plug has a limited heat range that may not be adequate for some applications. An engine may require a relatively cold running plug at full throttle, but may need a hotter plug at low speeds when the engine is cool and not working very hard. Spark plug heat range can be extended somewhat by using an extended insulator tip.

A plug of this design places the electrodes and insulator tip deeper in the combustion chamber than does a conventional plug. This takes advantage of **charge cooling** at high engine speeds. At low speeds, the small incoming air-fuel charge cools the plug only slightly, and the plug remains hot. As the engine speeds up, the incoming air-fuel charge is greater (and more frequent) and tends to cool the plug more. This gives the plug an extended heat range, quite suitable to the type of driving most people do today. Figure 10-18 shows the difference in appearance between a conventional firing plug end and a plug with an extended tip that is designed to take advantage of charge cooling. Figure 10-19 shows the cooling effect of the incoming air-fuel charge on an extended plug tip.

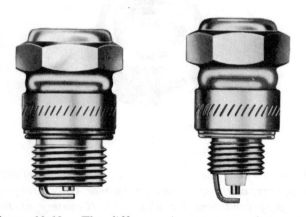

Figure 10-18. *The difference in appearance between a conventional firing plug end (left) and a plug with an extended insulator tip. (Courtesy of Champion Spark Plug Company of Canada, Limited)*

Resistor Plugs

As has been mentioned, most cars and trucks are factory-equipped with resistor- (suppression-) type ignition cables. Many cars also have resistor spark plugs. **Resistor plugs** further reduce radio and television interference from the vehicle ignition system. See Figure 10-20.

COIL POLARITY

Reversing the polarity of the coil secondary voltage can cause poor performance that may be mistaken for spark plug failure. The voltage polarity at the coil tower should be negative, which will make the voltage negative at the plug terminal and give a positive ground through the spark plug shell. Should the polarity be reversed, the voltage needed to fire the plugs could rise 20 to 40 percent. This could cause poor plug operation and misfiring under severe engine loads or speeds.

Figure 10-19. *The incoming air-fuel charge flows across the extended plug tip, cooling it more at high speeds than at low speeds. (Courtesy of Champion Spark Plug Company of Canada, Limited)*

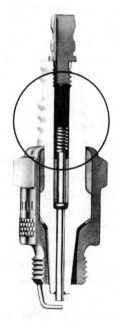

Figure 10-20. *A resistor plug. (Courtesy of Champion Spark Plug Company of Canada, Limited)*

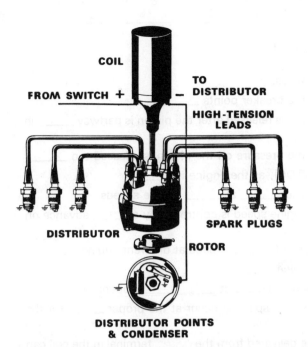

Figure 10-21. Coil polarity should always be negative at the spark plug terminals. If polarity is wrong, reverse the two primary leads at the ignition coil. (Courtesy of Champion Spark Plug Company of Canada, Limited)

The center electrode, which is encased in porcelain, gets much hotter than the side electrode, which is cooled through the steel shell. Electrons are agitated by heat. Hot electrons are much easier to ionize (release) than cool electrons. Since electrons move from negative to positive, it is better for the center electrode to have negative polarity, because it is the hotter electrode and will release electrons easier than the side electrode. In other words, it takes less voltage to move electrons from a hot object to a cool object than it takes to move electrons from a cool object to a hot object.

The polarity of the coil primary terminals is marked, and the coil should be connected properly. See Figure 10-21. If the primary terminals are connected backward, then the secondary circuit polarity will be backward. Train yourself to look at these connections when you are doing a tune-up. If a positive ground coil is installed on a negative ground system,

Figure 10-22. The side (ground) electrode will have a dished-in appearance if the coil polarity is reversed. (Courtesy of Champion Spark Plug Company of Canada, Limited)

it will have the wrong secondary polarity. In this case, the coil will not match the ignition system and must be replaced.

Checking Coil Polarity

Below are several different methods for determining coil polarity.

1. When you are using an ignition scope, the pattern will be upside down if the coil polarity is reversed.

2. Certain tune-up testers test spark strength and show a reversed reading if the coil polarity is reversed.

3. Electrode condition can help determine reversed coil polarity. If the plugs have been installed long enough to show it, the side (ground) electrode will have a dished-in appearance if the coil polarity is reversed. See Figure 10-22.

□ ASSIGNMENT 10-E □

1. Describe the appearance of a plug that has too hot a heat range, one that has the correct heat range, and one that has too cold a heat range.

2. Explain charge cooling.

3. List three different methods of checking coil polarity.

☐   SELF-TEST   ☐

Complete the following sentences by filling in the missing words.

1. The ignition _____ is delivered to the cylinders when the breaker points _____ .

2. If the ignition spark occurs later than it should, the _____ is released after the piston is partway _____ in the cylinder, and some power is _____ .

3. If the ignition spark takes place earlier than it should, the pressure on the piston is released too _____ .

4. Initial timing is usually set near _____ _____ _____ (TDC), as the engine is _____ .

5. An advance mechanism causes the ignition spark to occur _____ at _____ engine speeds.

6. The amount that the ignition is advanced to allow for engine speed is controlled by a _____ advance on the _____ shaft.

7. The centrifugal advance causes the correct spark advance for _____ loads at different engine _____ .

8. Spark timing is affected by engine _____ as well as engine _____ .

9. A vacuum advance mechanism provides the extra advance needed at _____ -_____ openings.

10. Timing devices time the breaker point _____ and cause the spark to occur at the proper _____ for the most efficient _____ at different engine speeds.

11. The high voltage produced by the ignition coil has to be delivered from the _____ terminal in the coil cap tower to the distributor _____ and _____ , and from the distributor cap _____ to the spark plugs.

12. Adding a controlled amount of resistance in the _____ circuit results in _____ of radio and television interference.

13. The inductive stage of the _____ is suppressed by the _____ resistance wires or _____ .

14. Care must be exercised when you are handling resistance high-tension wires. They are not as _____ as wires with an inner _____ conductor.

15. A spark plug conducts the _____-_____ current from the ignition _____ into the engine cylinder, where it can spark between the _____ in the plug and ignite the air-fuel mixture in the cylinder.

16. If a plug with too short a reach is installed in an engine, the unused _____ in the cylinder head will fill with _____ , and installation of the correct plugs will be difficult.

17. Spark plugs should be tightened to the proper degree with a _____ wrench.

18. The difference between a hot and a cold plug is the difference in _____ at which each is designed to operate.

19. Plug heat ranges are indicated by _____ .

20. Spark plug heat range can be extended somewhat by using an _____ insulator tip.

21. The voltage polarity at the coil tower should be _____ , which will make the voltage _____ at the plug terminal and give a _____ ground through the spark plug steel shell.

22. If a positive ground coil is installed on a negative ground system, it will have the wrong _____ polarity.

11

IGNITION SYSTEM SERVICE

After studying this chapter, you will be able to:

1. Perform a compression test.

2. Explain and demonstrate how to service spark plugs.

3. Perform diagnostic electrical tests on the ignition system.

4. List the problems to look for when inspecting ignition system parts.

5. Remove and replace a distributor.

6. Service a distributor.

7. Explain the tests that can be done on a distributor test machine.

8. Demonstrate how to check and adjust ignition timing.

9. Demonstrate how to use a timing light to check advance mechanisms.

10. Discuss the reasons for early battery failure.

11. Describe how to test a battery using a hydrometer.

12. Define and/or discuss the following terms:

compression test	point spring tension
wet test	ignition timing
voltage-drop test	overcharging
resistance test	undercharging
carbon paths	undercapacity battery
distributor shaft side play	hydrometer
point alignment	low-maintenance battery

157

INTRODUCTION

This chapter covers ignition system service procedures. In previous chapters, you learned fuel system fundamentals, carburetor servicing, and electrical and ignition system fundamentals. This knowledge, together with the material in this chapter, should help you advance toward becoming a competent tune-up technician. The following service procedures are outlined in this chapter:

Procedure 1.   Compression test.
Procedure 2.   Spark plug service.
Procedure 3.   Ignition system electrical tests.
Procedure 4.   Ignition system parts inspection.
Procedure 5.   Distributor installation marking.
Procedure 6.   Distributor service.
Procedure 7.   Distributor installation in an engine with no installation marks.
Procedure 8.   Ignition timing adjustment and distributor advance mechanism checks with a timing light.

COMPRESSION TEST

A **compression test** must be performed each time you think that one or more engine cylinders have lost compression. A compression test is often done before any ignition system service is undertaken. An engine with low compression in one or more cylinders will not operate correctly. A tune-up will not improve poor compression. When there is poor compression in a cylinder, the power stroke will give less power than it should. If there is no compression, the piston will provide no power at all.

Poor compression is a result of either air leaking into and out of a cylinder, or compression leaking past the piston rings. Cylinder vacuum, compression, and power pressure can all be lost by leakage through burnt or warped valves; loose, worn piston rings; worn or damaged cylinder walls; cracks or holes in the pistons; or a poor fitting or blown head gasket. A cylinder with low or no compression will not deliver power to the piston on the power stroke. The expanding gases developed during ignition will escape, rather than force the piston down into the cylinder.

Compression Test Procedure

In order to perform this procedure, you will need a compression tester, jumper wire, remote starter button, air hose, oil can, and a device to hold the throttle and choke open.

1.   The battery must be in good condition. Test the battery and clean the battery terminals if necessary.

2.   Idle the engine until it has reached operating temperature. Then stop the engine.

3.   You should not leave the ignition system operational during a compression test. The sparks from dangling plug wires could cause a shock or could set fire to oil or fuel on the engine. Moreover, the ignition system can be permanently damaged.

Most ignition systems have a ballast resistor that is bypassed during cranking. Because the ballast resistor is bypassed, extra power is sent into the coil during starting. The bypassed ballast resistor, along with the open circuit at the dangling plug wires, will cause the voltage from the coil to rise much higher than usual. This high voltage will jump around the distributor cap.

High-voltage sparks may also arc through the high-tension wires and over the coil tower. These sparks can **carbon track** (burn) the distributor cap, rotor, wires, and coil. The spark can also arc inside the coil and cause coil failure. If you pull out the coil high-tension wire, sparks will still jump inside the coil and over the coil tower. Therefore, the ignition system must be completely disconnected when you are doing a compression test.

Disconnect the ignition system, using one of the following methods:

(a)   On point-type ignition systems, connect a jumper wire from the distributor side of the coil to ground.

(b)   On electronic ignition systems that have a separate coil, remove the high-tension wire from the center terminal of the distributor cap and connect the end of the wire to ground with a jumper wire.

(c)   On GM High-Energy Ignition systems, remove the battery supply wire that connects to the distributor.

4.   Remove the spark plug wires carefully. Remember to twist the rubber boots to break the seal. Do not pull on the wires. This may break the carbon resistance centers in the wires. Use the rubber boot to

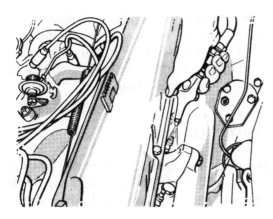

Figure 11-1. Blow any dirt from around the plugs with compressed air. (Courtesy of Ford Motor Company, Dearborn)

pull the wire off, or use special rubber-coated pliers designed for this operation.

5. If dirt enters the cylinders and lodges in the valve seats, it will cause false low compression readings. You should blow the dirt from around the spark plugs before you remove them. See Figure 11-1. **Caution:** Whenever you use an air hose, observe all safety precautions associated with air hose use. Safety glasses are a must when using air hoses!

6. Remove the spark plugs. Keep them in cylinder order for inspection. Spark plug appearance can often help you diagnose a cylinder problem.

7. As shown in Figure 11-2, lock the throttle and choke linkages to hold the throttle and choke wide open. This allows maximum air flow to enter the engine during the compression test. If you lock the throttle and choke open during a compression test, you can avoid opening and closing the throttle during each separate cylinder test. Each time you open and close the throttle, gasoline is pumped from the acceleration pump into the engine. This gasoline washes oil from the cylinder walls. The oil on the cylinder walls acts as a seal between the piston rings and the cylinder wall. If this oil is washed away, compression readings will be lower.

8. Look up the manufacturer's specifications to find the compression readings for the engine you are working on.

9. Compression test readings must be taken while the engine is being cranked. A **remote starter button** can be connected to the starter solenoid or relay to crank the engine while you take the test. **Caution:** The ignition system on many vehicles is

grounded by the ignition switch when the ignition switch is turned off. To prevent damage to the wiring and ignition switch, turn the ignition switch on before using a remote starter button. If you are in doubt about whether the system you are working on is grounded with the ignition switch in the off position, always turn the switch to the on position before using a remote starter button.

If you do not have a remote starter button, have someone sit in the vehicle and turn the key to crank the engine while you take the compression test.

10. Insert the compression tester hose into the first cylinder, as shown in Figure 11-3. Crank the en-

Figure 11-2. Lock the throttle and choke in the wide-open position. (Courtesy of General Motors of Canada Limited)

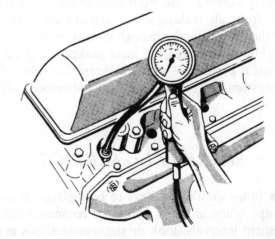

Figure 11-3. Compression test. (Courtesy of Ford Motor Company, Dearborn)

gine over four to six compression strokes (count them by the compression bumps visible on the compression gauge). Record the highest reading.

11. Repeat this procedure on each cylinder, using the same number of compression strokes for each.

Diagnosis

The closer the compression readings are for each cylinder, the better. A compression difference of 15 to 25 psi (105–175 kPa) is generally acceptable. Extreme compression differences (over 25%) between cylinders are not acceptable. Equally low readings in two cylinders that are side by side could indicate that the head gasket is blown between them. If you suspect a blown head gasket, look for signs of water leaking into the cylinders.

If the readings in the cylinders are uneven, try a **wet test**. Put about a teaspoonful of 30-weight motor oil into each cylinder through the spark plug hole. Crank the engine for a moment to spread the oil over the cylinder walls, and retest the compression in each cylinder. If the wet-test readings test higher, but are even in all cylinders, the piston rings are leaking. If the wet-test readings are higher, but still low and uneven from cylinder to cylinder, the engine has leaking valves, defective pistons, or a blown head gasket.

FACTS TO REMEMBER

Engine compression should be checked before ignition system service. Without proper compression, the engine will not operate correctly, even if the ignition system is working well. Poor engine compression can result from air leaking either around the cylinders (past the piston rings), through the valves, or between the cylinders (through the head gasket). A compression test is performed with a compression tester. Any compression leaks should be corrected before ignition service.

SPARK PLUG SERVICE

Spark plugs should not have to be replaced at every tune-up. When in doubt about the recommended replacement intervals, look up the specifications in the manufacturer's shop manual. If there is no way of telling when the spark plugs were installed, you will have to determine their condition visually and decide to replace them or to service and reinstall them. Remember that plug service is usually performed only if you feel confident the plugs will provide good service until the next engine tune-up.

Procedures

To inspect and service spark plugs, you will need a spark plug cleaner, spark plug gauge, file and bending tool, wire brush or wheel, and cleaning solvent.

1. Spark plugs should be inspected externally and internally. Externally, look for signs of compression leakage. These will show as dark streaks running up the plug insulator from the steel shell. Look for chips and cracks in the insulator, damaged threads, or a loose, dirty, or corroded terminal. It is normal for plugs to be dirty below the rubber boot.

Internally, look at the condition of the insulator and the amount of wear on the electrodes. If the gap between the electrodes has increased more than .010″ (.22 mm), the plug should be replaced. Use a round wire feeler gauge when checking the spark plug gap. Look at the condition and color of the insulator tip to determine if the heat range is correct, or if replacement with a different plug is needed. Use a chart similar to Figure 11-4 as an aid in your diagnosis. Consult the manufacturer's specifications to determine if the correct plug is installed in the car.

2. Remove any oil from the plugs with solvent, and dry the plugs. This prevents cleaning abrasive from clinging to the plugs during cleaning.

3. Open the side electrode wide enough to permit cleaning and filing.

4. Place the plug in the proper adapter in the spark plug cleaner. As shown in Figure 11-5, use the "cleaning blast" position for three to five seconds while rotating and moving the plug back and forth. This forces abrasive cleaning material around the insulator tip and electrodes. Give the plug an "air blast" for a few seconds to remove all of the abrasive. Then remove the plug for inspection. Repeat the cleaning process if necessary. Do not overdo the cleaning, however, because the cleaning abrasive can erode the plug insulator.

5. As shown in Figure 11-6, file both the electrodes flat with a small file. The type of file supplied in an ignition kit or attached to the plug gauge is best for this purpose. Ignition sparks tend to jump from the outer edges of the plug center electrode. If you keep this edge sharp, the plug will have a better spark.

6. As shown in Figure 11-7, clean the plug threads with an electric wire brush. Do not clean the ceramic insulator with the wire brush, because metal

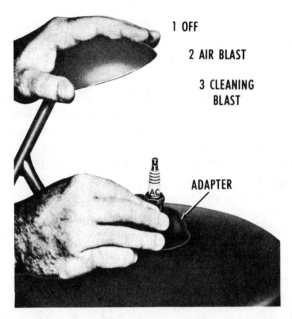

1 OFF

2 AIR BLAST

3 CLEANING BLAST

ADAPTER

Figure 11-5.   A spark plug cleaning machine. (Courtesy of General Motors of Canada Limited)

1. NORMAL OPERATION

Brown to grayish-tan deposits and slight electrode wear indicate correct spark plug heat range and mixed periods of high and low speed driving. Spark plugs having this appearance may be cleaned, regapped and reinstalled. When reinstalling spark plugs that have been cleaned and regapped, be sure to use a new engine seat gasket in each case.

2. CARBON FOULING

Dry, fluffy black carbon deposits may result from overrich carburetion, excessive hand choking, a faulty automatic choke, or a sticking manifold heat valve. A clogged air cleaner can restrict air flow to the carburetor causing rich mixtures. Poor ignition output (faulty breaker points, weak coil or condenser, worn ignition cables) can reduce voltage and cause misfiring. Excessive idling, slow speeds under light load also can keep spark plug temperatures so low that normal combustion deposits are not burned off. Fouled "spark plugs" are the result - not the cause - of this problem: AFTER THE CAUSE HAS BEEN ELIMINATED, SPARK PLUGS HAVING THIS APPEARANCE CAN BE CLEANED, REGAPPED AND REINSTALLED.

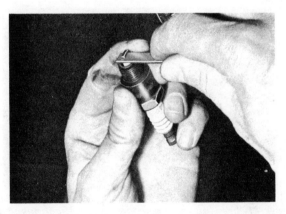

Figure 11-6.   File the electrodes flat with a small file. (Courtesy of General Motors of Canada Limited)

Wet, oily deposits with very little electrode wear may be caused by oil pumping past worn rings. "Break-in" of a new or recently overhauled engine before rings are fully seated may also result in this condition. Other possibilities of introduction of oil into the combustion chamber are a porous vacuum booster pump diaphragm or excessive valve stem guide clearances and/or defective intake valve seals.

Usually, these spark plugs can be degreased, cleaned and reinstalled.

A HOTTER TYPE SPARK PLUG WILL REDUCE OIL DEPOSITS, but too hot a spark plug can cause preignition and, consequently, severe engine damage. An engine overhaul may be necessary in severe cases to obtain satisfactory service.

3. OIL FOULING

Red, brown, yellow and white colored coatings which accumulate on the insulator are by-products of combustion and come from the fuel and lubricating oil, both of which today generally contain additives. Most powdery deposits have no adverse effect on spark plug operation; however, they may cause intermittent missing under severe operating conditions, especially at high speeds and heavy load. IF THE INSULATOR IS NOT TOO HEAVILY COATED, THE SPARK PLUGS MAY BE CLEANED, REGAPPED AND REINSTALLED. Sometimes, even after cleaning, an invisible shunt path remains. The only remedy under such circumstances is to replace the plug.

4. DEPOSIT FOULING "A"

Most powdery deposits, as shown in "A" have no adverse effect on the operation of the spark plug as long as they remain in the powdery state. However, under certain conditions of operation, these deposits melt and form a shiny yellow glaze coating on the insulator which, when hot, acts as a good electrical conductor. This allows the current to follow the deposits instead of jumping the gap, thus shorting out the spark plug. Glazed deposits can be avoided by not applying sudden load, such as wide open throttle acceleration, after sustained periods of low speed and idle operation. IT IS ALMOST IMPOSSIBLE TO EFFECTIVELY REMOVE GLAZED DEPOSITS, SO WHEN THEY OCCUR THE PLUGS SHOULD BE REPLACED.

5. DEPOSIT FOULING "B"

Excessive overheating is evidenced by burned or blistered insulator tips and badly worn electrodes. It is brought on by preignition**, cooling system defects, lean fuel air ratios, low octane fuels, overadvanced ignition timing, improper installation procedures (also see illustration 8), and stuck closed heat riser valves.

INSTALL A NEW PLUG OF THE RECOMMENDED HEAT RANGE AFTER PROBLEM HAS BEEN CORRECTED.

6. EXCESSIVE OVERHEATING

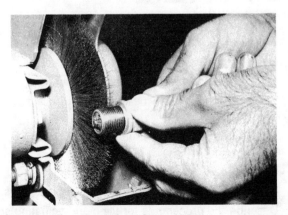

Figure 11-7.   Clean the plug threads with a wire brush or wheel. (Courtesy of General Motors of Canada Limited)

Figure 11-4.   Typical spark plug conditions and their causes. (Courtesy of General Motors of Canada Limited)

from the brush will become imbedded in the ceramic insulator. This will cause spark flashover from the plug insulator to the steel shell when the plug is operating.

7. Gap (set to the proper opening) the electrodes to specifications, as shown in Figure 11-8. Use a round wire gauge or a special plug gapping tool. Only bend the side electrode. If you try to bend the center electrode, you will crack the insulator tip. A plain, flat feeler gauge cannot accurately measure the true width of the plug gap. See Figure 11-9.

8. Place the plugs in a cleaning solvent such as carburetor cleaner to remove any remaining abrasive, filings, or dirt. Then dry the plugs.

9. Install the plugs in the engine and tighten them finger tight.

10. Finish tightening the plugs to torque specifications.

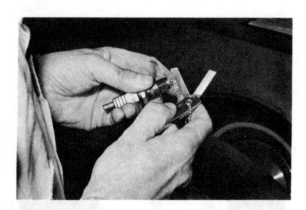

Figure 11-8. Gap the electrodes to specifications using a round wire gauge. (Courtesy of General Motors of Canada Limited)

□ ASSIGNMENT 11-A □

1. Describe the procedures for a compression test.
2. How do you perform a wet test?
3. What information can be gathered from a compression test?
4. What information can be gathered from a wet-compression test?
5. When should spark plugs be replaced?
6. Describe the procedures for cleaning spark plugs.
7. Describe the procedures for filing and adjusting spark plugs.

Figure 11-9. A plain flat feeler gauge cannot accurately measure the true width of the spark plug gap. A round wire gauge or special spark plug gapping tool must be used. (Courtesy of General Motors of Canada Limited)

IGNITION SYSTEM ELECTRICAL TESTS

In order for the ignition system to function properly, it must have the proper amount of voltage available. This is only possible if there is a minimum amount of voltage drop in the electrical devices and connections in the circuit. Procedures for determining the condition of the ignition circuit are described below. You may find it helpful to refer back to the section on meter care and operation in Chapter 8 before attempting any of the tests described below. Remember that meters are precision instruments. They must be handled properly and adjusted correctly in order to give you accurate readings.

Refer to Figure 11-10 for the places in the ignition system that you have to test. The procedures given for these tests are as simplified as possible and require a minimum of test equipment. To perform these tests, you will need a voltmeter, an ohmmeter, a low-reading ammeter, the necessary tools for tightening electrical connections, a metal probe, and jumper wires.

Voltage-Drop Tests

1. Examine the condition of the primary wiring and connections. They must be in good condition (not cracked or frayed) for this test. Clean the wires with solvent, if necessary, so that you can examine them easily.

2. Select the correct voltage scale on the voltmeter. If you are working on a negative ground system, connect the negative (black) lead from the voltmeter to a clean ground. If you are working on a positive ground system, connect the positive (red) lead from the voltmeter to ground. You can connect the voltmeter lead to the battery ground cable if the cable is clean. Do not connect the voltmeter leads to painted, rusted, or dirty metal.

3. Use the voltmeter to determine battery voltage (Connection 1, Figure 11-10). Use the ungrounded voltmeter lead for this and all the other tests listed here. Record the battery voltage and all of the following readings.

4. Connect a jumper wire from the distributor side of the ignition coil (Connection 5, Figure 11-10) to ground. This will ensure a good circuit to ground even if the points are bad.

5. Turn the ignition switch on, but do not start the engine. Turn off all accessories, such as the radio or lights. These accessories will cause an unwanted voltage drop.

6. Test the voltage at the ballast resistor input (Connection 2, Figure 11-10). If the car does not have

a ballast resistor in the system, you will have to probe in the fire wall plug for the ballast wire. The reading you get should be within .5 volts of battery voltage. If the reading is lower, you will have to find the ignition switch terminals and fire wall plug, and trace back to the ballast resistor to find out what is reducing the voltage to the resistor. Often a poor connection, or bad ignition switch, will be the problem.

7. Test the voltage at the battery side of the ignition coil (Connection 4, Figure 11-10). It should read 5 to 8 volts on ballast resistor systems. On systems that have no ballast resistor, the reading should be within .5 volts of battery voltage. Faulty readings indicate poor connections or a faulty ballast resistor.

8. To test if the ballast resistor bypass is working during cranking, first read the voltage at the coil battery terminal (Connection 4, Figure 11-10) while cranking. Then read the voltage at the battery (Connection 1, Figure 11-10) while cranking. The coil

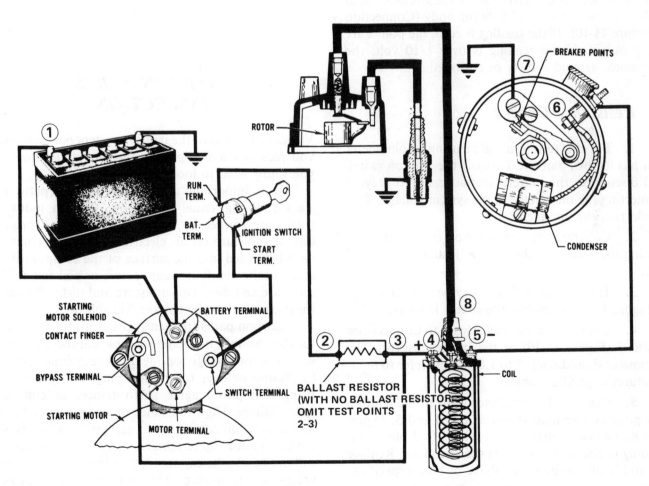

Figure 11-10.   An ignition system schematic showing the places to test the ignition system. (Courtesy of General Motors of Canada Limited)

voltage reading should be within one volt of the battery voltage.

9. Remove the jumper wire from the ignition coil distributor terminal (Connection 5, Figure 11-10), and attach the voltmeter lead on the terminal. The reading you get should be less than 1/10 volt when the points are closed. Higher readings indicate that the points are burned or oxidized and have high resistance, that there are bad connections in the distributor, or that the distributor contact to ground is causing excess resistance.

If the reading is exactly battery voltage, the points are open. Crank the engine, a little at a time, until the reading drops to near zero, indicating that the points are closed. Then take a voltmeter reading. This reading should be less than 1/10 volt.

10. If the above reading was too high, take a voltage reading at the points (Connection 6, Figure 11-10). If this reading is 1/10 volt or less, the distributor lead is defective. Move the voltmeter lead from the points to the distributor body (Connection 7, Figure 11-10). If the reading is zero, the points are the problem. If the reading is over 1/10 volt, the distributor ground is dirty or corroded.

Resistance Checks

1. For this test, you will be using an ohmmeter that has its own battery. Turn off the ignition switch and disconnect the battery ground cable to prevent connecting the ohmmeter to the system voltage. This would ruin the ohmmeter.

2. Calibrate the ohmmeter on the low scale by joining the leads together and adjusting the control dial.

3. Take off the coil primary wire (Connection 5, Figure 11-10) to isolate the circuit from ground.

4. Connect the ohmmeter leads to Connections 2 and 3 (Figure 11-10) at the ballast resistor. The ohmmeter should read .5 to 1.85 ohms (refer to manufacturer's specifications).

5. Connect the ohmmeter leads to the ignition coil primary terminals (Connections 4 and 5, Figure 11-10). The ohmmeter should read 1 to 3 ohms, according to the manufacturer's specifications. Replace the coil if the readings are above or below specifications.

6. Calibrate the ohmmeter on the high scale.

7. Connect the ohmmeter to the coil primary

terminal and to the terminal inside the coil tower (Connections 4 and 8, Figure 11-10). The meter should read 7,000 to 14,000 ohms (see manufacturer's specifications). A reading that is much lower than it should be indicates a short-circuited winding in the coil. If the reading is extremely high or infinite, the windings are open-circuited. In either case, replace the coil.

□ ASSIGNMENT 11-B □

1. Explain where to test ignition circuit voltage and what the readings should be.

2. Explain where to test ignition circuit resistances and what the readings should be.

IGNITION PARTS INSPECTION

Visual inspection of the ignition system parts can help you pick out many ignition system faults, provided you know what to look for.

It is important to look for carbon paths (or tracks) during visual inspection. **Carbon paths** or tracks are formed by high-voltage shorting through dirt or moisture on an electrical component until a path is burned into the surface of the component. A crack in the distributor cap, rotor, or coil can collect moisture and dirt. This moisture and dirt will form a short-circuit that the voltage will follow.

Carbon paths frequently occur inside a distributor cap. Should this happen, these carbon paths will short out the voltage for one or more cylinders, either to ground or over to another plug, and cause misfiring and poor engine performance, or complete spark failure. High resistance or open-circuited ignition cables can contribute to carbon tracking. When the distributor cap terminal is dirty or wet, the spark will arc across the cap to another terminal tower that offers less resistance. This will also cause carbon paths.

There are several conditions you should look for when you are inspecting ignition system parts.

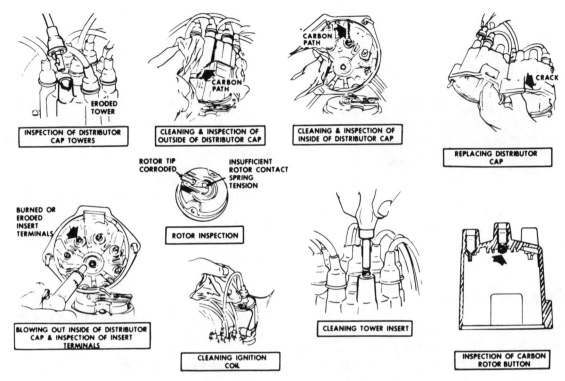

Figure 11-11. Cleaning and inspecting the distributor cap, rotor, and coil can often reveal defects. (Courtesy of General Motors of Canada Limited)

Distributor Cap

If the cap is dirty, it should be cleaned with detergent soap and hot water. Pull out the plug wires one at a time, and look for cracked, burned, or corroded towers and inserts. See Figure 11-11. Inspect the inside and outside surfaces of the cap for signs of crossfiring, carbon paths, and cracks between the towers or down the sides of the cap. The amount of burning and erosion on the metal insert terminals inside the cap is an indication of the cap's condition. Any **tower inserts** that are corroded should be cleaned with a wire brush designed for this operation. If a special brush is not available, wrap fine sandpaper around a pencil and spin it in the tower hole.

The **carbon rotor button** in the cap must be inspected for deterioration or carbon buildup. A rotor button that is spring-loaded may become stuck, which will leave a gap between the button and the rotor. A suppressor- (resistor-) type button may be open-circuited, which will make the spark jump the opening. The resistance of suppressor buttons should be checked with an ohmmeter.

Rotor

Check the **rotor tip** for corrosion and wear. Make sure there is enough spring tension for rotor contact. Check the rotor for cracks and carbon paths. The rotor should fit snugly on the distributor shaft. This will prevent the rotor from misaligning with the distributor cap inserts. Make sure the rotor is the correct length for the distributor cap. Some rotors have a suppressor that must be checked with an ohmmeter. If necessary, the rotor can be cleaned with detergent soap and hot water or parts cleaning solvent.

Ignition Coil

Clean off the coil tower before you inspect it. Remove the center wire and look inside the tower for signs of deterioration. Examine the coil top and terminal for burns, corrosion, carbon paths, or cracks. Figure 11-12 shows what happens to a coil tower if the coil wire is defective or is not pushed all the way in.

Figure 11-12. *This coil tower was burned and corroded by the spark because the wire was defective or not pushed in all the way. (Courtesy of Chrysler Corporation)*

Ignition Cables

Examine the rubber boots on both ends of the wires. Squeeze the boots with your fingers. If they crack, the rubber has deteriorated and the boots or wires should be replaced. Examine the wires for cuts, breaks, or pinholes. Also look for road deposits (salt), oil soaking, drying out, burning, or terminal and metal insert deterioration.

If the ignition wires pass inspection, check their resistances with an ohmmeter. See Figure 11-13. Use the following procedure:

1. Zero the ohmmeter on the high scale. Use the recommended manufacturer's specifications for the vehicle you are working on. A rule of thumb is that the wires should show 5,000 to 10,000 ohms resistance per foot.

2. Join one ohmmeter lead to a metal probe in the spark plug end of the wire, and connect the other ohmmeter lead to the distributor end of the wire. Record the readings taken on each plug wire and on the coil wire.

3. Wires that read beyond manufacturer's specifications or show an open circuit should be replaced. You can replace individual wires, or replace the whole set. Copper conductor wires should read zero ohms resistance. Copper wires are not recommended for modern cars, because they cannot suppress radio interference.

4. The ignition wires should be cleaned with detergent soap and hot water before reinstallation.

Breaker Points

The condition of the distributor breaker point contacts can indicate a problem in the ignition system. Several different possible conditions are described below.

Gray and Level: Points that are gray and level are operating normally, without a condenser prob-

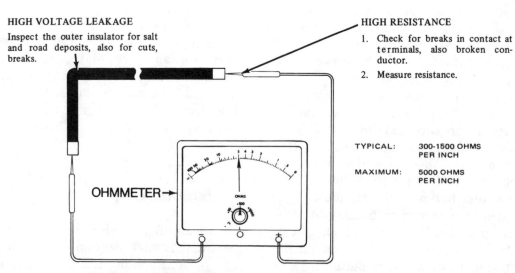

HIGH VOLTAGE LEAKAGE

Inspect the outer insulator for salt and road deposits, also for cuts, breaks.

HIGH RESISTANCE

1. Check for breaks in contact at terminals, also broken conductor.

2. Measure resistance.

OHMMETER →

TYPICAL: 300-1500 OHMS PER INCH

MAXIMUM: 5000 OHMS PER INCH

Figure 11-13. *After inspection, resistance wires should be checked with an ohmmeter. (Courtesy of Ford Motor Company, Dearborn)*

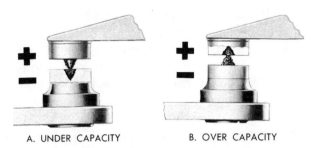

A. UNDER CAPACITY   B. OVER CAPACITY

Figure 11-14. An under- or over-capacity condenser can pit the points. (Courtesy of General Motors of Canada Limited)

lem. Use the thickness of the remaining tungsten as a guide to determine if the points need replacement.

Gray and Pitted: Points that are gray and pitted indicate that the condenser is preventing point burning, but that the condenser capacity is wrong. On negative ground systems, pitting on the ground point indicates an undercapacity condenser. Pitting on the moving point indicates an overcapacity condenser, as shown in Figure 11-14. A radio suppression condenser that has been connected to the distributor side of the coil instead of the battery side is another possible cause of point pitting.

Burned Black: If the points are burned black, there has been excessive point arcing. This could be caused by a faulty condenser, as shown in Figure 11-15. If the condenser has failed, there may be yellow spots or a yellow haze over the black deposit. Deposits of oil or grease thrown off the distributor shaft lubricator wick or the point opening cam would cause the points to burn. A plugged **Positive Crankcase Ventilation** (P.V.C.) system could cause excessive crankcase pressures that could force oil vapors up the distributor shaft and into the distributor. This would cause blackened points and give a messy, oily appearance inside the distributor.

Burned Blue: It takes a lot of heat to turn tungsten blue. Points that are burned blue have been burnt by excess current flow from one or more sources. The excess current that burns points could be caused by several different problems.

1. A voltage regulator that is set too high or is defective and allows the voltage to rise could cause excess current.

2. A shorted ignition coil primary winding will result in burned points.

3. An incorrect or defective ballast resistor will not provide enough resistance. Not all ballast resistors have the same resistance. The ballast resistor must match the ignition system.

4. A ballast wire that was replaced with a copper wire by mistake will allow excess current flow. The copper wire will allow almost double the normal amount of current to flow through the system.

5. Short start and stop drives in the winter will result in burned points. The ballast resistor and coil primary have less resistance when they are cold and pass more current until they warm up. The voltage regulator also causes a higher voltage when it is cold. This is called **temperature compensation**. A cold battery needs more voltage when it is charging. Temperature compensation causes extra current to flow in the ignition system, until the voltage regulator warms up.

6. Hard starting with long periods of cranking can also cause excess current flow. The ballast resistor is bypassed during cranking. Long periods of cranking will cause excess current flow for too long a time.

7. Cranking the engine while boost charging with portable boosters that put out 20–25V will burn the points.

CONDITION	CAUSED BY
 **BURNED**	Points any color other than slate grey should be considered to be burned. Failing condenser. Grease or oil burned on points. Excessive current flow from one or more sources. Poor alignment.
 **EXCESSIVE METAL TRANSFER OR PITTING**	Improper capacity condenser. Radio condenser connected to the distributor side of the coil.

Figure 11-15. Point conditions can be used to detect ignition system faults. (Courtesy of Ford Motor Company, Dearborn)

Condenser

When you are inspecting the condenser, look for deterioration on the lead wire or its connection, or signs of failure on the insulator or the seal on the condenser can. Do not take chances on a condenser—it is inexpensive to replace. If the points show any signs of indicating a condenser problem, replace the condenser. If there is a condenser tester available, use it to check a condenser you intend to reuse. Test a new condenser to be sure it is in good condition, as shown in Figure 11-16.

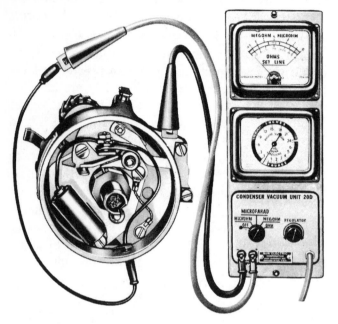

Figure 11-16.   Testing a distributor condenser. (Courtesy of Ford Motor Company, Dearborn)

Vacuum Advance

The easiest and safest way to test a vacuum advance is with a hand vacuum pump or a distributor test machine vacuum pump. The test will determine if the diaphragm holds vacuum. Figure 11-17 shows a hand vacuum pump. If a pump is not available, push in on the diaphragm arm and seal the fitting with your finger. Hold the vacuum advance near your ear, and release your finger. You will hear the hiss of the air entering the advance if the diaphragm is good. A badly rusted vacuum advance should be replaced, even if it tests correctly.

Centrifugal Advance and Shaft Side Play

To check the centrifugal advance while the distributor is still installed on the engine, try to turn the rotor with your fingers. If the shaft is not seized, the rotor should turn freely for a short distance in the direction of rotation and spring back when you release it. It should not turn the other way.

To check for **shaft side play**, align the point rubbing block on the high point of a cam lobe, and press the shaft back and forth (at a 90° angle to the points). Note the distance that the points move when you press on the shaft. As measured with a feeler gauge, the difference should not exceed .006 inches (.15 mm). Excess distributor shaft side play can result from a worn distributor shaft or bushing, or from wear between the point cam and the inner shaft. Excess side play causes the shaft to move back and forth while it is turning. This causes point dwell and ignition timing to be irregular and results in a rough-running, poorly operating engine.

You must remove and inspect the distributor to determine the condition, need for lubrication, or necessary repairs on the centrifugal advance. When you remove the distributor, you can also do further checks for excess distributor shaft side play.

Breaker Point Cam

The cam lobes should be shiny and smooth. If the cam is scored, it must be replaced. A scored cam will act like a file and wear down the point rubbing block.

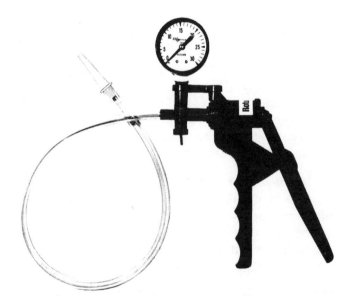

Figure 11-17.   A hand vacuum pump can be used to test a vacuum advance. (Courtesy of Ford Motor Company, Dearborn)

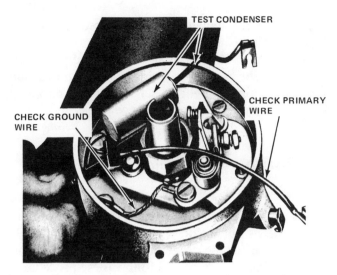

Figure 11-18. *The condition of the primary lead wire, ground wire, and condenser should be checked. The condenser should be tested. (Courtesy of Ford Motor Company, Dearborn)*

Distributor Primary Lead and Ground Lead

The primary and ground lead are made of very fine copper strands that are braided over steel wires. This gives the wires flexibility. Primary leads are insulated, but most ground leads are not. These leads must move back and forth with the breaker plate. If the wires are frayed or have cracked insulation, replace them. See Figure 11-18. Do not use ordinary copper wire for these leads. Ordinary copper wire is not flexible and will soon break.

FACTS TO REMEMBER

To function properly, the ignition system must have a minimum of voltage drop in wire connections and electrical devices. You should test for voltage drop and resistance during ignition system testing. All ignition system parts should be visually inspected for damage and wear. This inspection can help you diagnose ignition system faults.

□ ASSIGNMENT 11-C □

1. Explain how to test ignition cables.
2. Describe what to look for when inspecting a distributor cap.
3. List five causes of burnt points.

DISTRIBUTOR SERVICE

During ignition service, you often need to remove the distributor from the engine and give it a thorough inspection, cleaning, and service. There is a set procedure for this operation. Follow this procedure as closely as possible.

Distributor Removal and Installation

The distributor shaft is turned in time with the camshaft by a gear on the end of the distributor shaft that mates with a gear on the camshaft. The distributor must be marked before it is removed to ensure that the position of these two gears will be exactly the same when a distributor is reinstalled.

Procedure

1. Remove the distributor cap and wires, but do not remove the rotor. Look down into the open distributor and view it as a clock face with the distributor rotor as an hour hand.

2. Crank the engine until the rotor faces exactly the 6-o'clock position. This position is selected because it is an easy position to visualize. Put a chalk mark on the fire wall or inner fender to indicate the direction the distributor is facing. This will serve as a reminder for installation purposes.

3. Scribe a line on the edge of the distributor body in line with the rotor tip, as shown in Figure 11-19.

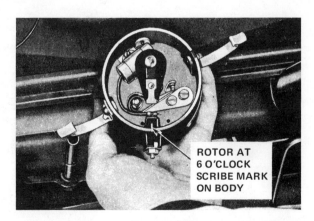

ROTOR AT 6 O'CLOCK SCRIBE MARK ON BODY

Figure 11-19. *A distributor should be marked before it is removed from the engine so that it can be installed in the same exact position. (Courtesy of General Motors of Canada Limited)*

4. Unbolt the distributor clamp, and pull straight up on the distributor housing to remove the distributor.

5. After repairing the distributor, install it so that the gear on the distributor shaft (Figure 11-20) meshes with the drive gear on the camshaft, and the distributor is fully seated in the engine block with the rotor in the same position it was in before removal.

If the distributor does not seat fully into the engine, the oil pump drive gear may be blocking the distributor shaft. Lift the distributor out again and use a long screw driver or socket (depending on the type of pump drive) to turn the oil pump drive gear until you get the right alignment. When you place the distributor back in the engine again, it should seat fully.

6. Once the distributor is fully seated, turn the distributor housing to align the line scribed on the housing with the rotor. Bolt the distributor in place and put on the cap, wires, primary lead, and vacuum line. Use a timing light to set the timing correctly. This step is covered later in this chapter.

Distributor Overhaul

The following is a general service procedure that can be applied to most distributors. Information and specifications not included here may be found in the shop manual for the distributor you are working on. Refer to Figure 11-20 as you follow these procedures.

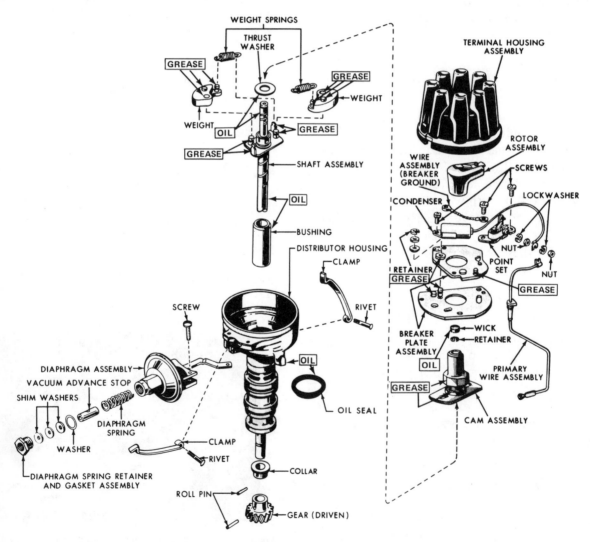

Figure 11-20.   An exploded view of a distributor with the lubrication points identified. (Courtesy of Ford Motor Company, Dearborn)

1. Use a vise with soft jaw caps to hold the distributor.

2. Clean the dirt off the distributor.

3. Remove the vacuum advance, and test it with a hand vacuum pump or the pump on the distributor test machine. When a strong vacuum is applied, the operating lever should pull in. The vacuum should remain steady after the pump is stopped. If the vacuum drops back or fails to come up to strength, there is a leak in the diaphragm and the advance unit must be replaced.

4. Remove the points and condenser and examine them.

5. Remove the breaker plate, and examine the pivots and slides for excess wear.

6. Check the centrifugal advance mechanism to determine if it is seized, has worn parts, damaged springs, or is in need of cleaning and lubrication. If the weights or the inner shaft of the point opening cam are seized, you will have to completely disassemble the centrifugal advance mechanism. Once the advance is disassembled, you can remove the dirt and rust and lubricate the parts.

7. Check the distributor shaft and bushing side play. Some distributors have no bushing on the lower section of the shaft. These distributors are steadied by a bushing inside the engine. If you do not account for this bushing when you measure side play on these distributors, they will show an extreme amount of side play. A special jig is available for checking such distributors. The jig slips over the shaft to steady it while you check the side play.

Figure 11-21 shows one method of checking side play by hooking the loop (handle) of a tension gauge over the distributor cam. Apply about 16 oz. (430 grams) of tension in several different directions, with the distributor shaft revolving in the test machine at about 500 rpm. The change in point dwell for each different direction in which the tension is applied should not exceed 3°.

An easy bench check is to press the shaft firmly toward the open point with the point rubbing block on a high peak of a cam, and measure the point gap. Release the pressure, and measure the gap again. The difference between the two measurements should not exceed .006 in. (.15 mm).

8. Check shaft end play against specifications with a feeler gauge between the shaft collar and body. A long distributor will have a lot of end play to allow

Figure 11-21. *Test for shaft and bushing wear. (Courtesy of Ford Motor Company, Dearborn)*

for heat expansion. A distributor with no end play when cold will probably seize when it is hot and could damage the gear teeth.

9. It is rarely necessary to replace a distributor shaft unless the vehicle has extremely high mileage. If you have to do so, follow the instructions in the shop manual.

10. Wash the centrifugal advance mechanism and all other dirty parts.

11. Refer to the lubrication points in Figure 11-20. On the centrifugal advance mechanism, grease the pivots and any parts that rub together. Oil the distributor shaft and cam guide shaft, and put a few drops of oil on the wick if there is one.

12. Install the breaker plate, and grease its moving parts.

13. Install the vacuum unit, and grease the pivot on the breaker plate.

14. Install the points and condenser, primary lead wire, and ground wire if there is one.

15. Install the point cam lubricator if there is one. On distributors without a point cam lubricator, grease the cam with special high-temperature distributor cam grease or a similar grease. If you do not apply cam grease, the cam and the point rubbing block will wear out.

16. Check the **point alignment**. Improperly

aligned points will burn because they never attain full contact. Figure 11-22 shows the contact area on misaligned points. Figure 11-23 shows how to use a special tool to bend the stationary point contact. Many tools have been made for this purpose. **Never** bend the moving point arm because it is easily broken.

17. Check to make sure that the point spring tension meets specifications. If there is too little point spring tension, the points will bounce or float away from the cam and cause the engine to cut out at some speeds. Too much spring tension causes excess wear on the rubbing block and cam. Excess spring tension also causes the distributor shaft and bushings to wear and results in early point failure or breakage.

Figure 11-24 shows how to test and adjust point tension. Read the statements on the illustration in order from one to four. On many point sets, spring tension is adjusted by sliding the spring back and forth in a slot on the spring plate, as shown in the illustration. On other point sets, you have to bend the spring. The spring on a pivotless point set is not adjustable.

18. Adjust the point gap to specifications with a feeler gauge while the point rubbing block is resting on a high peak on the distributor shaft cam, as shown in Figure 11-25. The proper point gap should give a dwell angle that is within tolerance.

19. If you reuse the rotor, cap, or wires, you should inspect and test them. If they are reusable,

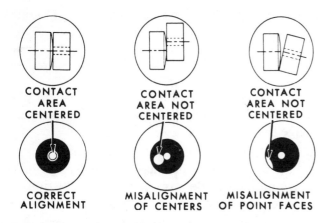

Figure 11-22. The breaker points must line up correctly for long life and good service. (Courtesy of Ford Motor Company, Dearborn)

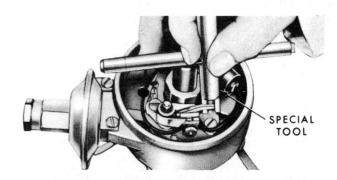

*Figure 11-23. Use an alignment tool to bend the stationary contact. **Never** bend the moving arm. (Courtesy of Ford Motor Company, Dearborn)*

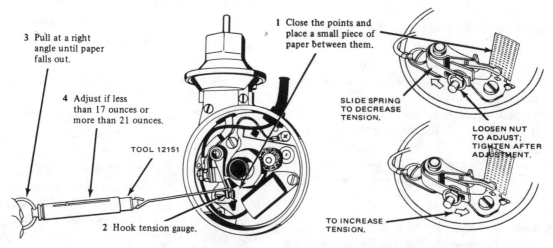

Figure 11-24. Point tension test and adjustment. (Courtesy of Ford Motor Company, Dearborn)

wash them in detergent soap and hot water. Use a short-bristle brush to clean the oxide, dirt, and oil off the cap and rotor. Do not be afraid to immerse the wires in water for a good scrubbing. Rinse the parts in hot water, and let them dry.

20. Test and calibrate the distributor. The points and the centrifugal advances are checked according to specifications, with a distributor test machine.

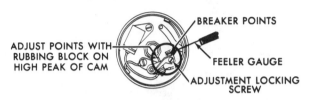

Figure 11-25. Adjust the point gap to get the proper dwell angle. (Courtesy of Ford Motor Company, Dearborn)

Using a Distributor Test Machine

There are a number of different distributor test machines on the market, but they all operate in almost the same manner. **A distributor test machine** converts electrical signals from the points into visual signals that show you:

1. the point dwell angle;
2. how the centrifugal advance is working;
3. how the vacuum advance is working; and
4. if the ignition sparks are occurring at an equal distance from each other. This verifies acceptable point lobe and shaft bushing wear.

Some machines can also be used to check breaker point resistance and test the condenser.

If you have not used one of these machines before, you should read over the manufacturer's instruction book until you are familiar with the machine. Then follow the book, step by step, as you test a distributor.

Figures 11-26 and 11-27 show two important tests that a distributor tester can perform. During the centrifugal advance test, the speed control can be regulated by the operator. The arrows on the test dial in Figure 11-26 appear at 45° apart, because an eight-cylinder distributor is being tested. In the centrifugal advance test, the arrows will change position to indicate the amount of timing advance provided by the centrifugal advance at different speeds.

Distributor test machines show the number of sparks per distributor shaft revolution and the number of degrees apart that each spark is delivered. The arrows (which represent the spark) appear every 90° for a four-cylinder distributor, every 60° for a six, and every 45° for an eight. You can adjust the amount of centrifugal advance on some distributors by

Figure 11-26. A centrifugal advance test. (Courtesy of Ford Motor Company, Dearborn)

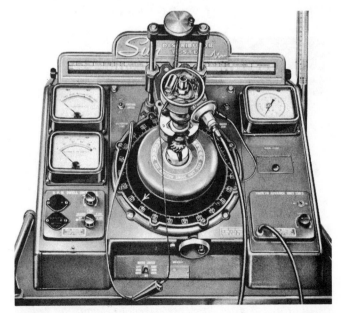

Figure 11-27. A vacuum advance test. (Courtesy of Ford Motor Company, Dearborn)

bending the spring brackets, as shown in Figure 11-28. Some advances are not adjustable.

To perform the vacuum advance test (Figure 11-27), you must connect the vacuum hose to the distributor vacuum advance. Run the test machine at a fixed speed, suggested in the manufacturer's instructions, and adjust the vacuum. The arrows will change position to indicate the amount of advance, according to the strength of the vacuum. Figures 11-29 and 11-30 show how to change the spring tension to adjust the amount of advance supplied by the vacuum advance. This adjustment is done by turning the

spring tension adjuster with an Allen wrench (Figure 11-29) or by adding or subtracting spacing washers (Figure 11-30).

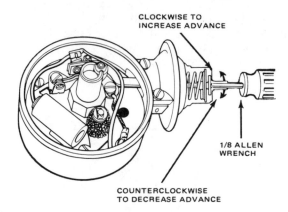

Figure 11-29.   Using an Allen wrench to adjust vacuum advance. (Courtesy of Ford Motor Company, Dearborn)

BEND BRACKET AWAY FROM CENTER

TOO MUCH ADVANCE

BEND BRACKET TOWARD CENTER

NOT ENOUGH ADVANCE

FACTS TO REMEMBER

During ignition system service, you must sometimes remove, clean, and service the distributor. The distributor should be marked before it is removed so that it can be reinstalled in the exact position that it was in before it was removed. Once the distributor is removed, it should be checked and lubricated. Distributor test machines can be used to test the distributor before and after a distributor overhaul.

Figure 11-28.   Adjust the centrifugal advance on a Ford distributor by using a screwdriver to bend the spring bracket. (Courtesy of Ford Motor Company, Dearborn)

Figure 11-30.   Adding or subtracting spacing washers to adjust vacuum advance. (Courtesy of Ford Motor Company, Dearborn)

□ ASSIGNMENT 11-D □

1. Explain how to mark the distributor for removal and reinstallation.

2. List the points to lubricate and the type of lubrication to use when servicing a distributor.

3. Explain why the following adjustments have to be made and checked during distributor service:
   point alignment
   point spring tension
   point gap

4. List four important tests that can be done on a distributor test machine.

INSTALLING AN UNMARKED DISTRIBUTOR

One of the most difficult tasks for a novice mechanic is the installation of a distributor when there are no prior installation marks with which to line up the distributor. This could happen when a new engine is installed, or if the engine was accidently cranked with the distributor removed.

If you recall the four-stroke cycle, you should realize that the ignition spark fires only every other time a piston is at top dead center. The timing marks on the crankshaft pulley line up with the reference mark on the engine when #1 cylinder is at top dead center on the compression stroke. The marks also come together when #1 cylinder is at top dead center on the exhaust stroke. If the distributor is incorrectly timed to #1 cylinder on the exhaust stroke, all of the cylinders will fire at 180° out of time. The engine will not operate, and it will backfire when you crank it over.

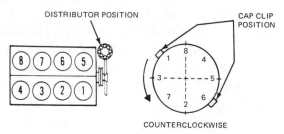

FIRING ORDER – 1-3-7-2-6-5-4-8

Figure 11-31.   A typical chart for firing order, wire positions, and distributor position. (Courtesy of Ford Motor Company, Dearborn)

Procedure

1.   Look up the ignition specifications in the manufacturer's shop manual or a specifications book.

2.   Clean the crankshaft pulley timing marks. Put chalk or paint on the mark that is used for initial timing and on the pointer or reference line, so they can be easily seen.

3.   Remove #1 spark plug. The front cylinder on four- and six-cylinder in-line engines is #1. If #1 is not marked on the intake manifold of a V-8, look up its location in the specifications book.

4.   Look up the position of #1 spark plug wire in the distributor cap and the position the distributor body should have when it is installed in the engine. Most specifications books give this information. An example is shown in Figure 11-31. If the cap and wires have not been removed from the engine, it will be easy to determine which is the #1 spark plug wire by following the wire from the #1 spark plug back to the cap.

5.   Fit the cap over the distributor, and put a scratch line on the distributor body in line with #1 plug wire.

6.   Place a compression whistle or a compression tester in #1 spark plug hole, or place your finger over the hole.

7.   Crank the engine over, a bit at a time, until compression is apparent by the loud whistle, shows on the compression tester, or blows around your finger. The crank pulley timing marks should line up at this point. See Figure 11-32.

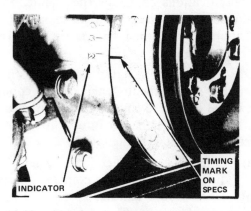

Figure 11-32.   Number 1 cylinder is at top dead center on the compression stroke when the timing marks line up and compression is apparent. (Courtesy of General Motors of Canada Limited)

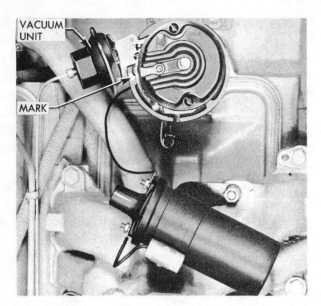

Figure 11-33. The rotor should face the mark on the distributor body. (Courtesy of General Motors of Canada Limited)

If the timing marks end up past their position for cylinder #1 on the compression stroke, the crankshaft will have to be brought back to the mark. This can be done by using a socket on the crankshaft pulley nut or by cranking the engine completely around again. If the timing marks become lined up without any signs of compression, then #1 cylinder is on the exhaust stroke instead of the compression stroke, and the crankshaft must be rotated 180°.

8. Install the distributor fully seated into the engine block with the rotor facing the scratch mark you made on the distributor body, as shown in Figure 11-33. The body should be positioned the same way as in the specifications chart for the engine. Put the distributor clamp in place just tight enough to allow the distributor to be turned, and connect the distributor wire to the ignition coil.

9. You can now static time the distributor. **Static timing** will bring the engine close enough to correct initial timing so that you can start it and set the initial timing. The procedure below should be followed during static timing:

(a) Connect a voltmeter (or test light) to the distributor side of the coil and to ground.
(b) Turn on the ignition switch, but do not start the engine.
(c) Rotate the distributor a little in the direction of distributor shaft rotation (retarding it) until the points close and the voltmeter reads zero (or the test light is off).

(d) Slowly turn the distributor in the direction opposite to distributor shaft rotation (advancing it) until the points open and voltage shows on the meter (or the test light is on). Repeat this procedure again to be certain that the setting is correct.

10. Tighten the distributor clamp in this position and complete the installation. Make sure you connect the correct plug wire to each plug.

11. Start the engine and check the ignition timing with a timing light, as described in the next procedure.

ADJUSTING IGNITION TIMING

You must check and set the ignition timing when the distributor has been removed, when the points have been replaced, when the dwell (point gap) has been changed, or if the engine performs poorly due to incorrect timing. For this procedure you will need a timing light, tach-dwell meter, and tools to loosen and tighten the distributor clamp.

Procedure

1. Look for a decal under the hood or use a shop manual or specifications book to obtain the following information:

(a) the speed the engine should be operating while you check the timing;
(b) which degree mark on the crankshaft pulley should be used during timing; and
(c) which vacuum lines to remove and whether they should be plugged or left open.

It is difficult to find the timing mark on some vehicles, or to decide which timing mark to use unless you have a shop manual or specifications book.

2. The engine should be warmed up to the point where it will run with the choke open and maintain a normal idle speed.

3. Remove and plug the vacuum lines according to the specifications.

4. Find the timing marks, clean them, and mark them with chalk or white paint.

5. Adjust the tach-dwell meter (calibrate the meter, and select the number of engine cylinders and

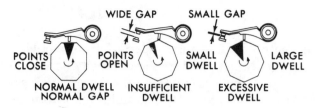

Figure 11-34. *Point gap affects dwell angle. (Courtesy of Ford Motor Company, Dearborn)*

proper scale). Connect the leads to the distributor side of the coil and to ground. Connect the black wire to ground on negative ground systems.

6. Connect the timing light to #1 spark plug.

7. Start the engine and observe the dwell. It should read according to specifications. If it does not, the points should be regapped before you proceed. Changing the point gap (dwell) changes the timing. If the dwell reads too high, the points are set too close. If the dwell reads too low, the points are set too wide, as shown in Figure 11-34. If the points are not pitted, you can reset them with a feeler gauge. If they are pitted, any attempt to set them with a feeler gauge will result in a gap that is wider than it should be. See Figure 11-35.

To regap the points, first remove the distributor cap and rotor. Crank the engine over and observe the dwell while you adjust the points with a screwdriver. Points with an Allen key adjuster can be adjusted while the engine is running.

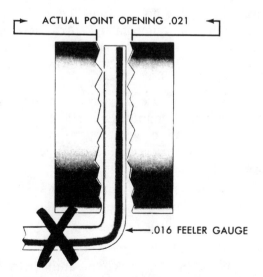

Figure 11-35. *A feeler gauge will not accurately measure the point gap if the points are rough. (Courtesy of General Motors of Canada Limited)*

8. Before you time the engine, it should be idling at the speed indicated in the specifications. Adjust the engine idle speed screw if necessary.

9. Point the timing light so that it flashes at the timing marks. View the marks at right angles, as shown in Figure 11-36. The correct timing marks should align when the light flashes. Because the timing light flashes only when #1 cylinder fires, the timing mark appears to be standing still next to the reference marks.

10. To change the timing, loosen the distributor mounting clamp and rotate the distributor a bit at a time while you watch the timing marks. When the marks line up, tighten the distributor clamp. Recheck the marks to be sure that the timing is still correct after you have tightened the distributor clamp.

Checking Distributor Advance with a Timing Light

A timing light can be used to check the operation of the distributor advance mechanism. Follow the steps below for this procedure.

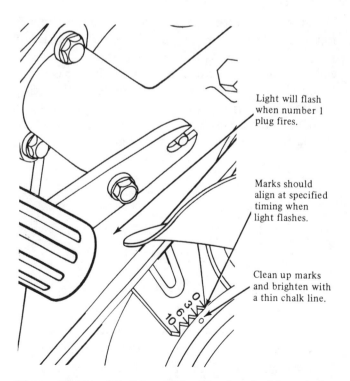

Figure 11-36. *Checking and adjusting ignition timing using a timing light. (Courtesy of Ford Motor Company, Dearborn)*

Procedure

1.   Remove and plug the vacuum advance hose to disconnect the vacuum advance. If there is a dual-vacuum advance, remove and plug both hoses.

2.   To check centrifugal advance operation, start the engine and use the timing light to observe the timing marks while you gradually increase engine speed. The timing should advance as the speed increases and return to the basic setting again at idle.

3.   To check vacuum advance operation, operate the engine at 2000 rpm, while observing the timing marks with the timing light. Then install the vacuum line on the vacuum advance (on dual units, install the advance side line only). When the vacuum hose is installed, the timing should advance the amount stated in the manufacturer's specifications, and the engine should speed up.

On dual-advance units, return the engine to idle and observe the timing as you install the hose on the retard side of the advance. The spark should retard 4° to 10°, as stated in the manufacturer's specifications.

FACTS TO REMEMBER

Often a distributor that has no installation marks must be installed in an engine. There is a set series of steps that must be followed to complete this procedure. You must ensure that the distributor ends up timed to the engine when #1 cylinder is in the firing position near top dead center on the compression stroke. After installation, the distributor advance should be checked with a timing light.

☐   ASSIGNMENT 11-E   ☐

1.   Explain how to find #1 cylinder firing position.
2.   Explain how to static time a distributor.
3.   What information is needed in order to set the timing?
4.   Describe the use of a timing light to check the timing.
5.   Describe how to check the operation of a single-vacuum advance mechanism with a timing light.

BATTERY SERVICE

The battery is an important part of an automobile ignition system. It provides the electricity necessary to start the car and to run the electrical accessories when the engine is turned off. The following information and illustrations on battery maintenance, testing, and service are taken in part from information supplied by the Ford Motor Company, Dearborn.

Safety Precautions

The principal hazards in battery service occur when you are charging the battery or handling acid. The following is a list of safety rules that must be observed when handling or charging batteries:

1.   When you are mixing battery electrolyte, always pour the acid into the water. Never pour water into acid.

2.   When you are working with acid, such as when you are filling batteries, wear splashproof goggles. Other articles of protective clothing, such as rubber gloves, should also be worn if batteries are handled frequently.

3.   When you are adding water or electrolyte to a battery, always use plastic containers and funnels.

4.   Never store acid in warm areas or in direct sunlight.

5.   If you burn your skin or eyes with acid, rinse the burned area immediately with clear water. Continue rinsing for no less than five minutes. Get medical attention immediately! Acid-neutralizing agents, such as baking soda, should always be kept close by to neutralize spilled acid. However, never put anything but clean, clear water in your eyes!

6.   When you are charging a battery, manufacturer's recommendations should be followed. These recommendations will ensure that you charge at a safe rate. This prevents the rapid generation of hydrogen gas. Hydrogen gas is extremely explosive!

7.   Open flames or smoking should not be allowed near batteries that are being charged.

8.   Avoid letting tools or metal objects fall across battery terminals.

9.   Never break a live circuit at the battery terminals. A spark usually occurs whenever charger or booster cable leads are disconnected. Any spark

could ignite the hydrogen gas that has accumulated around the battery. Make sure the charger is switched off before disconnecting the charger leads from the battery.

10. Use fender covers to protect the vehicle finish from acid.

Reasons for Shortened Battery Life

There are four general reasons for battery failure:

1. Poor physical condition (battery cracked or terminals corroded).
2. Prolonged undercharging or overcharging (improperly functioning voltage regulator, alternator, or generator).
3. Undercapacity application (battery too small for the vehicle).
4. Lack of proper maintenance (electrolyte level too low, terminals corroded).

The physical condition of a battery is an important factor in battery performance. One cause of poor battery condition is normal deterioration as the battery gets old. Repeated charging and discharging cycles slowly wear away the active materials in the battery plates and deposit them in the sediment area beneath the elements. A point is eventually reached where the surface area of the plates that is available for reaction with the electrolyte is too small to allow the battery to be fully recharged.

A low supply of electrolyte will cause early deterioration of the active material in the battery plates. If this should happen, there will not be enough plate area left to produce the power needed for the load on the battery.

Other factors that contribute to poor battery condition include damage, manufacturing defects, and lack of preventive maintenance.

Too much or too little charging power can also damage a battery. This applies to the vehicle charging system, or an external charging device. Some typical results of improper charging, undercapacity use, and poor battery maintenance are listed below.

Improper Charging

Improper charging may be caused by one or more of the following problems:

1. faulty voltage regulation;
2. incorrect generator or alternator output;

3. faulty conductors and/or connections in the circuit; or
4. poorly operating circuit control components (such as relays, solenoids, or switches).

Overcharging: Overcharging causes severe corrosion of the positive grids. When a battery is overcharging, the water in the battery decomposes into hydrogen and oxygen gas. This tends to lower the electrolyte level in the battery. This may damage the battery plates, because they are exposed to air or a high concentration of electrolyte.

The excess heat from overcharging will intensify the normal chemical reaction in the battery and damage the plates, separators, case, and sealing compounds. Excess heat can cause severe positive plate warpage and separator perforations. This is most likely to occur if overcharging follows a period of undercharging.

Electrolyte may blow out of the battery cells if overcharging is excessive. If this electrolyte is not neutralized, it may damage the cables, battery mounting bracket, and other engine compartment components.

Undercharging: Undercharging causes the density of sulfate on the battery plates to increase. This heavy sulfate deposit resists the normal electrochemical reaction that occurs when the battery is being charged. Also, an undercharged battery has a high water content in the electrolyte. During cold weather, this increases the possibility of battery freezing.

Undercapacity

When an automobile manufacturer specifies a battery of a given capacity as original equipment, this capacity rating takes into consideration the known demands that starting, accessory operation, etc., will place on the battery. The accuracy of this rating assumes that the demand on the battery will not change.

Several factors that might alter the demand on the battery are:

1. Poor starting that causes excess battery drain during starting because starting is prolonged.
2. An electrical circuit problem will frequently drain the battery.
3. The addition of electrical accessories in the battery circuit that exceed the charging capacity of

the battery could lead to very gradual battery discharge and eventual battery failure.

Poor Maintenance

The service technician who understands the operation of the starting and charging system will be a better-qualified troubleshooter for battery problems. Since battery operation depends on proper charging system operation, charging system maintenance is important to battery life. Remember that even a new battery cannot function correctly for very long without proper charging.

BATTERY PREVENTIVE MAINTENANCE

Preventive maintenance in battery service means performing those service operations that contribute to maximum battery life and operating efficiency. Most battery failures can be prevented by proper battery care.

Service Procedures

One of the most important service procedures that you can perform on a battery is cleaning the corrosive deposits off of the cables and the top of the battery case. Battery manufacturers have designed one-piece covers to help stop acid seepage on the tops of their batteries. Battery cleaning is very simple and should be done frequently. However, cleanliness is only part of a battery maintenance program. Several other service procedures must often be undertaken.

The following service procedures are a step-by-step guide for battery maintenance.

1. Raise the hood and put a fender cover in place.

2. Remove the battery cables from the battery posts (negative cable first). Clean the cable terminals with an acid-neutralizing solution and wire brush.

3. Remove the battery hold-down clamps.

4. Remove the battery from the vehicle.

5. Place the battery over a suitable drain.

6. Wash the battery exterior with an acid-neutralizing solution (ammonia, or baking soda and water). Do not allow any neutralizer to get inside the battery cells. When the exterior is clean, rinse the battery with clean water. Then dry the battery.

7. Wash the battery tray with a neutralizing solution. Then rinse the tray with clear water. Scrape off any excess corrosion or rust deposits, and open the water drain holes in the bottom of the tray. Dry the tray. If the tray is badly corroded, paint it with acid-resistant paint.

8. Test the battery and determine if it should be placed back in service, recharged, or replaced.

9. Clean the battery posts with a wire brush.

10. Add water to the battery if necessary.

11. Place the battery back in the vehicle.

12. Tighten the hold-down clamp (do not overtighten).

13. Replace the felt washers if so equipped.

14. Install the battery cables (positive cable first). Replace the cables if they are old, worn, frayed, or cracked. Coat the terminals and wire connectors with grease.

15. Check the charging system and/or ignition system if the battery tests indicate that there is still a problem.

BATTERY TESTING AND DIAGNOSIS

Battery tests determine the battery's state of charge and general condition. Battery tests will determine if the battery is good, needs and can receive recharging, or should be replaced.

Before any test procedures are undertaken, you should give the battery a thorough visual examination to determine if it has been physically damaged. A battery with a cracked and leaking outer case should always be replaced. Check the cable connections. Clean and tighten them if needed.

Check the electrolyte before attempting any tests. Rated capacity is available only when all battery plates are covered by the electrolyte. If the electrolyte level is low, add water as needed.

Electrolyte is a clear liquid with a slight smell of rotten eggs. Any discoloration or the presence of a strong rotten-egg smell suggests one of the following:

1. an excessively high charging rate;

2. constant overcharge/undercharge cycles;

3. impurities in the electrolyte; or

4. an old battery near the end of its service life.

Test Procedures

There are a variety of battery testing instruments available for many different battery tests. You are limited to those tests that your equipment will handle. For that reason, we will describe only tests that can be made with simple test equipment. Refer to equipment manufacturer's specifications for the operation of more complex test equipment.

You must find out certain initial information about a battery in order to proceed with any detailed testing.

Battery Charge: You must find the present state of battery charge. How you measure battery charge depends on the type of battery you are testing. On batteries with soft covers and exposed cell connectors, you can use a **cell voltage tester**. This is known as **open circuit voltage testing** (O.C.V.T.). On one-piece or **hard-cover** batteries, you can use a **hydrometer** to find the **specific gravity** of the electrolyte. This will determine the state of charge. You can also use a **cell analyzer** that measures individual cell voltages by inserting probes into the cell openings. Follow the instructions furnished with the unit.

Battery Condition: You must decide if the battery will respond satisfactorily to charging. This is where your accumulated knowledge of battery testing becomes valuable. You must know the battery age, condition, and load demands; specific charging rates available in the vehicle; owner experience; service specifications; and visual clues.

Testing for State of Charge

Specific Gravity Tests with a Hydrometer: The electrolyte in each battery cell is a mixture of water and acid. The acid content drops as the charge level drops. By measuring the acid content of a battery cell, you can determine the cell's state of charge. Cell acid content is measured with a **hydrometer**. See Figure 11-37. The hydrometer has a floating bulb of a known weight. Since the acid in the electrolyte is heavier than water, more acid content in the electrolyte causes the bulb to float higher, and less acid makes it float lower.

The hydrometer bulb is calibrated to tell you the acid content of the electrolyte. Pure water will float the bulb at exactly 1.000 (the specific gravity of water). A fully charged battery will float the hydrometer bulb at a specific gravity of about 1.260–1.280.

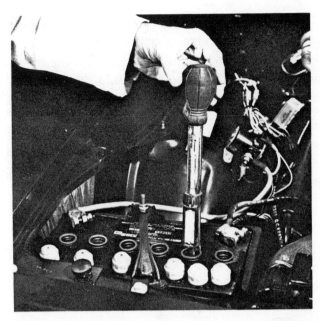

Figure 11-37. A typical hydrometer has a scale for specific gravity and a temperature correction scale. (Courtesy of Ford Motor Company, Dearborn)

See Figure 11-38. However, temperature affects specific gravity. Thus, the readings hold true only if the electrolyte is measured at exactly 80°F. This is why a battery hydrometer is equipped with a thermometer in addition to the bulb. The specific gravity is read with the hydrometer and then corrected according to the temperature of the electrolyte. This gives a true specific gravity reading for different temperatures. A hydrometer is fairly simple to use.

1. Make sure the electrolyte is high enough to draw enough acid into the hydrometer barrel. Do not take readings directly after adding water to the battery. The battery must be charged to thoroughly mix the water with the electrolyte before the hydrometer readings will be accurate.

SPECIFIC GRAVITY	STATE OF CHARGE
1.260-1.280	100% CHARGED
1.230-1.250	75% CHARGED
1.200-1.220	50% CHARGED
1.170-1.190	25% CHARGED
1.140-1.160	VERY WEAK
1.110-1.130	DISCHARGED

Figure 11-38. The specific gravity reading (corrected for temperature) will give an indication of the battery charge. (Courtesy of Ford Motor Company, Dearborn)

2. Insert the hydrometer pickup tube into a cell while holding the squeeze bulb collapsed.

3. Slowly release the pressure on the bulb to draw electrolyte into the bulb. Hold the hydrometer straight up and down so that the glass bulb floats freely.

4. Hold the hydrometer at eye level and note the number on the float scale that is intersected by the upper surface of the electrolyte in the hydrometer barrel.

5. Check this number against the temperature correction scale.

6. Note this reading and proceed to test the remaining cells in the same manner.

FACTS TO REMEMBER

Safety precautions should be observed when you service a battery, particularly when you are charging a battery or handling acids. Batteries fail for a number of reasons. Among these are poor physical condition, excess under or overcharging, using a battery that is undercapacity for the vehicle in which it is installed, and lack of proper battery maintenance. Battery service requires few tools, is simple, and can prolong battery life. A hydrometer can be used to check the state of charge in battery cells and determine battery condition.

LOW-MAINTENANCE BATTERIES

A number of newer batteries, called **low-maintenance** or **maintenance-free batteries**, have less maintenance requirements than the older lead-acid batteries. The important difference in these new batteries is that electrolyte gassing is reduced by using less **antimony** or by the use of **calcium** instead of antimony to harden the lead plate grids. The loss of battery water through gassing is so reduced in low-maintenance batteries that they can have a sealed top with no cell filler caps. However, some battery companies still put cell filler caps on their low-maintenance batteries.

A **charge indicator** is built into some maintenance-free batteries. One example of a battery with a charge indicator is distributed by General Motors. See Figure 11-39. The indicator is actually a built-in hydrometer located in one battery cell. It provides visual information on the battery state of charge. In-

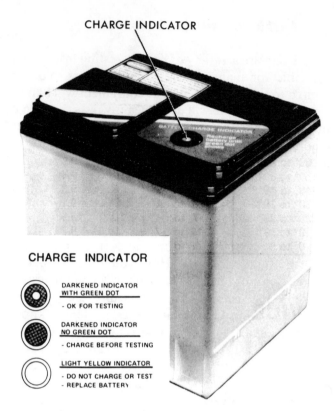

Figure 11-39. The General Motors maintenance-free battery has a charge indicator that changes color to indicate the state of battery charge. (Courtesy of General Motors of Canada Limited)

formation on how to read the charge indicators and the service procedures for specific low-maintenance batteries can be obtained from battery manufacturers or shop manuals.

☐   ASSIGNMENT 11-F   ☐

1. List four general reasons for shortened battery life.

2. List the possible causes of battery explosions.

3. List the safety considerations that should be observed during battery service.

4. What would the specific gravity reading be for a battery in the following different states of charge?
   100% charged
   75% charged
   50% charged
   25% charged
   Discharged

☐ SELF-TEST ☐

Complete the following sentences by filling in the missing words.

1. A compression test must be performed each time you think that one or more engine _____ have lost _____ .

2. Poor compression is a result of either _____ leaking into and out of a _____ or compression leaking past the _____ rings.

3. If you lock the throttle and choke open during a compression test, you can avoid opening and closing the _____ during each separate cylinder test.

4. A compression difference of _____ to _____ psi (105–175 kPa) is generally acceptable.

5. Ignition sparks tend to jump from the _____ edges of the plug center _____ . If you keep this edge _____ , the plug will have a better spark.

6. In order for the ignition system to function properly, it must have the proper amount of _____ available. This is only possible if there is a minimum amount of voltage _____ in the electrical devices and _____ in the circuit.

7. During resistance checks, you must turn off the _____ switch and disconnect the battery _____ cable to prevent connecting the ohmmeter to the system voltage. This would _____ the ohmmeter.

8. Carbon paths (or tracks) are formed by high-voltage _____ through dirt or moisture on an electrical component until a _____ is _____ into the surface of the component.

9. If the ignition wires pass inspection, check their _____ with an _____ .

10. The ignition wires should be cleaned with _____ _____ and _____ water before reinstallation.

11. Points that are burned blue have been burnt by excess _____ flow.

12. The easiest and safest way to test a vacuum advance is with a hand _____ pump or a distributor test machine _____ pump.

13. Excessive distributor shaft side play can result from a _____ distributor shaft or _____ , or from wear between the point _____ and its inner shaft.

14. Never bend the _____ point arm because it is easily broken.

15. If there is too little point spring tension, the points will _____ or _____ away from the _____ and cause the engine to cut out at some speeds.

16. On many point sets, spring tension is adjusted by _____ the _____ back and forth.

17. The timing marks on the crankshaft _____ line up with the reference mark on the engine when _____ cylinder is at top dead center on the _____ stroke.

18. If the distributor is incorrectly timed to #1 cylinder on the _____ stroke, all of the cylinders will fire _____ out of time.

19. You must check and set the ignition timing when the _____ has been removed, when the _____ have been replaced, when the _____ has been changed, or if the engine performs poorly due to incorrect timing.

20. The principal hazards in battery service occur when you are _____ the battery or handling _____ .

21. A low supply of electrolyte will cause _____ deterioration of the _____ material in the battery _____ .

22. Even a new battery cannot function correctly for very long without proper _____ .

23. Battery tests will determine if the battery is _____ , needs and can receive _____ , or should be _____ .

24. By measuring the acid content of a battery _____ , you can determine the cell's state of _____ .

25. A fully charged battery will float the hydrometer bulb at a specific gravity of about _____ – _____ .

26. The specific gravity is read with a _____ and then corrected according to the _____ of the electrolyte.

12

ELECTRONIC IGNITION SYSTEMS

☐ LEARNING OBJECTIVES ☐

After studying this chapter, you will be able to:

1. Describe the difference between a point-type ignition system and an electronic ignition system.

2. Describe how the spark is produced in an electronic ignition system.

3. Describe the procedure used to diagnose and test Chrysler, Ford, and General Motors electronic ignition systems.

4. Describe the purpose of the main components in a Chrysler Electronic Spark Control system.

5. Define and/or discuss the following terms:

solid state	stator
transistor	engine sensors
electronic ignition	control unit
pickup coil	vacuum transducer
reluctor	

INTRODUCTION

There appears to be no end to the things that can be done with electronic circuitry. **Electronic ignition systems** use electronic circuitry to produce the ignition spark. Most new electronic equipment is **solid state**. Solid state devices have no tubes or relays. Instead, they use a number of different **transistors** and **diodes**. The term "solid state" refers to the fact that transistors are solid, rather than hollow glass tubes. One major advantage of transistors is that they do not break.

The automobile ignition system is one example where transistors are used. Recall that ignition spark advance on a conventional ignition system is controlled mechanically. This is done with a cam lobe that opens the breaker points, and with centrifugal and vacuum advances. Most electronic ignition systems also use centrifugal and vacuum advances. Other systems use a solid state control unit to control ignition spark. It would not be possible to discuss all of the solid state devices and other components that make up the control units used in electronic ignition systems. To do so would require a complete book. The control unit circuitry is sealed. Control units cannot be serviced, but are replaced if they break down. However, by comparing a conventional ignition system with an electronic ignition system, we can get an idea of the differences between the two systems. Once we understand the differences between the two, we can become familiar with how the electronic ignition system produces an ignition spark. A comparison between a conventional and an electronic ignition system is shown here.

Electronic components have not changed ignition system fundamentals. The principles of operation are similar for both conventional and electronic ignition systems. An ignition coil is still used in an electronic ignition system, but an **electronic control unit** or **module** turns on the current flow into the coil primary winding. This current builds up a magnetic field inside the coil. The electronic control unit turns off the primary current by using a signal from a **pickup coil** inside the distributor. When the primary current is turned off, the magnetic field collapses and cuts across the conductors of the coil secondary winding. This collapse induces a high voltage into the coil secondary winding. The high voltage fires the spark plug through the distributor cap, rotor, and high-tension cables.

In this chapter, we will discuss the operation of an electronic ignition system, using a Chrysler electronic system as an example. If you understand one system, you should be able to understand the other systems, because they all operate in a similar manner.

CONVENTIONAL	ELECTRONIC
Ignition Coil	Identical in some systems. Others have a different turns ratio. General Motors systems use a transformer.
Breaker Points and Cam	Replaced by pickup unit and reluctor (Chrysler); stator and armature (Ford); pickup coil and timer core (G.M.).
Primary Current: breaker point closing and opening turns the primary current on and off.	A control unit is used to turn the primary current on and off, based on signals from the pickup coil.
Ballast Resistor: used to help regulate current flow in the primary circuit.	A ballast resistor is used in some systems, but not in others.
Secondary Ignition Parts	Identical on some systems. Other systems use a similar design, but with better insulating material. Better quality high-tension cables are used.
Spark Plugs	Identical in some systems. Other systems use plugs that are widely gapped.

THE CHRYSLER ELECTRONIC IGNITION SYSTEM

The following information and illustrations are taken in part from information provided by Chrysler Corporation.

Figure 12-1 shows a Chrysler electronic ignition system electrical circuit. Chrysler Corporation uses the same ignition coil on both their electronic and their point-type ignition systems. As shown in Figure 12-2, the distributor has a **pickup coil** and a **reluctor** instead of breaker points and a cam. Otherwise the distributor is unchanged and still provides centrifugal and vacuum advance. The ballast resistor pictured in Figure 12-3 has dual resistances. One resistance is for the coil, and one is for the control unit. The control unit is shown in Figure 12-4.

As pointed out by the arrows in Figure 12-2, the pickup coil is wound around one pole of a permanent magnet. The pole that the pickup coil is wound around is called the **pole piece**. Because the pickup coil is wound around a magnet, it is surrounded by a permanent magnetic field that passes into the reluctor. The reluctor and pickup coil work together to produce an electrical signal. The signal causes the control unit to interrupt the current flow in the primary circuit and induce the high voltage in the coil. This high voltage jumps the spark plug gap.

Reluctor

The reluctor is shaped like a gear and has a tooth for each cylinder. It is attached to the distributor shaft in the same position as the cam would be in a breaker-point distributor. The reluctor is not a magnet, but it does provide a better magnetic path than air. In other words, it is capable of reducing **reluc-**

Figure 12-2. An eight-cylinder Chrysler Electronic Ignition System distributor. (Courtesy of Chrysler Corporation)

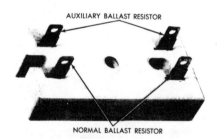

Figure 12-3. The dual-ballast resistor for the Chrysler system. (Courtesy of Chrysler Corporation)

Figure 12-4. The Chrysler control unit. (Courtesy of Chrysler Corporation)

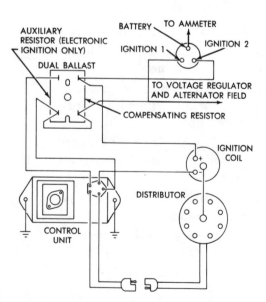

Figure 12-1. A Chrysler Electronic Ignition System schematic. (Courtesy of Chrysler Corporation)

tance (resistance to magnetic flow), which is why it is called a reluctor. In a very general way, the reluctor and pickup coil in an electronic ignition system do electrically what the cam and rubbing block do mechanically in a breaker-point ignition system. However, although the reluctor and pickup coil replace the cam and breaker points, they operate quite differently. The pickup coil is not a set of points, and there is no contact between the reluctor and the pickup coil.

Pickup Coil

A permanent magnet in the pickup coil produces a magnetic field. The magnetic field passes through the pickup coil that is wound around the pole piece. The magnetic field is relatively weak when there is an air gap between the pole piece and the magnet because air does not provide a good magnetic path between the two. See Figure 12-5.

Figure 12-6 shows that as a reluctor tooth approaches the pickup coil, it provides a better magnetic path than the air gap, and the strength of the magnetic field in the pickup coil is increased. The increasing field strength in the pickup coil induces a positive voltage at one terminal of the pickup coil winding. This voltage is induced by the changing (increasing) magnetic field strength and not by the movement of the magnetic field or the pickup coil. The positive voltage continues to build in the pickup

coil terminal until the reluctor tooth is exactly opposite the pole piece.

As soon as the reluctor tooth passes the pole piece, the air gap starts to increase and, as shown in Figure 12-7, the magnetic field strength in the pickup coil begins to decrease. The decreasing field strength through the pickup coil winding induces a reversed or negative voltage at the same terminal of the pickup coil winding. Notice that the polarity signs change in Figures 12-6 and 12-7.

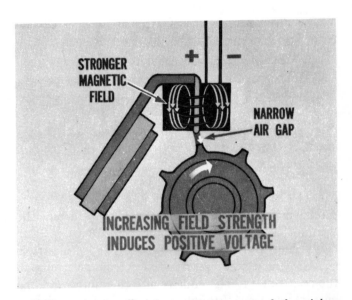

Figure 12-6. *As the reluctor moves toward the pickup coil, the magnetic field strength increases. (Courtesy of Chrysler Corporation)*

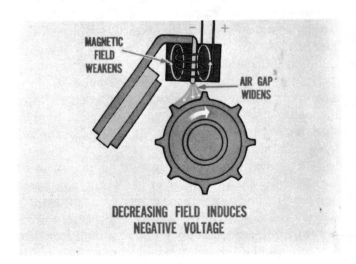

Figure 12-7. *The strength of the magnetic field decreases as the air gap increases. (Courtesy of Chrysler Corporation)*

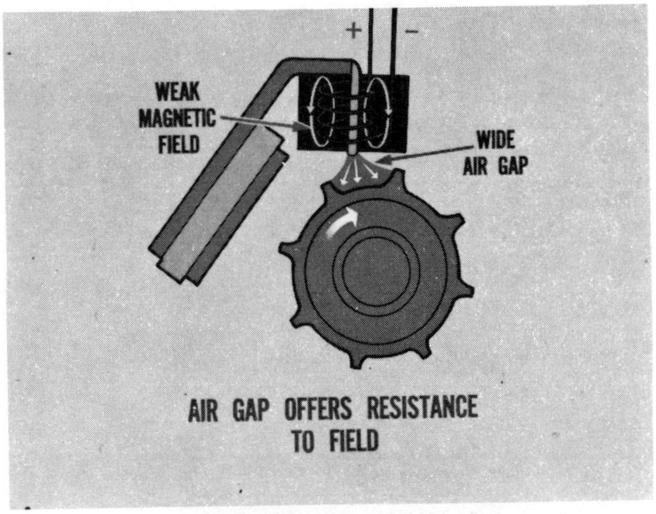

Figure 12-5. *An air gap offers resistance to the magnetic field when the reluctor is pointing away from the pickup coil. (Courtesy of Chrysler Corporation)*

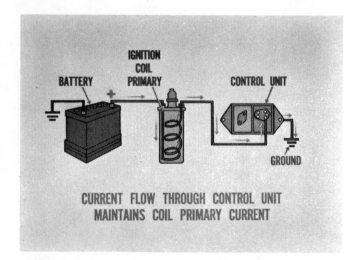

Figure 12-8.   As long as a positive voltage is applied to the control unit, the current flows through the ignition coil primary winding. (Courtesy of Chrysler Corporation)

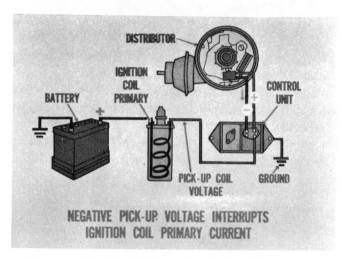

Figure 12-9.   When the reluctor passes the pole piece, a negative voltage is sent through the pole piece to the control unit, and the ignition primary current is turned off. (Courtesy of Chrysler Corporation)

The induced voltage in the pickup coil is very small. It provides a tiny electrical signal that is fed into the electronic control unit. The function of the voltage induced in the pickup coil is not the same as that of the voltage through the contacts in a breaker-point ignition. Breaker points open to interrupt the primary current in the ignition coil, but the pickup coil voltage only provides a precisely timed electrical signal. This signal triggers the electronic circuitry in the control unit. The control unit then interrupts the current flowing through the ignition coil primary winding.

In the electronic ignition system, battery current flows through the coil primary winding and then through the grounded control unit. This current flow causes a magnetic field to build up inside the coil. See Figure 12-8. This maintains current flow in the ignition coil primary winding in much the same manner as the closed contacts do in a breaker-point ignition. The control unit remains "on," and current flows through the ignition coil primary winding as long as there is a positive voltage from the pickup coil applied to the control unit.

As shown by the polarity signs and an arrow in Figure 12-9, when the reluctor passes the pole piece and the pickup voltage turns negative, it "turns off" the control unit circuitry. At this point, current cannot flow through the control unit to ground, and the current through the ignition coil primary winding is interrupted. As in a breaker-point-type ignition system, this current flow interruption in the primary circuit causes the magnetic field in the ignition coil to

collapse and induce a high enough voltage in the coil to jump the spark plug gap.

Control Unit

Figure 12-10 shows the electronic components contained in the control unit. The control unit electronically determines how long the ignition coil primary current is allowed to flow before it is interrupted. In other words, the control unit determines the dwell in the electronic system. Since the control

Figure 12-10.   The circuitry in a control unit. (Courtesy of Chrysler Corporation)

unit circuitry is sealed and has no moving parts, the dwell cannot be changed. The reluctor and pickup coil determine ignition timing. However, the reluctor and pickup coil must work together with the control unit to time the ignition coil primary current interruption and the firing of the plugs.

There is no reason to use a dwell meter when you are testing or checking an electronic ignition system. Dwell will be correct unless the control unit has been damaged. This possibility can be easily and quickly checked with an electronic ignition tester. A tachometer and timing light can be used to test an electronic ignition system in the same way they are used on a breaker-point system.

The ballast resistor for the electronic system is a **dual-ballast resistor**. See Figure 12-11. The .55 ohm side serves the same purpose as the ballast resistor in a breaker-point system. It regulates primary current while there are variations in engine speed. This protects the ignition coil against high current flow at low engine speed and raises the voltage applied to the coil at higher speeds. Like a breaker-point ballast resistor, this side of the dual-ballast resistor is bypassed during cranking, to apply full battery voltage to the coil for starting. The other side of the dual-ballast resistor is a five-ohm resistor. It protects the control unit by limiting current flow in the circuit.

FACTS TO REMEMBER

No voltage is induced in the pickup coil unless the reluctor is moving. The rapid increase and decrease of the magnetic field, as the rotating reluctor teeth approach and pass the pole piece, is what induces the positive, then the negative, voltage in the pickup coil. It is these voltage polarity changes that cause the control unit to break the current flow in the ignition coil. This causes the magnetic field to collapse and induce the voltage necessary to fire the spark plugs.

□   ASSIGNMENT 12-A   □

1. Compare a point-type ignition system with an electronic ignition system.
2. Briefly describe the operation of an electronic ignition system as it produces a spark.

TESTING ELECTRONIC IGNITION SYSTEMS

Most factory-installed electronic ignition systems work in a similar manner, but they all have some differences in construction and wiring. You must diagnose and troubleshoot each system somewhat differently. Each manufacturer publishes the specifications that you need to know in order to test its systems. Special testers are sold for checking each system. These testers should be used when they are available. However, if you do not have these testers, it is possible to check the systems with a voltmeter and an ohmmeter.

The material in this chapter will not cover the checks done with special testers, since each company supplies instructions for using its test equipment. Instead, we will discuss some easily applied methods of diagnosing and servicing Chrysler, General Motors, and Ford electronic ignition systems. These tests will rely on visual inspection and checks made with a voltmeter and ohmmeter. The spark output of each system should be checked before you use these meters.

The following information and illustrations are taken in part from information supplied by Echlin, Limited.

Ignition Secondary Checks

When you are doing electronic ignition systems tests, check the secondary circuit first.

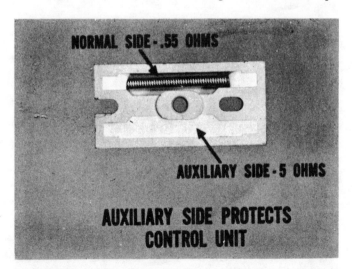

Figure 12-11. A ballast resistor for an electronic ignition system. (Courtesy of Chrysler Corporation)

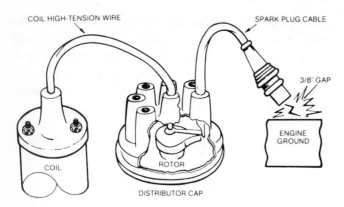

Figure 12-12. Testing for a good spark from the distributor cap. (Courtesy of Echlin, Limited)

1. Remove a spark plug wire from the spark plug and hold it approximately 3/8″ (10 mm) from a good engine ground, as shown in Figure 12-12.

2. Crank the engine, and see if a good spark is produced. If a good spark is present, the problem is most likely not in the ignition system, and other areas must be looked into, such as the fuel system, spark advance, etc. If no spark was produced, go on to step 3.

3. Remove the coil wire (except on General Motors High Energy Ignition systems) from the distributor cap and hold it approximately 3/8″ (10 mm) from ground. See Figure 12-13.

4. Crank the engine and see if a good spark is produced. If a good spark is present in this test, the problem will probably be in the cap, rotor, or spark plug wires. Always inspect the condition of the cap, rotor, spark plug wires, and spark plugs prior to beginning any primary tests on the ignition system.

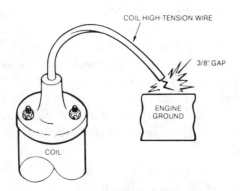

Figure 12-13. Testing for a spark from the coil. (Courtesy of Echlin, Limited)

This will save you time. Problems in these parts are easy to correct.

If the system has failed the above test, or by your estimation requires further testing, follow the procedures below.

CHRYSLER ELECTRONIC IGNITION TESTS

Specifications and Precautions

Always use the manufacturer's shop manual for the circuit and electrical specifications for the year engine you are servicing. A system wiring diagram is shown in Figure 12-14.

Caution: When you are doing these tests, you should observe certain precautions.

1. The control module must be grounded.
2. Disconnect the system power when performing a compression test.
3. Disconnect the battery before you disconnect the control module.
4. Do not touch the switching transistor on the control module while the engine is running. You may be shocked by the high voltage.
5. Do not file the edges on the reluctor teeth. They must be sharp. The reluctor can be replaced if necessary.

Distributor Test Procedure

The distributor may be tested with a voltmeter

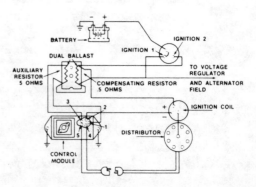

Figure 12-14. A system wiring diagram. (Courtesy of Echlin, Limited)

and an ohmmeter. When ignition problems are suspected, the following procedure can be used.

1. Check the battery and the battery connections for tightness and cleanliness. Clean them if necessary.

2. Check the air gap between the reluctor tooth and the pickup coil. To set the air gap, loosen the pickup coil hold-down screw. Insert a .008″ (.2 mm) nonmagnetic feeler gauge between a reluctor tooth and the pickup coil pole piece. Adjust the pickup so that the .008″ (.2 mm) feeler gauge is snug. Then tighten the hold-down screw.

3. Rotate the engine two complete turns and make sure that the gap is no less than .006″ (.15 mm) or more than .010″ (.25 mm) at any reluctor tooth. See Figure 12-15.

4. Check the distributor cap for cracks, excess tower corrosion, and carbon tracking. If there is evidence of any of these problems, replace it with a new cap.

5. Check the primary wires at the ignition coil and ballast resistor for tightness.

If the above checks do not determine the problem, the following tests will determine if a component is faulty. When making these tests, a 10-ohm, 2-watt resistor may be connected between the circuit being checked and ground. See Figure 12-16. This resistor will serve as a load on the circuit and result in more accurate readings.

Circuitry Tests

Test A: Cavity #1 Circuitry

1. Remove the multiwiring connector from the control module and expose the wiring harness connector cavities. **Caution:** When you are removing or installing the wiring connector at the control module, the ignition switch must be "off." Otherwise, the control module could be damaged.

2. Turn the ignition switch on and connect the negative (−) lead of a voltmeter to a good ground.

3. Connect the positive lead of the voltmeter to the wiring harness connector cavity #1.

4. Available voltage at cavity #1 should be within one volt of battery voltage, with all accessories turned off. If there is more than a one-volt difference between battery voltage and the reading taken in

cavity #1, the circuitry connected to cavity #1 must be checked and replaced as necessary. The thick black line in Figure 12-17 outlines the circuit connected to cavity #1.

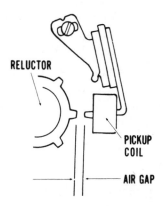

Figure 12-15. The air gap should be between .006″ and .010″. (Courtesy of Echlin, Limited)

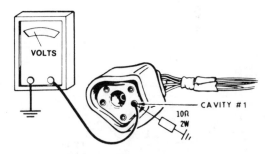

Figure 12-16. Testing cavity #1. Use a 10-ohm, 2-watt resistor during these tests. (Courtesy of Echlin, Limited)

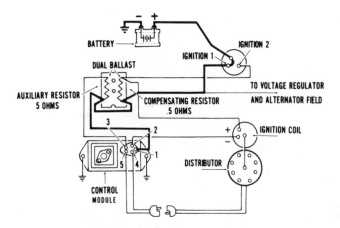

Figure 12-17. Circuit for test A: Cavity #1. (Courtesy of Echlin, Limited)

Test B: Cavity #2 Circuitry

1. Connect the voltmeter positive lead to the wiring harness cavity #2, and the 10-ohm, 2-watt resistor to ground. See Figure 12-18.

2. Available voltage at cavity #2 should be within one volt of battery voltage, with all accessories turned off. If there is more than one volt difference, check the wires and connections, as outlined in the circuit diagram in Figure 12-19.

3. The components that would cause an ignition failure in this test would be the ignition coil, dual-ballast resistor, ignition switch, or the related wires and connections.

Test C: Coil

1. If you suspect problems in the ignition coil, connect an ohmmeter across the coil primary terminals, as shown in Figure 12-20. The reading should be between 1.41 and 1.79 ohms.

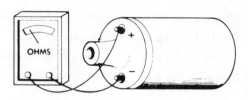

Figure 12-20. *Checking the coil primary windings. (Courtesy of Echlin, Limited)*

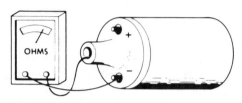

Figure 12-21. *Checking the coil secondary windings. (Courtesy of Echlin, Limited)*

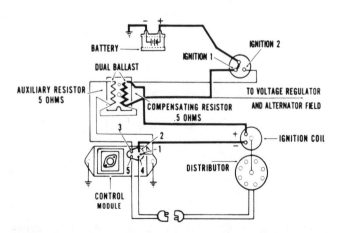

Figure 12-18. *Testing cavity #2. (Courtesy of Echlin, Limited)*

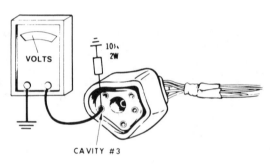

Figure 12-22. *Testing cavity #3. (Courtesy of Echlin, Limited)*

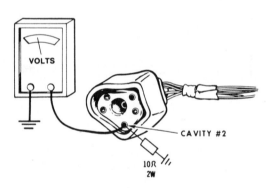

Figure 12-19. *Circuit for test B: Cavity #2. (Courtesy of Echlin, Limited)*

2. To check the secondary coil windings, connect the ohmmeter to the negative (−) terminal and the secondary tower, as shown in Figure 12-21. The reading should be between 8,000 and 11,700 ohms.

3. If the coil is defective, replace it.

Test D: Cavity #3 Circuitry

1. Connect the voltmeter positive lead to connector cavity #3, and the 10-ohm, 2-watt resistor to ground, as shown in Figure 12-22.

2. The available voltage at cavity #3 should be within one volt of battery voltage. If there is more than a one-volt difference, repair the wires or connections, as outlined in Figure 12-23.

Test E: Ballast Resistor

1. Calibrate an ohmmeter in the ×1 scale. Be sure the ignition switch is turned off. Connect the ohmmeter to the ballast resistor, as shown in Figure 12-24.

2. The auxiliary resistor that is molded into the unit should read 4.75 to 5.75 ohms of resistance. The open, wire-wound resistor should read .5 to .6 ohms. If either resistor varies from these specifications, the ballast resistor must be replaced.

Test F: Cavities #4 & #5, Pickup Coil

1. Turn the ignition switch to the off position. Calibrate an ohmmeter in the ×100 scale.

2. Connect the ohmmeter to the wiring harness connector cavities #4 and #5. See Figure 12-25. The ohmmeter reading should be between 150 and 900 ohms.

3. If the reading is higher or lower than specified, disconnect the dual-lead connector coming from the distributor. See Figure 12-26. Use the ohmmeter to check the resistance at the dual-lead connector coming from the distributor. If the reading is not within specifications, replace the pickup coil in the distributor. If the reading is within specifications, check the wiring harness from the dual-lead connector back to the control module.

4. To test the insulation of the pickup coil, connect one ohmmeter lead to a good ground and the other to either dual-lead connection terminal in the distributor harness. The ohmmeter should show an open circuit. If the meter shows continuity, the pickup coil is shorted out and it must be replaced.

Test G: Continuity

1. Connect one ohmmeter lead to a good ground and the other lead to the control module connector pin #5, as shown in Figure 12-27.

2. The ohmmeter should show continuity between the ground and the connector pin. If continuity does not exist, clean the control module ground connection and tighten the bolts that hold the control module to the fire wall.

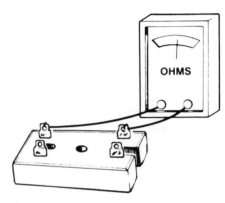

Figure 12-24. Checking the ballast resistor. (Courtesy of Echlin, Limited)

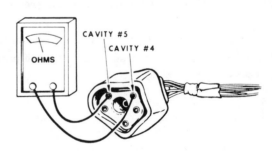

Figure 12-25. Testing cavity #4. (Courtesy of Echlin, Limited)

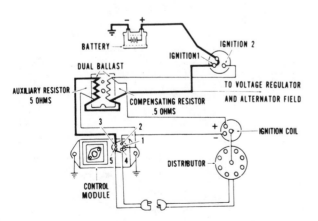

Figure 12-23. Circuit for test D: Cavity #3. (Courtesy of Echlin, Limited)

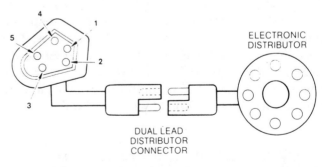

Figure 12-26. Checking the dual-lead connector from the distributor and from the wiring harness. (Courtesy of Echlin, Limited)

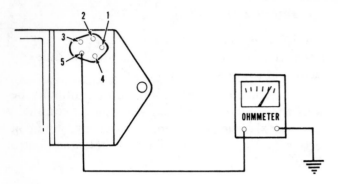

Figure 12-27. Checking for continuity to ground. (Courtesy of Echlin, Limited)

3. Recheck for continuity. If the meter still does not show continuity, the control module must be replaced.

4. If all tests are within specifications and the vehicle does not perform properly or is still inoperative, replace the control module.

□   **ASSIGNMENT 12-B**   □

1. Describe the adjustment procedure used to set the air gap between the reluctor teeth and the pickup coil pole piece.
2. Describe the procedure used to test the pickup coil.
3. Describe the procedure used to test the coil primary and secondary windings.

FORD ELECTRONIC IGNITION TESTS

Now that we are familiar with the procedures for diagnosing a Chrysler electronic ignition system, we can discuss the test procedure for Ford systems. The Ford system uses the names **stator** and **armature** instead of "pickup coil" and "reluctor." The following information and illustrations are taken in part from information supplied by Echlin, Limited.

Specifications and Precautions

Always use the manufacturer's shop manual for circuit and electrical specifications for the year engine

you are servicing. Some electrical specifications change each year.

1. Always disconnect the battery before you disconnect the control module wires.
2. Control modules cannot be interchanged on models from different years.
3. A knife switch should never be used on the battery terminal when you are testing the alternator.
4. Disconnect the ignition system while you are performing a compression check.

Circuitry Tests

Test A: Stator

1. Calibrate an ohmmeter in the ×100 scale.

2. Make sure that the ignition switch is turned off. Connect one of the ohmmeter leads to the purple stator lead in the wiring harness connector, and the other to the orange lead. See Figure 12-28.

3. If the reading is not between 400 and 800 ohms, the stator must be replaced.

Test B: Ground Circuit

To check for an open circuit in the black ground wire:

1. Connect one ohmmeter lead to the black ground wire terminal in the wiring harness connector, and the other ohmmeter lead to a good ground. See Figure 12-29.

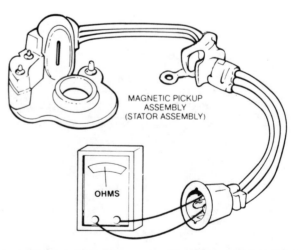

Figure 12-28. Checking stator resistance. (Courtesy of Echlin, Limited)

2. You should get a full continuity reading. If a full continuity reading is not shown, repairs or replacements in the ground circuit will have to be made, because this black ground wire grounds the control module.

Test C: Stator Shorts

To check for shorts in the stator:

1. Connect one ohmmeter lead to either the orange or purple pickup lead and the other ohmmeter lead to ground. See Figure 12-30.

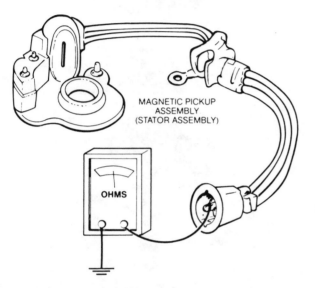

Figure 12-29. Checking the ground circuit. (Courtesy of Echlin, Limited)

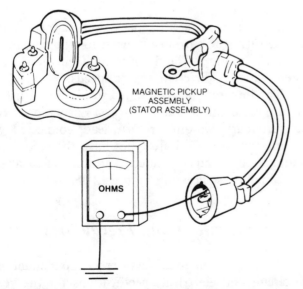

Figure 12-30. Checking for stator shorts. (Courtesy of Echlin, Limited)

Figure 12-31. Checking the coil primary. (Courtesy of Echlin, Limited)

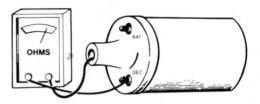

Figure 12-32. Checking the coil secondary. (Courtesy of Echlin, Limited)

2. If a reading of continuity is shown here, the stator is shorted and must be replaced.

Test D: Coil

1. To test the coil primary, connect an ohmmeter to the coil DEC and BAT terminals, as shown in Figure 12-31. The reading should be 1 to 2 ohms. If not, replace the coil.

2. To check the secondary coil windings, connect the ohmmeter to the DEC terminal and the secondary tower, as shown in Figure 12-32. The reading should be 7,000 to 13,000 ohms. If not, replace the coil.

Test E: Continuity Connections

When making the following voltage checks, a 10-ohm, 2-watt resistor may be connected between the circuit being checked and ground. This resistor will serve as a load on the system and result in more accurate readings.

1. Use the wiring diagrams to check the continuity of the wires in the system.

2. Check all electrical connections to be sure they are clean and tight.

3. Turn the ignition off and unplug the control module connections.

4. Turn the ignition on, and use a voltmeter to check the system **power input** circuit at the control module connector. To find this circuit, refer to the wiring diagram for the vehicle you are testing. The reading should be within one volt of battery voltage in the "run" and "start" positions. If it is not, replace or repair the battery cables, ignition switch, or related wiring.

5. Use the voltmeter to check the ignition coil DEC terminal wire at the control module connector. To find this connection, refer to the wiring diagram for the vehicle you are testing. The reading should be within one volt of battery voltage. If it is not, the ignition coil and related circuitry should be repaired or replaced.

6. If the system still does not operate or its operation is unsatisfactory, replace the control module.

☐ ASSIGNMENT 12-C ☐

1. Describe the voltage test generally made on Ford electronic ignition systems.

2. List the procedures that require the use of an ohmmeter to check the Chrysler and Ford electronic ignition systems.

GENERAL MOTORS ELECTRONIC IGNITION TESTS

The two systems covered so far have similar features. The General Motors High Energy Ignition (H.E.I.) system works electronically in a similar manner, but all of the electrical components on this system may be mounted inside the distributor. See Figure 12-33. As shown in Figure 12-34, some General Motors systems have the ignition coil mounted separately.

In the General Motors system, the control module turns on the coil primary current to build up magnetism. The pole piece is turned by the distributor shaft. Signals are induced into the pickup coil when the teeth on the pole piece align with the pickup coil. The signal is sent to the control module mounted inside the distributor. The control module turns off the current in the primary circuit and causes the magnetic field to collapse. This induces high voltage into the ignition coil secondary. The ignition coil is mounted in the distributor cap, or it is mounted separately near

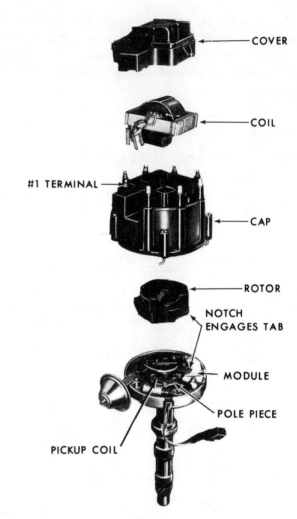

Figure 12-33. *General Motors High Energy Ignition with all components mounted inside the distributor. (Courtesy of General Motors of Canada Limited)*

the distributor. After the spark occurs, the control module turns the current on again for the next magnetic field buildup. The dwell in the General Motors system varies at different engine speeds.

The **integral coils** (mounted inside the distributor cap) are connected in two ways. Early types have the secondary winding return lead connected to the primary circuit. Late types have the secondary winding return lead connected to ground. These alternate circuits are shown in Figure 12-35.

Specifications and Precautions

Always use the manufacturer's shop manual for the circuit and electrical specifications for the year engine you are servicing. Disconnect the system when you are performing a compression test.

The following information and illustrations are taken in part from information supplied by Echlin, Limited.

Circuitry Tests

Test A: Battery Terminal Connector Plug

When making the following voltage checks, a 10-ohm, 2-watt resistor may be connected between the circuit being checked and the ground. This resistor will serve as a load on the system and result in more accurate readings.

1. Remove the battery terminal connector plug from the distributor cap.

2. Turn the ignition switch on and connect the negative lead (–) of the voltmeter to ground.

3. Connect the positive lead (+) of the voltmeter to the battery terminal connector plug, as shown in Figure 12-36.

4. Voltage at the battery terminal connector should be battery voltage in the "run" and "start" positions.

5. **Caution:** Starting and engine-missing problems will result if the distributor battery terminal connector plug is not put back properly in the distributor cap.

Test B: Coil Primary (Integral Coil)

This test is for eight-, six-, and four-cylinder integral-type coils.

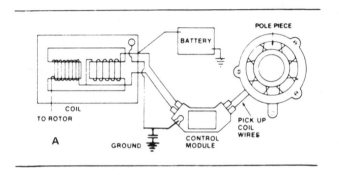

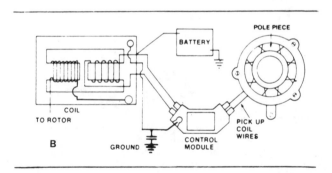

Figure 12-35. Late type: secondary winding is grounded to the frame (B). Early type: secondary winding is connected to primary circuit (A). (Courtesy of Echlin, Limited)

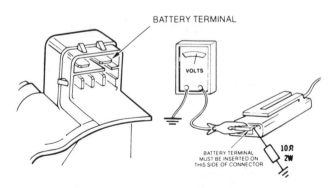

Figure 12-36. Testing the battery terminal connector plug. (Courtesy of Echlin, Limited)

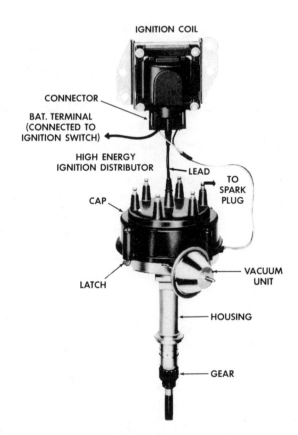

Figure 12-34. General Motors High Energy Ignition distributor used on some four- and six-cylinder engines. The coil is separate from the distributor. (Courtesy of General Motors of Canada Limited)

1. Remove the distributor cap and wires as an assembly.

2. Calibrate an ohmmeter in the ×1 scale.

3. Connect one ohmmeter lead to the tach terminal and the other lead to the battery terminal in the distributor cap. See Figure 12-37. If the reading is not .4 to 1.0 ohms, the ignition coil must be replaced.

4. Remove the ohmmeter lead from the battery terminal and connect it to the ground terminal on the distributor cap. If the reading is anything other than infinity (no reading), replace the coil.

Test B: Coil Primary (External Coil)

This test is for four- and six-cylinder engines with external coils.

1. With the ignition off, remove the primary and secondary wires from the ignition coil.

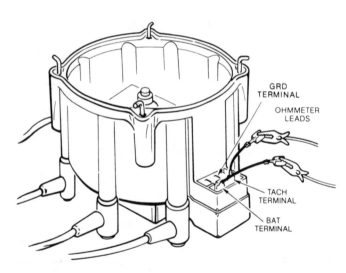

Figure 12-37.   Testing the coil primary, integral-type coil. (Courtesy of Echlin, Limited)

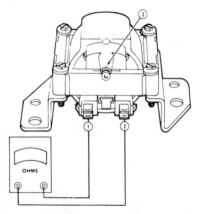

Figure 12-38.   Testing the coil primary, external-type coil. (Courtesy of Echlin, Limited)

2. Calibrate an ohmmeter in the ×1 range.

3. Connect an ohmmeter lead to each of the coil primary terminals, as shown in Figure 12-38. If the reading is not 0 to 1.0 ohms, the coil must be replaced.

4. Remove one ohmmeter lead from either of the primary terminals and connect it to ground. If the reading is anything other than infinity (no reading), replace the coil.

Test C: Coil Secondary (Integral Coil)

1. Calibrate an ohmmeter in the ×1000 scale.

2. Connect one ohmmeter lead to the coil secondary contact (carbon brush) and the other lead to the tach terminal on early types (Figure 12-39), or to the middle terminal of the module connectors (shown dotted in the illustration) on late types.

3. Either reading should be approximately 16,000 to 40,000 ohms. If the reading is too low, too high, or infinite (no reading), replace the ignition coil.

Test C: Coil Secondary (External Coil)

1. Calibrate an ohmmeter in the ×1000 scale.

2. Connect one lead to one of the primary terminals and the other lead to the secondary terminal. See Figure 12-40. The reading should be between 6,000 and 30,000 ohms. If not, replace the coil.

It is important to note that the tests mentioned above will not indicate if the windings are shorted. This condition can only be detected with **scope analysis** or a **coil tester**. If shorted windings are suspected and these instruments are not available, substitute a new coil to test the system.

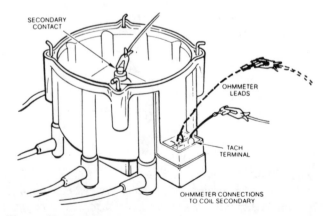

Figure 12-39.   Testing the coil secondary (integral type). (Courtesy of Echlin, Limited)

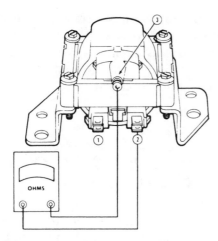

Figure 12-40. Testing the coil secondary (external type). (Courtesy of Echlin, Limited)

Test D: Pickup Coil

1. Calibrate an ohmmeter in the ×100 scale.

2. Disconnect the pickup leads from the control module and connect the ohmmeter leads to the pickup leads, as shown in Figure 12-41. The reading should be between 500 and 1500 ohms. If it is not, the pickup coil should be replaced. Also, the readings should not vary as you wiggle and flex the pickup leads.

Test E: Pickup Coil Shorts

To test for shorts between the pickup coil and ground:

1. Connect one ohmmeter lead to either one of the two pickup coil leads.

2. Connect the other ohmmeter lead to a good ground, as shown in Figure 12-42. The reading should be infinite (no reading). If the reading is anything other than infinite, replace the pickup coil.

Test F: RFI Capacitor

To check the Radio Frequency Interference (RFI) capacitor:

1. Calibrate an ohmmeter in the ×1000 scale.

2. Disconnect the RIF capacitor. Place one ohmmeter lead on the capacitor terminal. Place the other ohmmeter lead on a good ground, as shown in Figure 12-43. The meter should move slightly and return to infinity. If there is any continuous reading other than infinity, replace the RFI capacitor.

If the system still does not operate, or if it operates improperly, and all of the electrical connections

and wiring have been checked, replace the control module.

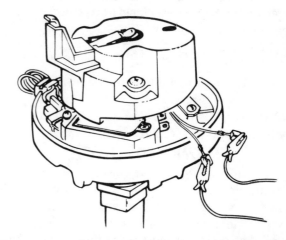

Figure 12-41. Checking the pickup coil. (Courtesy of Echlin, Limited)

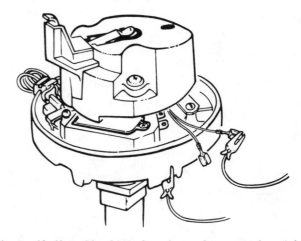

Figure 12-42. Checking for shorts between the pickup coil and ground. (Courtesy of Echlin, Limited)

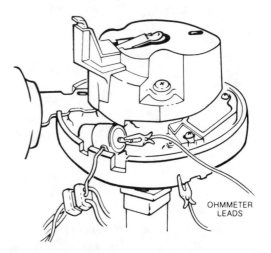

Figure 12-43. Checking the radio frequency interference capacitor. (Courtesy of Echlin, Limited)

1. Describe the function of the components in the General Motors High Energy Ignition system.
2. Describe how to test the integral-type ignition coil.
3. Describe how to test the pickup coil.

ELECTRONIC SPARK ADVANCE

Electronic circuitry can also be used to provide spark advance according to engine speed, load, and temperature. A system designed for this purpose uses a distributor that does not have a vacuum or centrifugal advance. Instead, the advance is provided by an electronic control unit, based on input signals it receives from various engine sensors. Chrysler Corporation was the first to use this method. They first named it the Electronic Lean Burn System and later, the Electronic Spark Control System. We will discuss both of these systems. However, since the testing and diagnosis procedure is outlined in the manufacturer's shop manual, we will not discuss it here.

CHRYSLER ELECTRONIC SPARK CONTROL

The following information and illustrations are based in part on information supplied by the Chrysler Corporation.

The Electronic Spark Control (E.S.C.) system shown in Figure 12-44, or its forerunner, the Electronic Lean Burn (E.L.B.) system, consists of a **spark control computer**, engine sensors, and a specially calibrated carburetor. By electronically controlling ignition advance, the system provides a method for the engine to burn a lean air-fuel mixture.

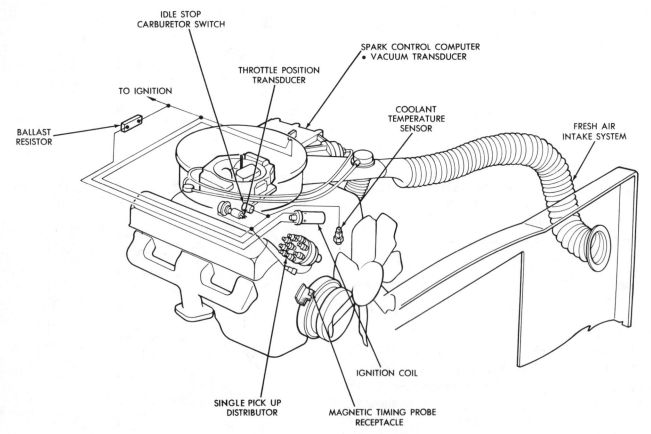

Figure 12-44. The Electronic Spark Control (E.S.C.) system. (Courtesy of Chrysler Corporation)

Spark Control Computer

The **spark control computer** is the heart of the entire system. See Figure 12-45. The spark control computer contains the **ignition spark module** and the circuitry needed to control spark timing. Spark timing is precisely controlled according to differences in engine operation. The spark control computer is capable of igniting lean air-fuel mixtures because it times the spark to the moment of greatest cylinder compression pressure.

The computer consists of a single electronic printed circuit board for the late-type systems. On the early systems, two circuit boards were used. The computer receives signals from all the sensors at the same time, computes them to determine how the engine is operating, and then advances or retards the ignition timing.

In other words, the computer determines the exact instant when the ignition spark is required. It then causes the ignition coil to produce the electrical impulses that fire the spark plugs.

Sensors

There are several sensors that supply the spark control computer with the necessary information needed to fire the spark plugs at the right time. These sensors are listed below.

Pickup Coil: The E.S.C. and late-type E.L.B. systems have one **pickup coil** in the distributor that supplies the basic timing signal to the computer. See Figure 12-46. Except during cranking, this signal tells the computer to create the maximum amount of timing advance available for any engine rpm. This signal also allows the computer to determine engine speed and when each piston is coming up on its compression stroke.

The early E.L.B. system uses two pickup coils in the distributor, as shown in Figure 12-47. The **start pickup** supplies the signal to the computer that causes the spark plugs to fire at a fixed amount of advance during cranking. The **run pickup** supplies the basic timing signal to the computer and performs the same functions as the single pickup in the other systems.

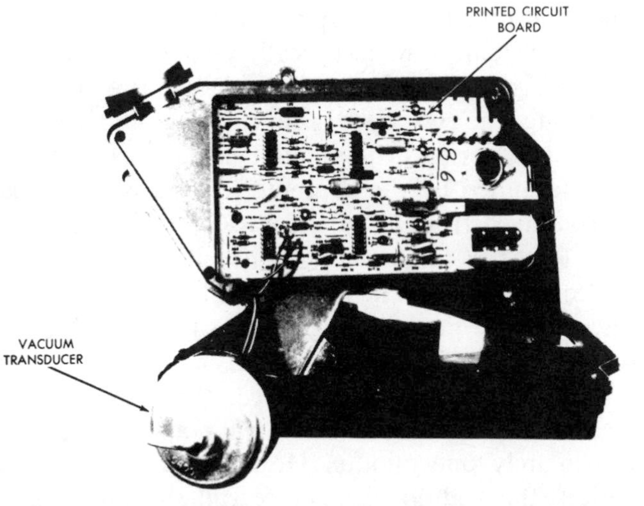

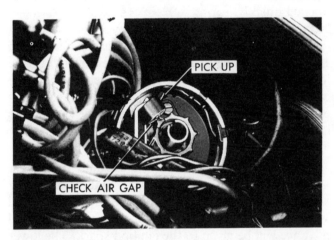

Figure 12-46. *An Electronic Spark Control distributor containing one pickup coil. (Courtesy of Chrysler Corporation)*

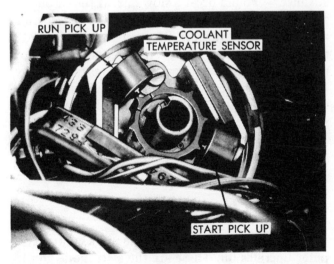

Figure 12-47. *Early Electronic Lean Burn System distributor with a "start" and a "run" coil. (Courtesy of Chrysler Corporation)*

Figure 12-45. *The spark control computer. (Courtesy of Chrysler Corporation)*

Coolant Temperature Sensor: The **coolant temperature sensor** is located on the water pump housing (E.L.B.) or on the intake manifold housing (E.S.C.). See Figure 12-47. It supplies a signal to the computer when the engine coolant temperature is below 150°F (66°C).

Throttle Position Transducer: The **throttle position transducer** is located on the carburetor, as shown in Figure 12-48. Its signal tells the computer the position and the rate of change of the throttle plates. Additional spark advance will be given by the computer when the throttle plates start to open, and in every other position to full throttle. Even more advance is given for about one second if the throttle is opened quickly.

Carburetor Switch Sensor: As shown in Figure 12-48, the **carburetor switch sensor** is located at the idle stop. The curb idle speed adjuster contacts the carburetor switch sensor. The signal from the carburetor switch sensor tells the computer if the engine is at idle or off-idle.

Vacuum Transducer: The **vacuum transducer** is located on the computer. See Figure 12-45. Its signal tells the computer the strength of the manifold vacuum. The higher the vacuum, the more additional advance will be given to the ignition spark. The lower the vacuum, the less spark advance is provided.

In order to obtain the maximum amount of advance, the carburetor sensor switch must remain open for a specified amount of time. During that time the advance will build up at a slow rate. If the carburetor switch closes before the predetermined time period, the buildup of advance at that time will be canceled in the ignition system. However, the computer will put this advance into memory and slowly return it to zero. If the switch is reopened before the advance has returned to zero, the buildup of advance starts at the point where the computer still has it in memory. If the switch is reopened after the advance has returned to zero, the buildup of advance must start all over again.

System Operation

There are two **modes** that the spark control computer operates on. These are the **start mode** and the **run mode**. The start mode only functions during engine cranking and starting. The run mode only functions after the engine starts and during engine

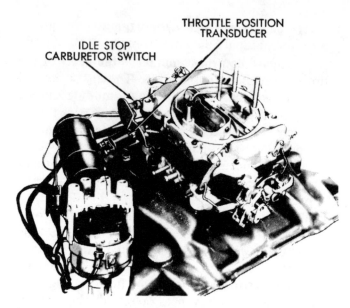

Figure 12-48. Location of the carburetor sensors. (Courtesy of Chrysler Corporation)

operation. The two will never both operate at the same time.

For cranking and starting, the pickup coil in the distributor feeds its signal to the computer. During this time, the start mode is functioning and the run mode is bypassed. A fixed amount of starting advance is established in the ignition system because of the position of the pickup coil. The amount of advance in the start mode is determined by the distributor position, in the same way that initial advance is determined by the position the distributor is set in when a breaker-point-type system is timed.

After the engine starts and during engine operation, the pickup coil signal continues to feed into the computer on single pickup types. However, the early E.L.B. system would electrically switch over from the start pickup to the run pickup. While the engine is operating, the run mode is functioning, and the start mode is bypassed. The amount of advance will now be determined by the computer, based on information received from all of the sensors.

The start mode will take over in the event of a run mode failure. The engine will keep running but, since the start mode timing remains fixed, engine performance will be below standard.

After the engine is started, the computer will create additional advance and will maintain it for approximately one minute. However, after that time period, the additional advance will slowly be eliminated. If the engine is running and the engine coolant temperature is below 150°F (66°C), the coolant temperature sensor will signal the computer to prevent any additional spark advance from the vacuum transducer signal. After the engine reaches operating temperature, normal system operation will begin.

The pickup coil signal is a reference signal. When it is received by the computer, the maximum amount of timing advance is provided. Based on data it receives from all the sensors, the computer determines how much advance is needed at any instant.

If there is a failure in the computer, the system will go into what is called the **limp-in mode**. This will enable the driver to continue to drive the vehicle until it can be repaired. However, while in this mode, the system will deliver very poor performance and fuel economy. If the pickup coil or computer start mode or the start pickup on early E.L.B. systems fails, the engine will not start or run.

□ ASSIGNMENT 12-E □

Explain the purpose of the following:
   pickup coil (single-type)
   throttle position transducer
   carburetor switch sensor
   vacuum transducer
   spark control computer

□ SELF-TEST □

Complete the following sentences by filling in the missing words.

1. Solid state devices have no _____ or relays. Instead, they use a number of different _____ and _____ .

2. The electronic control unit turns off the primary current by using a signal from a _____ coil inside the _____ .

3. The reluctor is shaped like a gear and has a _____ for each _____ .

4. A permanent _____ in the _____ coil produces a magnetic field.

5. The pickup voltage only provides a precisely timed electrical _____ .

6. The control unit electronically determines how _____ the ignition coil _____ current is allowed to _____ before it is interrupted.

7. When you are removing or installing the wiring connector at the control module, the _____ switch must be _____ . Otherwise, the control module could be _____ .

8. In the General Motors High Energy Ignition system, the pole piece is turned by the distributor _____ . Signals are _____ into the _____ coil when the _____ on the pole piece align with the pickup coil.

9. Dwell in the General Motors system _____ at different engine _____ .

10. The Chrysler Electronic Spark Control (E.S.C.) system consists of a _____ _____ computer, engine _____ , and a specially calibrated _____ .

11. In the Electronic Spark Control system, the computer determines the exact instant when the _____ spark is required.

13

EMISSION CONTROL SYSTEMS

☐ LEARNING OBJECTIVES ☐

After studying this chapter, you will be able to:

1. List the pollutants emitted from vehicles and explain the formation of smog.
2. Describe the purpose and operation of the following systems:
   - positive crankcase ventilation
   - thermostatically controlled air cleaner
   - lean-calibrated carburetor and choke
   - distributor advance control
   - evaporative emission control
   - exhaust gas recirculation
   - air injection
   - catalytic converters
3. Define and/or discuss the following terms:
   - smog
   - hydrocarbon
   - carbon monoxide
   - nitrogen oxides
   - carbon dioxide
   - emission standards
   - PCV valve
   - lean calibration
   - retarded spark timing
   - charcoal canister
   - evaporative emissions
   - catalyst

INTRODUCTION

In the early 1960's, government emission standards made it mandatory that emission controls be installed on all automobiles. This was done because the air we breathe was becoming dangerously contaminated by automobile exhaust pollutants.

There have always been natural sources of air pollution. When Mount Vesuvius erupted in 79 A.D., many people who were not trapped in the doomed city of Pompeii choked to death on the ash fallout in the air. Every year people suffer from what is loosely termed "hay fever," which often includes allergies and asthma, caused by certain weeds, flowers, and trees. Conifer (evergreen) trees give off terpene hydrocarbons, and rotting vegetable matter in forests gives off methane hydrocarbons.

People who live in cities are exposed to man-made pollution in the form of chemical fumes from factories, smoke stacks, chimneys, and harmful exhaust emissions from many types of vehicles. This pollution is often called **smog**, a combination of the two words "smoke" and "fog." Smog is made worse by air inversions, because when there is an air inversion, air cannot move upward to spread out the pollutants. See Figure 13-1.

AIR POLLUTION AND SMOG

It is a well-known fact that warm air rises and cooler air stays on a lower level. Cool air moves into an area during the night. As the daytime temperature rises, the cooler air is warmed and should be able to move up through the atmosphere. However, when there is an **air inversion**, the cool air cannot rise, because it is trapped by a covering barrier of hot air. This top

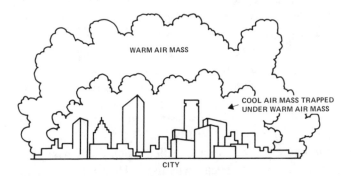

Figure 13-1. *During an air inversion, a warm air mass traps a cold air mass close to the ground.*

layer of hot air is heated by a combination of the sun's heat and the dense concentration of heat and smoke from factories and vehicles. Not until a wind blows the top barrier of hot air away, can the cooler air be released and carry away the pollutants. Meanwhile, the city is choked with smog.

A city's geographical location has a lot to do with its smog problem. A city located near a large body of water and surrounded by hills or mountains is more likely to have a smog problem than a city on a flat plane.

Smog results from a photochemical reaction in the atmosphere. This reaction takes place between **hydrocarbons** (compounds of hydrogen and carbon) and **nitrogen oxides** when they are exposed to sunlight. Unburnt hydrocarbons (HC) are particles of fuel that have not been burned during engine combustion. Nitrogen oxides (NOx) are formed by a chemical union of nitrogen molecules with one or more oxygen molecules. Nitrogen oxides form more quickly under extreme heat conditions (such as in the combustion chamber of an engine). No emission standard was proposed to control nitrogen oxides until 1973.

Carbon monoxide is an odorless, poisonous gas that is emitted along with the other gases from an automobile exhaust. If one carbon molecule is united with two oxygen molecules, a harmless gas called carbon dioxide (CO_2) is produced. Carbon monoxide (CO) is produced when one carbon molecule is united with only one oxygen molecule. If it is inhaled in sufficient quantities, carbon monoxide can cause nausea, headaches, and even death. Carbon monoxide is not an ingredient in smog formation, but it is emitted from automobile exhausts.

Some people feel that we are going to destroy our atmosphere with pollution and thus destroy ourselves. This is definitely possible. Thinking people, and government and law enforcement agencies, are taking the responsibility for eliminating the harmful gases emitted by motor vehicles. These gases cause smog and endanger everyone. Perfecting fuel emission controls is a serious and necessary challenge. If you study and understand the operation and service procedures for vehicle emission controls, you can help to meet this challenge.

Progress in Reducing Vehicle Emissions

Vehicles produced before emission controls emitted large quantities of pollutants. In fact, they

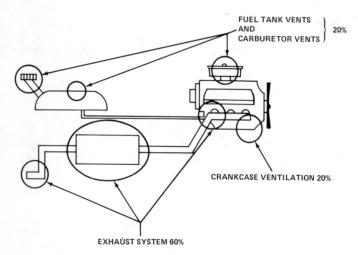

Figure 13-2.   Four places where unburned hydrocarbons are emitted from vehicles.

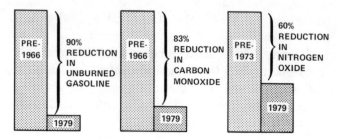

Figure 13-3.   Emission reductions as of 1979.

Model Year	Test Procedure	Grams Per Vehicle Mile		
		HC	CO	NOx
1968-69	FTP	3.4*	35*	NS
1970-71	FTP	2.2*	23*	NS
1972	CVS-C	3.4	39	NS
1973-74	CVS-C	3.4	39	3.0
1975	CVS-CH	1.5	15	3.1
1976	CVS-CH	1.5	15	3.1
1977-79	CVS-CH	1.5	15	2.0

FTP   Federal Test Procedure, concentration measure.
CVS-C   Constant Volume Sample, Cold start mass test.
CVS-CH   Constant Volume Sample, Cold/Hot weighting mass test.
NS   No Standard.

*Converted from parts per million.

Figure 13-4.   Comparison of emission standards for different years.

did so at the rate of over 900 parts per million (ppm) of hydrocarbons, and over 3% carbon monoxide. Compare this to the initial government emission standard of not over 275 ppm of hydrocarbons, and 1½% of carbon monoxide! On vehicles that were produced before emission controls, hydrocarbon emissions came from the exhaust systems (60% of total), the engine crankcase (20%), and evaporation through the fuel tank vents and the carburetor bowl (20%), as shown in Figure 13-2.

There are now effective emission control systems for all sources of vehicle emissions. Today, crankcase emissions and fuel evaporation from the fuel tank and carburetor (which accounted for about 40% of the pollution before controls) have been eliminated. Exhaust emissions have been so reduced by various controls that by the year 1979, the total reduction of pollutants was as much as 90% for unburned hydrocarbons, 83% for carbon monoxide, and 60% for nitrogen oxides. See Figure 13-3.

The chart in Figure 13-4 shows the Federal Automotive Standards for the years 1968 through 1979. Notice that they become tighter each year. Because of emission controls, a dramatic decrease in automobile emissions has occurred. Emissions are expected to keep decreasing as government agencies keep the pressure on for tighter emission standards.

□   ASSIGNMENT 13-A   □

1. List the dangerous pollutants emitted from vehicles.
2. Name the ingredients of smog.
3. Describe the conditions under which smog is formed.

POSITIVE CRANKCASE VENTILATION

Before emission controls, air was directed into the crankcase through a mesh-type filter in the **oil filler cap**. Air passed out of the crankcase through an open tube called a **draft tube** that extended below the engine. As shown in Figure 13-5, some unburned air-fuel mixture escapes past the piston rings on the compression and power strokes. This unburned mixture, called **blow-by**, would cause oil contamination and excess crankcase pressure if it were not vented out of the crankcase. A vacuum was created in the draft tube as the vehicle was driven. This vacuum drew away piston blow-by gases and crankcase fumes and expelled them through the draft tube into the atmosphere where they became pollutants.

Crankcase emissions were easily controlled with **Positive Crankcase Ventilation** (PCV) systems. On some early PCV systems, called **open PCV systems**, an oil filler breather cap was used. However, this cap was a source of pollutants under severe engine loads, when excess blow-by pressures would reverse the flow of air in the crankcase and cause smoke to come out the oil filler cap. A hose from a sealed oil filler cap, or from the rocker cover (through a filter), into the air cleaner was used to make the **closed PCV system**. The closed system is the system presently in use.

Closed PCV Systems

In a closed PCV system, as shown in Figure 13-6, the air flow begins at the air intake to the air cleaner. The air used for crankcase ventilation travels around the air cleaner element into the connecting hose, through a breather cap filter, and into the valve cover. From the valve cover, it flows into the crankcase through the valve train and oil return passages. The air circulates and mixes with the blow-by gases and oil vapors and is drawn up through the opposite side of the engine into the valve cover. Here it passes through the PCV valve, which controls the flow rate. It is then drawn through a connecting hose to the intake manifold and mixes into the air-fuel mixture that is leaving the carburetor. The intake manifold provides the vacuum that is needed to keep the air circulating while the engine is running.

When the engine is operating under heavy loads and very high speeds, blow-by pressures increase. Manifold vacuum, which is lower at high speeds and heavy loads, may not create enough flow to cope with this added blow-by pressure. Under these conditions, some of the flow will reverse direction and leave the

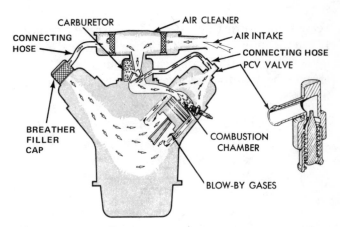

Figure 13-6.   A closed PCV system. (Courtesy of Chrysler Corporation)

crankcase, pass through the oil breather cap filter, through the connecting tube, and into the air cleaner. Here it will be drawn down through the carburetor to become part of the incoming air-fuel mixture. In this way, no blow-by gases or hydrocarbon pollution can escape into the atmosphere from a closed PCV system.

The flow rate of the gases through a PCV system must be regulated for correct engine operation. This is the job of the **PCV valve**. PCV valves come in a variety of shapes and sizes, but they all operate in the same manner. A few engines use a **metered orifice** (or **flow jet**) instead of a PCV valve.

To learn how a PCV valve operates, follow the numbers and explanations shown in Figure 13-7.

After studying Figure 13-7, you can see that the flow rate of 1 to 3 cubic feet per minute (.03 to .09 cu. meters) is a small flow that will not interfere with proper engine idle or low-speed operation. Higher flows during idle or low-speed operation could cause stalling and hesitation. At higher speeds, or when the engine load is heavy, the PCV valve opens to allow the higher flow rate of 3 to 6 cubic feet per minute (.09 to .17 cu. meters). This flow is absorbed into the air-fuel mixture and does not affect engine performance.

PCV System Problems

If the PCV system fails to draw away crankcase blow-by gases, excess pressure could build up in the crankcase. This pressure would cause oil leaks at the crankshaft seals or engine gaskets and contamination of the crankcase oil. The air cleaner and element, and PCV filter, could become soaked with oil from the re-

On compression stroke, unburned air and HC "blow-by" the piston into the crankcase.

On power stroke, combustion (exhaust) gases "blow-by" the piston into the crankcase.

Figure 13-5.   Crankcase blow-by gases are produced on the power stroke. (Courtesy of Ford Motor Company, Dearborn)

versed flow during heavy-load, high-speed operation. If the incoming line or PCV filter is plugged, oil can be drawn out of the crankcase through the PCV system by the manifold vacuum and be burned in the cylinders.

FACTS TO REMEMBER

The PCV valve vents the crankcase blow-by gases and fumes either through the air cleaner or directly into the intake manifold. When the blow-by pressures are low (low-speed, light-load operation), the gases are

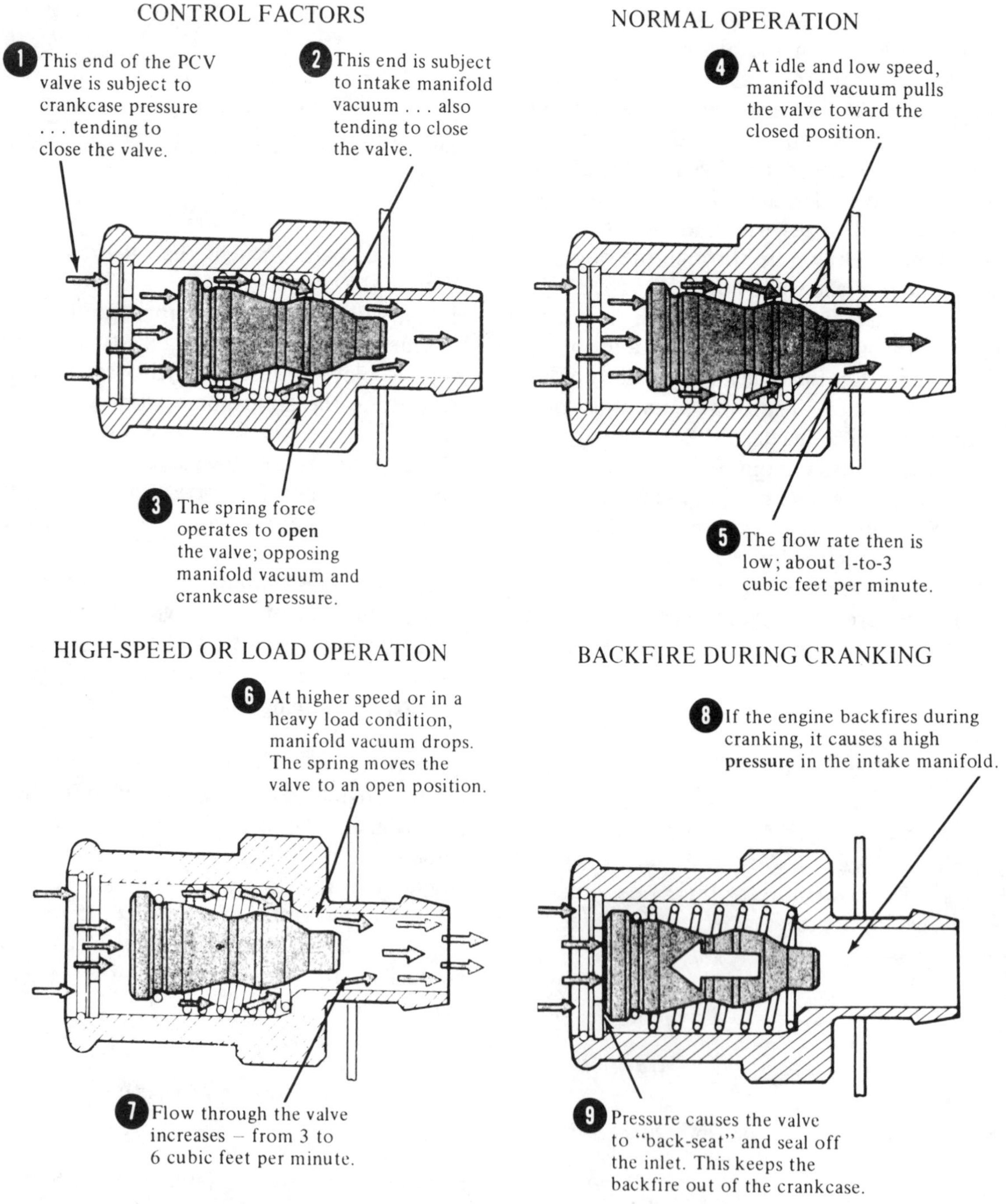

CONTROL FACTORS

1 This end of the PCV valve is subject to crankcase pressure . . . tending to close the valve.

2 This end is subject to intake manifold vacuum . . . also tending to close the valve.

3 The spring force operates to **open** the valve; opposing manifold vacuum and crankcase pressure.

NORMAL OPERATION

4 At idle and low speed, manifold vacuum pulls the valve toward the closed position.

5 The flow rate then is low; about 1-to-3 cubic feet per minute.

HIGH-SPEED OR LOAD OPERATION

6 At higher speed or in a heavy load condition, manifold vacuum drops. The spring moves the valve to an open position.

7 Flow through the valve increases — from 3 to 6 cubic feet per minute.

BACKFIRE DURING CRANKING

8 If the engine backfires during cranking, it causes a high **pressure** in the intake manifold.

9 Pressure causes the valve to "back-seat" and seal off the inlet. This keeps the backfire out of the crankcase.

Figure 13-7.   Operation of the PCV valve. (Courtesy of Ford Motor Company, Dearborn)

delivered directly into the intake manifold. When the blow-by pressures are high (very high-speed or heavy-load operation), some of the crankcase gases are delivered to the air cleaner to be mixed with the incoming air for the air-fuel mixture.

☐ ASSIGNMENT 13-B ☐

1. Describe the flow of the crankcase gases through the PCV system.
2. Describe the positioning of the PCV valve at different engine speed and load conditions.

THERMOSTATICALLY CONTROLLED AIR CLEANER

Another method of reducing emissions is to burn leaner air-fuel mixtures from the carburetor. Engineers have determined that the ratio of the air-fuel mixture reaching the cylinders has an influence on exhaust emissions. Extremely high or low air-fuel ratios cause hydrocarbon pollution. Air-fuel ratios with more than 15 parts of air to one part of fuel reduce carbon monoxide and hydrocarbons, because the extra oxygen in these leaner mixtures causes more complete combustion. This is true as long as no other factors, such as defective spark plugs or poor piston rings, offset the process. Emission control devices are defeated by a worn and poorly tuned engine.

A **lean-calibrated carburetor** that is designed to provide lean air-fuel mixtures performs better if the temperature of the air entering the carburetor is kept above 100°F (38°C). This is particularly important in cold weather. Preheated air coming into the carburetor continuously on severe winter days, and during the engine warm-up period in warmer weather, causes better fuel vaporization and distribution. This results in leaner fuel requirements, permits the use of a weaker, faster-acting choke spring, and a leaner carburetor calibration. Also, stalling that is caused by carburetor icing during the warm-up period is greatly reduced through the use of preheated inlet air.

Heated Inlet Air

The **Heated Inlet Air** system, shown in Figure 13-8, has a **manifold shroud** covering the exhaust manifold with a **heated air tube** leading to the bottom of the **air cleaner snorkel**. A **vacuum motor** or **chamber**, which is a spring-loaded diaphragm, will close the **heat control door** (control damper assembly) when the air coming into the snorkel tube is cold. A **temperature-sensing vacuum valve** (also called an **air bleed valve**) is mounted inside the air cleaner, and a hose line to the intake manifold vacuum is connected through the valve to the vacuum motor. The temperature-sensing vacuum valve controls the closing and opening of the heat control door. It does this by regulating the strength of the vacuum to the vacuum motor, according to air temperature.

Thermostatic Air Cleaner

Figure 13-9, View A, shows the parts of a **thermostatically controlled air cleaner**. In this view, the control damper assembly is open. View B shows that the temperature sensitive air bleed valve is closed at temperatures below 85°F (29°C). View C shows that the air bleed valve is fully open at temperatures above 128°F (53°C). At this temperature, the vacuum is so reduced by the air bleed that the vacuum chamber does not respond. The control damper is fully open to outside air, thus blocking the hot air flow from the manifold shroud. When a widely opened throttle causes low manifold vacuum, the control damper will open fully and allow for maximum air flow to the engine.

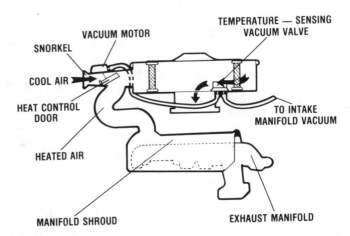

Figure 13-8. A Heated Inlet Air system. (Courtesy of Chrysler Corporation)

View D shows that between 85°F (29°C) and 128°F (53°C), the temperature-sensitive air bleed valve is bleeding in a little air, and the control damper is in a partly closed position. During these temperatures, **ambient** (outside) air is blended with preheated air.

□ ASSIGNMENT 13-C □

1. Explain the result of keeping the temperature of the air entering the carburetor to above 100°F (38°C).

2. Explain how the air cleaner control damper is regulated to the closed and open position.

LEAN CARBURETOR CALIBRATION

A thermostatically controlled air cleaner gives better performance with a lean-calibrated carburetor. Carburetors with fuel jets that have smaller metering orifices (openings) can produce a leaner air-fuel mixture than carburetors with larger metering orifices. This is one approach used to provide lean air-fuel mixtures. There are a number of other carburetor devices for lean calibration. The examples covered here are a cross section of a large number of carburetor alterations used to produce leaner air-fuel mixtures.

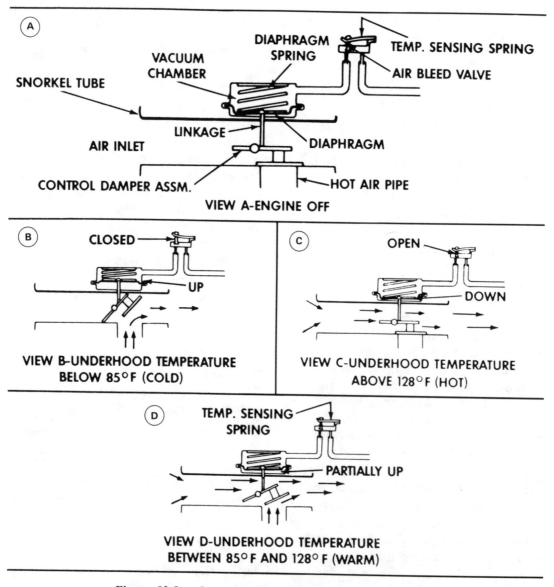

Figure 13-9. Operation of a Thermostatic Air Cleaner.
(Courtesy of General Motors of Canada Limited)

Off-Idle Adjustment Screw and Idle Compensator

Figure 13-10 shows a carburetor with an **off-idle air adjustment screw**. This screw controls the flow of air in an air bleed into the two idle systems. It is adjusted at the factory to a precise air-fuel mixture with the engine just above idle, then capped over to prevent the setting from being changed. Figure 13-10 also shows an **idle channel restriction** that helps to regulate the fuel flow more precisely.

The circled inset in Figure 13-10 shows an **idle compensator** (sometimes called a **hot idle compensator valve**). When the engine is overheated, the gasoline in the carburetor bowl boils and the vapors are drawn into the air-fuel mixture. This makes the idle mixture rich, which raises hydrocarbon and carbon monoxide emissions.

At normal engine temperatures, the idle compensator bimetal strip will close the attached valve. When the engine is oveheated, the bimetal strip will lift up and open the valve, permitting some air to pass through the air passage. This extra air will mix with the air-fuel mixture, leaning it out, and reducing the exhaust emissions. The leaner air-fuel mixture will cause the engine idle speed to increase, thus increasing the coolant flow and helping to cool the engine in heavy traffic. The valve will close again when the engine cools down.

The idle adjustment needle shown in Figure 13-10 has a **limiter cap** installed after the idle needle is

Figure 13-11. Idle limiter caps of this style allow about a 7/8" turn of the mixture adjusting screw. Other types lock and allow no adjustment. (Courtesy of Ford Motor Company, Dearborn)

adjusted at the factory. Some idle limiter caps prevent any movement of the mixture adjusting screw. Others allow a movement of about 7/8 turn for fine adjustment. See Figure 13-11. If you remove the limiter caps to adjust the carburetor, you must install new ones when you have finished the adjustment.

Idle Enrichment Diaphragm

Figure 13-12 shows a carburetor with an **idle enrichment diaphragm** (valve). The idle enrichment diaphragm increases the richness of the idle circuit to reduce cold engine stalling. The diaphragm receives its vacuum signal from the intake manifold through a

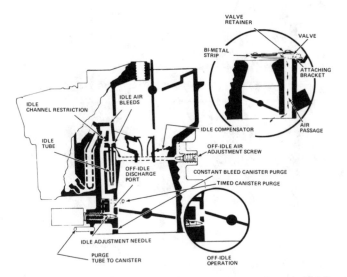

Figure 13-10. A two-barrel idle system, with an off-idle adjustment screw and an idle compensator. (Courtesy of General Motors of Canada Limited)

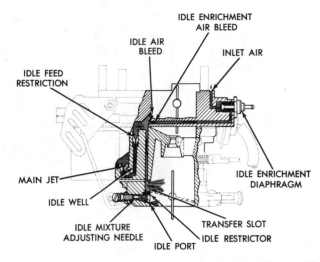

Figure 13-12. A carburetor with an idle enrichment diaphragm (valve). (Courtesy of Chrysler Corporation)

thermostatic vacuum switch that senses engine coolant temperature. When it is cold, the sensor is open. It passes vacuum to the diaphragm that moves a valve to block the idle enrichment air bleed. This increases the idle vacuum signal to the idle well, and the fuel flow increases.

During warm-up, the thermostatic vacuum switch closes, and cuts off the vacuum to the diaphragm and valve. The action opens the idle enrichment air bleed, which reduces the idle vacuum signal to the idle well, and the fuel flow decreases. Figure 13-12 also shows an idle restrictor in the passage between the idle port and the transfer slot. This prevents excessively rich idle mixtures, even when the idle mixture adjusting needle is out of adjustment.

PART-THROTTLE AND POWER SYSTEMS

The part-throttle and power systems have also been designed to provide leaner mixtures. The part-throttle air-fuel mixture is factory adjusted on some carburetors. See Figure 13-13. The **metering orifice** can pro-

vide up to 5% of the main metering fuel flow. The fuel flow is through the metering orifice, past the part-throttle adjustment screw, into the power valve cavity. From the power valve cavity, fuel flows through the power restrictions into the two main wells behind the two main metering jets. The part-throttle

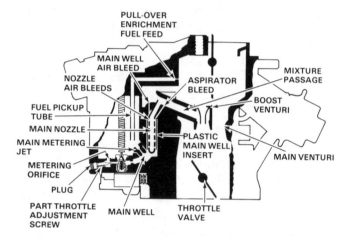

Figure 13-13. *This carburetor has a part-throttle adjustment screw that is factory adjusted. (Courtesy of General Motors of Canada Limited)*

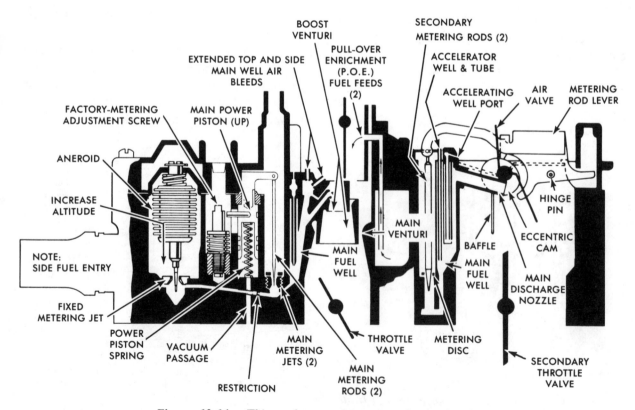

Figure 13-14. *This carburetor has many lean mixture features. (Courtesy of General Motors of Canada Limited)*

adjustment screw is capped over after it is adjusted at the factory. This prevents anyone from changing the mixture adjustment.

Engineers have designed the power system to provide as lean an air-fuel mixture as possible for moderately heavy loads, but to ensure enough fuel at heavier loads or very fast speeds. Increased air velocity through the carburetor bore will draw fuel from the **pull-over enrichment fuel feed** during extreme speed or load conditions. See Figure 13-13. The carburetor shown in Figure 13-14 also has this system.

METERING JETS AND VALVES

Many carburetors have metering jets and valve systems to help provide lean air-fuel mixtures. The carburetor shown in Figure 13-14 has several such lean-mixture features to prevent excess fuel emissions. The main power piston has a rod extending from its side that comes to rest on top of the factory-set **metering adjustment screw** at part throttle (when the manifold vacuum is strong). This positions the main metering rods in a precise position for the best fuel mixture through the main metering jets.

This carburetor also has an altitude compensation feature. An **aneroid**, which responds to altitude pressure changes, extends its bellows at higher altitudes. This moves the attached metering rod downward, decreasing the fuel flow through the **fixed metering jet** to the main metering jets by a small amount. This prevents the air-fuel mixture from becoming richer at higher altitudes as is the tendency of most other carburetors. At lower altitudes, the aneroid bellows contract and raise the metering rod, allowing a small increase in the fuel flow.

This carburetor has three venturis on the primary side for finer mixture control. It also has a number of air bleeds in the fuel circuits for better fuel atomization so that the fuel and air will mix easily. The secondary side has an air valve, eccentric cam, metering rod lever, and two secondary metering rods. As the secondary throttle valves open, the air valves open and lift the secondary metering rods in their metering discs to precisely control the secondary air-fuel mixture.

FACTS TO REMEMBER

One method of reducing exhaust emissions is by burning leaner air-fuel mixtures. Leaner air-fuel mixtures can be burned by preheating the air coming into the carburetor. This helps vaporize the incoming fuel. Carburetor modifications can help to provide leaner mixtures. Thermostatically controlled air cleaners are used to trap hot air and transfer it to the air cleaner to provide preheated air to the air-fuel mixture. Off-idle adjustment screws, idle enrichment diaphragms, modified part-throttle and power systems, as well as a number of different metering jets and valves, are adapted to carburetors to provide lean air-fuel mixtures.

CHOKE

A carburetor-mounted, **electric-assist choke** system is shown in Figure 13-15. The heating element is connected in series with a temperature-sensitive thermostatic switch. The switch contacts are open below 60°F (15°C) to prevent electric heat assist. When the contacts are open, the choke receives heat only through the heat pipe. When the temperature rises above 60°F (15°C) either during engine operation or starting, the temperature-sensitive contacts close and the heating element provides additional heat to open the choke quickly.

Electricity for this type of choke is usually supplied from the alternator. Thus, the choke will receive electricity only while the alternator is operating. Some

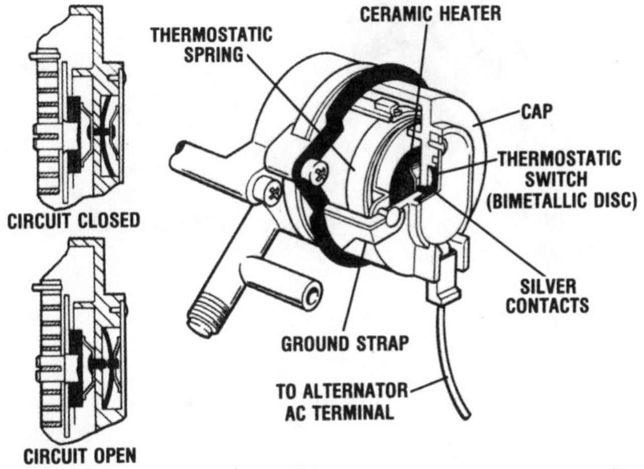

Figure 13-15. An electric-assist, carburetor-mounted choke. (Courtesy of Ford Motor Company, Dearborn)

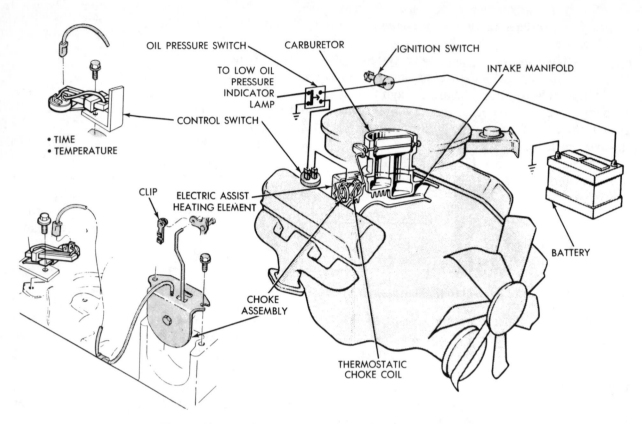

Figure 13-16.   An electric-assist, engine-mounted choke system. (Courtesy of Chrysler Corporation)

carburetor-mounted choke springs are continuously electrically heated and receive their electric power supply from either the ignition switch or the alternator. **Continuously electrically heated chokes** require no other heat source.

An **engine-mounted, electric-assist choke** assembly is shown in Figures 13-16 and 13-17. As shown in Figure 13-17, this choke has a metal heating element next to the thermostatic choke coil. The assembly is mounted in a recess in the intake manifold and receives heat from the exhaust crossover passage. See Figure 13-16. When the control switch, which is mounted on the engine, senses engine temperature above approximately 80°F (27°C), it turns on the heating element to cause a fast and positive choke opening. The control unit turns the heating element off after about five minutes.

Some Chrysler chokes have extra heat assistance when the engine is cold. These chokes have a **series resistor** across the control switch terminals that flows a reduced current through the heater when the contacts are open. The oil pressure switch also opens the circuit to the heating element until the engine starts.

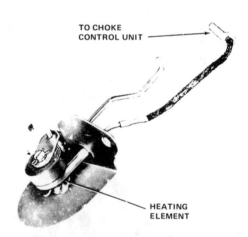

Figure 13-17.   An engine-mounted, electric-assist choke heating element. (Courtesy of Chrysler Corporation)

□   **ASSIGNMENT 13-D**   □

Explain the operation of an electric-assist choke thermostatic spring assembly.

CONTROLLING DISTRIBUTOR ADVANCE

Many different emission control systems have been employed to control distributor spark advance. A separate discussion of each of these systems would be beyond the scope of this book. However, you should understand some of the approaches used to control distributor spark advance and the reasoning behind their use. We will discuss the systems that have been used most frequently, or have been the most effective.

Retarding the spark is one of the common methods used to control exhaust emissions. The combustion flame is late in starting with a retarded spark, but it lasts further into the power stroke. This keeps the metal engine cylinder surfaces warmer, which results in more complete combustion.

A retarded spark also allows the engine to burn leaner air-fuel mixtures, as shown in Figure 13-18. In the illustration, two identical engines are shown to be idling at 700 rpm. The first engine has its initial timing set at 8° BTDC (Before Top Dead Center) and operates with relatively little air flow past the carburetor throttle plate. The second engine has its initial timing retarded to 4° BTDC. Since retarded timing places less power push on the pistons, the engine slows down, and a larger throttle plate opening is needed to allow more air into the fuel to achieve 700 rpm. The mixture is somewhat leaner and provides a larger volume of air for compression in the compression chamber. This leads to more complete combustion that results in less exhaust emissions. Retarding the spark at idle was one of the first emission control methods employed.

Most distributors have two spark advance sys-

tems—the centrifugal advance system (which is controlled by engine speed), and the vacuum advance system (which is controlled by the intake manifold vacuum). In order to meet emission standards, manufacturers retarded the initial timing 4° to 10° on their vehicles. This had a direct effect on the centrifugal advance during engine idle. The weights and springs on the centrifugal advance were reworked so that they would compensate for this retarded spark during high-speed advance requirements.

Retarded Idle Advance

One method used on the vacuum advance does not actually retard the vacuum advance, but prevents it from operating during idle. The system shown in Figure 13-19 places the spark advance vacuum port a fraction above the leading edge of the throttle valve at idle. The manifold vacuum is cut off from the vacuum advance at idle, but as the throttle is opened to the off-idle position, the port is exposed to the vacuum needed to operate the vacuum advance. This system is called a **ported spark advance**.

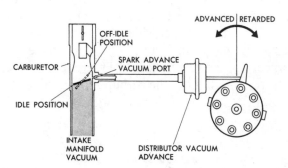

Figure 13-19. A ported spark advance. (Courtesy of General Motors of Canada Limited)

Another method of achieving retarded spark at idle is by using a **dual-action vacuum advance**, as shown in Figure 13-20. Notice that a ported spark advance is used on the advance side of the vacuum chamber in a dual-action vacuum advance. From a port below the throttle plate (some manufacturers use manifold vacuum from a fitting on the intake manifold), manifold vacuum is applied to the retard side of the diaphragm. This retards the timing an extra 4° to 10° during idle when the ported vacuum is not applied to the advance side. When the throttle opens and ported vacuum is applied to the advance side, the

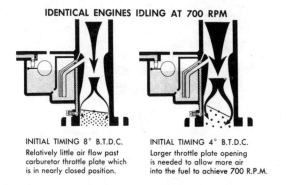

Figure 13-18. Exhaust emissions can be reduced by retarding initial timing. (Courtesy of General Motors of Canada Limited)

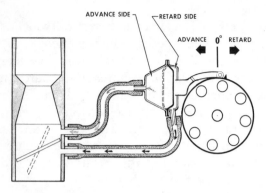

Figure 13-20. A dual-action vacuum advance. (Courtesy of General Motors of Canada Limited)

advance side overrides the retard side, and normal advance takes place. A Ford Motor Company system of using a dual-diaphragm vacuum advance mechanism is shown in Figure 13-21.

An engine that idles for some time in warm weather with a retarded spark tends to overheat. Therefore, it is necessary to override a retarded advance system if the engine becomes overheated. Figures 13-22 and 13-23 illlustrate the use of a **temperature-sensitive vacuum control valve** in the advance unit hoses. As shown in Figure 13-22, when the coolant is at normal temperature, manifold vacuum is applied to the retard side, and carburetor ported vacuum to the advance side of the dual-diaphragm control. As shown in Figure 13-23, when the engine is overheating, the vacuum control valve senses the temperature, switches off the carburetor ported vacuum, and applies manifold vacuum to both sides of the

unit. The advance side overrides the retard side, and the timing is severely advanced. This makes the engine race at idle and causes faster coolant circulation to cool the engine. Advanced timing also creates less combustion heat. When the engine cools, the system returns to normal.

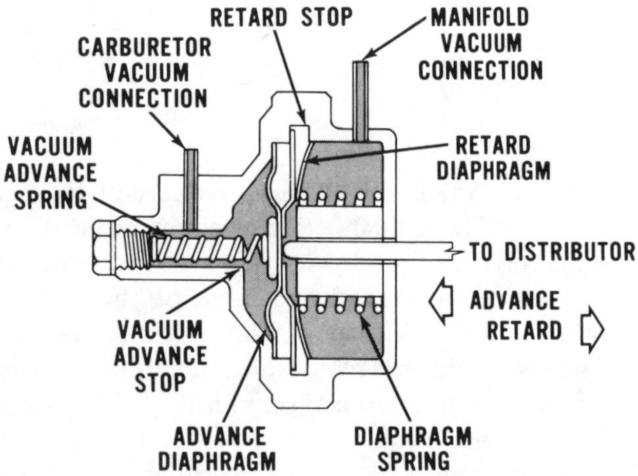

Controlling Spark Advance at Moderate Speeds

During periods of moderate acceleration with normal distributor spark advance, combustion temperature rises and causes excess nitrogen oxides. Retarding the spark a little by denying the full spark

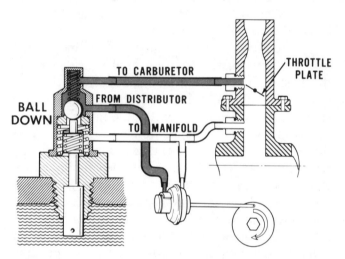

Figure 13-22. A vacuum control valve in the normal position. (Courtesy of Ford Motor Company, Dearborn)

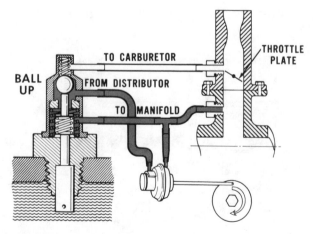

Figure 13-23. A vacuum control valve in the engine overheating position. (Courtesy of Ford Motor Company, Dearborn)

Figure 13-21. A Ford dual-diaphragm vacuum advance mechanism. (Courtesy of Ford Motor Company, Dearborn)

advance from the vacuum unit helps to reduce nitrogen oxides during moderate acceleration.

Many systems have been used to retard the spark during moderate acceleration. Most of these systems used electrical components and electronic control units attached to the transmission, and most were used for only a year or two. These systems denied the vacuum advance throughout lower gear operation and allowed it to work in high gear only after about 36 mph (60 km/h). Over a period of time it was found to be more effective to delay the vacuum advance operation only momentarily each time the throttle was opened, rather than continuously throughout the range of lower gears.

One device for controlling nitrogen oxides during moderate acceleration is called an **Orifice Spark Advance Control (OSAC)** valve. The OSAC valve has been used by the Chrysler Corporation for some time. See Figure 13-24. The OSAC valve is usually mounted on the fire wall or on the side of the

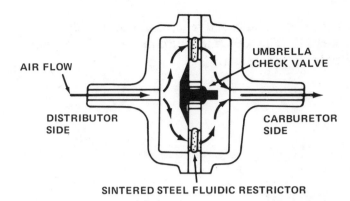

Figure 13-25. A Ford Spark Delay Valve (SDV). (Courtesy of Ford Motor Company, Dearborn)

the distributor vacuum advance. The SDV delays the vacuum going to the vacuum unit when the throttle is opening, but allows a quick change in vacuum when the throttle is closing. The Ford SDV is a small, round plastic unit that comes in several colors. The colors designate the delay time that the valve provides.

Some OSAC valves contain a thermostatic override that provides better drivability during the engine warm-up period. On some engines, a **Thermal Ignition Control (TIC)** valve senses engine temperature and switches manifold vacuum directly to the vacuum advance if the engine overheats. See Figure 13-26. Advanced spark causes cooler combustion and speeds up engine idle, which cools down the engine.

As shown in Figure 13-27, the Ford Motor Company uses a similar valve called a **Ported Vacuum Switch (PVS)**. Ford also uses another system that senses ambient (outside) temperature. When ambient temperature is below about 65°F (18°C), this system causes the spark delay valve to be bypassed for im-

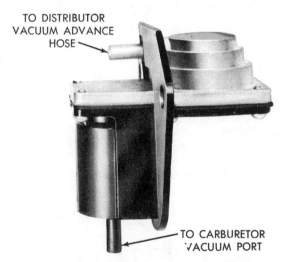

Figure 13-24. A Chrysler Orifice Spark Advance Control. (Courtesy of Chrysler Corporation)

air cleaner. The OSAC valve has a small orifice called a **timing delay orifice**. This orifice delays the change in ported vacuum to the distributor advance by 10 to 27 seconds when the throttle is moved from idle to part throttle. When going down from part throttle to idle, the change in vacuum retards the spark instantly by using a special valve inside the OSAC valve that bypasses the timing delay orifice.

Figure 13-25 shows a similar unit that is used by the Ford Motor Company. This unit is called a **Spark Delay Valve (SDV)**. It is located in the hose leading to

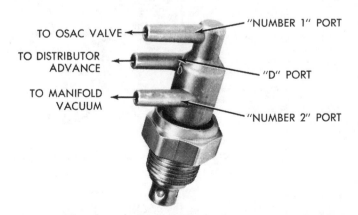

Figure 13-26. A Thermal Ignition Control (TIC) Valve. (Courtesy of Chrysler Corporation)

proved drivability and reduced nitrogen oxides in cold weather. This system is called the **Delay Vacuum Bypass (DVB)** system.

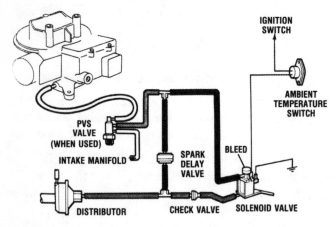

Figure 13-27. *A Ford Ported Vacuum Switch (PVS) and Delay Vacuum Bypass (DVP) system. (Courtesy of Ford Motor Company, Dearborn)*

FACTS TO REMEMBER

Retarding the spark advance is important for controlling hydrocarbons and nitrogen oxide emissions. Many methods have been used to retard spark advance. One of the first was to simply retard the initial timing. Further improvements involved retarding the spark advance at idle and at moderate speeds and loads. Systems designed to retard idle advance generally involve the centrifugal and vacuum advance. Systems that retard advance at moderate speeds concentrate on controlling advance momentarily when the throttle is opened.

□ ASSIGNMENT 13-E □

State the purpose of each device in the following list:
    ported spark advance
    dual-diaphragm vacuum advance
    OSAC valve
    PVS and TIC valves
    DVB systems

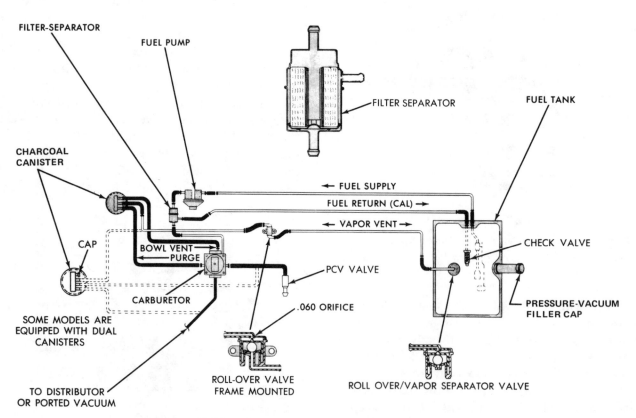

Figure 13-28. *An evaporation control system. (Courtesy of Chrysler Corporation)*

EVAPORATIVE EMISSION CONTROLS

Any gasoline released from the fuel tank or carburetor in a liquid or vapor form enters the atmosphere as 100% hydrocarbon pollution. Reduction of liquid and vapor fuel losses are accomplished with a variety of different devices. So many systems have been tried and discontinued that it is not possible to discuss them all here. However, some proven, workable devices commonly used for controlling evaporation and liquid fuel losses from fuel systems are discussed below.

Vapor Control

The **evaporation control system** shown in Figure 13-28 is a Chrysler Corporation system. This system prevents the emission of gasoline vapors from the fuel tank and carburetor. When fuel evaporates in the carburetor float chamber or the fuel tank, vapors are formed. These vapors pass through the bowl vent line from the carburetor, or the vapor vent line from the fuel tank, to a **charcoal canister**. Here they are temporarily held until they can be drawn into the intake manifold during engine operation. The **purging** (drying out) of the canister is done by manifold vacuum through the **purge hose line**, connected from the canister purge fitting to the **carburetor purge port**. This purge port is a calibrated opening that prevents too much vapor flow from the canister. Too much flow would upset the air-fuel mixture that is delivered to the cylinders by the carburetor.

Some vehicles, particularly those designed to meet California emission standards, have a **filter separator**, as shown in Figure 13-28. This permits some fuel to recirculate (along with vapors) into the fuel return line, back to the tank, and out of the one-way check valve at the end of the fuel return line. The check valve blocks fuel from the tank from entering the return line. Recirculation cools the fuel, which reduces the amount of vapor formed and the risk of vapor lock. Vapor lock could make the fuel pump ineffective and stall the engine.

A **roll-over valve** is placed either at the midpoint or tank end of the vapor vent line (depending on the car model). This valve permits a 360° vehicle rollover without fuel leakage from the canister. The roll-over valve is incorporated into a **roll-over vapor separator valve** on some models. The separator valve separates any liquid fuel from the fuel vapor and prevents liquid fuel from flowing with the vapor into the vapor vent line.

If a carburetor with no canister vent was factory installed on the engine, the canister carburetor vent fitting will be capped. Some systems have two charcoal canisters. The second canister is shown in Figure 13-28 by dotted lines connected into the vapor vent line. This second canister is purged by the PCV valve line and the ported vacuum for the distributor.

Charcoal Canisters

Careful study of Figures 13-29 and 13-30 will help you understand the operation of the **charcoal canister**. When the engine is turned off, the vapors that form in the fuel tank (particularly in hot weather) force their way along the vent line and into the charcoal canister, along with vapors formed in the carburetor fuel bowl. This is shown by the arrows in Figure 13-29. The air and vapors pass through the activated charcoal, which absorbs the fuel vapor. Once cleaned of vapor, the air passes out into the atmosphere through the filter in the bottom of the canister.

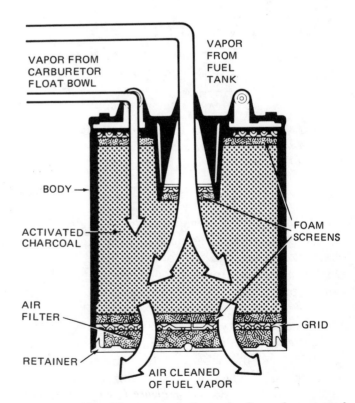

Figure 13-29. *The arrows indicate the flow of vapor and air into the charcoal canister. (Courtesy of General Motors of Canada Limited)*

As shown by the arrows in Figure 13-30, when the engine is operating the purge line vacuum draws air into the air filter in the bottom of the canister, and through the activated charcoal. This evaporates the gasoline trapped in the charcoal. These fumes are carried into the intake manifold and burned in the cylinders.

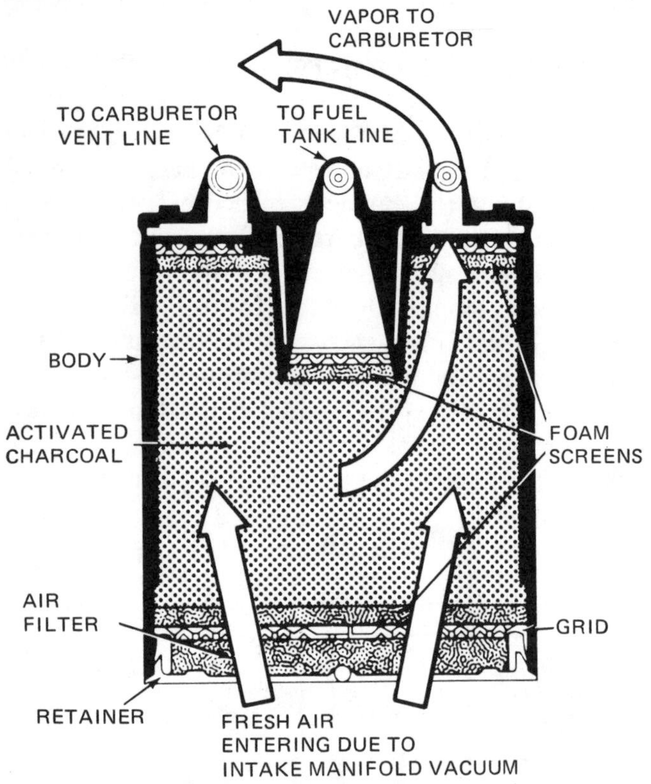

A float-type vapor-liquid separator operates by allowing a float to rise with the liquid gasoline and shut off a needle valve in the vent line. The valve remains shut until the fuel drains back to the tank. See Figure 13-33.

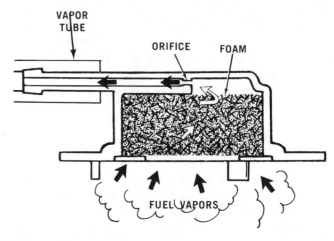

Figure 13-31.   *A vapor-liquid separator that uses open-cell filter material. (Courtesy of Ford Motor Company, Dearborn)*

Figure 13-30.   *The arrows indicate the flow of air and vapor during canister purging. (Courtesy of General Motors of Canada Limited)*

Different types of vapor-liquid separators have been used to prevent liquid fuel from entering the charcoal canister. One type of vapor-liquid separator passes the vapors through open-cell foam. Liquid cannot pass through the foam, as shown in Figure 13-31.

A standpipe-style vapor-liquid separator is shown in Figure 13-32. Vapors cool and condense in the standpipe and drain back to the tank through the drain opening. When the vehicle is parked on an incline, liquid fuel stays inside the standpipe, since it is higher than the fuel tank. This eliminates flooding of the charcoal canister.

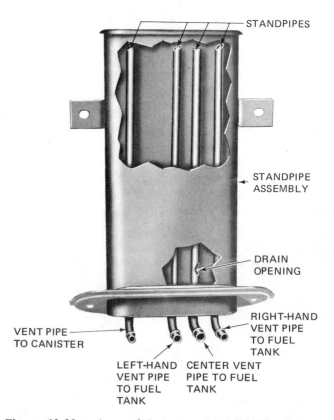

Figure 13-32.   *A standpipe-type vapor-liquid separator. (Courtesy of General Motors of Canada Limited)*

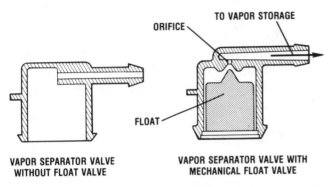

Figure 13-33. A float-type vapor-liquid separator. (Courtesy of Ford Motor Company, Dearborn)

Fuel Tanks

A modern fuel tank is sealed with a specially engineered **pressure-vacuum relief filler cap**, as shown in Figure 13-34. The relief valves in the cap are only a safety feature and operate only to eliminate excess pressure or vacuum in the tank. Excess pressure or vacuum could be caused by a malfunction in the system or damage to the vent lines. The relief valve in the cap prevents fuel vapors from escaping and is not intended as a constant atmospheric tank vent. The atmospheric pressure required to move the fuel into the fuel lines and fuel pump enters the tank through the carbon canister and vent line.

A fuel tank that is overfilled can spill fuel. This can happen at the gas pump or after the tank has been filled. Fuel expansion and evaporation in an over-filled tank will produce pressure that forces fuel out of the tank. For this reason, modern fuel tanks usually have some type of overfill limiting feature. One simple solution uses a filler pipe that is extended down inside the fuel tank. The fuel tank will not accept fuel after the end of the filler pipe inside the tank is covered with fuel. This leaves a space for fuel and vapor expansion.

Some fuel tanks have an **internal expansion tank** that takes up about 1/10 of the main tank's volume. See Figure 13-35. The ports leading into the expansion tank are so small that it takes 10 to 15 minutes for gas from the main tank to fill the expansion tank. This slowly filling expansion tank inside the main tank lowers the fuel level in the main fuel tank after the main tank has been filled at the fuel pump. This provides room for fuel expansion and vapors in the main tank.

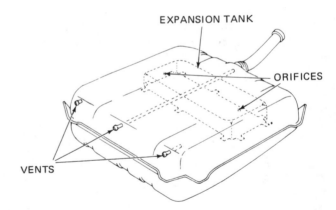

Figure 13-35. A fuel tank with an internal expansion tank. The vent lines are connected to a vapor-liquid separator. (Courtesy of General Motors of Canada Limited)

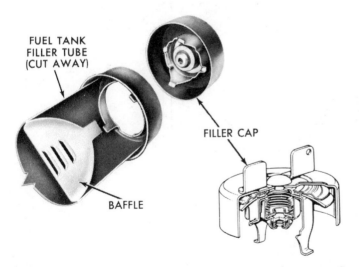

Figure 13-34. A pressure-vacuum filler cap. (Courtesy of Chrysler Corporation)

FACTS TO REMEMBER

Any liquid fuel or fuel vapor that is released into the atmosphere is a pollutant. Vapor vent hoses and lines from the carburetor and fuel tank into a charcoal canister are used to control fuel vapor leaks into the atmosphere. Special fuel tanks with internal expansion tanks and vacuum relief filler caps are used to prevent liquid fuel leakage and vapor loss.

□ ASSIGNMENT 13-F □

Explain the purpose of each device in the following list:
  pressure-vacuum relief cap
  vapor vent line
  charcoal canister
  roll-over valve
  expansion tank
  purge line

EXHAUST GAS RECIRCULATING SYSTEM

Most of the systems that reduce hydrocarbon emissions have a negative effect on nitrogen oxides. At about the point where hydrocarbon emissions are made acceptable, nitrogen oxide emissions are increased beyond acceptable levels. Nitrogen oxides are produced by high combustion temperatures. Most emission controls, however, increase combustion temperature. **Exhaust Gas Recirculating** (EGR) systems of various designs are used to reduce nitrogen oxides.

The EGR system dilutes the air-fuel mixture in the intake manifold with a small amount of exhaust gas. The exhaust gas does not contribute oxygen or burn during combustion, but it does absorb some of the combustion heat. This lowers the cylinder combustion temperature and reduces nitrogen oxides.

EGR System Operation

EGR systems all operate through the use of a basic system. For information about control devices added to this basic system by individual manufacturers, you can refer to their shop manuals.

Figure 13-36 illustrates a basic EGR system. The EGR vacuum port is located above the throttle plate at idle, preventing a vacuum signal until the throttle is opened. If exhaust gases were allowed to dilute the idle mixture, the engine would idle poorly or stall. At normal speeds, exhaust dilution of the air-fuel mixture does not affect engine performance. However, if the engine is cold, exhaust dilution can have an effect on drivability. Therefore, when the engine is cold, exhaust dilution is prevented by a temperature-controlled vacuum valve in the vacuum line to the EGR valve. Until the engine warms up, the EGR valve remains closed.

Exhaust dilution will affect power on acceleration or during faster than normal engine speeds with

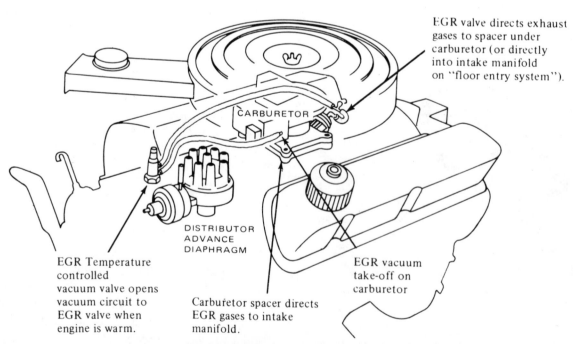

EGR valve directs exhaust gases to spacer under carburetor (or directly into intake manifold on "floor entry system").

CARBURETOR

EGR Temperature controlled vacuum valve opens vacuum circuit to EGR valve when engine is warm.

DISTRIBUTOR ADVANCE DIAPHRAGM

Carburetor spacer directs EGR gases to intake manifold.

EGR vacuum take-off on carburetor

Figure 13-36. A basic EGR system. (Courtesy of Ford Motor Company, Dearborn)

wide throttle openings. Since the manifold vacuum decreases drastically at wide throttle, the EGR valve closes from lack of vacuum strength, cutting out exhaust gas recycling automatically.

To understand the operation of the basic EGR system, and the EGR valve, study Figure 13-37. Read the statements in Figure 13-37 in order from one to twelve.

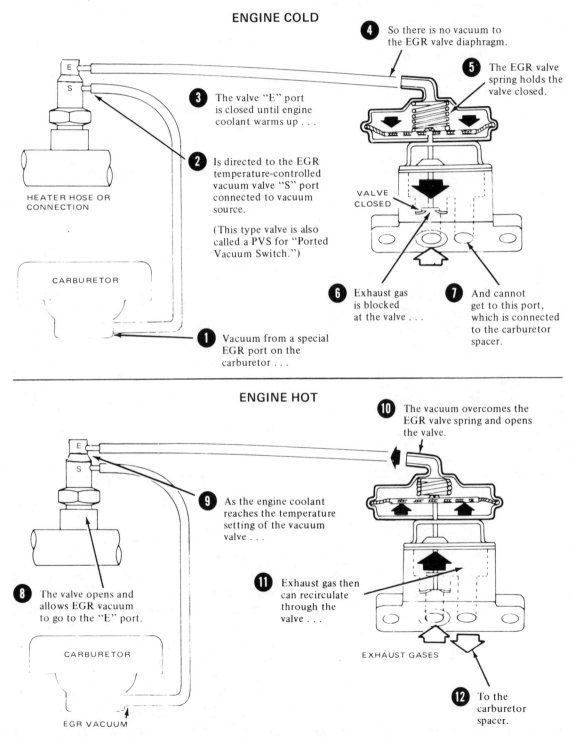

ENGINE COLD

4 So there is no vacuum to the EGR valve diaphragm.

5 The EGR valve spring holds the valve closed.

3 The valve "E" port is closed until engine coolant warms up . . .

2 Is directed to the EGR temperature-controlled vacuum valve "S" port connected to vacuum source.

(This type valve is also called a PVS for "Ported Vacuum Switch.")

HEATER HOSE OR CONNECTION

VALVE CLOSED

CARBURETOR

6 Exhaust gas is blocked at the valve . . .

7 And cannot get to this port, which is connected to the carburetor spacer.

1 Vacuum from a special EGR port on the carburetor . . .

ENGINE HOT

10 The vacuum overcomes the EGR valve spring and opens the valve.

9 As the engine coolant reaches the temperature setting of the vacuum valve . . .

8 The valve opens and allows EGR vacuum to go to the "E" port.

11 Exhaust gas then can recirculate through the valve . . .

CARBURETOR

EXHAUST GASES

EGR VACUUM

12 To the carburetor spacer.

Figure 13-37. Operation of the EGR valve. (Courtesy of Ford Motor Company, Dearborn)

Figure 13-38 shows two methods used to route the exhaust gas into the engine. One method, known as **carburetor spacer routing**, picks up exhaust gas from the exhaust crossover, passes it through the spacer to the EGR valve, then back through the spacer just below the carburetor, and into the intake manifold. In the other method, known as **floor entry routing**, the EGR valve is mounted on the intake manifold and receives exhaust from the exhaust crossover through a built-in passage. This directs the exhaust gas flow to another built-in passage that ends at ports in the floor of the intake manifold below the carburetor.

Some EGR systems have **vacuum amplifier** units that raise the strength of the vacuum from which they operate. These systems work off of venturi vacuum instead of manifold vacuum. Venturi vacuum needs strengthening to be able to operate the EGR valve.

Some systems have a **speed sensor** and **electronic control unit** to cut off the operation of the EGR valve at high speeds and provide better high-speed drivability.

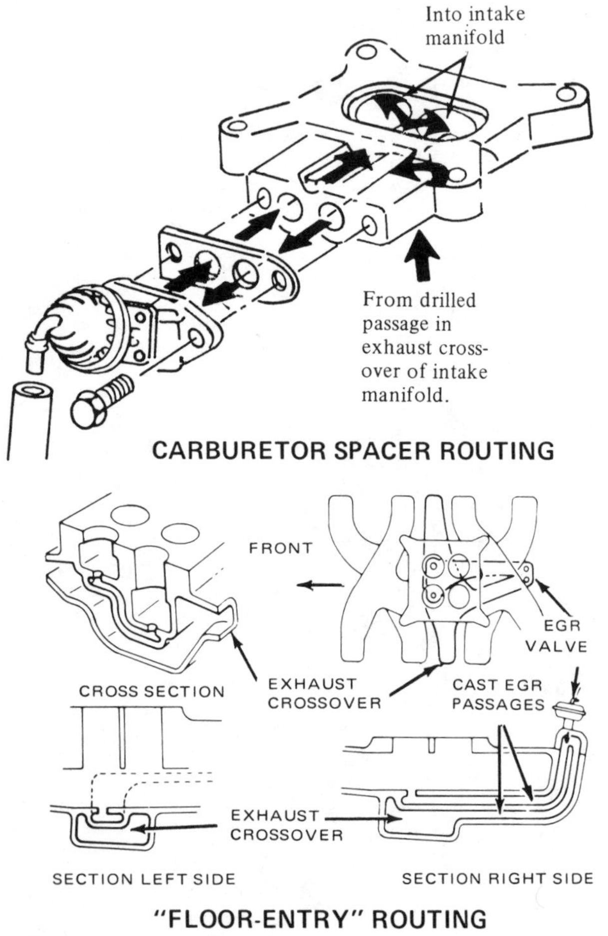

☐   ASSIGNMENT 13-G   ☐

1. Briefly explain how exhaust gas recirculation can reduce nitrogen oxides.
2. Tell whether the EGR valve would be open or closed under the following driving conditions:
   during the warm-up period
   at idle
   at normal speeds and normal engine temperature
   on acceleration
   at speeds above regular cruising

CARBURETOR SPACER ROUTING

"FLOOR-ENTRY" ROUTING

Figure 13-38.   Two methods of routing EGR valve exhaust gas into the engine. (Courtesy of Ford Motor Company, Dearborn)

AIR INJECTION SYSTEMS

Air injection systems are designed to introduce fresh air (and, thus, oxygen) into the exhaust as the exhaust gas is leaving the exhaust ports. This causes further oxidation (burning) of the hydrocarbons and carbon monoxide left in the hot exhaust. The process is like fanning a dying fire. Oxygen in the air combines with hydrocarbons and carbon monoxide to reduce their concentration, allow them to oxidize, and produce harmless water vapor and carbon dioxide.

Air Injection System Operation

In order to understand the operation of the air injection systems, you should study Figures 13-39 and 13-40. The **Thermactor Air Injection System** produced by Ford is representative of the systems used by most other companies. An **air pump**, driven by the engine through a belt and pulleys, provides a large-volume, low-pressure air supply. This air is pumped through a hose to a **bypass valve** (sometimes called a **diverter valve**). Air passes from the bypass valve through another hose to one **check valve**, and out into an **air manifold** that connects to a passage at the rear of each exhaust manifold. See Figure 13-40.

The air travels through passages built into each exhaust manifold to mix with the exhaust gas as it leaves the exhaust valves. In Figure 13-39, which shows an early-type air injection system, the air that leaves the bypass valve divides into two check valves attached to **air distribution manifolds** fastened into the cylinder heads. Only one side of an eight-cylinder engine is shown in Figure 13-39. The air passes through stainless steel tubes that direct it into each exhaust valve port just outside the exhaust valve. A six-cylinder engine would have one air distribution manifold with six tubes.

The air pump shown in Figure 13-41 is a rotating vane, lifetime lubricated type that is usually serviced as a unit. If the unit has a **centrifugal filter fan** that stops dirt and water from entering the pump, the fan alone can be replaced.

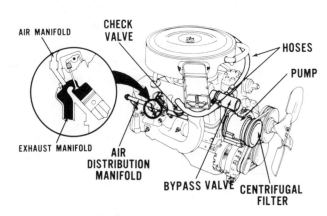

Figure 13-39.   An early-type Thermactor Air Injection System used by the Ford Motor Company. (Courtesy of Ford Motor Company, Dearborn)

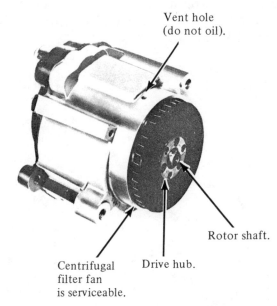

Figure 13-41.   An air pump used on the Ford air injection system. (Courtesy of Ford Motor Company, Dearborn)

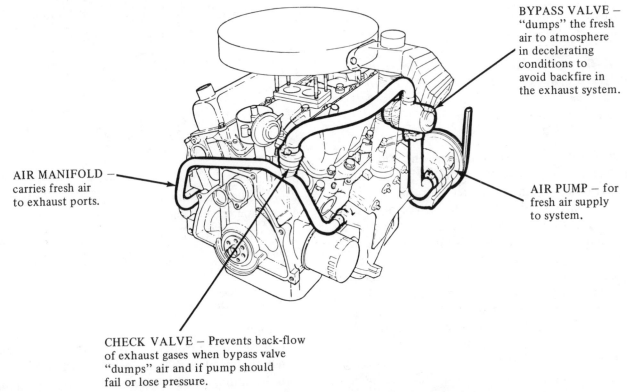

BYPASS VALVE – "dumps" the fresh air to atmosphere in decelerating conditions to avoid backfire in the exhaust system.

AIR MANIFOLD – carries fresh air to exhaust ports.

AIR PUMP – for fresh air supply to system.

CHECK VALVE – Prevents back-flow of exhaust gases when bypass valve "dumps" air and if pump should fail or lose pressure.

Figure 13-40.   A late-type Ford Thermactor Air Injection system. (Courtesy of Ford Motor Company, Dearborn)

The check valve shown in Figure 13-42 is a one-way valve that permits air from the pump to pass through, but prevents a back flow of exhaust gases when the bypass valve diverts the air flow, or if the pump should fail or lose pressure. The cross section of the check valve shown in Figure 13-42 shows the spring-loaded metal diaphragm that lets air flow in the direction of the arrow, but does not allow exhaust gases to back flow.

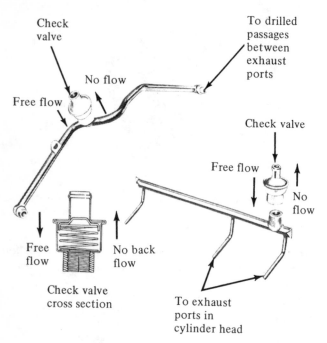

Figure 13-42. *Check valves used in the Ford air injection system. (Courtesy of Ford Motor Company, Dearborn)*

Bypass Valve

On sudden deceleration, the throttle closes quickly and cuts off the air to the carburetor bore. However, fuel, which is heavier than air, tends to discharge from the high-speed nozzle for an instant after the air flow has stopped. This momentarily causes an air-fuel mixture that is too rich to burn. If this unburned fuel meets the injected air, it becomes combustible. An instant later, when the air-fuel mixture is normal again, the hot exhaust gases ignite the mixture in the exhaust system. This will cause explosions known as **backfiring** in the exhaust system.

The **bypass valve** on the air injection system prevents backfiring on this initial deceleration stage by diverting the pumped air flow from the injection system to the atmosphere for a few seconds. Some sys-

tems divert the air into the air cleaner. In some cases a valve, called a **gulp valve**, is used. The gulp valve diverts the air flow into the intake manifold, where it mixes with the fuel and produces a burnable air-fuel mixture.

To understand the flow through the bypass valve during normal operation where the air is passed through to the injection system, follow the numbered statements in Figure 13-43. The air flow for bypass (deceleration), where the air flow is bypassed from the system and discharged into the atmosphere for a short interval, is explained in Figure 13-44. The bypass operates for an instant whenever there is a sharp rise in manifold vacuum, such as when the engine is coasting with a closed throttle or during rapid deceleration.

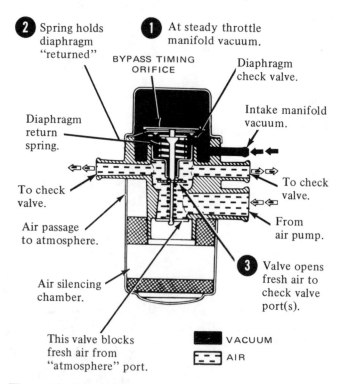

Figure 13-43. *A bypass valve under normal operation. (Courtesy of Ford Motor Company, Dearborn)*

Switching Systems

Figure 13-45 shows an air injection system used by Chrysler Corporation. This system has a **switching system** that ensures that air injection will not interfere with the ability of the EGR system to control nitrogen oxide emissions. During cold engine operation, this

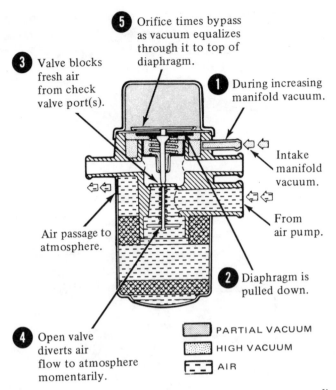

⑤ Orifice times bypass as vacuum equalizes through it to top of diaphragm.

③ Valve blocks fresh air from check valve port(s).

① During increasing manifold vacuum.

Intake manifold vacuum.

From air pump.

Air passage to atmosphere.

② Diaphragm is pulled down.

④ Open valve diverts air flow to atmosphere momentarily.

PARTIAL VACUUM
HIGH VACUUM
AIR

Figure 13-44. A bypass valve under deceleration conditions. (Courtesy of Ford Motor Company, Dearborn)

system performs in the same way as the Ford Thermactor system. Air is injected at the exhaust ports for a time during engine warm-up when the mixture tends to be richer, without ill effects to the EGR System. When the engine reaches normal operating temperature, the injected air is switched from the exhaust ports to a point lower in the exhaust manifold by the **air switching valve.** This valve receives vacuum through the **coolant control engine vacuum switch** when the engine warms up. The injected air can still assist oxidation in the exhaust system and catalytic converter, but it will not interfere with exhaust gas recirculation.

Aspirator Valves

A very simple type of system that permits air to be injected into the exhaust system without using an air pump uses an **aspirator valve.** This system is shown in Figure 13-46. It consists of a steel tube flanged to the exhaust manifold with a one-way aspirator valve threaded onto it, and a length of hose from the valve to the air cleaner.

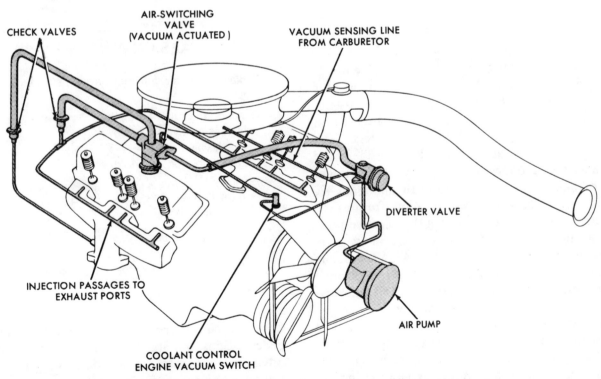

CHECK VALVES

AIR-SWITCHING VALVE (VACUUM ACTUATED)

VACUUM SENSING LINE FROM CARBURETOR

DIVERTER VALVE

INJECTION PASSAGES TO EXHAUST PORTS

AIR PUMP

COOLANT CONTROL ENGINE VACUUM SWITCH

Figure 13-45. An air injection system. (Courtesy of Chrysler Corporation)

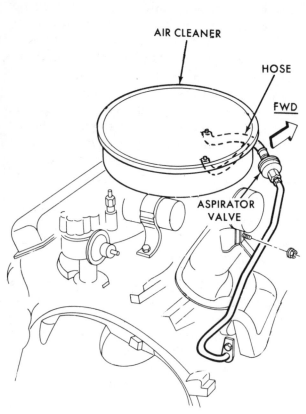

Figure 13-46. *An air injection system with an aspirator valve. (Courtesy of Chrysler Corporation)*

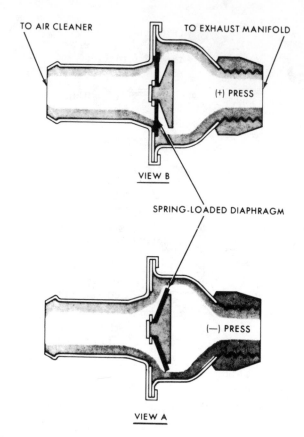

Figure 13-47. *An aspirator valve. (Courtesy of Chrysler Corporation)*

The aspirator valve uses exhaust pressure pulsations to draw fresh air into the exhaust system. This reduces carbon monoxide and, to a lesser degree, hydrocarbon emissions. Aspirator valves are used on vehicles equipped with catalytic converters. The aspirator valve draws air from the "clean" side of the air cleaner past a one-way, spring-loaded diaphragm made of high-temperature rubber. In Figure 13-47, View A, the diaphragm opens to allow fresh air to mix with the exhaust gases during the negative pressure (vacuum) pulses that occur in the exhaust ports and manifold passages. In Figure 13-47, View B, the diaphragm closes if the exhaust pressure is positive (above atmospheric), and no exhaust gases can flow back to the clean side of the air cleaner.

The aspirator valve works most efficiently at idle and off idle when the exhaust pulses are maximum. At higher speeds, the aspirator valve remains closed. Some aspirator valves have a metal **reed valve** instead of a diaphragm, but they operate in the same manner.

□   ASSIGNMENT 13-H   □

1. Explain how air injection systems reduce exhaust emissions.

2. Describe the function of the following:
   bypass or diverter valve
   check valve
   air distribution manifold
   air pump
   air switching valve
   aspirator valve

CATALYTIC CONVERTER SYSTEMS

Catalytic converters were designed to help meet Federal Emission Standards. A catalytic converter, often called a **catalytic muffler**, is similar in appearance to a small muffler and is installed in the exhaust system between the engine and regular muffler.

Converter Operation

The Chrysler catalytic converter is made up of two stainless steel shells that are welded together. As shown in Figure 13-48, inside the converter are two ceramic cores that are protected against breakage by a stainless steel mesh.

The ceramic material is capable of withstanding very high temperatures. The ceramic core has thousands of passages—about 240 per square inch (6.45 sq cm). See Figure 13-49. These passages present an enormous surface area for contact with the exhaust as it passes through the converter. Normal operating temperature is 900° to 1200°F (480° to 650°C), but the converter will become much hotter if the fuel mixture is rich or the engine is misfiring.

The ceramic passages are coated with **platinum** and **paladium** metals. These metals provide the catalyst. When properly contained in the mufflerlike shell, the catalyst will reduce hydrocarbon and carbon monoxide pollutants by changing them into harmless water vapor and carbon dioxide. The catalyst operates only when it is hot, and remains unchanged during catalytic action.

Ford catalytic converters are similar to Chrysler converters, but contain only one honeycombed ceramic core. General Motors catalytic converters contain ceramic beads that are coated with platinum and paladium. See Figure 13-50.

All vehicles equipped with catalytic converters have shielding around the converter to protect the vehicle floor and reduce the heat inside the vehicle.

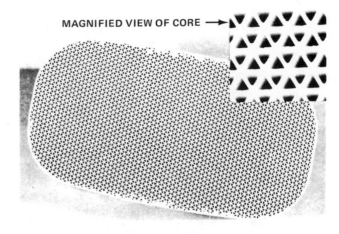

MAGNIFIED VIEW OF CORE →

Figure 13-49. End view of a catalytic converter core showing the thousands of passages that help in the catalytic action. (Courtesy of Chrysler Corporation)

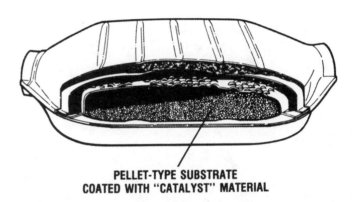

PELLET-TYPE SUBSTRATE COATED WITH "CATALYST" MATERIAL

Figure 13-50. A General Motors catalytic converter contains catalyst covered beads. (Courtesy of General Motors of Canada, Limited)

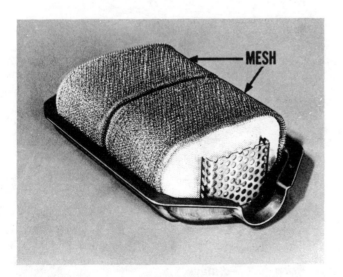

← MESH

Figure 13-48. A Chrysler Corporation catalytic converter. (Courtesy of Chrysler Corporation)

Secondary Air Supply

A catalytic converter may be supplied with a **secondary air supply** by an air injection system that uses an air pump or aspirator valve. The purpose of this secondary air is to provide oxygen to aid the catalytic action of the platinum and paladium. The resulting oxidation (burning) produces a high temperature. High temperatures are one of the main requirements for breaking down hydrocarbons and carbon monoxide into water vapor and carbon dioxide.

Three-Way Catalytic Converters

The catalytic converters that we have studied to this point effectively reduce hydrocarbons and carbon

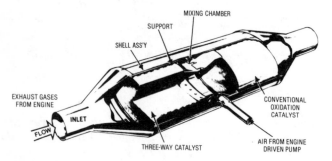

Figure 13-51. *A cutaway view of a dual-bed, three-way catalytic converter. (Courtesy of Ford Motor Company, Dearborn)*

monoxide, but have no effect on nitrogen oxides. It was found that **rhodium** (a metal), used one part to five parts of platinum, along with proper carburetor mixture control, could be fairly effective in reducing nitrogen oxide. This led to the manufacture of **three-way catalytic converters**.

One style of three-way catalytic converter, used by Ford, is shown in Figure 13-51. The flow of exhaust gas first enters the three-way catalyst where reaction to all three pollutants—hydrocarbon, carbon monoxide, and nitrogen oxide—is promoted. Air is then introduced from an air injection pump, and the exhaust passes through a conventional oxidation catalyst where hydrocarbon and carbon monoxide are further reduced.

The types of controls used in this type of a system are complicated, as shown in Figure 13-52. Con-

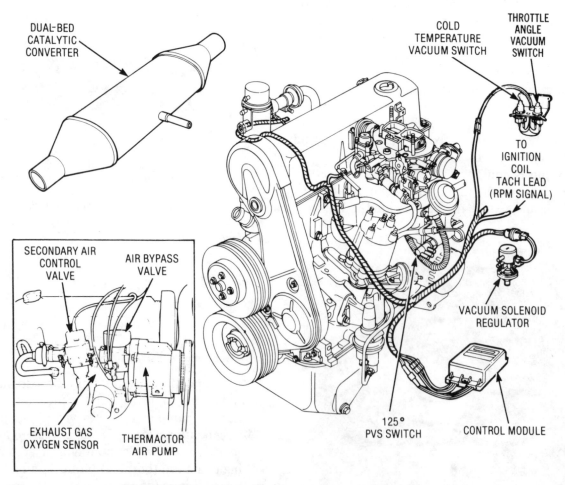

Figure 13-52. *A view of an engine with a dual-bed, three-way catalytic converter. Notice the parts necessary to operate this system. (Courtesy of Ford Motor Company, Dearborn)*

trol devices aid in carburetor mixture regulation through the use of an oxygen sensor in the exhaust manifold, electronic devices to control the carburetor mixture, and the control and routing of the air from the air injection system. See Figures 13-53 and 13-54.

Care of Catalytic Converters

Only unleaded gasoline can be used in catalytic-converter-equipped vehicles. Leaded gasoline causes the catalyst to become coated with lead, thus destroying its effectiveness. A smaller fuel tank filler neck, trap door, and a decal stating, **Use Unleaded Fuel Only,** help provide safeguards against the use of leaded fuels in cars equipped with catalytic converters. See Figure 13-55.

The catalyst in the converter must be protected from overheating during periods of cold running with a rich mixture, periods of high engine heat caused by

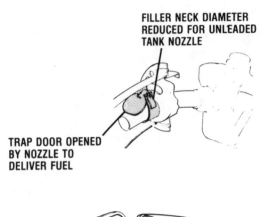

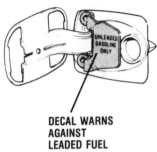

Figure 13-55. Several safeguards are used to prevent the use of leaded fuel in catalytic-converter-equipped cars. (Courtesy of Ford Motor Company, Dearborn)

long idle intervals on a hot day, or during deceleration. Many catalyst protection devices are used by various companies. Information on different catalyst protection devices can be found in the manufacturers' shop manuals.

If more than normal amounts of unburned fuel reach the catalytic converter, it can become severely overheated, damaged, and can cause damage to the vehicle floor. Engine maintenance is critical. Misfiring of one or more spark plugs or other malfunctions that cause richness in the exhaust gases will overheat the catalytic converter.

Do not idle the engine more than 10 minutes. When you are testing plugs and wires, do not operate the engine more than 30 seconds with one spark plug wire removed or shorted. Use an oscilloscope, if available, for isolating cylinders, instead of shorting or removing wires. Avoid excess cranking when you are starting a flooded engine. Repair the cause of flooding first, and dry the engine by removing the spark plugs if necessary. If the engine diesels (runs after it is switched off), readjust the idling speed. Excess dieseling can damage the converter.

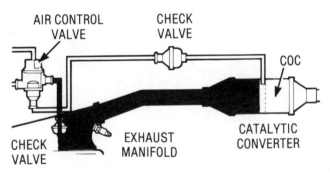

Figure 13-53. Air is injected into the exhaust manifold during engine warm-up. (Courtesy of Ford Motor Company, Dearborn)

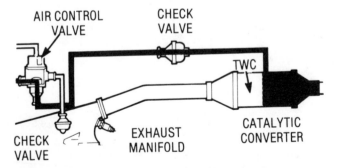

Figure 13-54. Air is injected into the "mid-bed" of the catalytic converter during normal hot engine operation. (Courtesy of Ford Motor Company, Dearborn)

FACTS TO REMEMBER

Automobile exhaust gases contain harmful hydrocarbon and carbon monoxide pollutants. Several methods are employed to reduce these emissions. Exhaust gas recycling systems route exhaust gases into the cylinders to cool combustion temperatures during normal driving and reduce nitrogen oxides. Air injection systems inject fresh air into the exhaust system to mix with the hot exhaust gases and aid in changing them into water vapor and harmless carbon dioxide. Catalytic converters use a metal catalyst in the presence of heat to convert hydrocarbons and carbon monoxide. Catalytic converters can only be used with unleaded fuel and must be protected from overheating.

☐ ASSIGNMENT 13-I ☐

1. Explain the function performed by a regular catalytic converter and a three-way catalytic converter.

2. Why can you use only unleaded fuel in catalytic-converter-equipped vehicles?

3. List four precautions you must observe on catalytic-converter-equipped vehicles to protect the catalytic converter from overheating.

□ SELF-TEST □

Complete the following sentences by filling in the missing words.

1. Smog is made worse by air inversions, because when there is an air inversion _____ cannot move _____ to spread out the pollutants.

2. Smog results from a photochemical reaction in the atmosphere. This reaction takes place between _____ and _____ _____ when they are exposed to sunlight.

3. On vehicles produced before emission controls, hydrocarbon emissions came from the _____ systems (60% of the total), the engine _____ (20%), and evaporation through the fuel tank vents and carburetor _____ (20%).

4. A hose from a sealed oil _____ cap, or from the rocker _____ , into the air cleaner was used to make the closed PCV system.

5. The flow rate of the gases through a PCV system must be _____ for correct _____ operation. This is the job of the _____ valve.

6. If the PCV system fails to draw away crankcase blow-by gases, excess _____ could build up in the _____ . This pressure would cause oil leaks at the crankshaft _____ or engine _____ and contamination of the crankcase oil.

7. Extremely high or low air-fuel ratios cause _____ pollution.

8. Preheated air coming into the carburetor causes better fuel _____ and _____ . This results in _____ fuel requirements.

9. The idle enrichment diaphragm increases the _____ of the idle circuit to reduce _____ engine stalling.

10. Engineers have designed the power system to provide as _____ an air-fuel mixture as possible for moderately heavy loads, but to ensure enough _____ at heavier loads or very fast speeds.

11. Many carburetors have metering _____ and _____ systems to help provide lean air-fuel mixtures.

12. The combustion flame is _____ in starting with a retarded spark, but it lasts further into the _____ stroke.

13. An engine that idles for some time in warm weather with a retarded spark tends to _____ .

14. During periods of moderate acceleration with _____ distributor spark advance, the temperature of combustion _____ and causes excess nitrogen oxides.

15. Any gasoline released from the fuel tank or carburetor in a liquid or _____ form enters the atmosphere as 100% _____ _____ .

16. The evaporation control system prevents the emission of gasoline vapors from the _____ _____ and _____ .

17. When the engine is turned off, the vapors that form in the fuel tank force their way along the _____ line and into the _____ _____ along with vapors formed in the carburetor fuel bowl.

18. A modern fuel tank is sealed with a specially engineered pressure-vacuum relief _____ _____ .

19. Nitrogen oxides are produced by high _____ temperatures. Most emission controls, however, _____ combustion temperature. Exhaust Gas Recirculating (EGR) systems are used to _____ nitrogen oxides.

20. Air injection systems are designed to introduce fresh _____ into the _____ as the exhaust gas is leaving the exhaust ports.

21. The catalyst in the converter must be protected from overheating during periods of cold running with a _____ mixture, periods of high engine heat caused by long _____ intervals on a hot day, or during deceleration.

22. Only _____ gasoline can be used in catalytic-converter-equipped vehicles. Leaded gasoline causes the catalyst to become coated with _____ , destroying its effectiveness.

14

EMISSION CONTROL SYSTEMS: DIAGNOSIS AND SERVICE

□   LEARNING OBJECTIVES   □

After studying this chapter, you will be able to:

1. Explain the purpose of an infrared exhaust analyzer.

2. Explain and demonstrate the use of the infrared exhaust analyzer to adjust the carburetor idle mixture.

3. Explain why you would use a propane-assisted idle adjusting procedure.

4. Explain and demonstrate propane-assisted idle mixture and idle speed adjustment.

5. Describe and demonstrate the diagnostic and service procedures for the following emission control systems:
   PCV system
   thermostatic air cleaner
   electrically heated chokes
   distributor advance controls
   evaporative emission control system
   exhaust gas recirculation system
   air injection system
   catalytic converters

6. Define and/or discuss the following terms:
   infrared analyzer
   propane enrichment

INTRODUCTION

This chapter covers the service procedures for the emission control systems described in Chapter 13. Before you can check emission controls, you have to be certain that the ignition system is in good working order and that the carburetor is operating correctly. Emission control system service may require that you do some testing and make some ignition system adjustments. Always check the operation of the advance mechanisms and the ignition timing. These procedures were covered in Chapter 11.

Carburetor checks and proper adjustment can be done with an infrared exhaust analyzer or with a propane-assisted idle adjustment procedure. Which of these you use will depend on the manufacturer's recommendation. We will discuss these adjustment methods before covering the service procedures for emission controls.

INFRARED EXHAUST EMISSIONS ANALYZER

The **infrared exhaust emissions analyzer** takes a sample of a vehicle's exhaust gases and determines the hydrocarbon level and the amount of carbon monoxide in the sample. With the readings you get from an infrared analyzer, you can determine if the engine is performing efficiently and meeting emission control standards.

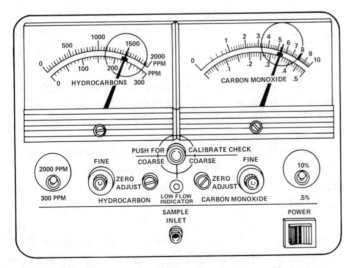

Figure 14-1. *Warm up and calibrate the infrared analyzer before you begin a test. (Courtesy of Chrysler Corporation)*

Hydrocarbon content is measured in **parts per million** (ppm), by volume. A hydrocarbon reading of 100 ppm means that for any million parts of the sample, 100 parts are hydrocarbons. Carbon monoxide is measured as a percentage of the volume of the sample. A reading of 1% carbon monoxide means that 1% of the test sample is carbon monoxide.

Proper engine maintenance is vital. A poorly tuned engine raises hydrocarbon and carbon monoxide emission levels and gives high analyzer readings. Emission control devices that are not operating properly can also cause high readings. With proper training and practice, and by following the manufacturer's shop manuals, you can use the infrared exhaust analyzer as a valuable diagnostic tool.

Infrared Analyzer Operation

Be sure the analyzer is properly warmed up and calibrated before you begin the test. Figure 14-1 shows the controls and meters on a typical infrared analyzer. Calibrate this type of analyzer by pressing the "calibrate" button. Calibration should be done with the hydrocarbon meter selected on the 2000 ppm scale and the carbon monoxide meter on the 10% scale. Turn the "zero adjust" knobs to reach a zero adjustment on the meter scales.

Some infrared exhaust analyzers are adjusted differently and have a "span" as well as a "zero" adjustment. You should become familiar with the proper method of adjusting your analyzer. Always allow any infrared analyzer to warm up for five to ten minutes before calibrating it or using it for testing.

Idle Mixture Adjustments

The carburetor idle mixture is frequently checked and adjusted with an infrared analyzer. Before you do this test on a vehicle, you must determine which lines or devices to disconnect and whether the transmission should be in neutral or drive during the test. This information is usually recorded on an emission decal under the hood or in the manufacturer's specifications. Make sure the engine is fully warmed up before you begin any of these tests.

1. Engage the parking brake and turn off the engine. Place the transmission in neutral or in drive as recommended by the manufacturer. Turn off the air conditioning compressor and headlights. On Chrysler vehicles with Electronic Spark Control or Electronic

Lean Burn systems, use a jumper wire to ground the carburetor switch. Figure 14-5 shows how to ground the carburetor switch.

2. Place the infrared exhaust analyzer probe into the tail pipe, as shown in Figure 14-2, or if specified by the manufacturer, connect the probe into the tap provided at the front of the catalytic converter, as shown in Figure 14-3.

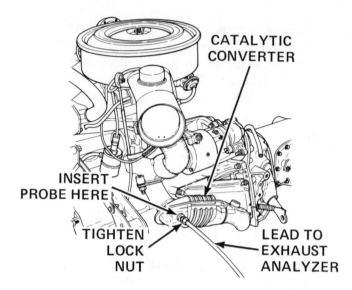

Figure 14-3. *The probe of the infrared analyzer can be connected into a tap provided at the front of the catalytic converter. (Courtesy of Chrysler Corporation)*

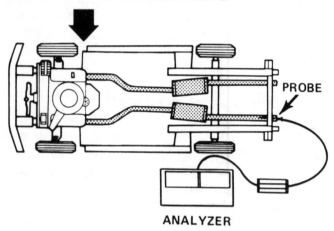

Figure 14-2. *Place the infrared analyzer probe at least six inches into the tail pipe. On dual-exhaust-equipped vehicles, insert the probe into the side without the manifold heat control valve. (Courtesy of Chrysler Corporation)*

3. Connect a tachometer to the engine.

4. Disconnect the air pump diverter valve (bypass valve) outlet hose and plug it if the vehicle is so equipped. See "Air Injection System Service" in this chapter for the location of the valve.

5. Start the engine and allow it to run for a few minutes. With the engine idling at the correct speed, compare the hydrocarbon and carbon monoxide reading from the analyzer to the recommended readings.

6. If you need to adjust the idle mixture, follow the manufacturer's recommended procedure. The hydrocarbon and carbon monoxide reading will become higher if the mixture screw is turned out (counterclockwise) and lower if it is turned in (clockwise). You may have to remove the idle adjustment limiter caps to make this adjustment. It is important to note that a mixture screw that is turned in too far will create a mixture that is too lean. This mixture will

cause high infrared analyzer readings because of **lean misfire**. Lean misfire occurs when the mixture becomes too lean, and the cylinders misfire.

Adjust the two mixture screws on a dual- or four-barrel carburetor only about 1/16 of a turn at a time. This will help you keep them in balance. The final mixture adjustment must achieve the lowest possible hydrocarbon and carbon monoxide readings with the best engine idle.

7. **Blow out procedure**: Excess idle time during adjustment can affect analyzer readings. To prevent this, you should accelerate the engine to about 2500 rpm for 10 seconds between measurements. Allow 30 to 60 seconds for the readings to stabilize after the engine returns to idle.

8. When you have adjusted the carburetor for the proper idle readings, increase the engine speed to approximately 2500 rpm. The hydrocarbon and carbon monoxide readings should both be lower at this engine speed than they are when the engine is idling. If they are higher, suspect a problem with the engine, carburetor, or emission controls. Further diagnosis and testing is required to determine the problem.

9. When the testing is completed, switch off the engine and remove the exhaust analyzer and tachometer. Reinstall the diverter (bypass) valve hose if the vehicle is so equipped. Remove the jumper wire, where used on Chrysler Electronic Lean Burn and

Electronic Spark Control systems. Install new idle adjustment limiter caps if they had to be removed for the idle adjustment.

□   **ASSIGNMENT 14–A**   □

1. Explain the purpose of the infrared exhaust analyzer.
2. Describe the effect that turning an idle mixture adjusting screw in and out has on the infrared readings.

PROPANE-ASSISTED IDLE ADJUSTMENT

The majority of manufacturers now recommend that you use **propane enrichment** when you are setting the idle mixture adjustment and the curb idle speed on their vehicles. All mechanics are required by law to adjust engines to manufacturers' specifications by using the methods outlined on the **emission control label** (or decal) that is mounted in the engine compartment.

Emission standards have resulted in carburetor idle mixtures that are so lean that it is difficult to detect the "lean-drop" position when you make the idle mixture adjustment. The lean-drop position was discussed in Chapter 4 of this text.

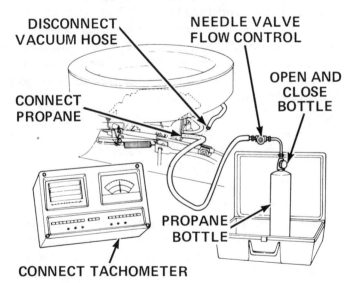

Figure 14-4. *The equipment needed to perform propane-assisted idle mixture adjustment. (Courtesy of Chrysler Corporation)*

Further, as an aid to producing low exhaust emissions, catalytic converters are being installed on many vehicles. Such low hydrocarbon and carbon monoxide readings result with catalytic converters that it is difficult to detect poor carburetor adjustment with an infrared exhaust analyzer.

A rich carburetor mixture will sometimes produce a rotten-egg smell at the exhaust. This smell can be reduced by propane-assisted idle adjustment. A carburetor that is properly adjusted with the manufacturer's recommended propane adjustment procedure should idle better and provide fewer drivability problems. If the carburetor has fixed limiter caps, you can use propane-assisted adjustment to determine if the mixture is correctly set without removing the limiter caps. It is only necessary to remove the caps if adjustment is necessary. Remember to remove the limiter caps with the correct tool and to replace the caps with new ones after you make the adjustment.

Equipment Needed

1. A bottle of propane gas from a small cylinder torch kit can be used for propane enrichment. Dealers and suppliers can furnish you with a metering valve kit to fit the propane bottle. If you cannot find a metering valve, you can make one of your own by fitting a needle-type flow control valve to the torch nozzle tube from a torch kit. See Figure 14-4.
2. A length of hose and suitable adapters are needed to attach the propane source to the carburetor or air cleaner.
3. A tachometer should be available for accurate engine speed readings.
4. You should also have a set of carburetor adjustment tools.

Procedures

A large number of companies require that the carburetors on their vehicles be adjusted with propane-assisted idle adjustment. Each company has slight differences in its recommended procedures. One method will be described here to familiarize you with the procedures. The Chrysler recommended procedure is described below. Make all adjustments with the engine fully warmed up.

1. Stop the engine. Put the parking brake on and place the transmission in neutral. Turn off the air conditioning compressor and headlights. On vehicles with Electronic Lean Burn (ELB) and Electronic Spark Control (ESC), use a jumper wire to ground the carburetor switch, as shown in Figure 14-5.

2. Connect a tachometer.

3. The PCV valve should be removed from the rocker cover before tests are made.

4. Disconnect the air cleaner heated door hose at the carburetor base. Connect the propane supply hose to the exposed fitting. Use a propane bottle equipped with a Chrysler metering device or a metering device of your own fabrication. See Figure 14-4.

5. Stand the propane bottle upright to maintain a constant flow. Start the engine, and adjust the flow rate to achieve the highest engine speed. Too much propane will reduce engine speed.

6. With the propane flowing, adjust the idle speed screw to the enriched idle rpm, as shown on the emission label.

7. Readjust the propane flow to obtain the highest idle speed, and then readjust the idle speed screw(s) to the enriched rpm.

8. Turn off the propane flow. Adjust the idle mixture screw(s) to achieve the smoothest idle at the curb rpm, as shown on the emission label. Do not turn the idle speed screw at this time. The mixture

screw limiter caps may have to be removed for this setting. If the limiter caps are removed, install proper replacement caps.

9. Turn on the propane, and check the enriched rpm. If the enriched idle speed is more than 15 rpm from the recommended enriched rpm, repeat steps 5, 6, and 7.

10. Turn off the engine and remove the tachometer and propane equipment.

11. Reinstall the air cleaner vacuum hose on the carburetor. Remove the jumper wire from the carburetor switch if one was installed.

□   ASSIGNMENT 14-B   □

1. Explain the reason for using propane-assisted idle adjustment.

2. Describe how a propane-assisted idle adjustment is done.

FACTS TO REMEMBER

Before you attempt to service emission controls, the engine must be in good working order and properly tuned-up and the carburetor must be working properly. The infrared emissions analyzer is a valuable tool for checking carburetor adjustment and emission pollutant levels. The infrared analyzer samples exhaust emissions and "reads" their hydrocarbon and carbon monoxide levels. Propane-assisted idle enrichment is used to help adjust a lean-calibrated carburetor to the proper idle speed. Propane enrichment and the infrared analyzer provide a convenient method for adjusting carburetor idle and checking the adjustment.

EMISSION CONTROL SERVICE

The infrared analyzer and propane enrichment procedures will help you determine if the emission control systems on the vehicle are operating properly. If the emission standards cannot be met by proper carburetor adjustment, the emission control systems must be checked to find and correct the problem. The rest of this chapter will cover the testing and service procedures for the emission control systems that were described in Chapter 13.

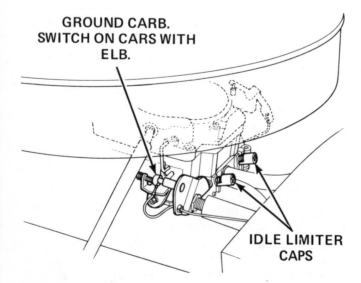

GROUND CARB. SWITCH ON CARS WITH ELB.

IDLE LIMITER CAPS

Figure 14-5.   Ground the carburetor switch on a Chrysler ELB- or ESC-equipped vehicle. The idle limiter caps are factory installed. (Courtesy of Chrysler Corporation)

PCV SYSTEM SERVICE

PCV system problems can cause drivability complaints, oil contamination, sludging of engine internal parts, or oil in the air cleaner. **Sludge** is a thick black jelly-like substance formed when water and dirt in the oil mix together over time. A well-ventilated crankcase evaporates the water before sludge can settle on the engine parts. PCV problems can also cause excess oil consumption and oil leakage from engine seals and gaskets due to excess crankcase pressures.

There are a number of testers on the market for testing PCV systems. Figure 14-6 illustrates the use of a Ford (Autolite) tester. When the tester is placed over the opening for the oil filler cap, it will respond to the vacuum that is supplied through the PCV valve at idle speed. If the ball in the tester settles in the pink area, the system needs service. If the ball settles in the green area, the system is working properly.

The PCV system can be checked without a tester by following the numbered steps outlined in Figures 14-7 and 14-8.

Figure 14-6. *Testing the PCV system with a Ford tester. (Courtesy of Ford Motor Company, Dearborn)*

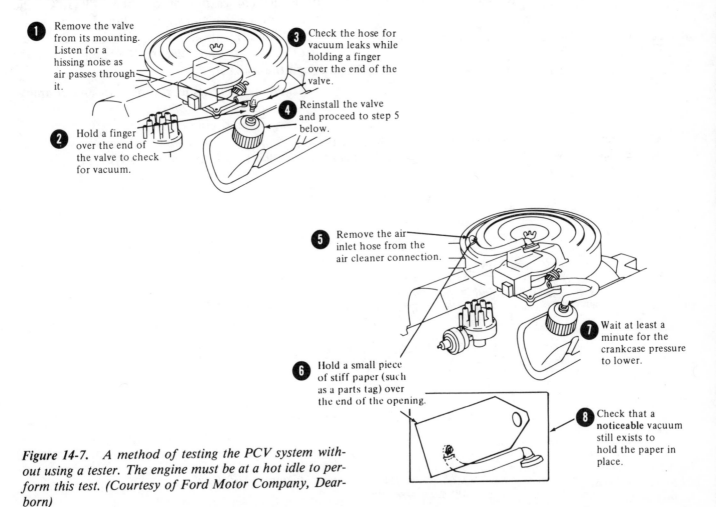

Figure 14-7. *A method of testing the PCV system without using a tester. The engine must be at a hot idle to perform this test. (Courtesy of Ford Motor Company, Dearborn)*

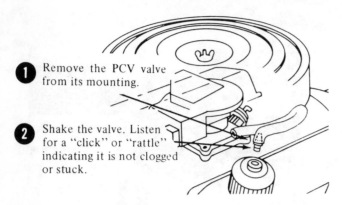

① Remove the PCV valve from its mounting.

② Shake the valve. Listen for a "click" or "rattle" indicating it is not clogged or stuck.

Figure 14-8.   A method of testing the PCV valve with the engine stopped. (Courtesy of Ford Motor Company, Dearborn)

If your tests show that the system requires service, and for scheduled maintenance as recommended by the manufacturer, follow the steps outlined in Figure 14-9.

□   **ASSIGNMENT 14–C**   □

1. Describe the problems that can be caused by a defective PCV system.
2. Explain how to test the PCV system.

THERMOSTATIC AIR CLEANER SERVICE

If the heated inlet air system fails to warm the air entering the engine, the vehicle will have drivability problems, such as hesitation, stalling, or carburetor icing during the warm-up period. The heated inlet air system must be kept clean and in good operating order.

Procedures

Chrysler Corporation uses the following procedure to determine if the thermostatic air cleaner system is functioning properly.

1. Make sure all the vacuum hoses and the flexible connector between the heat stove and the air cleaner are properly attached and are in good condition.

2. When a cold engine is running in an ambient (outside air) temperature of less than 50°F (10°C), the heat-control door in the snorkel should be in the up or "heat on" position. The position of the heat-control door can be checked by shining a light through the snorkel.

3. With the engine warmed up and running,

- Inspect hoses, tubes and connectors at 12 months or 12,000 miles.
- Replace PCV valve at 24,000 miles or whenever system fails functional test. Also, clean the system (hoses, connectors, etc.).

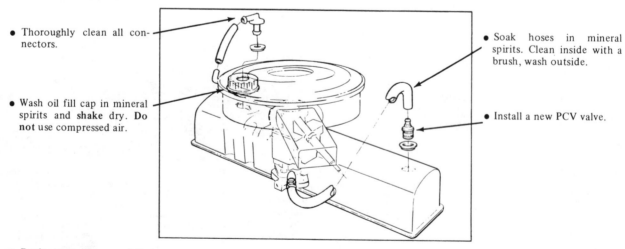

- Thoroughly clean all connectors.

- Wash oil fill cap in mineral spirits and **shake** dry. **Do not** use compressed air.

- Soak hoses in mineral spirits. Clean inside with a brush, wash outside.

- Install a new PCV valve.

- Replace any component that
  – shows signs of damage, wear or deterioration.
  – cannot be cleaned to allow free passage of air.

Figure 14-9.   PCV system service. (Courtesy of Ford Motor Company, Dearborn)

check the air temperature entering the snorkel or at the sensor inside the air cleaner. When the air temperature is 100°F (38°C) or higher, the heat-control door should be in the down or "heat off" position.

4. Remove the air cleaner from the engine and allow it to cool down. Blow compressed air on the sensor to speed up the cooling.

5. With 20 inches (67.5 kPa) of vacuum applied to the sensor, the door should be in the up or "heat on" position. If the door does not rise to the "heat on" position, test the vacuum diaphragm.

To test the diaphragm, apply 20 inches (67.5 kPa) of vacuum directly to the diaphragm, using a vacuum pump as shown in Figure 14-10. The diaphragm should not bleed down more than 10 inches (33.75 kPa) of vacuum in five minutes. The heat control door should not start to lift off the bottom of the snorkel at less than 5.5 inches (18.6 kPa) of vacuum, and it should be in the "full up" position with no more than 8.5 inches (28.7 kPa) of vacuum.

6. If the vacuum diaphragm does not perform correctly, replace it as described below, and repeat the checks in steps 2 and 3.

7. If the vacuum diaphragm performs correctly but proper intake air temperature is not maintained, or vacuum does not pass through the cold sensor, replace the sensor and repeat the temperature checks in steps 2 and 3. Sensor and vacuum diaphragm removal and replacement are covered below.

Vacuum Diaphragm and Sensor Replacement

Diaphragm Removal

1. Remove the air cleaner housing from the vehicle. Disconnect the vacuum hose from the diaphragm. Drill through the welded tab on the vacuum diaphragm, as shown in Figure 14-11. Then tip the diaphragm slightly forward to disengage the lock tabs, and rotate the diaphragm counterclockwise. When the diaphragm is free from the snorkel, slide the complete assembly to one side to disengage the operating rod from the heat control door, as shown in Figure 14-11.

2. When the vacuum diaphragm is removed, check the door for free travel. The door should fall freely when it is released from the up position. If it does not, check to make sure there is no dirt on the door, snorkel walls, or the hinge pin.

Diaphragm Installation

1. Insert the operating rod into the heat-control door. Position the diaphragm tabs into the openings in the snorkel, and turn the vacuum diaphragm clockwise until the lock is engaged. Pop rivet the tabs in place.

2. Apply 9 inches (30 kPa) of vacuum to the diaphragm hose fitting. The heat control door should operate freely. Do not attempt to operate the heat

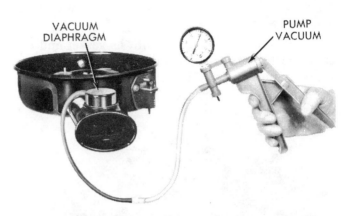

Figure 14-10. Testing the vacuum diaphragm. (Courtesy of Chrysler Corporation)

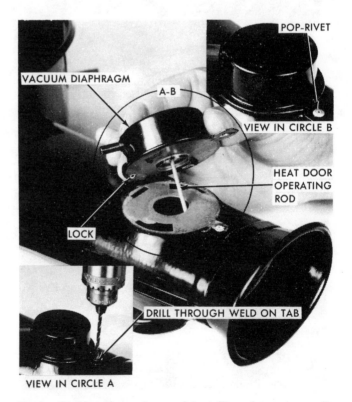

Figure 14-11. Removing and installing the vacuum diaphragm. (Courtesy of Chrysler Corporation)

control door manually. You could bend the operating rod or diaphragm by manually operating the door. This would cause the system to operate incorrectly.

3. Reassemble the air cleaner, install it on the vehicle, and repeat the tests for proper operation.

Sensor Removal

1. With the air cleaner housing removed from the vehicle, disconnect the vacuum hoses from the sensor and remove the retainer clips, as shown in Figure 14-12. Discard the retainer clips. New clips are supplied with a new sensor.

2. Remove the sensor with its gasket and discard the sensor. Do not attempt to adjust an improperly functioning sensor.

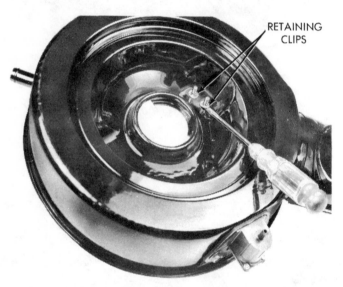

Figure 14-12. Removing the sensor retaining clips. (Courtesy of Chrysler Corporation)

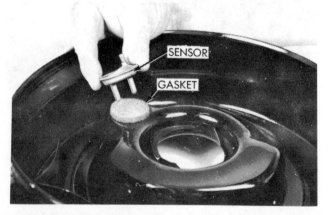

Figure 14-13. Installing the gasket and sensor. (Courtesy of Chrysler Corporation)

Sensor Installation

1. Position the new gasket on the air cleaner housing and install the sensor. See Figure 14-13.

2. Support the sensor on the outer edges, and install new retainer clips. Make sure that the gasket is compressed to form an airtight seal.

ELECTRICALLY HEATED CHOKE SERVICE

Heating Element Checks

An electrically assisted choke spring has a heat pipe between the choke housing and the manifold. An electrically heated choke has no heat pipe. The choke spring on a carburetor-mounted, electrically assisted choke must be heated to between 60°–80°F (16°–27°C), depending on the vehicle make, before the internal thermostatic switch turns on the heating element. If the choke is not already hot, heat it up with a heat gun or hair dryer. Never use an open flame to heat the choke, because the flame will burn and scar the choke and present a fire hazard around gasoline. All other electrically heated or assisted chokes, whether carburetor or engine mounted, can be tested while they are hot or cold.

1. Remove the wire connector from the choke and test from the choke terminal to ground with an ohmmeter. Readings of 4 to 12 ohms are acceptable. If the meter readings indicate open or short circuits, you will have to replace the heater assembly.

2. Connect a voltmeter (or test light) to the choke electrical supply feed wire and ground. Start the engine. The voltmeter reading should be full-system voltage. If you use a test light, the light should glow brightly. In some cases, you will have to heat the engine-mounted heat sensing switch to turn on the voltage to the choke. When you are in doubt, look up the details for testing the system in the manufacturer's shop manual.

If no voltage reading appears on the voltmeter, you will have to find out where the voltage is being lost. Voltage loss could be caused by a faulty temperature sensor. If the temperature sensor is open, no voltage will reach the heater. Another cause could be a faulty oil pressure switch. This switch is supposed to turn on the system only when there is oil pressure. Some electrical chokes are supplied by an internal alternator connection that is alive only when the alternator is turning. On these chokes, a defective alternator may also result in voltage loss. Faulty wiring connections are also a frequent cause of voltage loss.

□ **ASSIGNMENT 14-D** □

1. Describe how to bench test the sensor and vacuum diaphragm on a thermostatic air cleaner.
2. Describe how to test the choke heating element with a voltmeter.

DISTRIBUTOR CONTROLS SERVICE

Malfunctioning emission controls that affect the distributor advance can cause poor gas mileage and drivability problems. A vehicle that has any problems in the distributor advance emission controls will probably fail to meet emission standards. Dual-diaphragm or single-diaphragm vacuum advance distributors are easily checked with a timing light.

Connect the timing light and a tachometer to the vehicle. Go over the timing marks with white chalk and remove and plug one or both distributor vacuum hoses, depending on whether the vacuum advance is a dual or a single unit. Run the engine at the recommended timing speed and observe the initial timing, as shown in Figure 14-14. Adjust the dwell if necessary, and then adjust the timing to the manufacturer's specifications.

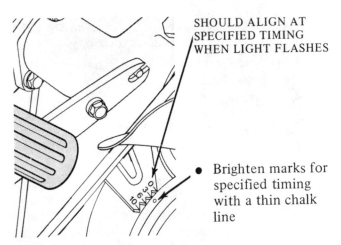

SHOULD ALIGN AT SPECIFIED TIMING WHEN LIGHT FLASHES

● Brighten marks for specified timing with a thin chalk line

Figure 14-14. Checking the initial advance on a dual-diaphragm distributor. (Courtesy of Ford Motor Company, Dearborn)

To check the centrifugal advance, increase the engine speed to 2000 rpm. The timing should advance smoothly, as shown in Figure 14-15. Make note of the amount of advance. To check the advance side of the vacuum unit, follow the text in Figure 14-16. A single-diaphragm vacuum advance has only one vacuum fitting. The retard side of the vacuum unit (on vehicles so equipped) can be checked by following the text in Figure 14-17.

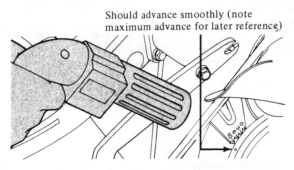

Should advance smoothly (note maximum advance for later reference)

Figure 14-15. Checking the centrifugal advance on a dual-diaphragm advance. (Courtesy of Ford Motor Company, Dearborn)

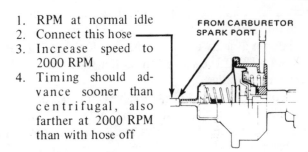

1. RPM at normal idle
2. Connect this hose
3. Increase speed to 2000 RPM
4. Timing should advance sooner than centrifugal, also farther at 2000 RPM than with hose off

FROM CARBURETOR SPARK PORT

Figure 14-16. A quick check for vacuum advance on a dual-diaphragm distributor. (Courtesy of Ford Motor Company, Dearborn)

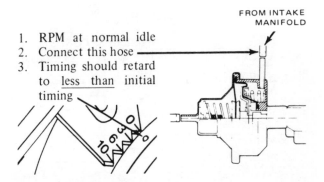

1. RPM at normal idle
2. Connect this hose
3. Timing should retard to less than initial timing

FROM INTAKE MANIFOLD

Figure 14-17. A quick check for vacuum retard on a dual-diaphragm distributor. (Courtesy of Ford Motor Company, Dearborn)

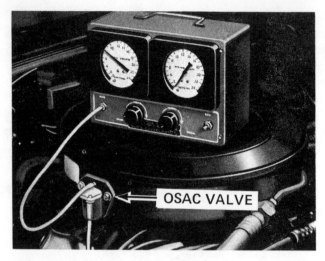

Figure 14-18.   Checking the Chrysler OSAC valve with a vacuum gauge while running the engine. (Courtesy of Chrysler Corporation)

A Spark Delay Valve (SDV-Ford) and an OSAC valve (Chrysler) are tested in a similar manner. Warm up the engine before you perform these tests. Connect a vacuum gauge on the valve fitting leading to the vacuum advance. Run the engine at 2000 rpm and observe the amount of time required for the vacuum to show a full reading on the vacuum gauge as indicated by manufacturer's specifications. The vacuum must drop down quickly as the throttle is closed to idle. See Figure 14-18. If the valve fails either test, a new valve should be installed.

Spark Delay and OSAC valves can also be tested by connecting a distributor tester vacuum pump to the manifold side of the valve and a vacuum gauge to the distributor side. Pump up the vacuum and observe the time required for the valve to pass the vacuum to the vacuum gauge. OSAC valves come in ranges of 10, 17, and 27 seconds. The time delays for

| | TIME IN SECONDS | |
TYPE VALVE	MINIMUM	MAXIMUM
Black & Gray	1	4
Black & Brown	2	5
Black & White	4	12
Black & Yellow	5,8	14
Black & Blue	7	16
Black & Green	9	20
Black & Orange	13	24
Black & Red	15	28

Figure 14-19.   A chart showing the time delays for different colored Ford Spark Delay Valves. (Courtesy of Ford Motor Company, Dearborn)

Ford Spark Delay Valves are listed in the chart in Figure 14-19.

EVAPORATIVE EMISSION CONTROLS SERVICE

When the evaporative emission system is not functioning properly, there usually is a strong odor of gasoline around the vehicle, and fuel may be dripping from the charcoal canister. Excess fuel or vapor losses from this system cause increased hydrocarbon emissions. The following tests and service procedures can be performed on the evaporative emission system.

1.   Inspect the hoses for cracks, bloating, stiffness from excess heat, or other forms of deterioration. Check them for proper routing and make sure that there are no hoses missing.

2.   Inspect the pressure vacuum fuel filler cap. Try to open and close the valve in the cap. It should blow open one way and be drawn open the other way with very little vacuum. Always replace the cap with the proper one for the vehicle.

3.   Inspect the charcoal canister for cracks and other damage. Replace the filter element in the bottom of the charcoal canister at the manufacturer's recommended change interval or sooner if it is dirty. See Figure 14-20. The change interval is usually 24

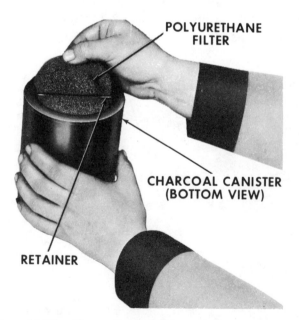

Figure 14-20.   Removing a canister filter. (Courtesy of General Motors of Canada Limited)

months or 30,000 miles (50,000 km). Some canisters have no filter, and the whole canister should be replaced at a specific mileage interval.

When the charcoal canister has a strong gasoline odor or has gasoline dripping from it, suspect trouble in the purging system. With the engine running, check for vacuum to the purge ports on the canister. Some purge lines have a **ported vacuum pickup**. The vacuum port is located above the throttle plate at idle and no vacuum will get through at idle. The engine has to be operated at 2000 rpm to check these systems. If the unit has a **purge valve** on it, you should also test the valve with a hand vacuum pump to see if the valve diaphragm retains vacuum. Since the purge valve is integral with the canister, you must replace the whole canister if the valve is defective.

A defective liquid vapor separator or liquid vapor check valve can also cause canister saturation. Replace the liquid vapor separator if it is damaged.

Overfilling the fuel tank can also cause canister saturation. When the fuel expands with heat, it has no expansion space in an overfull tank, and if there is no liquid check valve in the system, liquid fuel forces its way through the vapor vent line to the canister.

The tail-pipe probe of an infrared exhaust analyzer can be used as a "sniffer" to help you detect fuel odors and leaks. Pass the probe along the vent lines and fuel lines. Use it to sniff around the carbon canister, hoses, fuel tank, filler tube, and filler cap. At a point where fuel or vapor is leaking, the hydrocarbon gauge on the infrared analyzer will show a large response. Small responses here and there in the system (particularly around the carbon canister) are acceptable.

☐ ASSIGNMENT 14-E ☐

1. Explain how to test distributor advances with a timing light.
2. Explain one method of testing a SDV or OSAC valve.
3. List the usual tests performed on an evaporative emission system.

EGR SYSTEM SERVICE

A leaking Exhaust Gas Recirculation (EGR) valve will pass exhaust gases to the intake manifold while the engine is idling. This will cause a rough idle or stalling. A valve that does not operate may give no symptoms, or it may cause excess engine pinging because the combustion temperature is too hot. Improper operation of the EGR system causes increased nitrogen oxide emissions.

The EGR valve can be tested by connecting a vacuum gauge into the line to the valve, as shown in Figure 14-21. Run the engine at normal idle, and then check for vacuum increase as you open the throttle for a moment. At about 3/4 of an inch (2.5 kPa) of vacuum, the valve stem should begin to move inward toward the diaphragm to open the valve, and by 8 inches (27 kPa) of vacuum, the stem should be fully in and the valve should be fully open. If vacuum is present but the stem does not move, replace the EGR valve.

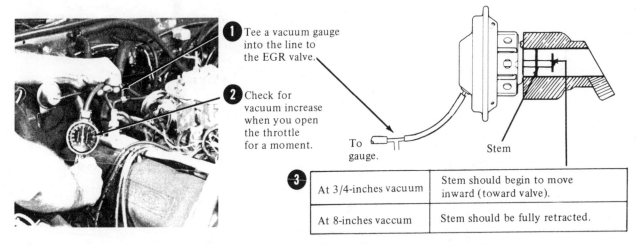

① Tee a vacuum gauge into the line to the EGR valve.

② Check for vacuum increase when you open the throttle for a moment.

To gauge.

Stem

③

At 3/4-inches vacuum	Stem should begin to move inward (toward valve).
At 8-inches vaccum	Stem should be fully retracted.

Figure 14-21. Testing the EGR system. (Courtesy of Ford Motor Company, Dearborn)

If no response in vacuum is noted, attach the vacuum gauge directly to the EGR vacuum port on the carburetor and check for vacuum. With the engine running, the vacuum should rise and fall as you move the throttle to halfway open and back to idle. Clear the vacuum port if no response is indicated.

Always perform an **unrestricted flow test** on EGR valves, as outlined in Figure 14-22. If the valve or passages are blocked, there will be no change in idle performance when the vacuum is applied. The system will need to be cleaned out to correct this problem.

Test the **Ported Vacuum Switch** (PVS), as outlined in Figure 14-23. Since all thermostatic vacuum switches are not the same, refer to the manufacturer's shop manual for details on the tests for each type.

These tests will determine if the EGR system is choked with carbon and requires cleaning out. The methods of cleaning Ford EGR valves and exhaust passages are shown in Figure 14-24.

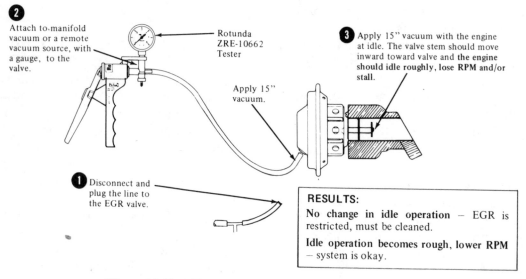

Figure 14-22. *Testing for unrestricted flow in the EGR system. (Courtesy of Ford Motor Company, Dearborn)*

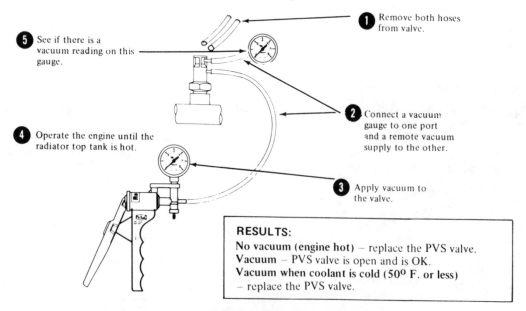

Figure 14-23. *Testing the PVS valve (two-port type). (Courtesy of Ford Motor Company, Dearborn)*

CLEANING VALVE ORIFICE

Important: Cover the manifold riser bores to keep dirt out.

Replace the valve if the orifice won't clean up.

CLEANING PASSAGES IN MANIFOLD

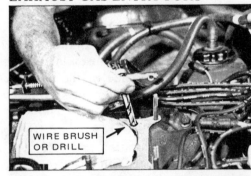

CLEANING SPACER PASSAGES

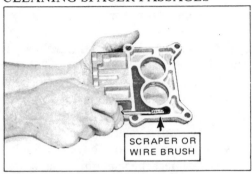

Drill Size
- 460, 429 — 1/2 inch
- Others — 7/16 inch
Use hand pressure only.

EXHAUST GAS ENTRY PORT

CLEANING MACHINED HOLES

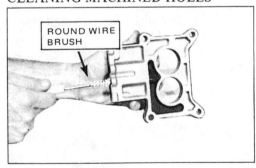

Clean 6-cylinder EGR tube with brush and compressed air.

REMOVE EGR TUBE FOR CLEANING

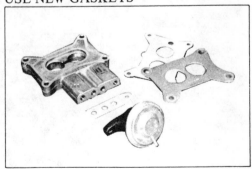

4-V CARBURETORS

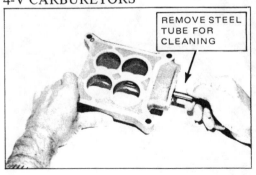

USE NEW GASKETS

Figure 14-24. Cleaning the EGR system. (Courtesy of Ford Motor Company, Dearborn)

□ ASSIGNMENT 14-F □

1. List the symptoms caused by an EGR valve that is stuck open.
2. Describe the tests used to determine if the EGR system is working properly.

AIR INJECTION SYSTEM SERVICE

Some typical problems related to the air injection system are: noisy air pump, seized air pump, squealing drive belt, leaking air hoses, and backfiring from the exhaust on deceleration. Improper operation of the air injection system causes increased hydrocarbon and carbon monoxide in the exhaust. Several different parts of the system need to be checked.

Drive Belt: Check the **drive belt** for wear, cracks, or deterioration and replace it if necessary. Check the belt tension using a tension gauge, as shown in Figure 14-25. Adjust the belt to specifications for the vehicle you are working on. A loose belt can be the cause of poor air flow from the pump. Be

careful not to pry on the pump housing and distort the housing while you are adjusting the belt.

Air Pump: Check the **air injection pump** by removing an outlet hose and speeding the engine up to about 1500 rpm. A properly operating pump will increase air flow as the engine speed increases. If flow does not increase or if there is no flow, check for a leaking pressure relief valve. If the pressure relief valve is leaking, you can hear air leaking from the valve. If the pump does not operate properly and the pressure relief valve is good, replace the pump.

If the pump is very noisy, it should be replaced. Do not put oil into the bearing vent hole in order to quiet the pump. This may make the pump quiet temporarily, but it will soon fail again.

Diverter or Bypass Valve: If the vehicle is backfiring from the exhaust, the most probable causes are loss of vacuum signal to the diverter (bypass) valve or a defective diverter valve. To check for loss of vacuum signal, check the condition and routing of the diverter valve vacuum signal hose. It must fit securely on the fittings and have no cracks, crimps, or leaks. Disconnect the vacuum signal line at the diverter valve. With the engine running, test for strong vacuum at the line. Make these tests by covering the end of the hose with your finger or with a vacuum gauge. See Figure 14-26.

To check the operation of the diverter valve, reconnect the vacuum signal line to the diverter valve. With the engine running at idle, no air should be es-

Figure 14-25. Checking the air pump belt tension. (Courtesy of General Motors of Canada, Limited)

Figure 14-26. Checking for vacuum at the diverter valve. (Courtesy of General Motors of Canada Limited)

the engine running at 1500 rpm. This test is shown in Figure 14-29.

Figure 14-27. Air should discharge from the diverter valve air outlet for a few seconds on deceleration. (Courtesy of General Motors of Canada Limited)

caping from the diverter valve air outlet. When you manually open and quickly close the throttle, a momentary (two-second) blast of air should discharge from the diverter valve muffler (or air) outlet, as shown in Figure 14-27.

Diverter valves are not repairable and should be replaced when they are defective. Use the correct valve for the vehicle you are working on.

Air Manifolds and Hoses: Inspect all air hoses for deterioration or holes. Inspect the air manifolds for cracks or rust holes. All connections must be tight and not leak air. Check for leaks on the pressure side of the system by pouring a soapy-water solution on the connections and components. When the pump is operating, bubbles will form in the soap mixture if a leak is present. See Figure 14-28. Be careful not to get water in the air pump inlet. This can cause pump seizure. If it is necessary to replace a hose, use only the proper type of high-temperature hose meant for the purpose.

Check Valves: Check valves should be checked whenever the hoses are removed. If the valves or hoses are sooty and black inside, exhaust gas is leaking back into the valve. You must remove the air supply hose(s) to check the check valve(s).

Visually inspect the check valve to make sure it is seated tightly against its seat. Then insert a probe to depress the valve, and check to see that it returns freely to the seated position. If the valve returns to the seated position, check for exhaust gas leakage with

Figure 14-28. Checking for air leaks with a soapy-water solution. (Courtesy of General Motors of Canada Limited)

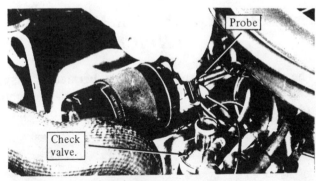

- Engine at normal operating temperature.
- Hoses inspected and leaks corrected.
- Air supply hose(s) to check valve(s) disconnected.

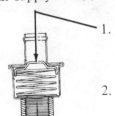

1. Check visually that valve plate is seated lightly against seat.

2. Insert a probe to depress the valve and check for free return to seated position.

3. Look for exhaust gas leakage to 1500 RPM.

Figure 14-29. Testing the check valve. (Courtesy of Ford Motor Company, Dearborn)

If the check valve fails any of the above tests, it should be replaced. If you have to replace the check valve, use two wrenches to remove it to avoid twisting the manifold tubing. See Figure 14-30.

Centrifugal Filter Fan: If the centrifugal filter fan is cracked, plugged with dirt and oil, or squealing on the housing, it can be replaced. You must remove the air pump from the engine and remove the pump pulley in order to remove the filter fan. Once the pulley is removed, insert needle-nosed pliers between the fan fins and break the fan from the drive hub, as shown in Figure 14-31. It is not possible to remove the fan without destroying it.

Avoid getting pieces of the fan into the air inlet passage in the pump. Install a new fan by pushing it into place. Use the pulley and bolts to press the fan into the recess in the housing, as shown in Figure 14-32. Do not attempt to hammer the fan into place. This will break the fan. The fan may squeal for 20 or 30 miles (32–48 km) after installation, until its outer sealing lip is worn in.

ASPIRATOR AIR VALVE SERVICE

The aspirator air system (or Ford Thermactor II system) has very few parts to check. Inspect the metal tube and rubber hoses and look for signs of exhaust or air leakage. Inspect the muffler or filter if there is one, and replace it if necessary.

Test the aspirator valve by removing the hose that connects it to the air cleaner (or its filter or muffler). When the engine is idling, pulses of air should be felt and heard entering the valve. There

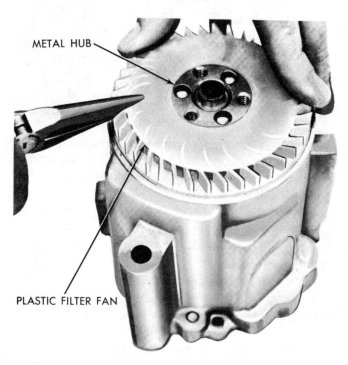

Figure 14-31. *Removing the centrifugal filter fan. (Courtesy of Chrysler Corporation)*

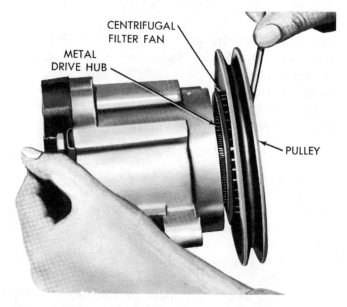

Figure 14-32. *Installing the centrifugal filter fan. (Courtesy of Chrysler Corporation)*

Figure 14-30. *Use two wrenches to remove the check valve. This will ensure that the air manifold tubing does not become twisted. (Courtesy of General Motors of Canada Limited)*

should be a purring sound as the aspirator valve pulsates (moves quickly back and forth) but no exhaust should discharge from it. Speed up the engine and check to be sure that no exhaust escapes from the valve at higher engine speeds. Replace a leaking valve to prevent carbon from getting into the system from the exhaust gases. A leaking valve will give very poor engine performance, particularly at idle and low speeds.

□ ASSIGNMENT 14-G □

1. Explain how to check the operation of a diverter (bypass) valve.
2. Explain how to test the air injection system for air leaks.
3. Explain how to check an aspirator valve.

CATALYTIC CONVERTER SERVICE

When a catalytic converter fails to function, the exhaust gas hydrocarbon and carbon monoxide content rises. Continued use of leaded gasoline can contaminate the catalyst in the catalytic converter with lead and make it inoperable.

One of the main causes of converter failure is excess heat. Continued operation of an engine that has one or more spark plugs misfiring, or any other form of ignition interruption, can cause excess heat in the converter. This heat will destroy the ceramic pellets or inner core. Extreme heat is generated as the converter burns the unburned fuel from the cylinders that were not igniting.

An engine that has a richer than normal air-fuel mixture will also cause extreme heat in the converter. The converter will have to burn the extra unburned fuel resulting from the rich air-fuel mixture. During long periods of engine idling in hot weather, the converter may overheat because there is poor air circulation around the converter when the vehicle is standing still. Physical damage to the outer shell of the converter can break the inner core and ruin the converter. At times a converter may become plugged with carbon. This will cause poor engine performance, because the carbon will block the free flow of exhaust gas.

There is no recommended service interval for catalytic converters. The physical condition of a converter should be checked each time the vehicle is raised on a hoist. In most cases, if the converter is defective, it must be replaced. Catalyst pellets can be removed and replaced on General Motors converters if special equipment is available. General Motors shop manuals should be checked for this procedure. However, if the converter shell is badly damaged (cracked or bent), the converter should be replaced.

Whenever there is a problem with a catalytic converter, the original cause of the trouble must be repaired before you install a new converter. Many different catalytic converter protection devices are employed by different companies. To learn how to test and service them, refer to the manufacturer's shop manual.

□ ASSIGNMENT 14-H □

1. List five causes of catalytic converter failure.
2. Describe three conditions that would cause a catalytic converter to overheat.

□ SELF-TEST □

Complete the following sentences by filling in the missing words.

1. The infrared exhaust emission analyzer takes a sample of a vehicle's _____ gases and determines the _____ level and the percentage of _____ _____ in the sample.

2. A poorly tuned engine raises _____ and _____ _____ emission levels.

3. The hydrocarbon and carbon monoxide reading will become higher if the mixture screw is turned _____ and lower if it is turned _____ .

4. The majority of manufacturers now recommend that you use propane enrichment when you are setting the idle mixture _____ and the curb idle _____ on their vehicles.

5. A _____ carburetor mixture will sometimes produce a rotten-egg _____ at the exhaust.

6. The _____ _____ and _____ _____ procedures will help you determine if the emission control systems on the vehicle are operating properly.

7. PCV system problems can cause numerous _____ complaints, _____ contamination, and _____ of engine internal parts.

8. If the heated inlet air system fails to _____ the air entering the engine, the vehicle will have drivability problems such as _____ , _____ , or carburetor icing during the warm-up period.

9. Never use an open flame to heat the choke, because the flame will burn or scar the _____ and present a _____ hazard around gasoline.

10. Malfunctioning emission controls that affect the distributor advance can cause poor _____ _____ and drivability problems.

11. When the evaporative emission system is not functioning properly, there usually is a strong _____ of gasoline around the vehicle, and fuel may be dripping from the _____ _____ .

12. When the charcoal canister has a strong gasoline odor or has gasoline dripping from it, suspect trouble in the _____ system.

13. A leaking Exhaust Gas Recirculation valve will pass exhaust gases to the intake _____ while the engine is _____ . This will cause a rough idle or stalling.

14. Some typical problems related to the air injection system are: noisy air pump, _____ air pump, squealing drive belt, _____ air hoses, and _____ from the exhaust on deceleration.

15. When a catalytic converter fails to function, the exhaust gas hydrocarbon and carbon monoxide content _____ .

16. Continued operation of an engine that has one or more spark plugs _____ , or any other form of ignition interruption can cause excess _____ in the converter.

SELF-TEST ANSWERS

Chapter 1

1. four, gasoline, spark
2. petroleum, hydrocarbons
3. octane
4. monoxide
5. air, fuel
6. steel, flexible
7. ignition, air-fuel
8. ignition, closed
9. cam, lobes
10. reciprocating, rotary
11. intake, exhaust
12. down, open, exhaust
13. one, revolution
14. crankshaft, two
15. power, stagger
16. twice, timing
17. oil, pressure
18. cleaner, carburetor
19. torque
20. drive shaft

Chapter 2

1. tank, pump, carburetor
2. filter, cleaned
3. separator, tank, return
4. 14.7
5. vented
6. steel, abrasion, breakage
7. one-way, direction
8. eccentric, push rod
9. outlet, float
10. pushed vacuum
11. 3-5, 1, 30

Chapter 3

1. vapor, air, air-fuel
2. fuel, oxygen
3. high-speed, light, medium
4. high-speed, 25
5. bleed, atomization
6. meters, high-speed, idle
7. atmospheric, vacuum
8. constriction, bore, speed up, less
9. primary, main, increases, boost
10. manifold, vacuum, throttle
11. acceleration, time
12. closes, opens
13. offset, thermostatic, increases

Chapter 4

1. vent
2. metal, spontaneous combustion
3. ignition, compression, timing
4. high-speed, shaft
5. rises
6. intake, cracked, blocked
7. idle, blocked
8. lean, diesel, rich, spark plugs.
9. piston, power, power
10. power, cut out
11. hesitation, wastes, lag
12. rich, cold, richness
13. flood, smoke, open

Chapter 5

1. number, make, model, year, size
2. cover, dirt, corrosion
3. impressions
4. scraped
5. bent, ridged
6. goggles, ventilated, solvents
7. gaskets
8. cover, staggered
9. plunger, fuel, throttle
10. chock
11. thermostatic spring
12. carburetor, cross-threading, binding

Chapter 6

1. air-fuel, cylinder
2. spray, manifold, intake, cylinder
3. manifold pressure, air flow
4. port injection
5. starting motors, thermoswitch
6. bypasses, throttle, fast
7. trigger
8. trigger, ignition points
9. throttle, valve
10. port, intake valve
11. pressure, constant
12. fuel, air, sensors, electronic, unit
13. filter, rail
14. vacuum, speed, load, altitude

Chapter 7

1. flow, circuit, negative, positive
2. electrons, move
3. pressure
4. volt, voltmeter
5. electrons, force
6. ampere
7. resists, flow, circuit
8. permanent, electromagnet
9. current, field
10. reverses
11. induction
12. chemical
13. shorted out
14. reactions, current

Chapter 8

1. excess
2. absence
3. path, source, circuit
4. one, device
5. voltage, resistance
6. two, one
7. open, stop
8. two, more, path
9. not, operate
10. break, open, current
11. short, current
12. excess

13. some, flowing, off
14. rest, error, range
15. parallel
16. series
17. separate, series
18. ground, remove

Chapter 9

1. air-fuel, spark
2. two, coil
3. magnetic field
4. secondary winding
5. coil, weak
6. close, open, pulses
7. coil, distributor cap, spark plug
8. secondary, spark plug
9. primary, magnetic field
10. capacity, point, hole
11. stabilizes, flow
12. points, reducing, voltage
13. bypassed, maximum
14. degrees, cam, close
15. closed

Chapter 10

1. spark, open
2. power, down, lost
3. soon
4. top dead center, idling
5. sooner, higher
6. centrifugal, distributor
7. heavy, speeds
8. load, speed
9. part-throttle
10. opening, time, combustion
11. secondary, cap, rotor, towers
12. secondary, suppression
13. spark, secondary, suppressors
14. strong, metal
15. high-tension, secondary, electrodes
16. threads, carbon
17. torque
18. temperature
19. numbers
20. extended
21. negative, negative, positive
22. secondary

Chapter 11

1. cylinders, compression
2. air, cylinder, piston
3. throttle
4. 15, 25
5. outer, electrode, sharp
6. voltage, drop, connections
7. ignition, ground, ruin
8. shorting, path, burned
9. resistance, ohmmeter
10. detergent soap, hot
11. current
12. vacuum, vacuum
13. worn, bushing, cam
14. moving
15. bounce, float, cam
16. sliding, spring
17. pulley, #1, compression
18. exhaust, 180°
19. distributor, points, dwell
20. charging, acid
21. early, active, plates
22. charging
23. good, recharging, replaced
24. cell, charge
25. 1.260 − 1.280
26. hydrometer, temperature

Chapter 12

1. tubes, transistors, diodes
2. pickup, distributor
3. tooth, cylinder
4. magnet, pickup
5. signal
6. long, primary, flow
7. ignition, off, damaged
8. shaft, induced, pickup, teeth
9. varies, speeds
10. spark control, sensors, carburetor
11. ignition

Chapter 13

1. air, upwards
2. hydrocarbons, nitrogen oxides
3. exhaust, crankcase, bowl
4. filler, cover
5. regulated, engine, PCV
6. pressure, crankcase, seals, gaskets
7. hydrocarbon
8. vaporization, distribution, leaner
9. richness, cold
10. lean, fuel
11. jets, valve
12. late, power
13. overheat
14. normal, rises
15. vapor, hydrocarbon pollution
16. fuel tank, carburetor
17. vent, charcoal canister
18. filler cap
19. combustion, increase, reduce
20. air, exhaust
21. rich, idle
22. unleaded, lead

Chapter 14

1. exhaust, hydrocarbon, carbon monoxide
2. hydrocarbon, carbon monoxide
3. out, in
4. adjustment, speed
5. rich, smell
6. infrared analyzer, propane enrichment
7. drivability, oil, sludging
8. warm, hesitation, stalling
9. choke, fire
10. gas mileage
11. odor, charcoal canister
12. purging
13. manifold, idling
14. seized, leaking, backfiring
15. rises
16. misfiring, heat

INDEX

Acceleration pump (*See also* Carburetor, acceleration pump system), 42
adjustment, 80
checking discharge, 63-64
diaphragm-operated, 63
discharge cycle, 43
problems, 61-64
test, 78
Air bleed, 27, 34, 35, 213
Air bleed valve, 209
Air cleaner, 7, 11, 28, 32, 54, 60, 63, 84, 207, 209, 250
service, 240-242
thermostatically controlled, 209, 210, 213
Air cleaner snorkel, 209
Air-flow sensor, 95-96
Air-Fuel mixture, 26, 28, 32, 38, 39, 45, 56, 58, 87, 93, 99, 106, 130,
lean, 145, 200, 209-213, 215, 236
rich, 211, 212, 226, 251,
spark plugs and, 150, 151, 153,
Air injection pump, 248
Air injection systems, 224-228, 231, 232
aspirator valves, 227-228
bypass valve, 226
reed valve, 228
service, 248-250
switching systems, 226-227
Air inversion, 205
Air manifold, 224-225, 249
Air meter, 87
Air pollution (*See also* Emission controls; Exhaust gases, 13, 28, 34, 205, 221, 230
Air pressure, 27, 32, 54
Air pump, 224-225, 248
Air switching valve, 227
Alternating current, 131
Alternator, 111, 114, 119, 213-214, 242-243
Ambient air, 210, 217, 240
Ammeter, 110, 125-127
inductive amps pickup, 126
Amperage (ampere), 110, 125
Amps-Volts Tester, 125, 126
Aneroid, 213
Antimony, 116, 182
Antipercolator valve, 32
Antisyphon air vent, 43
Aspirator valves, 227-228
service, 250-251
Atmospheric pressure, 12, 13, 18, 30-39, 42-47, 50, 94, 221
Atmospheric vent, 30
Atom, 109, 119
Atomization, 27, 34
Auxiliary air devices, 93-94

Backfiring, 226, 248
Baffle, 13
Ballast resistor, 3, 134, 138-139, 158, 167, 189
Bar, 101
Battery, 3, 109, 114-117, 119, 120
acid neutralizers, 178
charge indicator, 182
charging, 117, 179, 180, 181

Battery *(Continued)*
testing for state of charge, 181-182
discharge, 116
electrolyte, 114-116, 178
elements, 114
gassing, 116
grids, 116
grounded, 120
hard-cover, 181
lead-acid, 114
lead grids, 116
low-maintenance, 182
negative plate, 114, 115
operation, 116-117
plate bridges, 115
plate straps, 115
positive plate, 114-116
preventive maintenance, 180
principles, 114-116
sediment chambers, 115
self-discharge, 116
separator, 114-116
service, 178-180
reasons for failure, 179, 182
safety precautions, 178
testing and diagnosis, 180-182
soft-cover, 181
stiffeners, 116
terminals, 115
test, 158
voltage, 130
Battery acid, (*See also* Battery electrolyte) 178
Battery cell, 114, 115
Battery current, 188
Battery electrolyte, 114-116, 178-181
Benz engines, 26
Blow-by, 206-209
Bosch continuous injection system, 97-101
Bosch EFI-L and EFI-D systems, 89-97
Bosch, Robert, 88, 89, 97
Breaker points, 3, 134, 143, 147, 148
BTDC (Before Top Dead Center), 215
Bypass valve, 224-226, 236, 248-249

Calcium, 116, 182
Cam, 48, 94
Cam and linkage, 48
Camshaft, 6, 18, 19, 23
Camshaft fuel pump lobe, 19
Capacitor. *See* Condenser
Carbon, 28, 152, 153, 246, 251
Carbon canister, 11, 13, 34, 221
Carbon dioxide (CO_2), 2, 205, 224, 229
Carbon monoxide (CO), 2, 3, 28, 53, 205, 206, 209, 224, 228
measured, 236
Carbon resistors, 148
Carbon rotor button, 165
Carbon track, 158, 164
Carburetor, 2, 3, 11-14, 17, 19, 20, 25-71, 72-85, 87, 235
acceleration pump system, 29, 42-45
design, 42
operation, 42-43
parts, 42

Carburetor *(Continued)*
problems, 61-63
pump pullover, 43-45
choke system, 29-30, 45-50, 77
automatic, 45
operation, 49-50
parts, 45-49
design, 45
hand-operated, 45
problems, 64-66
quick service procedure, 66-69
dirt in, 61
float system, 29-33, 69, 78-79
problems, 55-56, 77
flooding, 20, 21, 31, 40, 55, 56, 73,
fundamentals, 25-50
gasoline vaporization, 26-28
simple systems, 29-30
high-speed system, 29, 37-38
operation, 38
parts, 37-38
problems, 59-61
venturi, 37
idle and low-speed systems, 29, 33-36, 69
operation, 36
parts, 35
problems, 56-57
improper idle speed and mixture adjustment 57-59
quick service procedure, 58-59
lean-calibrated, 209-212
idle channel restriction, 211
idle compensator, 211
idle enrichment diaphragm, 211-213
off-idle adjustment screw, 211, 213
loading up, 55
major repairs, 55
minor repairs, 69-70
power system, 29, 39-41, 70
operation, 39-41
parts, 39
quick service procedures, 55, 58-59, 66-69
cleanliness, 54-55, 70
safety precautions, 53-54
tools, 53
single-barrel, 56, 59
two-barrel, 36
two- or four-barrel, 56, 58, 59
with lean mixture features, 212-213
Carburetor overhaul, 72-84
cleaning, 74-75, 77, 78
disassembly and inspection, 75-77, 78
external adjustments, 79, 80-83
float system adjustments, 78-79
identification, 73
installation, 83-84
internal adjustments, 78-79
ordering parts, 73
overhaul kits, 73-74
reassembly, 78-79, 83
rebuilt carburetor, 73-74
removal, 74-75
Carburetor bore, 37, 46, 63
Carburetor checks, 235-238
infrared exhaust analyzer, 235-238

Carburetor checks *(Continued)*
  propane-assisted idle adjustment, 237–238
Carburetor cleaner, 53
Carburetor float bowl, 18, 55, 75, 78
Carburetor fuel bowl, 13, 38, 206
  fuel levels, 38
Carburetor purge port, 219
Carburetor spacer routing, 224
Carburetor switch sensor, 202
Carburetor throttle valve, 33, 34, 36
Catalytic converter, 59, 228–232, 237
  care of, 231
  operation, 229
  service, 251
  three-way, 230–231
Catalytic muffler. *See* Catalytic converter
Cell voltage, 181
Centrifugal filter fan, 225, 250
Charcoal canister, 13, 32, 219–221, 244–245
Check valves, 17, 18, 44, 224, 226, 249–250
Choke, 29, 84
  automatic, 45–48
    operation, 49–50
  bimetallic thermostatic spring, 46–48, 50,
    64–66, 68, 69
  electic-assist, 213–214, 242
    thermostatic choke coil, 214
  electric heater element, 65–66
    checks, 242–243
  fast idle cam and unloader, 48–49, 65, 67
  hand-operated, 45
  heat pipe, 65, 67
  integral choke, 66–68, 82
  offset choke plate, 50
  offset choke valve, 50
  parts, 55
  piston or diaphragm, 47, 50, 65
  plate, 45–46, 64, 65, 68
  problems, 64–66
    quick service procedure, 66–69
  sources of heat, 48
  spring, 209
  spring adjustment, 82–83
  vacuum diaphragm choke, 68–69
Choke break, 81–82
Chrysler air injection system, 226–228
Chrysler catalytic converter, 229
Chrysler Electronic Spark Control, 200–203
  operation, 202–203
  sensors, 201–202
  spark control computer, 200–201
Chrysler propane-assisted idle adjustment,
  237–238
Circuit. *See* Electrical circuits
Cleaning tank, 53, 54
Clutch, 7, 8
Coil Cap, 132
Coil case, 132
Coil-condenser oscillations, 137
Coil polarity, 154–155
Combustion, 26
Combustion chamber, 4
Compound battery element, 115
Compression stroke, 5–7, 28, 143
Compression test, 158–160
  tools needed, 158
Condeser, 3, 132–133
  testing, 167–168
Conductor, 109, 112–114, 149
Connecting-rod bearings, 6
Connection rod, 4, 6
Contact path, 96
Continuous port injection system, 97, 99

Coolant control engine vacuum switch, 227
Coolant temperature sensor, 202
Cooling fan, 7
Corona, 149
Corrosion, 123, 149–150
Crankcase, 239
  positive ventilation, 206–208
Crankshaft, 4–7, 143
  journals, 6
Crocus cloth, 67
Current, 110, 112, 122
  alternating, 131
  direct, 131
  flow, 114
  reversed, 117
  total, 121
Cylinder, 4, 6, 7, 11, 38, 56, 143
  compression test, 158–160
  firing order, 6
  inline, 87
Cylinder pressures, 143

Daimler, Gottlieb, 26
Delay Vacuum Bypass (DVB) system, 218
Detonation, 28
Diagnosing problems, 53
Diaphragm (carburetor), 40, 44–45, 61
Diaphragm cells, 95
Diaphragm spring, 18, 19, 146
Dielectric, 133
Dieseling, 231
Differential, 8
Diodes, 185
Direct current, 131
Discharge check ball, 42, 43
Distributor, 3, 6, 144
  breaker points, 166–168
  cap, 4, 135–136, 148, 164
    inspection, 164–165
    rotor, 135, 165
  centrifugal advance, 168, 171, 215, 243
  controlling advance, 215–218
    retarded idle advance, 215–216
    spark advance, 216–218
  installing an unmarked distributor, 175–176
  primary and ground leads, 169
  service, 169–174, 243–244
    checking advance with timing light,
    177–178, 243
    overhaul, 170–173
    point alignment, 171–172
    removal and installation, 169–170
    using test machine, 173–174
  shaft, 169, 186
    cam, 143
    side play, 168
  static timing, 176
  with vacuum advance, 146, 168, 171, 174,
    215
Distributor tester vacuum pump, 244
Diverter valve, 224, 248–249
Divorced choke coil, 48
Draft tube, 206
Drain plugs, 15
Drive belt, 248
Driveline components, 8
Drive shaft, 8
Dual-action vacuum advance, 215–216
Dual-diaphragm vacuum advance, 216
Duration spring, 42, 43, 62–63
Dwell, 176, 177, 188–189, 243

EFI-D (manifold-pressure-sensitive) fuel in-

EFI-D *(Continued)*
  jection, 89, 92, 94, 101
EFI-L (air-flow-sensitive) fuel injection, 89,
  96
EGR solenoid, 106
Electrical circuits, 110, 114, 119–123
  defined, 119–120, 122
  leakage, 123
  open circuit, 122
  resistance, 123
  short circuits and grounds, 123
  types, 119–122
    parallel, 121–122
    series, 120–121
    simple, 120
Electrical fuel pumps, 19–21
  bellows type, 20
  diaphragm type, 19
  impeller type, 20
  testing, 22
Electrical fundamentals, 109–117
Electrical heating element, 48
Electrical leakage, 149
Electrical meters, 124–128
  ammeter, 125–127
  care and reading, 124
  ohmmeter, 110, 124, 127–128
  scales on meters, 124, 125, 127–128
  voltmeter, 125
  zeroed, 124, 128
Electrical path, 119, 122, 123
Electrically heated choke service, 242–243
Electric assist choke system, 213–214
Electric lamps, 109
Electric starters, 109
Electrodes, 134, 135
Electromagnet, 111, 112
Electromagnetic field, 112
Electromagnetic induction, 113–114
Electromagnetism, 112–113
Electronic control unit (ECU), 88–89, 101,
  105–106
Electronic ignition systems, 185–203
  Chrysler electonic spark control, 200–203
    control computer, 201
    operation, 202–203
    sensors, 201–202
    spark advance, 200
  Chrysler system, 186–189
    control unit, 188–189, 224
    pickup coil, 187–188
    reluctor, 186–187
    tests, 190–194
      circuitry, 191–194
      distributor, 190–191
  Ford ignition tests, 194–196
  General Motors ignition tests, 196–199
  ignition timing, 189
  integral coils, 196
  testing, 189–194
    secondary checks, 189–190
  vs. conventional system, 185
Electronic Lean Burn System, 200–203,
  235–236, 238
Electronic Spark Control System, 200, 235,
  237, 238
Electronic Suppression, 148
Electron movement, 109, 113, 119, 155
Electrons, 109, 119
  free, 109, 119
  measuring flow, 110
  movement, 109, 155
Electron theory, 109

Elements, 109
Emission control label, 237
Emission control service, 238–251
    air injection system, 248–250
    aspirator air valve, 250–251
    catalytic converter, 251 (*See also* Catalytic converter)
    distributor controls, 243–244
    EGR system, 245–247
    electrically heated choke, 242–243
    evaporative emissions controls, 244–245
    PVC system, 239–240
    thermostatic air cleaner, 240–242
Emission controls (*see also* Air pollution; Exhaust gases), 32, 35, 36, 48, 57–59, 205, 222, 228
    evaporative, 219–221
    reducing vehicle emissions, 205–206, 215
Engine cooling system, 28
Engine crankcase, 206
Engine heat, 54
Engine manifold, 13
Engine sensors (*See also* Sensors), 87, 104
Engine torque, 88–89
Engines:
    causes of damage to, 28, 56
    cold, 48, 222
    eight-cylinder, 6, 225
    flooding, 34, 47, 49, 231
    four-stroke cycle, 2, 4
    multicylinder, 6–7
    overheated, 216, 217
    single-cylinder, 4
    six-cylinder, 225
    speed, 143–145, 147, 148
    stalling, 245
Evaporative emission controls, 219–221
    charcoal canisters, 219–220
    fuel tanks, 221
    service, 244–245
    vapor contol, 219
Exhaust gases (*See also* Emmission controls), 27, 28, 37, 59, 88, 91, 143, 147, 150, 153, 206, 209, 211, 215, 222, 232, 251
    analysis of emissions, 59
    catalytic converter and, 231
    precautions, 53–54
    recycling systems, 232
Exhaust gas recirculation valve, 106, 222–224
Exhaust gas recirculation (EGR) system, 222–224
    service, 245–247
    vacuum amplifier units, 224
    vacuum port, 222, 246
Exhaust pollutants (*See also* Air pollution), 205
Exhaust ports, 227
Exhaust stroke, 5
Exhaust valve, 4–6
Exhaust valve port, 225.
Exhaust ventilation system, 2
External idle vent valve, 32
External vent, 34

Fanbelt, 7
Fast idle cam or choke rod adjustment, 81
Fast idle valve, 103–104
Federal Automotive Standards, 206
Filler cap, 15
    pressure-vacuum relief, 221
Filler tube, 13
Filter separator, 219
Flare nut wrenches, 21–23, 83

Flat spot. *See* Hesitation
Flex line, 16, 23
Float-drop, 31, 79
Float-drop tang, 31
Float level, 31
    adjusting tang, 30
Float on pivot, 30
Float or pivot damage, 55
Floor entry routing, 224
Flow jet, 207
Flywheel, 7, 8
Ford catalytic converter, 229
    three-way, 230–231
Ford and Holley carburetors, 61
Ford (Autolite) tester, 239
Four stroke cycle engine, 2, 4–6
Fuel barrel, 99–100
Fuel bowl, 30–32
    venting, 31–32
Fuel bowl vents, 31–32, 38
    external capped vent, 32
    internal vent, 32
    modern vents, 32
Fuel delivery system (*See also* Fuel injection systems), 89
Fuel distributor, 99
Fuel filter, 11, 89
Fuel flow, 30, 31, 33, 99, 212
Fuel gauge, 14–15
Fuel injection systems, 86–107
    Bosch continuous injection, 97–101
    Bosch EFI-L and EFI-D systems, 89–97
        air-flow sensor, 99
        control units, 96–97
        detecting sensor elements, 92–96
        differential pressure valves, 100–101
        fuel barrel, 100
    components, 87
    electronic fuel injection, 88–89, 107
        service, 107
    General Motors electronic fuel injection system, 101–106
        operation, 106
        subsystems:
            air induction, 103–104
            electronic control unit, 105–106
            fuel delivery, 103
            sensors, 104–105
    Rochester system, 87
    systems, 87
    timed port injection EFI system, 101
Fuel leakage, 16
Fuel line hose, 22
Fuel lines, 3, 11, 13, 15, 16, 17, 22, 83, 99
    inspection and service, 16
    pressure, 91
Fuel loss, 150
Fuel meter, 87
Fuel mixture control unit, 99
Fuel nozzle, 27, 87, 92
Fuel outlet ports, 27
Fuel pickup pipe, 14, 15, 20
Fuel pressure regulator, 89, 91, 103
Fuel pump mounting flange, 23
Fuel pumps (*See also* Mechanical fuel pumps), 3, 11–13, 16
    average pressure, 21
    electrical, 19–21, 89
    failure, 14
    flow capacity, 21
    mechanical diaphragm, 18–19
    testing procedures, 21–23
        flow test, 22
        fuel tank line, 22–23

Fuel pumps (*Continued*)
    inlet and outlet vacuum and pressure, 22
    pressure test, 21–22
    tips on replacement, 23
Fuel return line, 11
Fuel savings, 89, 147
Fuel sending unit, 11, 13,
Fuel system, 3, 11
Fuel tank, 3, 11, 13–17, 221, 245
    filters, 14, 15
    fuel gauge tank unit, 14–15
    inspection and service, 15–16
    venting, 13
    vents, 206
Fuel tank internal expansion tank, 221
Fuel tank vent, 13
Fuel tank vent line, 13, 15, 22–23
Fuel vapors, 11, 31, 32, 44, 221
Full-load enrichment diaphragm, 95
Fuses, 123

Gas cap, 13
Gaskets, 75, 78, 83, 160
Gasoline, 3, 18, 19, 87
    combustion, 2
    handling, 15, 53–54
    leaded, 251
    metering and mix with air, 28
    unleaded, 231, 232
    vaporization, 26–28
General Motors:
    catalytic converters, 229, 251
    fuel injection system, 101–106
    ignition tests, 196–199
Generator, 109, 111, 114, 119
Glass insulation, 132
Gravity feed systems, 17
Grounded, 120, 122
Ground return, 120
Gulp valve, 226

Heat-control door, 240–242
Heated-air duct, 11
Heated Inlet Air system, 209
Heat pipe, 242
Hesitation, 42, 44, 61–63,207
High-tension voltage, 148
High tension wires, 4, 158
Hydraulic lock, 43
Hydrocarbons (HC), 2, 3, 56, 205, 206, 209, 219, 224
    emissions, 222, 228, 244
    measured, 235
Hydrogen, 28
    gas, 178–179
Hydrometer, 181–182

Idle air adjusting screw, 36, 57
Idle air bleed, 56
Idle air bypass system, 36
Idle fuel discharge port, 33, 35
Idle fuel passage, 34
Idle jet, 56
Idle limiter needle, 36
Idle mixture adjustments, 235–237
Idle mixture screw, 34, 35, 57–58, 84, 236
Idle speed adjusting screw, 57–58
Idle tube, 34, 35
    blocked, 56
Idle vent valve adjustment, 81
Ignition coil, 3, 131–132,165, 167, 185
Ignition condensers, 132–133, 137, 138
Ignition spark, 3
Ignition-spark timing, 143

Ignition-spark timing *(Continued)*
  advance mechanisms, 143-148
  centrifugal advance, 144-145, 148
  vacuum advance, 145-148
Ignition switch, 19, 159
Ignition system (*See also* Electronic ignition
    systems), 3-4, 54, 130-140, 235
  adjusting timing, 176-178
  ballast resistors, 134, 138-139, 158, 167
  ballast wires, 139, 167
  breaker point set, 134
    wear, 137-138
  cables, 166
  dwell angle, 139-140
  electrical tests, 162-164
    meters needed, 162
    resistance checks, 164, 169
    voltage-drop, 162-164, 169
  GM High-Energy, 158
  high-tension cables, 148-150
  initial timing, 140, 176
  point gap, 139-140
  primary circuit, 130
    components, 131-134
  producing a spark, 136-138
  secondary circuit, 130-131
    components, 134-136
  short circuit, 164
Impeller blades, 20
Infrared analysis, 59, 73, 84
Infrared exhaust analyzer, 235-237, 245
Initial timing, 140, 143, 176
Injection distributor, 94
Injection durations, 97
Injection valves, 88, 89, 91, 94, 99
Inlet check ball, 42, 43, 62
Inlet check valve, 18, 42
Inline cylinders, 87
Insulators, 110, 149, 151
Intake manifold, 7, 27-28, 32, 33, 37, 45, 209
  common, 95, 99
  fuel and, 87
  heat source, 48
  leaks in, 56-57
  pressure in, 94-95
  vacuum, 44-45, 50, 91, 215
Intake valve, 4-6
  ports, 99
Interference, 148-149, 154
Internal combustion engine, 4-6
Ionization, 151
Iron core, 112-113, 132
Iron shield, 132

Jet carburetter, 26

Lead grids, 116
Lead peroxide, 114, 115
Lean misfire, 236
Lean mixtures, 57, 59, 60, 237
Limiter cap, 211, 237
Liquid return line, 13
Liquid-vapor separator, 13, 245
Load, 120-122
Low-speed port, 35

Magnetic devices, 119
Magnetic field, 111-114, 185, 187-89
Magnetism, 111
Main air bleed, 38
Main bearings, 6
Main discharge tube or nozzle, 38
Main fuel nozzle, 27
Main metering jet, 35, 37-38, 59-60, 213

Main metering system, 29
Main power piston (*See also* Piston), 213
Main vent tube, 38
Main well, 38
Manifold absolute pressure sensor, 104
Manifold heat control system, 27-28
Manifold heat control valve, 67
Manifold shroud, 209
Manifold vacuum, 32-34, 37, 39-40, 91,
    146-148, 208, 215, 216
  loss, 60
  low, 207
  strong, 213, 226
Manifold vacuum passage, 39
Manifold vacuum pressure sensor, 94-95
Mechanical fuel pumps (*See also* Fuel
    pump), 17-19
Metal rollers, 90-91
Metering, 28-29
Metering adjustment screw, 213
Metering jets, 28, 42, 59-60, 213
  valves, 213
Metering orifice, 207, 210, 212
Metering rods, 40-41, 59, 60-61
  adjustments, 80, 213
Metering slits, 99-100
Metric tools, 53
Mixture
  lean, 57, 59, 60, 237
  rich, 56-60, 64
Modes (in spark control computer), 202-203
Molecule, 109
Muffler, 228, 250
Multibarrel carburetor, 26
Multimeter, 125, 126
Mutual induction, 137

Needle and seat valve, 19, 30-31, 76
  problems, 55
Negative charge, 119
Neoprene, 148
Neutrons, 109
Nitrogen oxide, 106, 205, 216-218, 222, 226,
    230, 245
North pole (N), 111, 112
Nozzle valve, 92

Octane number, 2
Off-idle air adjusting screw, 36
Offset choke plate, 46, 47
Ohm (Ω) 110
Ohmeter, 110, 124, 127-128, 166, 189, 242
Oil filler cap, 206-207
Oil pressure switch, 242
Oil pump, 6
Open circuit voltage testing (O.C.V.T.), 181
Orifice Spark Advance Control (OSAC)
    valve, 217, 244
Oscilloscope 231
Outlet check valve, 18
Oxidation, 224, 229
Oxygen, 3, 19, 26, 28, 229
Oxygen sensor, 231
Ozone, 149
Ozonic acid, 149

Paladium, 229
Part-throttle and power systems, 212-213
Part-throttle system, 29
Pickup coil, 185-189, 201
Pickup coil signal, 202-203
Pinging, 28, 245

Piston (*See also* Power piston), 4-8, 45, 67,
    68, 101
Piston pull, 47
Piston rings, 4
Piston and spring assembly, 41
Platinum, 229, 230
Plunger cup, 44
Plunger stroke, 61-62
Point alignment, 171-172
Point-opening cam, 144
Points, 94, 171-172
Polarity, 111, 113, 125, 187
  changes, 189
Pole piece, 186, 187, 189
Poppet valve, 46
Ported spark advance, 215
Ported vacuum pickup, 245
Ported Vacuum Switch (PVS), 217, 246
Positive charge, 119
Positive Crankcase Ventilation (PCV) system,
    167, 206-208
  closed system, 207
  hoses, 75
  open system, 206
  problems, 207-208
  service, 239-240
  valve, 207, 208, 219, 238
Power piston, 39-41, 60, 76, 143, 213
Power piston cylinder, 39
Power stroke, 5, 6
Power valve, 39, 40, 60, 61
Preheated inlet air, 209, 210, 213
Preignition, 153
Pressure relief valve, 32
Pressure-vacuum filler gas cap, 13
Primary winding, 3
Propane-assisted idle adjustment, 237-238
Propane enrichment, 59, 84
Protons, 109, 119
Pull-over enrichment fuel feed, 213
Pull rod, 18
Pulse, 103, 131
Pulse transformer, 131
Pulse width, 103
Pump discharge nozzle, 42, 43, 62
Pump housing, 90
Pump intake stroke, 18
Pump jet, 63
Pump linkage rod, 62
Pump override, 32
Pump plunger, 42, 62, 77, 78
Pump pressure stroke, 18-19
Pump pullover, 43-45, 62
Pump rotor, 90-91
Pump stroke, 61-62
Pump well, 44
Purge air, 13
Purge ports, 245
Purge valve, 13, 245
Push rods, 6, 18, 23

Quadrant slot, 47

Radio suppression, 148
Reluctance, 186-187
Reluctor, 186-187, 189
Reluctor tooth, 187
Remote starter button, 159
Resistance (R), 110, 120-122
  in a circuit, 123
Resistance cores, 149
Resistance wires, 148-150
Return spring, 42, 60-63
Rheostat, 14

Rhodium, 230
Rich mixtures, 56–60, 64
Ring gear, 7
Road test, 84
Rocker arms, 6, 18, 19
    movement, 18
Roller cell fuel pump, 90–91
Roll-over valve, 219
Roll-over vapor separator valve, 219
Rotor, 4, 105, 144
Rubbing block, 134, 168

Safety goggles, 54, 63, 77, 159
Secondary air supply, 229
Secondary winding, 3
Self-induction, 137
Semiconductor, 110
Sensing devices. *See* Sensors
Sensors, 87–89, 97, 101–105
    air-flow, 99
    Bosch systems, 92–96
    on Chrysler electronic spark control
        system, 201–202
    detecting sensor elements, 92–96
    pressure sensor, 94–95
    replacement, 242
    speed, 101, 105, 224
Series resistor, 214
Sludge, 239
Smog, 205
Solenoid armature, 92
Solenoid winding, 92
Solid state devices, 185
Solvents, 53, 54, 67
Source, 120
South pole (S), 111, 112
Spark, 5, 6, 130, 143, 148
    capacitive, 148–149
    high-voltage, 158
    inductive stage, 149
    retarding, 215–218
Spark Delay Valve (SDV), 217–218, 244
Spark plugs, 4–6, 28, 57, 131, 134–135, 251
    center electrode, 151, 153, 155, 160–161
    charge cooling, 154
    and coil polarity, 154, 155
    construction, 150–152
    flashover, 151
    gap, 149, 151, 188
    gasket and seat, 151
    ground electrode, 151, 153, 155, 160–161
    heat range, 153–154
    insulator, 151
    insulator tips, 151, 153, 154, 162
    internal connector, 151
    resistor plugs, 154
    seals, 151
    service, 160–162
    sillment, 151
    spark gap, 151
    steel shell, 151
    terminal, 150
    threads, 151–152
Specific gravity tests, 181

Speed sensor, 101, 105
Sponge lead, 115
Spring-loaded piston, 93
Starter, 7
Start valve, 92, 99
Start valve winding, 92
Static charge, 124
Step cam system, 64
Step-up rods, 40–41
Storage battery (*See also* Battery), 117
Stove, 48, 50
Stroke, 4, 6
    intake stroke, 5
Suction inlet, 90–91
Sulfuric acid, 114–115
Suppression resistance, 148–149

Tachometer, 189, 236, 243
Tail pipe, 236
Tank mounting straps, 15
Temperature compensation, 167
Temperature-sensitive vacuum control valve,
    216
Temperature sensor, 93, 105
Thermactor Air Injection System, 224–227,
    250–251
Thermal Ignition Control (TIC) Valve, 217
Thermostatic air cleaner service, 240–242
Thermostatic spring, 27, 64
Thermostatic switch, 242
Thermoswitch, 92
Thermo-time switch, 92
Throttle, 11, 40, 42, 43, 83
    fast opening, 43
    open setting, 26, 28, 35, 39, 42, 45, 47, 58
    wide opening, 147
Throttle plate, 147
Throttle position switch, 104
Throttle position transducer, 202
Throttle shaft, 75–76
Throttle stop screw, 58
Throttle valve, 33, 34, 36, 94, 99, 103, 147
Throttle valve switch, 96
Timed port injection EFI system, 101, 106
    subsystems, 101, 103–106
        air induction, 103–104
        electronic control unit, 105–106
        fuel delivery, 103
        sensors, 104–105
Timing advance, 173
Timing delay orifice, 217
Timing devices, 148
Timing gear, 6
Timing light, 177–178, 189
Torque converter, 7, 8
Transformer, 131
Transistors, 185
Transmission, 7, 8
Tungsten, 134
T.V.R.S. (Television and Radio Suppression),
    148

Universal joints, 8
Unloader, 49

Unloader adjustment, 82
Unrestricted flow test, 246

Vacuum, 12, 18, 27, 33, 37
    buildup, 13
    high, 12, 147
    low, 12
Vacuum advance, 146, 168
    dual-action, 215
Vacuum advance port, 147
Vacuum aneroids, 95
Vacuum break slot, 47
Vacuum control valve, 216
Vacuum diaphragm, 241–242
Vacuum diaphragm choke, 68–69
Vacuum gauge, 245–246
Vacuum motor or chamber, 209
Vacuum pressure gauge, 21, 22
Vacuum pump, 168, 241, 245
Vacuum retard solenoid, 106
Vacuum switch, 212
Vacuum transducer, 202
Vacuum valve, temperature-sensing, 209
Valve lifters, 6
Valve seats, 159
Valve springs, 6
Vapor, 26
Vapor delivery line, 11
Vaporization, 26–27
Vapor liquid separators, 220
Vapor lock, 16, 19, 103, 219
Vapor pressure, 44
Vapor recovery systems, 13
Vapor return line, 16, 23
Vapor separator, 11, 16
Vapor vent check ball, 44
Vapor vent hoses, 221
Venturi, 28, 37, 38, 42, 43, 47, 62, 213
    boost venturi, 37–39
Venturi vacuum, 224
Vent or vapor collection lines, 16
Volt, 110
Voltage, 110, 114, 115, 122, 130, 135–137,
    181
    high-tension, 148–149
    loss, 242–243
Voltage drop, 121
Voltage regulator, 167
Voltmeter, 110, 125, 176, 189, 242
Volumetric efficiency, 26

Warm-up regulator, 100
Water pump, 7
Wet test, 160
Winding, 112–113
    primary, 132, 167
    secondary, 132
    wrist pin, 4, 6

Zero correction button, 124